MAGNA CARTA
Legend and Legacy

MAGNA CARTA
Legend and Legacy

•

W I L L I A M   F .   S W I N D L E R

T H E   B O B B S - M E R R I L L   C O M P A N Y ,   I N C .

A Subsidiary of Howard W. Sams & Co., Inc.

PUBLISHERS   •   INDIANAPOLIS   •   KANSAS CITY   •   NEW YORK

TO OUR SON

William Rollins Clayton Swindler

CONTENTS

TO THE READER

MAGNA CARTA has become, in the course of seven and a half centuries, a household phrase meaning many things to many men, but all adding up ultimately (albeit rather vaguely) to a first principle of western freedom under law. Beyond this general understanding, however, many a layman, as well as many a professional, quickly becomes enmeshed in a confusion of alternative propositions. He will hear the charter extravagantly praised—particularly upon some atavistic occasion—as the starting point of our most fundamental liberties. Then comes the qualifying observation of the specialist, warning that Magna Carta was a medieval document aimed at satisfying the specific selfish interests of the privileged groups in feudal society. Next comes the discovery that it was one of the sparks which ignited the English Revolution four hundred years later—followed in the same instance with evidence that it was tailored as a propaganda piece by the Puritans, their purpose having been accommodated by Sir Edward Coke's broad interpretation of the charter out of all relation to the context of its own times.

For that matter, anyone inquiring into the story of Magna Carta must ask himself at the outset which document he is considering: John's short-lived grant of 1215, or Henry III's reissue of 1225, or the confirmation of 1297, in the context of the great constitutional legislation of Edward I. In any event, at the end of all this the evidence leads one back to the original proposition that, although virtually nothing in the charter has a direct operational force in modern law, the general principles it embodied are still an incalculably vital element in our constitutional heritage of today.

All of which is true—or partly true.

Obviously, then, what is needed on the seven-hundred-and-fiftieth anniversary of the Great Charter is a narrative summary of its origin and its progress to the present. And that is essentially the objective of the work which follows: not to attempt to add, in this brief study, anything new to the sum of scholarly comment, but to tell the story of Magna Carta as simply and yet as accurately as possible. The charter grew into a symbol for Everyman because for centuries it was part of the evolving political and legal institutions of the English-speaking world. It is part of Anglo-American folklore, but it is also part of the fabric of freedom to which Anglo-American society is committed. It is, as the subtitle of this small volume has it, partly legend and partly legacy.

To interpret both legend and legacy to the reader of the mid-twentieth century, the author has divided his work into two parts. The first takes Magna Carta as the hero of a narrative of English and early American history and seeks to answer certain questions in terms of the charter itself. If John's grant was an expression of feudal concepts, what was feudalism itself? As for John, was he really any worse than or different from the medieval kings who came before or after? What did the agreement at Runnymede actually contain? How did it differ from the reissues of 1216, 1217 and 1225? For that matter, why were there reissues? If there is not continuity, what attended the revival of the charter of the Middle Ages as the constitutional proposition which Coke stated in the seventeenth century? What is the evidence that the American colonists viewed it, on the eve of their own revolution, as one of their inalienable rights as Englishmen? And if it was one of the elements in the credo of the Founding Fathers, how may it be identified in the constitutional rationale of our own time?

Having undertaken to provide answers to such questions in the course of the narrative in Part I, this study then provides the reader with the documents of the legacy itself in Part II—the text of 1215 interpolated with the text of 1225, and accompanied by a brief annotation, chapter by chapter, which will, hopefully, develop the significance of the Great Charter for our time. Ten chapters, out of the original sixty-three of 1215 and the thirty-seven of 1225, are extant among the modern Statutes of the Realm on the seven-hundred-and-fiftieth anniversary of Magna Carta; but these are less important as rules of law than as the enduring propositions of government under law. Magna Carta was a highly practical document for its times; as the times changed, the symbol became more fundamental than the specific details which might be preserved.

Thus, the reader is admonished that this does not pretend to be a profound work; neither, its author hopes, will it be regarded as a superficial one. The story of the Great Charter is filled with drama from which legends are made; it is also endowed with much matter-of-fact concern with the details of the political economy which evolved in modern England and the United States. For those who seek further information, the Bibliographic Essay in the Appendix has been composed.

This study is an incident in the continuing research which the author has conducted, over a period of three decades, in Anglo-American constitutional and political history. He has undertaken to compose it as a guidebook for the layman, and for the professional who is not a specialist in legal history, in an excursion into the events which shaped the society *in* which we live and the convictions *by* which we live. If this excursion proves profitable and interesting to him who undertakes it, the author will be satisfied.

William F. Swindler

WILLIAMSBURG, VIRGINIA
MARCH, 1965

PART ONE

THE
MAKING
OF THE
LEGEND

Magna Carta is such a Fellow, he will have no Sovereign.

SIR EDWARD COKE.

I

The Feudal Age

B Y THE late afternoon of October 14, the Duke of Normandy had become William the Conqueror. The ear-splitting clang of sword upon helmet and shield had declined with the declining sun, and now King Harold of the Saxons, together with two of his brothers and a vast number of English thegns, lay silent and dead upon the narrow ridge. All day the battle had shifted from one side to the other, from the midmorning hour when the English axemen and archers had drawn up in a tight wall on the eminence above the French cavalry and waited for their opening charge. There had been some qualms as to the justice of Harold's cause, and before the issue was joined, the King's brother Gurth had urged him not to risk his person in the fray, "lest, fighting as a perjured man, you incur defeat or death." Harold had shaken off the advice. "May the Lord decide this day between William and me," he had cried, lifting his face toward heaven, "and may He pronounce which of us has the right."

William, on his part, had come to the field from a Mass where he had hung around his neck the sacred relics on which, he declared, Harold had sworn the oath he subsequently had broken. Rising from the holy service, the Duke had solemnly carried to the forefront of his own army the papal banner with which his expedition had been blessed. And thus, upon these appeals to divine judgment, the battle had been joined. Throughout the noontime the English in their tight formation had held the advantage; but by simulated flight the foe eventually had lured them down onto the plain, where the Norman cavalry had chewed them into fragments. And so it had been that, in the gathering twilight, the field finally was left to the French invaders, and the remnants of Harold's army began falling back into the forest of

3

Sussex. The Saxon standard collapsed under the final onslaught, and Harold, his eye pierced by an arrow, was ridden down and hacked to death.

Even contemporaries sensed that the Battle of Hastings was a turning point in history. The Bayeux Tapestry, woven within memory of the event and with partisan enthusiasm—the Bishop, after all, had been William's half-brother—nevertheless captured in the frozen details of the conflict the shadow of fate behind the wavering scales which finally tipped irrevocably toward the new order. All had been foretold, men said, by the appearance earlier that year of a heavenly portent which recalled an old prophecy:

> In the year of millennium and sixty-six
> The flames of a comet will scourge the English.

In later years a church—Battle Abbey—would be erected on this site, its high altar reputedly over the spot where Harold fell; but on this day Duke William himself came and stood here, and in the words of a contemporary chronicler, "rendered thanks to the King of Glory, through whom he had the victory." Then, continued the same writer, the Conqueror "ate and drank among the dead, and made his bed that night upon the field."

William the Bastard could sleep soundly after such a day. It was no new experience for him, for combat had become his rule of life. The illegitimate son of Duke Robert "the Devil," and thirty-eight years of age when he landed in Britain, he had already spent half his life in arms. He was accustomed to command; he had assumed the dukedom himself when he was seven, surviving the perils of a boyhood among men who devoted their lives to seeking for the chance to destroy him. Since attaining his majority, he had overwhelmed all rival claimants at home, added Maine to his French possessions, and invaded Brittany to some profit. The Northmen who had seized their stronghold on the coast of France a century and a half earlier had bred virile and aggressive warriors, and William was to prove himself the greatest of the line. A man of middling height, he was early given to baldness and later to corpulence; but his iron determination was reflected in the perpetual sternness of his visage, and his muscular strength was legendary.

On the field at Hastings, he had dominated the battle. "His sharp sword pierced shields, helmets and armor, and not a few felt the weight of his shield," sang the chronicler. Men long afterwards recalled, in song and story, how the Duke, his horse falling under him, had leapt to the ground and slaughtered the circle of foemen who had rushed in upon him. He fought with a fury that amazed his own men, and called upon them to put forth a like effort. There could be no retreat and no quarter. Saxons blocking the invasion, and Normans with their backs to the sea, had ventured everything in the moment of truth, and the combat would be to the death. When the long day ended, "the bloodstained ground was covered with the flower of the youth and nobility of England"; more—the Saxons' very lifeblood had been poured out upon that fatal field. Now William stood master of it all, and the victory was the sweeter for having been so desperately won.

The landing on the English coast was the type of calculated risk this skilled and confident general was prepared to take in consideration of the prize to be had—in this case, no less than a kingdom. For William had come to claim a throne vacated by Edward the Confessor, who had died only the previous January. Some fifteen years earlier, according to the Norman story, Edward had promised the succession to him, and the claim was plausible even if undocumented. Edward, childless himself, had been reared at the Norman court at Rouen and after his own accession to the throne had brought many Norman lords to seats in his domain. There was also more recent evidence, never very strongly disputed, that as late as 1064 Harold himself had visited William, either to confirm the earlier promise of Edward or to assure the Duke of Harold's own support of William's claim.

As the Normans told it, in that year Harold had landed on their coast as an envoy from Edward and had been rescued by William after being seized as a spy by a local magnate. As a guest at the ducal court, Harold had even been given the promise of William's daughter in marriage. But more binding than that, ran the story, had been the oath which Harold had taken to support William as Edward's successor, sworn upon a great chest covered with a cloth. After the oath, the cloth had been removed, and Harold had been staggered to find that he had sworn upon the sacred relics of many saints which had been placed in the chest. Solemn and irrevocable as such an oath was, Harold had nevertheless renounced it when he returned to England; the fact that the offer to take William's daughter to wife had been withdrawn had only aggravated the matter. Yet Harold had justified himself; for, said he, if a damsel's vow made in her father's house could be recalled as of no effect, much more ought an oath to be which had been made under duress.

In truth, it was not wholly within the power of either Edward or Harold to give the crown of the Saxons to anyone; and in any event, it was a matter of record that on his deathbed the Confessor—whether or not he was repudiating an earlier promise—had here named the Earl of Wessex as his successor. That earl was Harold, Edward's brother-in-law and of the ancient royal line, and "of old time a deathbed bequest the Saxons have held paramount to any other grant," Harold had told the Duke. These circumstances had been persuasive in the opinion of the English lords and justified ignoring the pretensions of Normandy. Harold, after all, had well earned his spurs by the savage standards of leadership of his day. As Edward's general, says the chronicler, he had ravaged Wales and had received the head of their own king in tribute from the Welsh people. Overcome with envy at Harold's favor with Edward for this and other warlike accomplishments, his brother Tostig had provoked a fight with him in the King's court, and when bested there, had proceeded to Hereford, where Harold was arranging a feast in Edward's honor. There Tostig had cut off the limbs of the servants preparing the feast and had thrust the arms and legs into the vessels of wine and mead, sending a message to the King that he should now find the food seasoned to his taste. For this insolence, Tostig was banished; but many said that God's vengeance would now inexorably be visited upon both brothers.

Thus it fell out that on the day that Edward was buried, Harold was crowned, in the full knowledge on his part and on the part of the Saxon nobles that they had invited Normandy to war. A man like William, with such a color of title to a kingdom and such a ready disposition to combat, would take up that challenge at the first opportunity. Unhappily for the English, the opportunity had come at the moment Harold was engaged in disposing of another threat, from the north, where Tostig and a Norwegian army had invaded the land. By the time Harold, with a brilliant march and a desperate battle at Stamford Bridge, had destroyed this foe, William had crossed the Channel and was fortifying a beachhead at Hastings. So the last of the Saxon kings, says the *Peterborough Chronicle,* "came from the north and fought against him before his [own] army had all come up." The odds were too great: the defenders fought with less than half of their men, exhausted from a forced march against the Norwegians and another southward to meet the Normans, who had been able to put ashore, unchallenged, their whole force of "horsemen, slingers, archers and foot-soldiers." Indeed, the difference between the two armies foretold the difference in the new order which was born of the slaughter that day: the Saxons fought on foot, in a cumbersome phalanx, while the mounted Norman knights dashed about them, and once the defense was breached, smashed it utterly.

And so Harold had died, and with him the Saxon civilization. For William understood, as he turned inland from the battlefield, that there could be no half measures if his reign was to be made secure; the whole of England must be infiltrated and the Saxon power destroyed forever. The English had hazarded everything at Hastings, and they had lost everything; now earldoms which had been established only a few generations after the last Romans had departed from Britain, and had survived and absorbed Danish and other Scandinavian adventurers, were to be supplanted by Norman baronies. Some surviving thegns would flee to Scotland, others to Flanders, and some to far Byzantium, the very distance testifying to the completeness of their catastrophe. The England into which William advanced was the product of a thousand years of sporadic invasions; he intended that his would be the last.

It was a pleasant and promising land that the Normans found; in spite of the years of Danish raids and the tribute, or Danegeld, by which invasions had been bought off, the country had prospered modestly under the last twenty years of Saxon rule. Most of the population lived in farms or hamlets clustered around a manor house, although the Danish kings had aided in the development of a few larger towns like York and London. King Edward had graced the ecclesiastical life of the latter with the construction of Westminster Abbey, which had been consecrated only a short time before his death. Across the downs the invading host now passed fields turning brown in late autumn, with the thatched roofs of cottages and the stone of village church and manor revealing the presence of the people who awaited their fate under their new lords.

In a sense, the Normans themselves were repeating British history. Six centuries earlier, it had been the Saxons who had swept across the water barrier from western Europe, and overrunning the native tribes, had gradually occupied the southern and middle parts of the island. Kent and Sussex, where William's forces first deployed, were the same spots where the Angles and Saxons had gained their early footholds. Here St. Augustine had landed in 597 to bring the gospel to the pagan dwellers in the land. From Salisbury in Wessex to Rochester in Kent, Alfred the Great had fought his ninth-century battles against the Vikings, bringing the Saxon crown to a point of primacy among the early English kings and gathering the various codes of these kings into something resembling a national collection of laws. In east Kent, too, was Canterbury, where St. Dunstan in the tenth century began the anointing of the Saxon rulers, thus enhancing the legitimacy of their claims to be overlords of all Britain.

But until the Conquest, no king was supreme in the island, and the overlordship which came to be attributed to the Saxon monarchs merely made them first among equals. A primitive council, the Witan, met on certain occasions to advise the overlord on the governing of the land, and upon the king's death to choose his successor, since the crown did not necessarily pass from father to son. Only half a century before William, the Danes under Canute had come to England and placed him on the throne, but the Danish interval had chiefly served to unsettle the country in general and thus make easier the Norman invasion. It was a shaky grasp which the Saxons put forth to the sceptre when it had returned to them in 1042.

Yet it was not an uncivilized country now. Crimes were

systematically inquired into by reputable men chosen in every locality, and the ownership of property and its sale was recorded on documents which could be produced before formal, even though crude, tribunals. The roots of the jury system would be traceable to Anglo-Saxon as well as to Norman English periods. As local petty kingdoms atrophied, becoming counties or shires, the overlord replaced the former royal house with his own officer, the reeve—the shire-reeve, or sheriff, becoming one of the first officers William encountered when he began the organizing of his new government.

The planting of Norman power in England was, as William realized, essential not only to securing his control but to rewarding those who had aided him in his venture. Men like William fitz Osbern, Roger de Montgomery, and Hugh d'Avranches were among many who would become in future the earls of such English seats as Hereford, Chester, or Warwick, in acknowledgment of the men and ships they had brought to the Duke's cause. Their names would be written large, and for a long time, among the great landholders of the realm—men with estates on both sides of the Channel, and often divided loyalties which made them aliens in the island until, at a distant future day, their descendants chose the new land as home and the French names changed to English. This would be the ultimate proof of the success of the Conquest; for the immediate present, however, William was concerned with creating earldoms to hold the country. This he did, first establishing them in southeastern England and adding new territories farther inland as the disjointed Saxon resistance was crushed. By the end of his reign, some 170 barons could trace their estates to grants for services performed in the course of the Conquest.

Little as they loved the Normans, the English could appreciate, once it was established, the practical value of the system of government which William brought with him. The island's very experience with successive alien inundations had emphasized, as it was impressed upon the medieval mind throughout western Europe, that security and order were hard-won necessities of existence. For almost six centuries, since the Roman world had disintegrated, Europe had been an unstable ferment of political particles which could not coalesce. Barbarian hordes, ravaging as they went, swept like storms across the land and desecrated the deserted citadels of pagan civilization, while the primitive Church struggled, generation after generation, to plant and nurture the Christian faith in this harsh and hostile environment. No man could know, when he sowed in the spring, whether he would be alive to reap in the fall—or whether, if he reaped, he could enjoy the fruit of his labor. His only recourse was to seek the shelter of a stronger one than he—and to offer part of his services and most of his land to the strong one in return for protection. Thus had medieval society taken shape.

England had followed, in its own fashion, this pattern of developing feudalism (as later generations were to call it) on the Continent; but it was in Normandy that the hierarchy of strength had attained its highest logic. The Normans had a genius for administration as well as for conquest which had made their duchy a relatively stable center amid the welter of anarchy in France and western Europe generally. The dukes, who had steadily extended their influence from Rouen, had not depended on loyalty and gratitude for land they bestowed upon their vassals—they had claimed obedience with their swords. Their barons were secure in their own estates so long as they supplied the dukes with well-armed and well-trained knights when they needed them. The paramount lord would insure his followers their rights so long as they were followers—and when they held back, his retribution was swift and devastating. William now determined to transplant the system to England, engrafting it upon Danish and Saxon customs as necessity might require.

The touchstone of security, as the Middle Ages understood it, was land and the power to defend it; for from the land—its fields for farming and minerals, its forests for game, grazing, and timber, its streams for fishing and transportation—came virtually all that was required to sustain life. As the small landholders clustered around a greater house for protection, so the lord of that house looked to another yet greater to protect him from the threats he could not meet. The Norman structure continued this pyramid, at least in principle, to the duke at the pinnacle; the Saxon structure was one of many small pyramids whose union

had been all too readily dissipated into rival sovereignties. Until
the Conquest, this resistance to concerted and sustained effort had
been one clue to England's vulnerability. As early as the Roman
invasions, Tacitus had written of the primitive Britons that "nothing helped us more . . . than their inability to unite." The Angles
and Saxons, as well as the Danes, had discovered the same
weakness.

Now William, following up his victory at Hastings with a
succession of skirmishes and occasional battles which eventually
won the submission of London, took vigorous steps to remake
English society. His coronation on Christmas Day marked the
beginning; through the next twenty years he would pursue his
goal of fashioning an Anglo-Norman state held firmly together by
the power of the throne. Finding the Danegeld at hand as a
precedent, William promptly decreed a nationwide levy which
provided him with a substantial treasury. In addition, declared
the new king, all freeholds of the realm were immediately forfeit.
The flower of Saxon aristocracy had perished at Stamford Bridge
or Hastings; some few surviving lords came to him and did homage and thus were permitted to redeem their lands in whole or
in part. But by far the greater portion of the English estates were
appropriated by the Norman Conqueror and went to his followers; some acquired vast holdings, so that a quarter of all the lands
William granted went to fewer than a dozen lords. But the central
fact was that the grants themselves came from the crown. The
Saxons had never made so unequivocal a claim, but it was a
logical extension of the Norman practice, and it could be made
more readily universal in a conquered land; William, as king,
was now an anointed sovereign, and all men were henceforth his
tenants, holding their estates of him.

With this absolute control of land, the essential commodity,
William could give full effect to the moral, personal, and military
commitments embodied in the ritual of homage. This binding
ceremony was well established by the Conqueror's day and epitomized the *mystique* of the feudal age. By the terms of the ritual
the tenant came before his lord, and kneeling, "put both of his
hands between the hands of his lord, by which is signified on the
lord's side protection, defense and warranty, and on the tenant's

side, reverence and subjection." Then, according to the ritual, the tenant vowed: "I become your man for the tenement I hold of you, and I will bear you faith in life and member and earthly honor against all men." The obligation assumed by each party to the ritual was manifest to all witnesses as well as to the principals: the king pledging himself to protect his tenant both by armed authority and by guarantee of his right to the land he received, the tenant in turn undertaking to provide his lord with a prescribed amount of service in men and produce as the lord might require them.

The crown tenants, or tenants in chief, held their estates of the king; and by subinfeudation these barons required homage of mesne lords who held of them. The mesne lords, intermediate in rank and power, in turn could make grants from their tenements to knights and minor nobles who, lacking authority to make further subinfeudation, were known to the feudal law as tenants paravail. Thus, with land as the literal foundation of power, the feudal system strove for stability through a process of interlocking loyalties and obligations.

This intricately stratified organization of tenancy affected only the upper fraction of Norman England; but the feudal law prescribed the duties of the humble as well as the privileged. The organization of local society was left largely unchanged; the hundreds and the counties continued to demand the service of all freeholders and yeomen at their monthly courts, where administrative as well as judicial matters were settled. The great majority of Englishmen spent their lives in scattered villages within these districts, or else sought homesteads in the forests, where William's officers periodically visited them to take payment for the forage used by their swine and cattle or for the timber and brush they gathered for their own livelihood. Deeper in the greenwood lived outlaws, men like Robin Hood of later renown, fugitives from the harsh forest laws which reserved for the king and the other great lords the deer and other game over large tracts. Whether figment of folklore or figure of history—a record dating from a century and a half after the Conquest speaks of a sheriff's accounts of the chattels of one Robert, or Robin Hood, *fugitivus*—the name captured men's imaginations in conceiving of what it might be like to live free of the tangled mass of duties which otherwise circumscribed medieval life.

For the average man, these duties were elaborately detailed and rigidly enforced. Peasants attached to an estate were required to pay forty pence at the autumnal equinox, four dozen bushels of wheat, and to plow three acres in the lord's demesne and sow them with their own seed. Each must mow half an acre of meadow, provide a stack of split wood and a separate bundle of poles for fencing, must shear the sheep in season, and "work as they are bidden every week save three—at midwinter, at Easter and at the Rogation Days."

The sporadic resistance to the Conquest, in the half-dozen years after Hastings, enabled William to advance his plan of organization with each new capitulation. An uprising in Northumbria and York, in the name of a youthful Saxon pretender, Edgar, led to a complete devastation of the country to the north. In the east, at Ely, another rebellion was crushed, and in 1072, King Malcolm of Scotland (the successor to Macbeth) was forced to swear his allegiance. So was England subdued; Norman barons built their castles on lands forfeited by Saxons, Scots, or Welsh— and when they themselves rebelled, they were replaced with other Normans. For feudal society, under the best of circumstances, was an always uneasy balance between the overlord and those who sought to be overlord in his place. When the king's attention was directed to beating down one challenger, others would in the very nature of the case be gathering strength behind his back. The physical impossibility of stamping out such threats over a vast region kept most feudal kingdoms relatively small.

With Malcolm's submission the Conquest was complete, and the King could at last discharge the large body of mercenaries whom he had retained for the great venture begun in 1066. Castles and other strong points, including the Tower of London, had been constructed to dominate strategic areas and lines of communication. But at the same time, ever mindful of the propensities of the military society in which he lived, William saw to it that most of his barons held their estates in scattered parcels, lest the ability to concentrate the retinue of their vassals should tempt them to a trial of strength with him or their neighbors. The temptation was constant and substantial, for, once England was nominally pacified, William hastened back to Normandy to put down insurrections fomented there during his absence.

One such effort at overthrow, says the chronicler, came about at Norwich while the King was in Normandy in 1075. At the wedding feast of Ralph, Earl of Norfolk and Suffolk, a plot was set afoot; but William's system of Norman infiltration and castle guard proved its effectiveness. Most strong points were held by mesne lords loyal to the throne, and they refused to turn them over to the plotters, declaring that the barons' own perfidy had absolved them of their feudal obligations. Meantime, the King was fully informed of the plot, returned to England, and seized the conspirators. Concludes the chronicle:

> Some were then made blind
> And some were driven from the land;
> Thus were William's betrayers humbled.

Much of English life remained undisturbed by William's statecraft. Freemen, churls, and villeins continued to follow the practices of the past, tilling alternate strips of land for themselves and their local lords, pasturing their few livestock in common fields or in the wastelands near the forests, and paying such taxes as they must. The local lords continued to hold their manorial courts for the settling of local disputes; the king's justices would not tour the land for some years to come. Thus, with the unbroken continuity of much local custom beneath the superstructure of feudal tenures, the Conquest could, with much truth, be said to have meant peace and security to a degree heretofore unknown. Still, the Saxons, even those who had never had the chance or inclination to resist the invasion, acknowledged the new order only grudgingly, and men spoke often of the old times. Occasionally, as in the rebellion of 1075, it was with a claim to trying to restore the former order; but more often, as the years wore on, the tales reflected a simple nostalgia.

Especially was there talk of the saintly Edward (who grew more saintly in retrospect) and of a vague, idealized body of his laws which it became patriotic to insist had been trampled under by the invaders. In time, the "good laws of Edward" came to stand for a heritage of fundamental rights which the Normans must somehow be brought to reaffirm. In this case the legend became substantial enough to persuade one of William's sons, when he became Henry I, that it was politic to acknowledge the "good laws" in a coronation oath. A century later, the appeal to this same heritage was to plague John at Runnymede. Long after that, John's own charter was to be abstracted and elevated to such an eminence that it would touch off a revolution in English life more complete even than the Conqueror's.

In his own time, William would have scoffed at the idea of a "return" to any earlier system. He was concerned exclusively with consolidating the kingdom he had captured, and he used Saxon and Norman practices interchangeably as his purposes might require. The "good laws of Edward" were little more than generalized statements of rudimentary old English or feudal concepts, and many of them William had already carried into his own system. Norman lords almost without exception continued the customs of the estates to which they succeeded, and William's own writs and charters carefully preserved the Saxon vernacular. His brief charter to the city of London is typical:

> King William greets in friendly wise William the bishop and Gosfrith the portreeve, and all the burgesses in London both French and English. . . . I will that you two be worthy of all the laws that you were worthy of in King Edward's day. And I will that every child be his father's heir after his father's day, and I will not endure that any man offer any wrong to you. God keep you.

In the great survey of 1085-86, William's census takers regularly referred to laws and customs obtaining in Edward's time. The Conqueror saw no necessity for expunging the past; indeed, one of the keys to his success was his preserving as much of it as he could.

A united, or at least a uniformly controlled, populace and a monarchy strong enough to enforce the king's will throughout the realm were William's objectives. The ecclesiastical power he centralized by making the See of Canterbury the Primacy of all England, while remaining deaf to suggestions from Rome that, in return for the Pope's blessing on his original mission, the land be made a papal fief. The royal forests, covering almost one-third of the realm, were policed by the King's men; and here the Conqueror's hand was heaviest of all, for William, like his successors, loved the hunt and appropriated all forests to his own pleasure, to the peril or ruin of the many who chanced to dwell therein. As for his dominance of his local lords, he accomplished this by holding court in various parts of the kingdom; "three times each year he wore his royal crown," reported a contemporary. "At Easter he wore it in Winchester, at Pentecost in Westminster, at Christmas in Gloucester, and then there were with him all the prominent men over all England, archbishops and suffragan bishops, abbots and earls, thegns and knights."

As his reign drew toward its close, William could rightfully consider that he had accomplished much of what he had set out to do. "Among other things not to be forgotten," says the chronicler, "is the good peace which he made in his country, so that a man who was of any importance could travel unmolested over his kingdom with his bosom full of gold; and no man dared kill another, even if he had done ever so great an injury to him; and if any man lay with a woman against her will, he immediately lost the members with which he had played."

There remained, in William's scheme of economic and political consolidation, two measures of fundamental importance to be undertaken, in order to leave the fullest legacy of security to his people and his heirs. The first of these was launched at Christmastide in 1085:

> . . . The king had a great council and spoke earnestly with his witan about this country—how it was occupied and with what men. Then he sent his men over all England into every shire and had them reckon how many hundred hides there were in the shire or what land and cattle the king himself owned in this county or what annual taxes he ought to receive from the shire. He also had them write down how much land his archbishops owned, and his suffragan bishops and his abbots and his earls, and—though I make my story too long—what or how much land and cattle each man who was a land-

owner in England possessed, and how much money it
was worth. He had it surveyed so very closely that there
was not a single hide or rood of land, nor—it is a shame
to tell, though it seemed to him no shame to do—was
there even an ox or a cow or a pig left that was not set
down in his writing; and all the writings were afterwards
brought to him.

The Domesday survey, in its precise recording of every chat-
tel and parcel of land in most of the counties of England, brought
the feudal system of William I to its highest stage of organization.
Spread upon the record in the *Domesday Book,* which was to
become the highest authority to which appeal could be made, was
the entire system of tenures in Norman England, as it had grown
up in the twenty years since Hastings. The survey traced the
descent of land from the crown, and in turn the rights to the
holding of this land were set out in charters which, preserved or
renewed, were themselves the incontestable proof of these rights.

The survey was exhaustive, as the "inquest" of the Abbot of
Ely illustrated: the canvassers "inquired what the manor was
called; who held it in the time of King Edward; who holds it now;
how many hides there are; how many ploughs in demesne and
how many belonging to the men; how many villeins; how many
cottars; how many slaves; how many freemen; how many sokemen; how much woodland; how much meadow; how much pas-
ture; how many mills; how many fisheries; how much has been
added to, or taken from, the estate; what it used to be worth
altogether; what it is worth now; and how much each freeman
and sokeman had and has. All this to be recorded thrice: to wit,
as it was in the time of King Edward, as it was when King William gave the estate, and as it is now. And it was also noted
whether more could be taken from the estate than is now being
taken."

The records set out the working system of feudalism: the
number of acres in a holding of land (hide); the villeins who
were bound to the service of the lord of this land, owing a portion
of time from their own fields to tend those in the dominion
(desmesne) of the lord; the lowlier labor performed by the cottars; the infrequent slaves, usually bond debtors; the freemen or

freeholders for whom the laws and their benefits were primarily intended; and the particular group of tenants called sokemen, who discharged their obligations by paying money rent for the lands they worked. Feudalism also emphasized frugality; the survey sought to inventory the productivity of estates and to make certain that nothing was wasted.

In the process of gathering statistics, the canvassers also provided the King with a summary of the laws and customs which obtained in various parts of his realm, thus fashioning guides for the justices of later times who would provide uniform royal courts throughout the land. The surveyors for Oxford and Oxfordshire thus succinctly reported on the prevailing customs of that area:

> Anyone breaking the king's peace given under his hand and seal to the extent of committing homicide shall be at the king's mercy in respect of his life and members. That is if he be captured. And if he cannot be captured, he shall be considered as an outlaw, and anyone who kills him shall have all his possessions.
>
> The king shall take the possessions of any stranger who has elected to live in Oxford and who dies in possession of a house in that town, and without any kinfolk.
>
> The king shall be entitled to the body and the possessions of any man who kills another within his own court or house excepting always the dower of his wife, if he has a wife who has received a dower.

Thus did William's men take the *descriptio* of the kingdom, as it was called; the rights, even where political in terms of their holders' position in the scale of power, were essentially economic. The *Dom-Boc* for the city of York thus opened with a general statement that

> . . . in the time of King Edward, besides the Ward of the Archbishop, there were six Wards; one of these was destroyed when the Castles were built. In the five Wards there were one thousand four hundred and eighteen inhabited mansions. The Archbishop has yet a third part of one of these Wards. In these, no one, except as a Burgess, was entitled to any customary payments, except . . .

four Magistrates, to whom the King granted this privilege by his writ, and that for their lives; but the Archbishop was entitled to all customary payments, in his Ward. Of all the above-mentioned mansions, there are now in the King's possession, three hundred and ninety-one inhabited, great and small, paying custom; and four hundred uninhabited, which do not yield customary services, but some only one penny rent, and others less; and five hundred and forty mansions so uninhabitable that they pay nothing at all; and Foreigners hold one hundred and forty houses.

Proceeding into Yorkshire itself, the surveyors reported to the King on the descent of part of the land granted to one Earl Edwin:

Ilbert de Laci has now this land, where he has twelve ploughs in the demesne; and forty-eight villanes, and twelve bordars with fifteen ploughs, and three churches and three priests, and three mills of ten shillings. Wood pastures two miles long, and one broad. The whole manor five miles long and two broad. Value in King Edward's time sixteen pounds, the same now.

So the inventory went, identifying the revenues which could be expected from each parcel of land, including the wards or administrative districts of towns and boroughs, and whether the customs or excises levied upon the produce of these parcels were to go to the King, to the Church authority, or to certain officers under a lifetime grant from the crown. The record also indicated the number of "mansions," or dwelling places, and whether these were inhabited by tenants or rented by adjacent freeholders. William could also learn, from the returns, into whose hands portions of his original grants had passed—as from Earl Edwin to Ilbert de Laci—and could then determine whether this subinfeudation was to his advantage or disadvantage, according to whether Ilbert was loyal or recalcitrant.

Of the total annual value of the properties surveyed by the *descriptio*, which was approximately £73,000, the King and his retinue were entitled to some £19,400, the Church to another £19,200, certain English peers to £4,000, while £30,000 of the remainder was distributed among the 170 baronies the Conqueror had created among his Norman followers. Well could William claim that his twenty-one years of administration had brought prosperity to his realm and to his vassals. And yet, realist that he was at all times, the information provided by the Domesday survey convinced him of the necessity for enacting the second fundamental measure for securing the realm, and this was undertaken in his final year. For the great canvass revealed a vast system of holdings which, in the course of two decades, had established the great barons as a powerful class with many subtenants. This class stood between the throne and the subtenants, in fact; for although the feudal theory held that all land came from the king, in practice the lesser lords held their estates of the lords directly above them. Their loyalty was therefore translatable only in terms of the crown tenants' loyalty.

When a subtenant died without heirs, his lands escheated to the lord of the fee or to the mesne lord, according as the one or the other had been the original grantor. In any case, it was not to the king; and from the holder of the estate or his heir the grantor alone received the services due from the estate, and the reliefs, fines, and dower gifts. William perceived that under a given combination of circumstances or conspiracies, the throne could well be cut off from the very support which in theory was insured to it by the feudal system. Precisely this was to happen to Stephen and John, the one because he proved weak in the face of such a challenge, the other because he had been shorn of power. To hold together the medieval system of tenures, two elements were vital—a strong king, and an accepted constitutional principle of higher loyalty, as when the mesne lords in 1075 held out against the plot to overthrow William I.

The Conqueror in his day had shown that he was powerful enough; now, on the heels of the Domesday survey, he undertook to confirm the constitutional principle. On August 1, 1086, he came to Old Sarum, or Salisbury, and according to the chronicler, "all the landowners who were of importance in all England, no matter whose men they might be, [came] and they all submitted to him and became his men and swore oaths of fealty to him that they would be faithful to him against all other men." Thus by the Oath of Salisbury did William seek to reaffirm and reinforce the central theme of Norman feudalism: All subjects held their estates ultimately of the paramount lord and their paramount obligation was to him. But in the end, as history was to prove, the principle rested upon the character and power of the king. The Normans who came after William I never attained the full authority which he enjoyed; possibly they lacked the momentum provided by the Conquest itself. Nor were the Plantagenets who followed Henry II such men as he, to impose by force of personality as much as by force of arms this inviolable loyalty upon restless and ambitious barons. The last of the Normans, Stephen, was to suffer the humiliation of seeing the constitutional principle openly flouted; the third Plantagenet, John, was to be compelled to qualify the principle with a counterbalancing principle of restraint upon the arbitrary use of power by the paramount lord.

The first of the Norman kings had shaped England into a centralized authority such as existed nowhere else in medieval Christendom; it remained to be seen whether the idea could survive him, and that issue was now at hand. Stricken in the course of an ill-starred invasion of France, the Conqueror clung to life long enough to receive the viaticum of the Church and to make his bequests to his sons: Normandy to his first-born, Robert; England to William Rufus (so called for his ruddy countenance); and money to his youngest, Henry. On September 5, William I died and was buried at Caen. To the funeral came many lords and prelates, but only one son; even before his father's death, Robert had raised a rebellion in Normandy, while William Rufus was already across the Channel and hurrying to London to secure his part of the patrimony. Henry alone came to Caen, and, so runs the report, "when the owner of the land where the King's body was buried made a difficulty about it, Henry pacified his anger by paying him a hundred marks of silver."

And now the empire that William I had built threatened to fall back into chaos. By dividing the kingdom and the duchy between two of his sons, he had divided the allegiance of the barons, particularly those with estates in both lands. Robert and Rufus would not be of William's brood if they accepted this division without a struggle, and the struggle was not long in coming. Odo,

Bishop of Bayeux and half-brother to the Conqueror, confirmed
Robert as Duke of Normandy and proceeded to England, where,
in his capacity as Earl of Kent, he was presumed to accept William II as King. But that truculent churchman and master intriguer had come for other purposes; after all, he had only been
released from imprisonment upon William's death, and lusted to
avenge himself on those he blamed for his humiliation. Lanfranc,
Archbishop of Canterbury, Odo held to be the principal conspirator against him, and since Lanfranc was adviser to Rufus, Odo
held them both his enemies. Once back in his own barony, Odo
sent letters to many, intimating that Robert alone was entitled
to the barons' loyalty and to adhere to Rufus was to risk losing
all the honors and tenures they had received after the Conquest.
The great lords wavered. If Odo was right, Robert alone could
guarantee the continued enjoyment of their estates in Normandy,
and if he replaced Rufus on the English throne, he would insure
the preservation of their lands on this side of the Channel also.

But it was William Rufus, and not Robert, who settled the
issue in the end. Appealing to the remnants of the English barons,
he offered them reduced taxes and greater freedom of the forests
in return for their support. Then, turning to the leader of the
Normans, Roger de Montgomery, William offered to go into
exile if the great lords so desired—but with the warning that the
Conqueror, "if he had erred about his son, might have erred
about them also," and thus the legitimacy of their earldoms
could be called into question. Roger grasped the King's meaning,
and "he who was the first after Odo to subscribe himself to this
conspiracy was the first of all who repented of it, and deserted
from it."

Thus strengthened, Rufus moved quickly and crushed the
rebels; the events which followed persuaded the Normans that
their real advantage lay with him rather than with Robert. The
King lost no time in re-establishing the dominance of the royal
house throughout England, compelled the renewed submission
of Scotland, and subdued much of Wales. "Bishop Odo, being
thus for a second time taken prisoner, abjured England for ever,"
says Roger of Wendover, adding that "all the rest returned to
their allegiance." At the end of ten years of this stern but effective

administration, Robert himself capitulated; he yielded his duchy to Rufus in return for ten thousand silver marks and a mission to join the First Crusade.

The Conqueror's legacy thus had survived its first test. When William II died in 1100—many said from a hunting accident arranged by Prince Henry—England had experienced thirty-four years of strong dynasty. This period was to be equalled by Henry's reign now beginning; although neither of the Conqueror's sons had his energy and insight, each in his fashion preserved and strengthened what the father had founded, so that the very ineptitude of Stephen's reign, when the barons had their way, demonstrated to them that their own best interest ultimately lay in maintaining the system of power which the Conqueror had devised. The Norman kings and the circumstances of their dynasty had given England a unity, if it was not yet a nation. It would be almost two and a half centuries after Hastings before Edward I would construct the first great organic laws suggesting an ultimate constitutional framework; three hundred more years would pass before the Tudors would forge, on the anvil of their own forceful personalities, the counterforce of the parliamentary revolution which would destroy the Stuarts in the century after that. By then, feudalism would be an empty shell; now, in the noon-time of Norman England, it was coming into full flower.

A million and a half people were said to live here in the twelfth century; of these, a few hundred were crown tenants, or the greatest lords, while a few thousand made up the rest of the peerage and the church hierarchy. These few thousands held virtually all of the land in the realm, and it was for them that the privileges and obligations of the feudal age were devised—a small power elite whose existence hardly had reference to the hundreds of thousands of men and women below. Only in London and a few other cities or boroughs might a yeoman achieve, as a burgess, a corporate identity and through this some voice in affairs. But the movers of events were the lords of the realm, both temporal and spiritual, and the number and nature of their rights and obligations were elaborately defined. Because their rights and duties were based on land, they were expressed in terms of the tenures by which the land was held—military tenure in the case of the barons and mesne lords, frankalmoin in the case of ecclesiastics, and socage in the case of those whose service obligations were essentially agricultural.

In the Conqueror's day, military tenure was of necessity the sole manner by which estates could be held; the overlord must know that the land could provide, on short notice, a prescribed number of armed and trained men and their retinue. Knight service was the most important function of a vassal in a military society, and indeed the only practical question under the circumstances was whether the paramount lord could expect these forces to be used for him or against him. To reduce the latter danger, tenancies often were held at the will of the grantor; it was not until the regime was settled and relatively quiet that estates were commonly granted for the life of the tenant, and still later to him and his heirs. As a matter both of military necessity and of economics, the feudal law required an heir to pay a relief, or a tax for the continuation of the grant after the original tenant died. If the heir was a minor and unable to bear arms, his overlord had the enjoyment and control of his estate until he came of age. If the heir was female, her marriage was a matter of policy, for her husband must be loyal to the grantor of the estate.

The tenure of land offered a variety of economic devices for the benefit of the lord, after the basic assessment of the estate in terms of a stipulated number of knights' fees. Some of the most immediately remunerative were called aids and included the obligation to ransom the lord's person if he were taken captive, or to provide men and money if the paramount lord was faced with war. Other aids were demanded to make the lord's eldest son a knight, "the intention of it being to breed up the . . . heir apparent of the seignory, to deeds of arms and chivalry, for the better defense of the nation," and to provide a suitable dowry for the eldest daughter, "for daughters' portions in those days were extremely slender; few lords being able to save much out of their income for this purpose," wrote William Blackstone. But the demands for aids did not always stop there; kings found it possible to raise revenues merely on the prospect of war, neglecting to refund if the prospect did not materialize. Eldest daughters of crown tenants might be married more than once—or younger daughters made the beneficiaries of dower gifts—so that money as well as pertinent alliances could be multiplied by giving in marriage. Widows could be compelled to pay a fine if they refused to marry at the lord's direction.

The Church, too, was expected to provide its share of material support, since the English kings after Domesday knew how substantial the Church's revenues were. At first the lords spiritual performed knight service under the military tenures required by William I: Bishop Odo had his personal army at hand whenever he was free from imprisonment. But soon the ecclesiastical tenants undertook to discharge their obligations by spiritual services— called frankalmoin, or "free alms"—for the poor who would otherwise be a drain upon the royal purse. This service substantially reduced the financial burdens on the churchmen; prayers and charitable offices were more economical than maintaining a following of armed men beyond the needs of their own holdings. Indeed, the lords temporal also found that, with the rising cost of equipping and training armored and mounted troops, it was cheaper to pay "shield money," or scutages, with which the overlord could hire his own fighting force. Before the end of the Norman regime, scutages had become general, and kings after Stephen regularly employed mercenary armies.

As he hastily mounted the throne following his brother's death, Henry I found it necessary to promise some reforms in the feudal system. The "good laws of King Edward" were to be observed, and all "bad customs, by which the realm of England has been unjustly oppressed" were to be repudiated. Such bad customs, which had grown up in his brother's time, Henry enumerated: Heirs had been compelled to buy back their estates at exorbitant prices rather than paying the reasonable relief fixed in terms of the number of knights' fees charged to the estate. Bishoprics had been left unfilled for long periods of time, so that the revenues from these estates would come to the king or the crown tenant instead of to an incumbent. Widows had been forced unwillingly into second marriages, or marriages of tenants' daughters had been dictated by the grantor. Debts and forfeitures to the crown which had been unreasonably exacted were forgiven, and restitution was to be made. Most important of all was the pro-

vision in Henry's charter of liberties that the promises now made
by the King to his tenants in chief were to be regarded as also
being made by these vassals to all their undertenants; as the lords
required justice of the crown, so they must do justice to their
own feudal dependents.

The coronation charter of that August 5, a century before
John was to meet the demands of his barons, confirmed the basic
elements of justice as the feudal age understood them. John was
cornered by his lords after military disasters abroad had left him
virtually defenseless at home; Henry kept the initiative by offering the guarantees before the lords could find a means of demanding them. In essence, the coronation charter of 1100 was an
extension of the coronation oath traceable to the ninth-century
Saxon king Ethelred; but it specified in detail the abuses which,
the tenants declared, had multiplied in Rufus's day. Henry thus
renounced the wrongdoings of one brother, to whose throne he
was succeeding, in order to strengthen his position with his vassals against his other brother. For Robert of Normandy had
returned in triumph from the First Crusade, flushed with determination to retrieve his dukedom, and since Rufus had died, to
extend a claim to the throne of England. Robert's invasion across
the Channel was turned back by the Treaty of Alton; then Henry
in his turn invaded Normandy and by 1106 had captured Robert
and ended the threat to his regime. Thereafter, Henry felt less
pressure to honor the coronation charter in every letter; but periodically throughout his reign he reissued it whenever he found
an appeal to the people needed to rally them against a common
foe.

Like his father, Henry I was concerned with development of
an effective administrative system once his control of the realm
was settled. He created a justiciar as a kind of vice-regent to act
for him whenever he was out of the land; a chancellor was
established to mind the domestic matters of the crown castles
and lands; and a royal treasurer now kept account of the revenues. The Anglo-Saxon Witan had gradually changed into a
general court which moved with the monarch as he proceeded to
various parts of his kingdom. As it was called upon to administer
justice, it came to be denominated the *curia regis;* when it gath-

ered to it all the great lords of the realm to deliberate with the King upon matters of government in general, it was the *magnum concilium*, the great council. The shape of a national government was very dimly becoming discernible, although it would be almost two centuries before conditions would call forth a regular assembly sufficiently representative to be called a parliament.

With the peaceful accession of Rufus and Henry, two crises for the legacy of the Norman Conquest had been passed; a third developed in 1120, when Prince William, Henry's only legitimate male heir, was drowned in a Channel crossing. The King was in the prime of life and career, but no man could foretell the course of events, and it became obvious that some provision must now be made for the future of the kingdom. The French monarch, Louis the Fat, was intriguing with the son of Robert and ready to support his bid for the ultimate succession. Henry's second marriage had produced no issue, and although he reportedly had fathered some twenty natural offspring, there remained only his second legitimate child, Maud, or Matilda, an empress by virtue of a German marriage, but now a widow and also childless. Still, this was better than nothing, and Henry proposed to his barons that they recognize her as heiress to the throne. The lords did not hesitate long, believing that a woman might be easier to dominate than the strong-willed sons of the Conqueror. In any event, they reasoned, at her death the choice of the succession would revert to them.

Things worked out differently. Henry in 1128 arranged a second marriage for Matilda, this time to Geoffrey, son of the Count of Anjou, and, in a promise reminiscent of Edward the Confessor's alleged offer to Duke William, offered him the thrones of both England and Normandy. Thus, the house of the Angevins —or Plantagenets as they were called, for the *genistas*, or broom plants, which they planted for hunting shelters—moved into the wings of history. Geoffrey and Matilda had three children, the eldest named Henry after his grandfather. Matilda, even more imperious and aggressive than her sires, showed every indication of holding the barons to their oath of support; but, writes William of Malmesbury, when she had remarried "all men were asserting, as though by some prophetic spirit, that after [Henry's] death

they would fail to keep this oath," for, said the lords, their swearing had been upon the condition that Matilda marry no one outside England unless with their consent.

Angevins were traditional foes of Normans, and the prospect
of an unbroken succession of Matilda's heirs dimmed the barons'
chances of regaining some of the control of affairs their fathers
had claimed in old times. The king in those days they had regarded as *primus inter pares*, and they would have this again.
Moreover, there was a candidate in the son of Adela, daughter
of the Conqueror. Theobald, Count of Blois, was the elder of two
sons of Adela and the natural candidate to whom the plotters
looked; but they reckoned without Stephen, Earl of Lancaster
and the younger of the two. As a member of Henry's court,
Stephen had familiarized himself with the techniques of seizing
power; it was his misfortune, and England's, that he lacked the
capacity to use it once it had been seized. In any event, when
Henry suddenly died in 1135, Stephen got across the Channel
before either Theobald or Matilda was aware of his intention.
He reached London and was elected king by the citizens, who
claimed to possess a special prerogative in such matters. Not
relying on this tenuous claim, however, Stephen then hurried to
Winchester and secured the royal treasury. Now possessed of this
strategic advantage, he then returned to London and was crowned
by the Archbishop of Canterbury.

Surprised as they were by this swift turn of affairs, the
lords of the realm took counsel with each other to determine
whether all might not be turned to their advantage. Theobald
was persuaded reluctantly to accept the dukedom in Normandy,
although his heart was never in statecraft after Stephen's *coup*,
and he soon resigned his new office in favor of his nimbler brother.
A stronger man than Stephen would now quickly have consolidated his power and confronted Matilda's certain challenge with
a maximum marshalling of his forces; but Stephen was not such
a man. "Of energy but little judgment," wrote a contemporary of
him; "lenient to his enemies and easily appeased, courteous to all;
though you admired his kindness in promising, still you felt his
words lacked truth and his promises fulfilment." The barons began
to gravitate toward one of the two camps: the Angevin party, with

its busy preparations for attack; or the royal party, which meas-
ured its loyalty to the throne by the concessions which could be
obtained from it.

Thus, the great lords at last were to have their voice in affairs;
but from the outset, the voice spoke only of self-interest. From
Stephen emanated another coronation charter, reissued with more
particulars the following year at Oxford; but the language differed
materially from the spirit of the charter of Henry I. Stephen did
not even pretend to have become king "by the grace of God,"
but specifically acknowledged that he ruled "by election and
assent of clergy and people" as well as by the confirmation of
the Pope. Moreover, the barons swore fealty to him only upon
receiving lavish grants secured by a torrent of private charters;
they did their homage perfunctorily. It was the unhappy beginning of an unhappy nineteen years. Stephen, a kindly man by
the standards of his age, was already a victim of the always
thinly disguised rapacity of feudalism. The drums rolled menac-
ingly across the Channel, and he knew not how to sound his
own trumpet but with an uncertain sound.

And now anarchy and chaos beset all of England; Matilda
moved deliberately to unseat her cousin and to avenge herself
on those who had falsely sworn to support her own right of
succession. Insecure on his throne, Stephen vacillated between
buying support—he "dealt out and scattered soothly" the royal
treasure that Henry had built up—and striking blindly at any
who aroused his suspicions. Before his reign was two years old,
he had outraged most of the lords in southern and western
England, thus pinpointing for the invaders the area of major
disaffection. In the spring of 1138 began a general uprising here,
and Matilda now crossed the Channel and raised her standard.
The Church withdrew its support, despite lavish grants the
King had made to it in his charters; and Stephen himself, deserted by his own armies at the Battle of Lincoln in 1141, though
he fought with desperate courage after all was lost, was taken
prisoner. At a Church council summoned by his younger brother,
Bishop Henry, now the papal legate, came the final humiliation;
Stephen was deposed, and Matilda recognized as the successor
to the throne.

But the tale of bitterness and division was only begun, and the ironic turns of fate buffeted all the claimants in succession. The Empress, with the throne now in sight, proceeded to Winchester to be formally elected *Domina Anglorum,* a title customarily bestowed upon a prince in anticipation of his coronation. But where Stephen had been too soft, Matilda was now proving too hard. The Londoners were turned out, as she entered the gates of the city, prepared to give her as tumultuous a welcome as they had a few years before given Stephen; but before she was even settled, she demanded a stern tallage, an arbitrary levy which was used to provide the sovereign with funds for his personal use. The cheers died away, to be replaced by the ringing of bells calling the citizens to arms. Matilda and her party hurriedly left by the city's western gate, for in addition to the aroused Londoners, there was Stephen's Queen at the head of a loyal army entering the city from the south.

Furious at being thwarted when the crown was virtually in her grasp, the Empress vented her wrath on her hapless prisoner, the erstwhile King, by putting him in irons. She returned to Winchester and laid siege to the Bishop's castle there; but the royalists raised the siege and drove the Empress in a rout to the west. Matilda's brother Robert was captured in the melee and in short order had been exchanged for Stephen. In December another Church council was convened, reversed its action of the previous April, branded Matilda as the usurper, and recrowned Stephen. The King was now back on his throne, but if possible, matters were worse than ever; his party held an uncertain grip on the east of England, and the Angevin party was entrenched in the south and west where the uprising had first occurred.

The realm was paralyzed, and the barons could hardly have wished for more; there were regular shifts of allegiance as particular lords crossed the lines and made particular bargains with the two parties. But the stalemate was the preferred order, for while it obtained, the barons could range freely across the realm, taking possession of such estates as caught their fancy and burning what they could not possess. William of Malmesbury wrote: "Undertenants, peasants, any who were thought wealthy, they kidnapped and compelled to promise anything by the severity of their tortures. After pillaging the dwellings of the wretched countrymen to the very straw, they bound the owners and imprisoned them, and did not let them go until they had spent for their ransom all they possessed or could in any way obtain." The contrast with former times was everywhere manifest. "Under King Henry many foreigners, displaced by troubles in their native land, sailed to England and lived in undisturbed peace under his wings; under Stephen many from Flanders and Brittany, who were wont to live by plunder, flew to England in the hope of great booty."

Of all who worked both sides of the troubled stream in those days, there was one whose name became synonymous with unprincipled advancement. Geoffrey de Mandeville, constable of the Tower of London, found himself in ideal position to turn the changes of fortune to his advantage. As a price for his loyalty in the control of this fortress, he obtained from Stephen, before the King's capture at Lincoln, a charter creating for himself the earldom of Essex. A grandson of one of the Conqueror's henchmen of the same name, Geoffrey readily persuaded himself that this honor was merely an overdue recognition of services rendered; but when Matilda entered London, he hastened to meet her and offer the Tower and its garrison. From the Empress he won a confirmation of his earldom and a grant of £100 yearly from crown revenues.

The concession had not even taken effect when Matilda was flying from London and Geoffrey was confronted with a newly crowned Stephen, with whom he proceeded to make peace. Indeed, it was Geoffrey's forces that helped rout the Angevins at the siege of Winchester and captured the lords who could be exchanged for the King. Stephen in acknowledgment of this service pardoned Geoffrey's treason, reconfirmed his earldom, and trebled the crown revenues which were to go to him. But there was yet no limit to Geoffrey's ambition or Stephen's readiness to buy his loyalty. Geoffrey was made sheriff and justice of Hertfordshire, London, and Middlesex—three counties which, with Essex, made the Earl virtual ruler of all eastern England.

In something less than two years, the Constable of the Tower had thus advanced to a position where no noble of the realm

surpassed him in wealth and authority. Barons listened to him
and obeyed his directions far more readily than they did Stephen.
Men envied rather than abhorred his open treachery, which continued as Geoffrey assessed the prospects of Matilda's ultimate
recovery of the crown. At Oxford in the early spring of 1142, the
Empress matched the King's gifts to Geoffrey, added a new earldom for his brother-in-law, Aubrey de Vere, and promised to
make no peace with any who were his enemies. Yet from Oxford,
Geoffrey went directly to Stephen's court and took up his duties
as a counsellor of the realm. It would be a year longer before
Stephen—or what is more likely, his stronger-willed Queen and
others more capable of decision—finally arrested Geoffrey and
charged him with treason.

The record of his indictment was the history of the anarchy
and a lesson in government without law. For months the Earl's
armed ruffians had ravaged the country so completely that across
vast tracts of land to the east there was no living thing to be
found. Uncut crops had rotted in the fields, blackened ruins out-
lined the site of former villages, and the skeletons of churches,
roofless and gutted, loomed above the ashes of the hamlets.
Scores of prisoners in his dungeons, done to death by unspeakable
tortures, had been dragged from the dwellings the Earl had ravaged in his search for riches. Famine, following in the wake of
the denuded lands, had taken hundreds more.

Geoffrey was slain in the course of a final rebellion against
the throne, after Stephen, in a characteristic turn of weakness,
had set him free upon the surrender of the Tower of London. For
his desecration of so much Church property during his bloody
career, the Earl died excommunicate, and his body was left unburied for twenty years until a son, making reparation for his
father's sins, was permitted by Pope Alexander to place the remains in the earth. By then Stephen, too, had passed from the
scene. A man of generally good intentions in a vicious age, he
ended his story as it had begun, subject to the decisions of others
who knew what they wanted. Matilda, having lost her own bid
for the throne, put her eldest son forward as next claimant, and
Stephen's last years were spent in security on the understanding

that Henry would succeed him. Thus passed ingloriously the Norman glory, giving place to the Plantagenets.

"To judge from the fortunate issues of chance, Henry II, King of the English, seemed to have obtained divine favor in almost everything," wrote Gerald of Wales. When he was crowned, said Gerald, "all those who before this had been oppressors of the kingdom and disturbers of the peace of the realm, including not only the foreigners but his own brothers and later their sons, were suddenly and as it were by a miracle destroyed by death. . . . Thus . . . he not only brought strong peace with the aid of God's grace to his hereditary dominions, but also triumphed victoriously in remote and foreign lands." At the age of twenty-one, the first of the Angevin rulers, whose successive reigns would reach to the end of the fourteenth century, proceeded to his throne across a land strewn with broken loyalties. Almost two decades of anarchy had eroded much of the order and security of Norman feudalism established by William and his sons; the times were ripe for a fresh advance in statecraft.

Henry, who had grown up marking Stephen's mistakes, set out at once to restore the power of the throne. Unlicensed castles, built in profusion and in defiance of royal authority, were torn down; lords who refused to disgorge what they had usurped were overpowered by the young King's knights and compelled to renew their homage. Thus, said an observer, "the ravening wolves were turned into sheep, or, even if they were not really changed, they were made through fear of the law to dwell harmlessly with the sheep." A squat, red-haired man of fierce determination, whose energy and ability. recalled legends of the Conqueror, Henry soon could consider England under his control; and his reign, for most of its thirty-five years, was a history of spectacular advancement, so that at its height the Angevin rule extended from the northern coast of Scotland to the slopes of the Pyrenees. Feudalism understood strength (Stephen had simply lacked it) and the barons submitted to Henry on these terms.

Now, aware of the depredations committed throughout the land in the years of anarchy, Henry II decreed that the king's justices should ride out on eyre (circuit) to inquire into the con-

duct of the crown's officers and to remove the worst offenders.
As the justices traveled about the realm, it became evident that
royal rights were unevenly maintained in different districts, and
also that many grave crimes, punished locally, were punished
unequally. By the Assize of Clarendon, in 1166, the King would
decree that serious offenses should thereafter be heard by the
justices on eyre, together with the cases involving royal rights.
Both matters would thus become a special body of adjudication
to be known as pleas of the crown. Henceforth the royal justices
would be regarded by many tenants as the preferred source of
justice, and one of the greatest powers of the barons and the
mesne lords, administration of the affairs of their subtenants in
the manorial courts, would be undermined. When property rights
also came to be the subject of royal justice, another intervening
power of the crown tenants would be vitiated.

But the brilliant advance in judicial procedure which ori-
ented the law of the land permanently toward the throne was
the concept of the returnable writ. By this writ, the sheriff became
personally answerable to the crown for the duty set out in the
command. "The King to the Sheriff, Greeting," ran the words.
"Command R. that he return to N. one hide of land in that village
where N. complains that he hath disseised him. And unless he do
so, summon him by good summoners to be before me or my justices . . . and do you have there the summoners and this writ."

William I, in one of the first decrees after the Conquest was
fairly established, introduced the Norman concept of trial by
battle, either between principals or between their hired cham-
pions, for the settlement of certain disputes between French and
English subjects. In an age when the strength to defend land was
an all-important consideration, the practical test of which party
was physically the more powerful was camouflaged by the religious proposition that God would support the right. But the possession and occupancy of land (seisin) and the protection of
seisin by the grantor had to be better insured in a society where
any unprincipled strong man might drive out the lawful occupants
and take up possession in the rightful tenant's absence.

Henry's first attempted remedy was the Grand Assize, a
choice between combat and the submission of the dispute to a

jury of recognition. The King and his great justiciar, Ranulph de Glanville, had high hopes for the new procedure, confirmed at Clarendon and renewed ten years later at Northampton. Wrote Glanville, or one of his colleagues:

> [The Grand Assize] flows from the most profound Equity. For that Justice, which, after many and long delays, is scarcely, if ever, elicited by the Duel, is more advantageously and expeditiously attained, through the benefit of this institution. . . . And by this course of proceeding, both the labor of Men, and the expenses of the poor are saved. Besides, by so much as the testimony of many credible witnesses, in judicial proceedings, preponderates over that of one only, by so much greater Equity is this institution regulated than that of the Duel. For since the Duel proceeds upon the testimony of one Juror, this constitution requires the oaths of twelve lawful men, at least.

But in practice, the device proved imperfect in reaching the basic problem, for it worked in favor of the person in possession of the land, who alone could elect to rest on the Grand Assize. It remained for Henry's learned men in the law—a class of specialists which developed as the royal courts created a need for them—to extend the principle from the Grand Assize into the petty assizes, called in Norman French the assizes of *novel disseisin, mort d'ancestor*, and *darrein presentment*.

By the writ of *novel disseisin*, the dispossessed tenant now simply alleged that a stranger by wrongful and recent (*novel*) action had disseised him of his estate. Said Glanville, in such case the plaintiff shall have this writ:

> The King to the Sheriff, Health. N. complains to me that R. has, unjustly and without a judgment, disseised him of his free tenement in such a vill, since my last voyage into Normandy; and therefore I command you, that if the aforesaid N. should make you secure of prosecuting his claim, then you cause the tenement to be reseised, with the chattels taken on it, and that you cause him with his chattels to be in peace until the Pentecost; and in the meantime, you cause twelve free and lawful

men of the neighborhood to view the land, and their
names to be imbreviated; and summon them, by good
summoners, that they be then before me, or my justices,
prepared to make the recognition; and put, by gage, and
safe pledges, the aforesaid R. or his bailiff if he be not
found, that he be then there to hear such recognition. . . .

The writ of *mort d'ancestor* was a palpable fiction, by which an
heir could assert that between the time of the death of the former
tenant and the time the heir could take possession, a stranger had
wrongfully occupied the land. The king's writ thereupon ordered
a jury to review the facts:

If *G.*, the son of *T.*, shall make you secure of prosecuting
his claim, then summon by good summoners twelve free
and lawful men of the neighborhood of such a vill, that
they be before me or my justices on such a day prepared
on their oath to return, if *T.* the father of the aforesaid
G. was seised in his demesne as of fee, of one Yardland
in that vill on the day of his death . . . and if the said *G.*
be his nearest heir. And in the meantime let them view
the land and cause their names to be imbreviated; and
summon by good summoners *R.*, who holds the land,
that he be then there to hear such recognition. . . .

More peculiarly feudal—although it would be the mid-nineteenth
century before it was completely repealed—was the action of *darrein presentment*, which concerned the privilege of advowson, or
the right to fill a vacant ecclesiastical position. Parish churches,
priories, and abbeys had been founded by local lords throughout
the realm. The Domesday survey, for instance, showed that Ilbert
de Laci had "three churches and three priests" in his estate. The
founder claimed the privilege of choosing the occupants of the
offices, an often fortuitous placement for a younger son or a
favored follower. By the new writ, the founder of the benefice
could allege that a stranger had usurped the right to fill the
vacancy since the last (*darrein*) presentment of a candidate to
the bishop for investiture.

Proof of innocence of accused in criminal cases was still primitive, including the ordeals of bearing red-hot irons in the hands
and being able to show the healing of the wounds within a pre-

scribed time, or thrusting one's arm into boiling water, or being bound and thrown into cold water where an innocent person supposedly would sink. But the developing speed and uniformity of the king's justice had already brought the law a great step forward from the dark ages. And where the king's peace was fundamentally involved in criminal matters, it was not difficult to argue that it was also involved in civil issues; the treatise attributed to Glanville contained more than forty writs offering undertenants and freemen generally a means of putting themselves upon the king's justice. However much the great lords might chafe at the narrowing jurisdiction of the seignorial courts, their acceptance of the principle of sovereignty in the king implied their obedience to his peace—and indeed the writ issuing from the chancellor required the crown tenants or the sheriffs not to hold the king's bidding in contempt.

Through Henry's statecraft, the gulf between Saxon and Norman, a century after Hastings, steadily diminished. The regular work of the justices on eyre meant the development of a trained class of lawyers and the emergence of a common law benefiting Saxon and Norman alike. But fate was to cloud the great advances of Henry's government with the bloody episode of the martyrdom of Thomas à Becket. Having established some fundamental propositions of the common law, the King now sought to regain jurisdiction over matters which Stephen had yielded to the canon law of the church. The matter brewed for several years, until at Clarendon in 1164—two years before the great Assize on jury functions—the Bishop of Oxford "made a recognition or inquisition, concerning certain customs and liberties of the king's predecessors, to wit, Henry, his grandfather, and others, which ought to be observed and held by all in the kingdom, on account of the dissentions and discords which often arise between the clergy and justices of our lord the king, and the nobles of the realm." The sixteen chapters of this "inquisition," later known as the Constitutions of Clarendon, were thereupon sworn to by the assembled spiritual and temporal lords. Observed Roger of Wendover: "In consequence of these constitutions, the lay-power was now extended without opposition to all ecclesiastical causes, whether of things or of persons, to the contempt of the ecclesiastical privileges; for the bishops were silent, or at least rather muttered their disapprobation than openly resisted."

But Thomas, Archbishop of Canterbury and Primate of All England, besought the Pope to absolve him from the oath. This was not the first, although it ultimately became the climactic, issue between Henry and his former chancellor and friend. The early disputes between them had been magnified out of proportion by Henry's courtiers, who, "seeking to win his favor and itching to gain his ear, defamed the archbishop and hated him without a cause." To them, says William fitz Stephen, were joined "many bishops, for fear of losing their land and goods." Two strong-willed paramount lords of the spiritual and temporal world were now committed to a struggle in which no compromise was possible.

Thomas saw the issue as an infringement of the temporal power upon prerogatives of the spiritual; Henry saw it as a logical and necessary step to make justice itself effective, not permitting a clerical class to escape the civil or criminal liability which fell on other men. The dispute over "criminous clerks" continued, and when Becket fled the kingdom to lay his case before the Pope, Henry's fury—a characteristic Plantagenet choler—could scarcely be contained. For five years, from Northampton to Rome to Montmartre, where an accord was almost reached, and to the final formal reconciliation at Fréteval, the issue was kept alive. The ultimate vindication of Becket in the arbitration arranged by the Pope might have been accepted by Henry in good part, had it not been for the excommunication of the Bishops of York, London, and Salisbury, three who had supported the King, although for their own purposes, in the course of the struggle. Their appearance before Henry in Normandy, with their version of the Archbishop's behavior upon returning to Canterbury, rekindled all the unreasoning anger in the King. In an impulsive and irrevocable outburst he appeared to call for Thomas's death. The Archbishop was murdered in his cathedral four days after Christmas, 1170; four years later, the King did public penance for the deed, and most of the Constitutions of Clarendon were eventually carried into effect.

The bitter conflict between king and prelate revealed the extent to which, in the century after William I, both canon and secular law had developed and overlapped. The veneer of civilization was still thin, but the civilization was genuine and would survive the succession of ills that the coming centuries would bring. The two Williams and the two Henrys had provided the land with a consistent example of the benefits of strong national rule which the anarchy of Stephen only threw into higher relief. But the true lesson of Stephen's period was that no one, whether the Conqueror or the first Plantagenet, ultimately could avoid the consequences of living in his own age. That age was medieval, not modern; the strong alone could survive, and only the strongest of all could lead and compel a following.

Henry II, one of the greatest of the early medieval monarchs, was to suffer in the end a denouement of the epic proportions of the Greek tragedies; his story warned of the long interval yet to be endured before a free society would be possible of conception. In the end, the chronicler would write of him:

> Though all the regions of the earth could not
> Suffice me once, eight feet of ground are now enough.

For more than three decades his reign had been a story of general advancement. The chronicle of Newburgh spoke glowingly: "In his ordinances he took great care of the poor, the widows and orphans, and in several places gave liberal alms with a bountiful hand." Except for the tragedy of his quarrel with Becket, he preserved scrupulously the ecclesiastic prerogative. "He never laid tribute on churchmen or monasteries on pretext of some necessity like other monarchs," the chronicle continued; and in temporal affairs he "strove diligently to keep the peace, wherever possible by gifts of money, but by armed force if he could not secure it otherwise. With these and other good qualities adorning his royal person, he was nevertheless not acceptable to many who had eyes only for his bad qualities. Ungrateful men and those bent on evil courses cavilled unceasingly against the wickedness of their own monarch and would not endure to hear good spoken of him. To such men especially the hardships of the days that followed alone brought understanding."

Part of Henry's troubles were of his own making, but part were born of the shifting weight of Continental politics which was to place a fatal strain on the far-flung Angevin empire. The threat of disaster was chronic, as in 1173, when, with the King deep in Poitou putting down a revolt, another rebellion broke out in his rear, on the Scottish border where William the Lion led a force southward gathering disaffected barons in an avalanche. But for the bold action of Glanville, then Sheriff of Westmoreland, and the surprise and capture of William in the fog-shrouded fields before the castle of Alwich, a catastrophe might have befallen the empire. And yet, aside from this great uprising, Henry's home front was relatively secure; and so long as the inept Louis VII sat on the throne of France, the shrewd opportunism of the Plantagenet was too much for foreign rivals. Aquitaine, that incalculably rich prize, Henry had long since added to his holdings by his marriage to Eleanor, whom he had stolen as wife from Louis. The heart of Normandy, the Vexin, he secured by arranging a marriage of the two-year-old French Princess Margaret to his six-year-old son Henry. To the west, the King simply annexed Brittany by announcing his succession when his brother, Count Geoffrey, died, although he had to enforce his claim by three years of hard fighting.

Now the Angevin rule extended from the Shetlands to the Pyrenees, and so great was Henry's influence on the Continent that the kings of Navarre and Castile submitted their disputes to him for arbitration. But winds of change were blowing; in 1180 Louis died and was succeeded by his son Philip, to be surnamed Augustus, a different breed of man. Louis might accept the stealing of his wife, but Philip was infuriated at the seduction of his sister; for, as rumor had it, among his many paramours Henry had indeed numbered the French Princess Alice, then betrothed to his son Richard. Philip's life was to be dedicated to the destruction of the Angevin power in France; against the father and both sons, the French monarch would pursue this objective singlemindedly until the Continental possessions of the English kings were all but expunged from history.

Yet another disruptive force was the worsening struggle in the Holy Land, where the zest of the First and Second Crusades

was rapidly giving way to despair, and the combined expedition-
ary forces of Christendom yielded ground to the infidel. A name
that sent a chill through the West—Saladin—momentarily stilled
the disputes between clashing European monarchies; in 1177,
Henry and Louis had executed a convention which in effect
established a truce, to last until each had completed a tour of
duty in the effort to save the kingdom of Jerusalem. The Pope
called for all available knights to take the cross, and when Philip
ascended the throne, he and Henry had agreed to continue the
truce, even though neither was personally in any hurry to embark
for the distant conflict. It was not until 1188 that Henry levied
the "Saladin tithe" in an effort to raise a war chest for the Crusade
—but by now his own time was running out, and fortune's smile
was fading.

To whom now should England look, as the great King's
strength and control over his family and his empire began to
wane? Henry had sought to guard against a disruption in the
affairs of the empire by having his eldest legitimate son, Henry,
crowned during his own lifetime. The legitimacy of this measure,
if not its legality, carried out by the Archbishop of York in the
heat of the controversy with Becket, had been rendered moot by
the death of the young king five years before. There now remained
the second and third sons, Richard and John. Although the
conjugal and filial relationships in Henry's household had long
since turned to the bitterest gall, the King was inclined to prefer
the youngest, John. Richard, after all, was too much his mother's
favorite, and Eleanor of Aquitaine had lived apart from her husband for most of the past fifteen years. The dashing warlike
accomplishments of Richard would have won his father's admiration had they not been in the service of the great province Eleanor
ruled virtually independent of the rest of the Angevin empire.

This state of affairs presented Philip with the opportunity he
was seeking. It was easy to play upon the estrangement of
Eleanor, and upon the concern of Richard that Henry might somehow maneuver him out of the succession. Even John could be
drawn into the combination now being forged against Henry,
for the removal of the father would mean his advancement at
least one step nearer the throne. In June 1188, Philip opened his

campaign by seizing Henry's castle of Chateauroux; Henry, who
had been busy in England with his Saladin tithe in anticipation
of the expedition to join the Third Crusade, was taken by surprise
but yet did not suspect the magnitude of Philip's challenge. The
aging king crossed the Channel with something less than a fully
mounted offensive force, intending to confront Philip with a
demand for a conference to explain why the truce had been
broken. At the meeting, the second and far more stunning blow
was dealt, as Richard formally deserted his father and swore
allegiance to the French king. Henry, dazed by the blow, was
caught in a trap. Richard's treachery had delivered to the foe
the whole might of Aquitaine, on which Henry would have relied
if, as it now was turning out, the conference led to war.

But more disasters were to come, for now many earls of
Anjou, Brittany, and Normandy itself followed Richard's banner.
The overwhelming host now pressed hard upon the reeling monarch; and, says the chronicler, "with the exception of the mercenaries, only a small number came to the assistance of the
king of England, and even those about him were wavering in
their loyalty." Le Mans, then Tours, and finally Angers fell to the
combined forces, and Henry, now a virtual fugitive, racked with
a fever, was brought to his final humiliation; Philip demanded
his unconditional surrender "without any reservation to be made
unless he himself of his mercy granted it."

At Colombières Henry, already in the last stages of his agony,
was led before Philip and compelled to "put himself in all things
at the advice and will of . . . [the] king of France." Richard was
declared heir to the throne and "none of the barons or knights,
who have withdrawn their allegiance to the king of England, in
the recent war, and have come over to Earl Richard, shall in
future return." Then came the final degradation—the kiss of
peace, by which Henry was directed to bless his son and "put
away all anger and indignation from his heart." The dying and
betrayed ruler mustered his wrath for one final verbal blow at
Richard; "God grant I die not before I have worthily avenged
myself on thee," he muttered in their embrace. Richard was sufficiently stricken to withdraw hastily from the meeting; but the

final exchange "aroused thereby the great mirth . . . of the French king and the whole court."

It was the knowledge of John's name, at the very head of the list of Angevin nobles arrayed against him, that had really done Henry in. He had raised himself from his sickbed at the news, to demand, "Is it true that John, my very heart, whom I have loved before all my sons, and for whose advancement I have endured all these ills, has deserted me?" The memory of that terrible report, and the bitterness of the final subjection before Philip, followed him back to the castle of Chinon and his bed. "Shame, shame on a conquered king!" were his last coherent words; he died cursing the day he had been born. Then, said Gerald of Wales, petty looters entered the death chamber and stripped the unguarded body, "so that for some while the body was exposed naked, . . . until a certain lad ran up and covered it as best he could with a short cloak, woven of fine thread, though it only reached to the knees, of the kind young men used to wear in summer. Thus was fulfilled . . . the nickname bestowed on him in his youth," when he was known as Henry Curtmantle.

The King's body was brought to Fontevrault for burial, and Prince Richard hastened from Poitou to attend the funeral. Bystanders said that at the moment Richard entered the church, blood began to flow from the dead King's nostrils and continued to flow for as long as his son remained there. For England, for Richard, and for John, the portent was grave for the quarter of a century which was now to follow.

Reaping the Whirlwind

RICHARD the Lionheart was many things to many men. Some observers had it that he was "bad to all, worse to his friends, and worst of all to himself." At thirty-two, he understood best the code of chivalry and the fierce physical competition of the tournament learned at Eleanor's fabled court at Aquitaine. The papal call to the Third Crusade had appealed to every instinct for glory and adventure that was in him, and impulsively, in 1187, he had taken the cross. Now, having wrested the patrimony from his father and preparing to ascend the throne as anointed sovereign, his thoughts turned impatiently to the Holy Land. Once his newly won kingdom was in order, he intended to be off; as matters turned out, he would spend only six months of his ten-year reign in England. He was a warrior rather than an administrator, and his gestures at statecraft more often than not sowed seeds of discord to be reaped by those who came after him. Many of his political moves were shortsighted, for like most men of action, he lacked the capacity to weigh the alternative consequences which might flow from certain decisions.

Two grave political considerations would have counseled a more prudent leader against subjecting his kingdom to an absentee government so soon after acquiring it. One was the fact that Philip of France, now flushed with the completeness of his triumph over Henry II and undiverted in his intention to drive England from the Continent, could scarcely be expected to relax his efforts because Richard had thrown in with him. The other was the fact that England itself was full of lords who had chafed at his father's iron domination of the realm, and who had just witnessed the gaudy rewards to be had through a well-executed rebellion. Against these odds, Richard had only one trump card to play—his reputation as a skillful and (for the most part) victorious fighter. It was a card he managed indeed to play with great effectiveness; the feudal age, after all, venerated physical courage and military prowess, and throughout his career Richard kept the sheen of gallantry.

Thus, it was Richard's fate to be able to put off the day of wrath—and John's to have to endure the full fury of the tempest when it finally broke. And in the quarter-century which was now beginning, the fortunes of the two brothers were to be intermingled and contrasted in many an ironic turn of fate. Ten years younger, John had been born at a moment when his father had no estate available to confer upon him; with his often sardonic humor, Henry had nicknamed him "Lackland." The King had made amends handsomely before the youth had reached the age of ten, and at Henry's death John was doubtless possessed of greater personal estates than Richard, until the latter ascended the throne. He was also considerably more intelligent, and in the uneven course of his own reign would accomplish several substantial feats of government which subsequent history tended to ignore. Both brothers, however, were also endowed with the worst of the Plantagenet faults: ungovernable rage, insatiable hunger for money and women, and consummate arrogance. They divided between them the family's talents for military brilliance and sporadic flashes of insight into statecraft.

Richard moved swiftly to establish himself in his dominions, to mollify Philip Augustus, and to prepare the way for his adventure on the Crusade. He dispatched messengers to England to order the release of his mother, whom Henry, in an attempt to break her independent power in Aquitaine, had long kept under restraints in France or in England. Richard directed that she should represent him until his coronation, which recalled to men's minds an old saying, "The eagle of the broken union shall rejoice in her third nestling." The new king was indeed the third of the five fierce males whom Eleanor had borne. Somewhat rashly, but with her son's approval, the Queen opened the doors of all the prisons in the land in a general amnesty. But Richard was not intent on vilifying his father's reign; rather, he warmly praised those nobles who had stood by the old King in his final

grim hours, and one faithful knight of Henry's—William Marshal
—he endowed with vast estates and gave to him in marriage one
of the greatest heiresses of the realm, Isabel of Pembroke. The
new King scattered largesses from the Norman and English treasuries; his settlement with Philip added four thousand marks to the
twenty thousand Henry had been forced to promise in tribute.
Already shiploads of gold and silver were being sent across the
Channel to pay the promise, although the prospect that his sister
Alice would now soon become Richard's wife stayed Philip from
demanding all at once.

In July, at Rouen, Richard received from the Archbishop the
sword of the duchy, of Normandy, thus investing himself with
the Angevin power on the Continent. The following month he
landed at Portsmouth and marched in a triumphal procession to
Winchester, the locale of the royal treasury in which Plantagenet
kings always had a consuming interest. There he "caused his
father's treasures to be weighed, and an inventory of them to
be made," and, says the probably exaggerated report, it was
reckoned at nine hundred thousand pounds of gold and silver. A
lordly sum indeed—but Richard intended to spend it in lordly
fashion, and to add to it by every means at his command. Within
a week after Richard's landing in England, Bishop Geoffrey of
Ely died, leaving an estate of three thousand marks of silver and
two thousand marks of gold which escheated to the King. There
was need for all available money, for at Rouen Richard had already invested his brother John with new estates and was presently to add to them. All of John's holdings in England, given by
Henry, were confirmed, and to these was added the great Norman
county of Mortaigne, while in England he was offered the hand
of the daughter of the Earl of Gloucester; although Isabel was
the third daughter of the lord, she was designated the heiress of
the great estates which went with this honor. John and Isabel
were related in the third degree of consanguinity, and because
of this, Archbishop Baldwin of Canterbury forbade the marriage,
but John espoused her in any case.

Geoffrey, his illegitimate brother, Richard had also honored
with nomination to the office of Archbishop of York, over the
opposition of Hubert Walter, dean of the cathedral and soon to

become Archbishop of Canterbury himself. Lord Geoffrey had
already been elected Bishop of Lincoln, so that his prospects
were substantially improved. But Richard's bounty had not yet
been exhausted; says Roger of Wendover, "he proceeded . . .
from one place to another, granting to all the objects of their
petitions and bestowing lands on many who before had none."
Thus heralded by popular acts and boons, the King came to Westminster to be crowned, after having conveniently sought and
received absolution for having borne arms against his father.
Because Richard, aside from this detail, had no impediment or
rival claimant to the coronation, the ceremony permitted a more
elaborate ritual and was a more splendid spectacle than any in
men's memory.

Four archbishops, as well as all the great spiritual and temporal lords, came to the event; two earls bore the two sceptres, the
one topped with the cross and the other with a dove; after these
came three barons bearing three swords in gold sheaths "taken
out of the king's treasury." Behind them came other nobles with
the crown and royal robes; and last came Richard, between two
bishops. Before the high altar, whereon had been placed the holy
Gospels and relics of certain saints, Richard swore to honor the
Church and its ordinances, and "that he would exercise true justice
towards the people committed to his charge, abrogating all bad
laws and unjust customs, if any such might be found in his
dominions." It was an indication of the stability of Henry's reign
that he did not, like some of his predecessors, find it necessary to
specify any particular reforms. After Richard was anointed, clad
in his vestments of office, and crowned, the Mass was sung and
the procession turned to the choir, "where the king put off his
royal robes, and taking others of less weight, and a lighter crown
also, he proceeded to the dinner table at which the archbishops,
bishops, earls and barons, with the clergy and the people were
placed, each according to his rank and dignity, and feasted splen-
didly, so that the wine flowed along the pavement and walls of
the palace."

Under the rich veneer of the coronation, there festered and
suddenly erupted a fierce cancer of hatred, which fell out in this
manner. Attending the ceremonies, said the chronicler, were many

Jews, although the proclamation had expressly forbidden them to come "on account of the magical incantations which take place sometimes at royal coronations." Some courtiers discovered them in the church and laid hands on them, "and when they had robbed and scourged them dreadfully they cast them out." A smouldering passion thus burst into flame. For more than a century the Jews had dwelt in the land under the king's protection, with little molestation amid the power struggles of the great landholders. But times had changed, in proportion as the Jews themselves had grown wealthy in the financing of many a baronial estate and most of the great new religious houses which had been built in the twelfth century. Pious myth soon developed to justify a Christian hostility to the segregated community; to the apocryphal stories of ritualistic murders committed by the Jews—a libel centuries later denounced by Pope Clement XIV—was added the fervor of the Crusades; for if the infidel could be slain in far Jerusalem, how much more should the vengeance of true believers be visited upon those at home. If, in the process, creditors of monastic communities and landed estates were destroyed, this could only be a gain for the followers of the Prince of Peace.

And now, touched off by the incident at Richard's coronation, a succession of massacres smote the Jewish communities in London and elsewhere. The citizens, said Roger of Wendover, rose up and slaughtered many; "and after they had put to death numbers of both sexes, and razed to the ground or burnt their houses, they plundered their gold and silver, their writings and valuable garments." Many Jews fled to refuge in the Tower of London, but not before the bloody business had decimated the quarter of the city in which they had lived. Richard, it is said, issued orders that the attacks were to be ended, but the fury by now was beyond control. Throughout the winter in English cities, Jews were to die under torture and ravage, in that period of time they had called their year of jubilee. So, after more than a hundred years of peace, the children of Israel returned to the sorrow-drenched fate that had dogged them through the centuries that they had been compelled to wander the earth homeless. But the ferocity of the attack which had followed the splendid coronation was an evil omen for England as well, if only men could have read it. Richard's time to leave on the Crusade was drawing nearer, and it would be one of many ultimate ironies that Jewish money would contribute largely to his ransom a few years later.

Money, in vast quantities, now became Richard's obsession, and, says one history of his busy life, everything was put up for sale: "powers, lordships, earldoms, shrievalties, castles, towns, manors, and such like." Indeed, the King was reported as saying, he would be ready to sell London itself if he could find a suitable buyer. He found plenty of other salable items, including writs of release for many who had rashly taken the vow to join the Crusade and now repented of their enthusiasm. Hugh de Puiset, Bishop of Durham and an active conspirator in domestic affairs, bought his release for a total of three thousand marks, with the sheriff's office and justiciarship of Northumberland thrown in. Another ready source of revenue developed in the practice of turning many officeholders out of their positions and then permitting their reinstatement upon payment of heavy fines. Thus, by one means or another, the Crusade fund grew, building alongside it a large accumulation of corruption and selfishness compounded of many plans to make the most of Richard's absence from the kingdom.

As for the King, his mind was on distant matters, and he was impatient to complete the arrangements for the governing of the realm ere his departure. His decisions on the matter were hasty and generally unwise. In the first place, he discharged his father's great justiciar, Ranulph de Glanville, and in the second place, he divided the authority of the regential office between two men: the aging Bishop of Durham, who had just bought his release from the Crusade, and William Longchamp, Chancellor of Aquitaine and a man of coarse and consuming ambition. Finally, having won John's support with his initial lavish gifts, Richard invited his resentment by stipulating that in the event of his dying without legitimate issue—and the long engagement with Princess Alice was still hanging fire—his successor should be his nephew Arthur, son of the fourth brother, Geoffrey, who had died in 1186 (and who was not to be confused with the natural brother of the same name who became Archbishop of York). Whether Arthur had a claim which was legally superior to that of the youngest brother, John, was a matter which Richard did not take time to argue. He had long since crossed the Channel to the Continent, and the more immediate problem was the welfare of the kingdom under his vice-regents.

Longchamp moved swiftly to the center of power; he first refused the Bishop of Durham the office of sheriff of Northumberland which he had purchased but not yet paid for. Soon thereafter, Longchamp arrested his coregent and, without apparent legal justification, forced him to surrender other estates which he had acquired by substantial payments to the crown. Finally, as De Puiset, still shaken from this experience, was returning home, his rival's henchmen seized him in Yorkshire and held him prisoner. Once more England was experiencing what it was like to have an unprincipled and uncontrolled deputy in such power; there were uneasy memories of Geoffrey de Mandeville. The comparison became more stark when, by the summer of 1190, Longchamp became sole justiciar, chancellor, and, through appointment of Clement III, papal legate. Wrote William of Newburgh, "the laity found him more than a king, the clergy more than a Pope, and both an intolerable tyrant." He traveled the country in a royal entourage, and to Richard's continual requisitions for more treasure, he added his own heavy claims upon the land.

Men now turned to John, the only prince of the blood royal who was in the land and therefore the logical center of the opposition. They found him ready and eager to act; Longchamp's arbitrary and tactless rule, however well within the scope of authority which Richard had unreflectingly conferred upon him, made him ripe for overthrow. Powerful in his own estates and backed by a substantial private army, John soon was gathering to him many barons eager for a trial of arms against the vice-regent. But if in this the younger brother saw a chance to seize power for himself, he was presently thwarted; for Walter de Coutances, Archbishop of Rouen, arrived in England at this point with a commission from Richard to investigate Longchamp's behavior and, if his removal was justified, to assume the vice-regency himself. At this time, too, Longchamp found his own position suddenly weakened, for Pope Clement died, and with him expired the commission as legate. The time had come to strike a bargain, and John made the most of it; Longchamp was to be permitted to continue as regent with John's support, in return for the Chief Justiciar's switching his influence from Arthur to John as the successor to the throne if Richard were to die on the Crusade.

Matters suddenly became still more confused. Archbishop Geoffrey of York, at last confirmed in his office, landed at Dover to enter upon his ecclesiastical duties. Longchamp did not relish the idea of another Plantagenet in the realm, and indeed had conspired to try to keep him from crossing the Channel; now his sister, wife of the Constable of Dover, claiming to enforce Longchamp's requirement that the Archbishop swear fealty to Richard and the vice-regent, took Geoffrey into custody. A new wave of alarm swept across the country; to the dim memories of Geoffrey de Mandeville were now added the more vivid memories of Thomas à Becket, and although Longchamp denied that he had condoned the Archbishop's arrest, it was a typically arrogant action which men readily attributed to him, and it spelt his doom. At a conference at Reading that October, Walter de Coutances recommended that he be deposed, and an armed host, led by John, drove the Justiciar into the Tower of London, where, seeing hope of relief vanished, Longchamp surrendered and was expelled from England.

The Archbishop of Rouen, by the terms of Richard's commission, now became vice-regent, but it was John who had advanced the most in the swift changing of sides that led to Longchamp's fall. His behavior was not lost on the barons who had joined in the overthrow; he could be approached again, they perceived, upon any pretext which would appear to bring him closer to the crown. This fact was noted also by Philip Augustus, who had come home from the Crusade well ahead of Richard to resume his plan for undermining the Angevin power. Alice, his sister and the perennial fiancée, was again a pawn in the strategy. Philip now offered her in marriage to John as a means of John's securing possession of the Continental possessions of the empire. Since Richard had gotten out of his engagement to Alice, and John was confident of being able to dissolve his childless marriage to Isabel of Gloucester, there seemed to be good prospects that the offer could be accepted.

Meantime, Richard was totally involved in other affairs that rose to greet him as he made his way slowly toward the Holy Land. Except for his piecemeal dealing with problems at home, by way of special envoys like Walter de Coutances, other complications of empire demanded his attention, such as the situation he encountered in Sicily when he landed there in the winter of 1190. His sister Joan, widow of the late king of the island, he found in prison and the crown claimed by a local usurper, Tancred. At the coming of the Lionhearted One, Tancred quickly released Joan, but he declined to disgorge her dowry, realizing that it might be his *quid pro quo*. Richard needed the money represented by the dowry, either to prepare the way for a strategic remarriage for his sister or to borrow against for the ever-mounting expenses of his expedition. Tancred bargained to keep his throne as a condition for the release of the funds; and although Sicily was nominally a fief of the German emperor, Richard eventually struck the bargain. Much time had been consumed in the process, and it was also a time for the final arrangement of his own wedding. This was Eleanor's doing, and it involved not the French Princess Alice, to whom Richard had been engaged since early childhood, but the Princess Berengaria of Navarre, whose union would secure the southern border of Aquitaine. Another bargain accordingly had to be negotiated with Philip, who agreed to dissolve the long engagement with his sister for ten thousand marks. Finally, in April 1191, the Crusaders were ready to leave Sicily in a fleet of two hundred ships, and made their first stop at Cyprus, where they overthrew the local tyrant and celebrated the marriage of Richard and Berengaria.

Now at last, his own kingdom many hundreds of miles behind, and the challenge of the Holy Land before him, Richard was ready for his great adventure. His fame had preceded him, and he immediately lived up to it. Before the port of Acre, the Christian armies for two years had maintained an ineffective siege, but within a month Richard had stormed the defenses of the city and compelled its surrender. The rest of the summer was spent in consolidating the Crusaders' positions along the coast and whipping up the enthusiasm of the Christian forces for the march inland toward Jerusalem. All of these dazzling deeds of Richard were well reported in England, and they had a certain deterring effect upon many men who might otherwise have taken even greater advantage of his long absence. But as the ensuing winter passed without winning the city of Jerusalem itself—twice Richard was within sight of it, and on one occasion, according to report, he even entered its walls—the King realized that he must soon start for home to keep the increasing number of conspirators in subjection. Philip Augustus was busy unhinging such castles and cities as he could from the network of Angevin strongholds, and Walter de Coutances had regularly reported to Richard on John's incessant schemes to secure the throne. The opportunity came in due course; having developed a personal regard for Saladin, his great opponent, Richard made a three-year truce with the Saracens and in October 1192, set sail for home; it was the beginning of a long odyssey.

The schemes of both Philip and John now received a great boon; as he passed near Vienna on his homeward journey, Richard was taken prisoner by Duke Leopold of Austria, whose enmity he had incurred on the Crusade. It was said that the King, traveling in disguise and seeking to avoid Philip's dominions, where he suspected his erstwhile ally of plotting to seize him, had been betrayed by one of his own servants, whom the Duke's men seized and threatened with having his tongue pulled off if he did not reveal Richard's whereabouts. In any event, the Duke in turn sold his prisoner to Emperor Henry VI of Germany for sixty thousand pounds of silver. Richard was shut up in the grim fortress of Treves until Henry could determine how to turn his capture to his own greatest advantage.

There were many high stakes involved in the savage game of European diplomacy at this time. Henry of Hohenstaufen had scores to settle with a number of German princes within his own realm, whose causes had been assiduously nurtured in London. He also held Richard responsible for confirming the usurpation of Sicily by Tancred, when in the normal course of feudal reversion it should have come to him. And he intimated that he would welcome the chance to trade Richard to Philip Augustus,

thus insuring the French monarch of the acquisition of Aquitaine and many of the Angevin provinces to the west, if he would
cease to interest himself in Germany to the east. This last prospect
thoroughly alarmed John, for he perceived that Philip would owe
him nothing if the King himself came into his power; accordingly,
John hurried across the Channel and agreed to the marriage with
Alice. The die was now cast; if anything was to come of this
commitment, Richard must quickly be thrust from the throne.
John therefore hastened back to England to raise the standard
of rebellion and to prepare the way for Philip's Flemish mercenaries, who were to back up John's own seizure of the throne.

In the end, all the parties overreached themselves; Philip
disappointed the Emperor Henry by making it clear that he
would continue to intrude himself into German politics, and the
Capetian ruler was himself disappointed by the refusal of the
Norman barons to betray Richard and turn over the strongholds
of the duchy to him. John found his mother, a veteran intriguer,
zealous to protect Richard's interests at home, so that the invading force was never able to put out from Flanders; and now
Hubert Walter, the great servant of three kings—Henry and both
his sons—arranged for Richard's ransom. The figure came to a
staggering sum—150,000 marks of silver—but on the promise that
it would be paid, the King of England was at last released, in
February 1194. Philip was dismayed to hear the news and sent
a warning to John: "Look to yourself, the devil is loosed."

It was indeed enough to make conspirators die of fright, as
one constable in northern England was reported to have done, to
hear that the conquering Crusader was at last coming home. The
barons who had planned to support John quickly renewed their
loyalty to Richard, and John suddenly found himself with neither
allies nor lands, for Walter de Coutances confiscated all of his
vast holdings. His gamble had been lost; against the glamor of
the warrior king and undoubted sovereign—Richard was recrowned at Winchester in April—the younger brother could not
hope to maintain an effective challenge. The Lionheart was
more than ever the hero; men said that a rainbow burst into the
sunlit sky when Richard first set foot on English soil, and the
throngs which turned out to greet him on his way to Canterbury,

where he paid homage to the shrine of St. Thomas, were likened to those which had attended his first coming as king.

Richard spent little time in wreaking vengeance at home; the French under Philip were his real concern, and in any event his need was for money and men. He was entirely willing to pardon treason where it involved the payment of heavy fines. Eleanor herself arranged for a reconciliation between the brothers, although the King was not hasty in returning to John all of his lands and castles. Nor did he tarry to consider the domestic state of his kingdom; he quickly perceived that he had a gifted minister in Hubert Walter, and his own interest, as always, was in battle. Thus it was that a month after his return, Richard crossed the Channel for a war which was to occupy the remainder of his reign. The problems of home government and foreign attack were chronic, but the Lionheart managed to remain the warrior hero to the end. The first few months of his new campaign only added to the legend; in quick order he drove the French from Anjou and Touraine, and overwhelmed a rebel host in Aquitaine. He had reached the zenith of his career; in the field and at home, he would postpone defeat and let it fall upon those who came after him. Wherever he and Philip met, Richard prevailed, until, with both sides exhausted, a five-year truce was arranged in January 1199. Three months later, struck by an arrow in the course of a punitive expedition against one of his own vassals, Richard the Lionheart died.

The ten years of his reign had been a significant interval in the growth of the nation. Except for the excesses of Longchamp—who, after his expulsion from England, continued to give Richard faithful service (by his standards) in Normandy—the administration of temporal affairs by Walter de Coutances and of spiritual government by Hubert Walter had given the realm a remarkably stable government. The king's justice, under the system initiated by Henry II, was regularly and effectively applied throughout the land; indeed, the establishment of formal records of pleas in this decade (although they probably originated in Henry's time) prompted Edward I a century later to proclaim that in certain areas of property law, the beginning of legal memory should be traced to the first year of Richard I. With the heroic image of the Lionheart to keep the great barons in check, and with the skillful administration of the Archbishop of Rouen and the Archbishop of Canterbury, both of whom had been trained under Glanville, the domestic institutions of the kingdom had prospered withal during Richard's long absence.

For his successor, however, the problems from the outset were forbidding ones. They were economic, military, and political, and inextricably intertwined. There was, first of all, the fact that the cost of everything had more than doubled in the past quarter-century. The goods which England purchased from its traditional markets in Flanders, the exotic new products of the Mediterranean and the East which the Crusaders had first encountered on their pilgrimage, and above all the cost of outfitting an army on the scale made necessary by the war with Philip Augustus—all helped account for high prices. The country in general benefited from good times; agricultural produce was in great demand and accounted for a major part of the island's exports. But the royal share of the national income had diminished steadily since the early years of Henry II, in large part because of the lavish grants of land by Henry and Richard, so that John had to meet rising prices of goods and services with revenues from diminishing holdings.

On the military side was the fact that, for all his gallant campaigns, Richard had not been able to win the war with France; Philip kept bringing up fresh armies and drawing upon great resources of income. Now the Capetian monarch was to be opposed by a king who, while he did not deserve the epithet of "Softsword" given him by his enemies, could not be compared with Richard as a general. The truce which had been agreed upon so shortly before Richard's death could be broken at any moment, and political events of the ensuing months were to give Philip the excuse he needed for breaking it.

A tremor of unrest swept through England at the news that the King had died; while the brief vacuum in the royal authority existed, men hastened to settle certain accounts in their own way. Powerful lords pushed tenants out of estates they claimed to be theirs, and some baronial raiding parties sallied across the land. On the whole, however, the justiciars kept a firm grip on affairs, and the chief cause of concern was the question of who would be king, Arthur or John. This was the first political issue on which Philip expected to capitalize; he chose to support Arthur, since the young Duke (not yet twelve years old) was preferred by the most restless provinces among the Angevin dominions on the Continent: Brittany, Anjou, Maine, and Touraine. Moreover, Arthur was at the moment actually living at Philip's court, in defiance of an order Richard had given several years before that the lad be brought to England for his training.

John moved swiftly upon the news of his brother's death, in part because he well knew the formula for gaining power, which was to secure the treasuries of Normandy and England. Even more urgent was the need to leave Brittany, where the word had reached him, before Arthur's henchmen there might make him their prisoner. He rode away to the north, obtaining the custody of the treasury of Anjou and its guardian castle of Chinon, and went on to Fontevrault, where Richard's funeral—like Henry's ten years before—had been held. It was not time for reminiscence, however, for Arthur's forces and Philip's were already executing a pincers movement on Anjou. John managed to escape the closing jaws of the trap, gaining the safety of Rouen and the Norman treasury which was held for him by Hubert Walter and William Marshal. Having received their homage, John dispatched them to England to reinforce William's deputy, Geoffrey fitz Peter, whom he had sent ahead as soon as the news of Richard's death had reached Rouen. On April 25, nineteen days after his brother had died, John was invested Duke of Normandy. A month and a day later, he was crowned King in Westminster.

Between these dates, however, a fateful meeting was called at Northampton. The three deputies upon whom John relied to secure the kingdom for him—Geoffrey fitz Peter, William Marshal, and Hubert Walter—found the barons demanding an understanding. In part this was a reaction to the realization that an end had come to the iron rule which Henry had imposed by his close surveillance of the affairs of the realm, and Richard by his reputation as a redoubtable warrior. There were, said the lords, unkept promises in abundance from Henry's reign on which they had never been able to get Richard's attention, and they did not propose to be put off any longer. In addition, however, it was insisted that where there was no clear succession indicated by feudal law, the barons had the right to determine who was entitled to ascend the throne. There were many who came to the meeting at Northampton, but particularly conspicuous among them were some of the men who would confront John himself at Runnymede fifteen years hence, like the Earl of Hertford, William de Mowbray, and Roger de Lacy. On two conditions then—the assurance of John's three deputies that old grievances would be redressed, and the claim that the magnates had a right to review the legitimacy of the candidate for the crown—the barons agreed to back John.

The chronicler Matthew Paris, in a striking passage, relates that Archbishop Walter at John's coronation made an unusual speech in which he said that "no one has an antecedent right to succeed another in the kingdom, unless he shall have been elected." The Archbishop is reported to have added: "But if any relation of a deceased king excel others in merit, all should the more readily and zealously consent to his election. We have said this to maintain the cause of Earl John, who is here present, brother of our illustrious King Richard, lately deceased without heirs of his body, and as the said Earl John is prudent, active, and indubitably noble, we have, under God's Holy Spirit, unanimously elected him for his merits and his royal blood." Such a speech, if it was made, reflected the sense of the council of Northampton and confirmed the fact that no hereditary formula existed to determine the succession to the English crown. Paris adds that Walter explained to curious questioners after the coronation that he perceived that John would "one day or another bring the kingdom into great confusion," and it was essential to establish that he owed his elevation to the throne "to election and not to hereditary right."

The legalistic language sounds plausible for one trained under Glanville. If this was to suggest, however, that a king so elected could be subjected to recall or deposition, it was a proposition unknown in feudal law. When the barons did seek at last to drive John from the throne, they would not rely upon such a proposition; Prince Louis of France would be invited to join in the uprising on more orthodox grounds. In any event, the coronation disposed of the possibility that Arthur would succeed to the throne; it now remained to reassert imperial authority over the Angevin provinces which had sworn fealty to the young Duke and were garrisoned by Philip's armies. Neither side was disposed at the moment to break the truce, and a settlement of John's claims to the remainder of the Angevin possessions on the Continent was effected by payment of a relief of twenty thousand marks to Philip, in the process of which Arthur was established in Brittany as John's vassal. Thus a tentative extension of the armistice was worked out, giving John time to look to long-neglected affairs in his kingdom and Philip time to add still further to his armed strength to be used when the proper opportunity was presented.

Although his ministers turned over to him a realm firmly under royal control, John was not a king to inspire confidence, not to mention enthusiasm. At best, he would have to dispel the memory of his failure as a ruler in Ireland, where, at the age of nine, Henry had declared him King. Hugh de Lacy, of the family which was to figure so prominently in John's later history, had been named his viceroy. When he was eighteen, his father had bidden John to embark for his new dominion and learn to govern it, but a callow arrogance defeated him from the outset. The Irish lords who greeted him at Dublin he treated with utter insolence, seizing their long beards and twisting them in their faces. Such insults drove the Irish to refuse him homage, and the young lord then invited them to open revolution by seizing their lands and giving them to others in his own retinue. Henry had provided John with a sizable army, but the prince appropriated the money with which they should have been paid to use in his own extravagant pleasures. The mercenaries accordingly went over to the rebels; thus, in five months John had managed to put the whole country in a state of revolt, and Henry called him home. The following summer his viceroy, Hugh de Lacy, was murdered by the rebels. The crown of peacock feathers set in gold, which the papal legates brought from Rome for his coronation in Dublin, he was never to use; when he returned to Ireland as King of

England, his brutality had matured, and it was by shocking violence that he brought the country to his obedience. Men marked
the lesson; if he could be challenged in the field, John might well
be overcome, but if he was secure in his power, the vanquished
could expect no mercy. Once, after a victory in Normandy, John
had ordered three hundred captives to be beheaded. He was a
mixture of good and evil qualities, but cruelty was one instinct
which was natural with him.

At the dawn of the thirteenth century, English feudal society
had developed to a degree considerably more complex than the
system which had been introduced with the Conquest, although
the basic forms were little changed. The number of barons had
increased steadily: from somewhat less than 200 in the day of
William I, it had grown to 236 when John came to the throne.
While it was now general practice to send "shield money" for
the employment of mercenaries rather than to assemble an equivalent number of knights in person, each baron's estate was still
reckoned in terms of the number of knights' fees it owed the
crown. This suggested the strength of the lord of the estate; but
in the more sophisticated economy of 1200, the monetary income
from the lands in the lord's demesne (dominion) was even more
important. In addition to the fees owed and the income from
demesne lands received, a lord might enjoy the revenues from
subtenancies which escheated to him. Early deaths, natural or
violent, left many minor heirs, whose estates were put "in ward"
to the lord of the fee, and he was entitled to the use and enjoyment of the land so long as the heir was under age. The lord could
also derive a small additional income from a variety of fees,
reliefs, aids, and fines, each covering a special duty in medieval
life.

On all these points, John found himself at a substantial disadvantage in dealing with his lords. While he was the largest
single estate holder when he began his reign, even a small combination of barons could surpass him in their combined military
strength and financial resources. Of more than seven thousand
knights' fees to be reckoned in the realm, nearly five thousand of
them were in the hands of some sixty lords, and half of these
were under the control of no more than twenty of the greatest

barons. While this was the number of armed followers these twenty magnates could assemble—a formidable force by the standards of that day—their financial power was even greater, for they often divided a single fee among two or more subtenants, so that when the King levied upon them in an amount of one pound for each knight's fee, they would pass the levy on to their own tenants. So it would frequently fall out that a crown tenant could demand the full one pound from each of sixty tenants supporting thirty knights' fees in the lord's estate, and he would pay his obligation to the King without cost to himself but with substantial profit instead.

Thus, on both economic and strategic matters, the King could easily find himself without adequate power to deal with barons who chose to defy him. There was now a legal issue which worked further to John's disadvantage. In the course of the one hundred and thirty years since the Conquest, a number of landholders had come to regard themselves as English, even though Norman in origin, the more so because they no longer held estates on the Continent. Thus, when John called upon them to perform their feudal obligations by following him to France against Philip, they insisted that they were not required to engage in foreign military service. The monetary substitutes they relied upon to discharge their duties were inadequate in two respects: they seldom were paid in full (and sometimes not at all); and in the face of the growing French strength, John needed men even more than money.

Faced with such problems at home and abroad, a king needed to be astute in his dealings with his vassals and so proficient as a military leader as to inspire loyalty. The situation in John's case cried for cultivating the good will of the strongest of his barons, and for the husbanding of his military strength until his foe had been spread thin. Unhappily both for John and for England, the King lacked the temperament to effect the one policy and the military vision to implement the other. Pathologically suspicious by nature, incapable of winning over wavering parties, impulsively or compulsively cruel in his vengeance, and above all, lacking Richard's dashing presence, John continually spread the seeds of his own ruin. Even so, had the pressure from Philip not been so deadly, he might have kept the upper hand at home; he had been able to bring Scotland, Wales, and Ireland into a degree of subjection which it was said no king before him had quite equalled. And in an effort to improve his economic position, he devised certain experiments in taxation which bespoke a shrewd administrative insight. A great deal more tact in dealing with his barons at home and a modest amount of good fortune in his military plans abroad might have saved him.

But now began a series of events which, in the span of four years, was to bring about the loss of Normandy, the great duchy upon which the Angevin empire had been established. In the summer of 1200 John was in Aquitaine seeking to settle a dispute between the two powerful houses of Angoulême and Lusignan. A tentative settlement had been effected and was to be cemented by the marriage of Hugh le Brun of Lusignan and Isabel of Angoulême, when the King, who had recently obtained a divorce from his first Isabel, suddenly sued for the hand of this one, a girl of fifteen. The Angoulême party was thus brought into firm alliance with the Plantagenets, but it remained to satisfy the Lusignan lords for the theft of their scion's bride. Instead of the customary payment of a fine, John ignored them, and accordingly drove them into Philip's camp. It would be a decade before the enmity was ended, and by that time John's own story would be careening toward its final tragedy.

For the next year and a half, Philip watched disaffection spread through Poitou and Aquitaine, while the separatist fervor in Brittany kept up a steady pressure on John's western front. When, in the spring of 1202, John ignored a summons from Philip to come to Paris to answer a series of Lusignan complaints, Philip announced that he had forfeited his rights to his holdings in France, under the feudal obligations John owed to Philip as paramount lord on the Continent. Now at length the truce was broken; and in the fighting which ensued, fortune swayed erratically from one side to the other. To advance Arthur of Brittany as his candidate to succeed to John's forfeited Continental dominions, Philip sent the Duke with an army plunging into Poitou, seeking to capture Queen Eleanor; and here John, in a surprise maneuver, captured the entire host, including his nephew and his wife's once-promised husband, Hugh le Brun.

With this good stroke of luck, a shrewd leader could now have turned back the French threat for years to come. Philip was already retiring from advanced positions he had taken up in Normandy, not only to avoid an attack from John's victorious armies on his flank, but to play the game, taken for granted, of bargaining for Arthur's ransom. But John's political acumen lay in deviousness rather than subtlety, and his obsession now was to dispose forever of the threats to his throne represented in the children of his late brother Geoffrey. Henry II certainly, and Richard I probably, would have seen the advantage of keeping Arthur and his sister Eleanor as invaluable pawns in the grim maneuvering against Philip; but the ferocious cruelty of John now took possession of him. Eleanor was sent under guard to a castle in England, where she would spend the rest of her life a prisoner. As for Arthur, his fate was known only as far as his imprisonment at Rouen; that he died within the year was authenticated, but no man could—or dared—confirm the dreadful rumor that John had strangled him with his own hands.

No strangers to wanton cruelty, the Angevin baronage nonetheless was staggered by the rumored murder. Brittany at once rose in open revolt, and Maine quickly followed. And now, as Philip returned to the attack with even greater fury, the Norman lords themselves began to lose heart in the cause of so violent a king. In the waning months of 1203, great fortresses which had held the French at bay for two centuries and more began to fall to them. In the case of Alençon and Vaudreuil, which guarded the gateway to Rouen itself, there was almost certain evidence of traitorous behavior by some of John's most highly placed captains. The duchy of William the Conqueror was now crumbling as John's inept military tactics, the disaffection of more and more of his own barons, and the ever-mounting power of the French attack made clear the ending of the Anglo-Norman age. On Midsummer Day 1204—one hundred and thirty-eight years after the Battle of Hastings—the Norman capital of Rouen surrendered to Philip Augustus. Thus ended that monarch's single-minded campaign, launched fifteen years earlier with the entrapment and ruin of Henry II, to secure the Seine and the northern seaboard and divide England from its restless and already semi-independent province of Aquitaine.

The loss of Normandy sent a violent tremor through society on both sides of the Channel. What now was to happen to those scores of tenants who held fiefs in both countries? Under feudalism's overlapping system of tenures, a tenant commonly held different estates of different lords, but when these estates were under different sovereignties a complex technical and moral question of proper loyalties presented itself. Both victor and vanquished declared that the great landholders must now choose one country or the other, although in practice they did not press too vigorously for an early division of the interests of lesser tenants. John, at least until the Battle of Bouvines a decade later, refused to sign a treaty conceding that the loss of the great duchy was final, and accordingly kept records of the Norman estates presently lost by barons in England, claiming that some day he would restore them.

More menacing was the prospect that Philip, with a victorious host at the water's edge, might now undertake to invade England itself. A navy, which had not been a serious requirement while the Channel had remained English, now had to be built, and the Five Ports—the towns of Dover, Hastings, Hythe, Romney, and Sandwich—which offered the first line of sea and land defense facing France, now had their original charters from Henry confirmed by John in 1205, and the castles guarding them were heavily reinforced. The whole of England was placed on a war footing "for the defense of the kingdom and the preservation of the peace against foreigners and other disturbers." An emergency levy of a fifteenth part of all movables was proclaimed in order to raise a war chest; had it not been for the refusal of many barons to promise to follow him abroad, John would now have considered carrying the war back to the Continent. In any case, the threat of immediate invasion was dispelled by these strenuous preparations.

But the seeds of another debacle in the story of John's reign were sown in July of 1205, when Archbishop Walter suddenly

died. He had served John and Richard well, and in Henry's lifetime he may indeed have been the author of the great treatise
attributed to Glanville. For the past dozen years he had been
first justiciar and then chancellor, and no man in England surpassed him in learning on the laws and customs of the country.
The beginning of regular records of pleas, fines, charters, and
official letters, supplemented by the documents known to history
as the Great Rolls of the Pipe, coincide with Walter's administration. Through him the independent power of the sheriff was
substantially reduced by the creation of the office of coroner to
look after the interests of the crown (*corona*) in the shires, particularly as these involved capital crimes which by now were
the exclusive concern of the royal courts. Within the framework
of his administration, which had kept the kingdom on so firm and
orderly a course amid the turbulence of Richard's and John's
reigns, a start had been made toward a more stable economy:
In 1199 had come the Assize of Wine, and in 1204 the Assize of
Bread, both aimed at establishing standards of weights and
measures for trade. Under Walter, though for varying reasons of
their own, both Richard and John had been persuaded to grant
or confirm a number of charters of liberties to the more important
towns of the land.

Now, in the matter of presenting a candidate for installation
in the See of Canterbury, John was to precipitate a long conflict
with the Church which would add substantially to the forces
which, ten years hence, would combine against him at Runnymede. The technical question of the process of nomination was
an involved one: the monastic community of Christ Church,
Canterbury, claimed the sole prerogative, but the bishops of the
archdiocese also demanded a voice in the matter, while John
considered that he himself had the greatest right to choose the
candidate. Even for a less grasping monarch than a Plantagenet,
there was a vital practical consideration involved, for not only
did a spiritual lord, who in such a position was a prince of the
Church, control enormous temporal estates and the fees for
military service which went with them, but as a man of secular
training, he was of necessity to be entrusted with the fundamental offices of government as well. It was therefore a respon-

sibility of the crown to see that the greatest prelates of the realm were men who would personally advance the royal interests.

At the time William I was extending his rule to both sides of the Channel, the revitalized and reformed papacy was undertaking to extend the rule of the Church into a uniform ecclesiastical administration throughout Christendom. Those kingdoms farthest from Rome, Germany and England, were the most vigorous in their resistance to the extension of papal dominion, and their quarrels with the Church's claims would one day fan the Protestant Reformation. Most of the feudal states of western Europe acknowledged the widening powers of Rome only grudgingly and were ever ready to assert their own primacy in ecclesiastical matters which they considered to be vital to their own national interests. William had sought to dispose of the problem by assigning to canon law the questions arising in the government of church affairs; Henry II had insisted, before and after the Constitutions of Clarendon and before and after the great quarrel with Archbishop Becket, that all wrongdoers, whether clerical or secular, were subject to the king's justice.

John thus spoke the same language as his father in the matter of selecting spiritual lords who were to assume their assigned responsibilities within the feudal structure. When sees and abbeys became vacant, the lord of the fee customarily had two prerogatives: to gather into his own hand the revenues from the spiritual tenement; and to present a candidate to the proper consecrating authority to fill the vacancy. Already John had filled a number of bishoprics with his own men—some competent, some not—and while he had never been a warm admirer of Walter, he now determined to have as Archbishop of Canterbury and Primate of All England a man who could, with equal competence and closer adherence to his own aims, continue the effective administration of government as well as the guidance of the Church. But John was never one to seek to persuade others to his view, and it was predictable that the monks of Christ Church would come up with one candidate and the King with another. Each party thereupon prepared the case for its candidate and dispatched a delegation to Rome to present the matter to Innocent III.

The issue did not come before the Holy Father, however, except as part of a succession of issues for which the Pope sought a settlement from John. Some of these had to do with internal ecclesiastical affairs in England, where several bishoprics were long unfilled while the revenues from their secular holdings poured into the royal coffers. Others concerned diplomatic movements in western Europe on which the Pope sought to enlist John's support. Finally, Innocent viewed the selection of an Archbishop of Canterbury as necessarily involving someone who, like Becket and Walter, could maintain the Church's interest in the face of a strong-willed monarch. It was not surprising therefore, that the Pope found both of the candidates—John de Gray, who was presented by the King, and the monks' subprior Reginald—improperly nominated and quashed both presentments. He invited the two parties to put forward new candidates, and when, two years after Walter's death, neither side would retreat from its original position, he himself proposed an alternate candidate, Stephen Langton, member of the papal court and professor of theology at the University of Paris.

On its face, the nomination was a highly rational one; Langton was an Englishman, although he had left the realm in 1180, and in contrast to the Bishop of Norwich, de Gray, who was little more than a military vassal in clerical vestments, he was an eminently qualified candidate. Nor was there any evidence that the prelate would be personally obnoxious to John, aside from the fact that in his professorial position at Paris he undoubtedly had a formal association with Philip Augustus. But as John wrote to Innocent, he could not accept a nomination by a third party; given the intimate association of the occupant of the See of Canterbury with the affairs of government, it was vital that the King of England make the nomination. If John exaggerated the importance of this point, Innocent certainly erred in deprecating it; and he now made matters much worse by proceeding to consecrate Langton as Archbishop in June 1207.

John struck back at the only object within his reach—the estates held by Canterbury itself. Save for a handful of aged monks, the community of Christ Church was dispersed; most of the monks fled to refuge in Flanders. On the whole, John found his lords, both spiritual and temporal, at one with him on the matter, and indeed the King himself acted with more restraint than was usually the case with him when he was thwarted. Now he suddenly found a means to strengthen his position still further; a quarrel with his brother Geoffrey, Archbishop of York, drove that prelate also into exile—whence he was not to return—and John now gathered into his hand the estates of the other great archdiocese. With Langton no closer to his new see than the Cistercian monastery at Pontigny, where Becket had waited for the settlement of his quarrel with Henry, the King had clearly won this round of the contest. Innocent was driven to the next step in the test of strength: he directed the bishops of Ely, London, and Worcester to place the kingdom under an interdict; they did this in March of 1208 and promptly fled to France themselves.

While a man as irreligious as John would not personally be cowed by this order to suspend all spiritual offices in the realm, the people in general were terror-stricken. Christian burial was no longer available to the dead, Christian marriage to the living except as it was surreptitiously celebrated, and baptism also was only to be had in secret. John still acted with comparative moderation toward the ecclesiastical establishments in his power and continued to enjoy the support of most of his barons. One story had it that John embarrassed the churchly authorities by arresting the mistresses of the clergy wherever he could find them and compelling the churchmen to ransom them; it was recorded as a rather lucrative source of revenue. Again, Innocent found himself unable to deliver a sufficiently telling blow at John, and in the fall of 1209 he took the ultimate coercive step. In November of that year, the King was excommunicated.

Now the unrelenting position of the Pope ignited John's rage, and his hand descended heavily upon all the ecclesiastical property in the realm. By various penalties and levies he drew vast sums into his exchequer from the Church: from 400 marks in 1209, the total climbed to 3,500 in 1210 and 24,000 in 1211. Some houses were bankrupted, and their communities fled to other religious orders for shelter or went into exile. Thus, so far as the material situation in England was concerned, the King still held the upper hand; and the long struggle over the See of Canterbury and its occupant had not substantially affected his freedom of movement in other areas of national policy. The new revenues captured from the spiritual realm were used for important temporal needs, including punitive expeditions into Scotland, Wales, and Ireland. Indeed, at the end of these adventures, the strength of his control at home gave John new confidence in the attempt he believed he must make to win back the lost Continental possessions.

More than the old Angevin prestige was at stake, for at Philip's court were a growing number of disaffected English barons, who had used the excuse of John's excommunication to flee from the kingdom and who busied themselves with plots for his overthrow. The French power was undiminished, and against it John would have to hazard the doubtful host of his own subdued tenants and the coalition of west German and Flemish princes. Still, the prospects were apt to become even less encouraging if he waited. Otto IV of Welf was now the Holy Roman Emperor, although the Pope had apparently repented of his coronation and was inclining toward the rival house of Hohenstaufen. The Counts of Toulouse, Boulogne, and Flanders were presently disposed to make common cause with Otto and John, and no man could foresee how long this would last. And finally, there came word that the Pope was prepared to call upon Philip Augustus to lead an invasion of England and depose the excommunicate king.

To remove this final threat, John perceived that the time had come to make a settlement with the Holy See, and after several exchanges of messengers, the seven years of conflict were now ended, with an agreement ratified by Pandulph, the papal legate, and a number of lords who would later claim that they had compelled the King to submit. The charter of settlement did indeed bear the phrase that it was agreed upon "with the counsel of our barons," but the initiative apparently was John's. In any event, the chasm was bridged; restitution of all seized ecclesiastical property was to be made, Archbishop Langton was to be welcomed to Canterbury, and a number of exiles, both spiritual and lay, were invited to return. But John now went even further

in strengthening the union of his throne with the Church; he surrendered the kingdoms of England and Ireland to the Pope's
deputy and received them back as a papal fief. The gesture
meant little more than when his father had done the same thing,
but it placed John under the Pope's protection against his vassals.
Innocent had proved himself to be a redoubtable opponent, and
John intended now to make him an equally formidable ally; a
tribute of one thousand marks a year was to be paid to the Holy
See in confirmation. So at last was the King's peace made with
the Church; the time was May of 1213.

Many asked themselves if this surrender of his crown by the
King to the Pope, and the receiving of it back, was the true
meaning of the prophecy of one Peter, a hermit of Yorkshire, who
had declared a year earlier that John would not be King of
England by the next Ascension Day. When John first heard the
prophecy he had caused Peter and his son to be seized and imprisoned. Now the settlement with Pandulph had been made on
the eve of Ascension, and all men looked to the morrow with
mistrust, says the chronicler. But when it passed without event,
John's instinctive cruelty returned with his confidence, and he
ordered the prisoners to be brought forth, tied to the tails of
horses, and dragged through the streets to a gibbet where they
were hanged. "To many," concludes the chronicler, "it did not
seem that [they] deserved to be punished by such a cruel death,"
but it was what they had come to expect of John. For now, as he
turned his attention to the effort to recapture the Continental
dominions, the King had to consider what foes he would have
at his back when he set out. All feudal monarchs accepted as a
matter of course that loyalties were both short-lived and relative;
if men were faithful, it might either be that they lacked ambition
or had been adequately paid.

John had now been in power for more than fourteen years,
and at the moment there was no serious threat to him at home.
The country had continued to prosper, and the business of the
royal courts had kept order throughout the realm. The real danger was beneath the surface, where tremors of bitterness warned
of the brooding eruption, awaiting a weakening of the violent
force that contained it. There was no question that the King's

hand had been heavy; it was a matter of record that in these fourteen years, John had demanded no fewer than eleven scutages, as against two in the ten years under Richard I and eight in the thirty-five years of Henry II. Nor was there serious dispute that John's lusts were chronic; says Roger of Wendover: "There were at this time in the kingdom of England many nobles whose wives and daughters the king had violated to the indignation of their husbands and fathers." Still, adultery and bastardy were only incidents of the age, and heavy taxation was ever a source of grumbling; it would require a vortex of deeper hatreds and higher principles upon which to mount a rebellion.

In the final analysis, it was the nemesis of empire that ultimately destroyed John; for a decade he had not only brooded over the loss of the great provinces across the Channel, but had never forgotten the treason of many of his vassals in the losing days of 1203. These were the same men who feared and hated him for his passionate cruelty, his greed, and his violent pressing of every royal prerogative, and they only waited for a disastrous turn in his fortunes to set upon him. Under close scrutiny, their causes might be little more justified than they would have been under Henry II or would be under Henry III; in terms of the effective administration of government he had given the land, John often equalled his father and would substantially surpass his son. Moreover, it could not be argued that the King was adamant on the matter of concessions of proper liberties; he had made important grants to many parties in his day, and between the opening of the Plantagenet dynasty and the last year of John's reign, no fewer than eighteen charters had established or confirmed privileges of a long list of English towns and boroughs. While Richard and John had hit upon the idea of regranting existing charters as a revenue device—and John in fact suggested the rule that all grants of earlier sovereigns had to be reconfirmed by him—the Plantagenets to this time had been disposed to honor such promises when they had been made. This was true of specific charters; in the case of more general promises made at coronation or absolution, the kings were apt to treat them more vaguely or to agree to them anew without intention of being significantly restricted by them.

Now, with his peace imposed at home, John returned to the Continental adventure which, if it succeeded, might well recover the former Angevin power, reduce the French to their one-time secondary position, and destroy all hopes of his enemies to challenge him. No man could say that the prize was not worth the gamble, or that the plan now devised was not reasonably likely to succeed. As it turned out, the strategy was simply too ambitious for the Middle Ages, involving as it did a carefully timed giant pincers movement of Otto's armies from the northeast and John's forces from Poitou in the south. When, at Bouvines in July of 1214, the French decisively defeated the imperial host, while John's vassals refused to follow him into pitched battles in the south, all was lost. Thereafter France would be supreme in western Europe, and it was a beaten and ruined force that straggled with John back across the Channel. No one could deny now that the Norman empire was gone forever; and it was clear that the breach in the royal control at home was at last inviting the revolt that had smouldered for so many years.

The conspirators began to come together rapidly. At St. Paul's Church in London on August 25—less than a month after the disaster in France—Archbishop Langton called to him a number of nobles and reported to them that "a charter of Henry the first king of England has just now been found, by which you may, if you wish it, recall your long-lost rights and your former condition." Whether the coronation charter of Henry I, issued more than a century before, had literally been forgotten or whether, as is more likely, the archbishop simply recognized the latent legal propositions in it, the effect was galvanic; the barons as they listened to its passages perceived the long precedents for their claims to feudal security and interrelated obligations; the ancient document spoke of reasonable reliefs, protection of heirs and widows, security of testamentary disposition of properties, reasonable forest laws, and the defined limits of knight service. Says the chronicler, "when this paper had been read and its purport understood by the barons who heard it, they were much pleased with it, and in the archbishop's presence swore that when they saw a fit opportunity they would stand up for their rights, if necessary would die for them."

More than forty barons, many of them boasting hundreds of armed retainers, would ten months later bring the King to bay. Their names and grievances were typified by the record of the twenty-five barons who would be named, in Chapter 61 of the great "concord," as sureties for John's adherence to the grant they would wring from him that day. There were the earls of Aumâle, Gloucester, Hereford, Hertford, Norfolk, Oxford, and Winchester, William d'Albini, Hugh Bigod, Gilbert de Clare, John fitz Robert, Robert fitz Walter, William of Huntingfield, John de Lacy, William de Lanvelei, William Malet, William Marshal, Roger de Montbegon, Richard de Montfichet, William de Mowbray, Richard de Percy, Robert de Ros, Eustace de Vesci, and William Hardell, mayor of London. Some ghosts would be present also, like the house of Briouse, whose lord had fled into exile and whose lady and youngest son had starved to death in John's dungeons; and the twenty-eight sons of Welsh chieftains hanged in 1212 as punishment for their fathers' attempt at insurrection.

The conspiracy against John was animated by lords who had the closest ties of family and of geography; although the term, "northern barons," did not accurately describe the whole area of disaffection, it was the group of lords under the Scots border and in the east of England who were the most vehement in their complaints against the King. It was to the north in 1209 that John had gone in search of conspirators, chief of whom he suspected as Roger de Lacy, sheriff of Cumberland and Yorkshire; when Roger died two years later, the King delayed two years more before granting his son John his inheritance, and for it demanded a heavy fine of seven thousand marks and various hostages for his good behavior. A cryptic letter from Philip Augustus had suggested that an uprising to coincide with a French invasion had been under consideration in 1209, and the King had evidently learned enough about the correspondence to identify John de Lacy as one of the probable leaders in the plot.

De Lacy was a neighbor of three other northern lords who would figure actively in the rebellion: the Count of Aumâle, Robert de Ros, and Eustace de Vesci. Of these, De Vesci was one of the bitterest of John's foes; he had used the excuse of the interdict to flee to the Continent and had been an active plotter at the

court of Philip Augustus, at the same time convincing the Pope
that he had suffered all for his devotion to the Church. John had
singled him out for harassment after the exile and let it be
known that he was among those whose titles to their estates were
being searched for flaws. Matters had not been helped by Eustace's refusal to follow the King on the ill-fated expedition to
France in 1214. As in the case of De Lacy, John's enemies spread
a story that the King desired to sleep with De Vesci's wife, and
that his hatred had grown after the baron had the temerity to
send in her place a common woman to the royal bedchamber.
Eustace still nursed a deep resentment at the demand of the
King that, as one of De Lacy's vassals, he contribute to the relief
which John had levied upon the De Lacy estate some years
earlier.

The clearest evidence of the magnitude of the enmity for
John was the northern uprising of 1212 and 1213, which threatened briefly to raise all of Scotland and Wales in revolt at the same
time. The King had been able to overcome the insurgents on all
fronts, demanding of all parties a number of hostages who now
were in his custody. Eustace and Robert fitz Walter, two of the
chief conspirators, gathered their families and fled hastily to
Scotland and France; Eustace, indeed, was brother-in-law to the
King of Scotland. Fitz Walter, who would be elected by the rebels
"marshal of the army of God and of Holy Church," had betrayed
John in the surrender of Vaudreuil in 1203; and there were other
events in his service which had fed the hatred that obtained between him and the King. Almost as vehement in his personal
animosity for John was William de Mowbray, for he maintained
that his own services (he had remained several years in Germany
as a hostage for the ransomed Richard) had never been rewarded.
To aggravate matters, when he returned to the realm, he had been
made a defendant in a suit challenging his title to his barony, and
when he had lost in this action, he was still compelled to pay the
fine customarily required of the victor.

Thus did the coalition develop—among men who had the
bitterest personal grievances against John and who hoped to rally
the many other lords of the kingdom whose long-standing dislike
of the Plantagenet rule in general would make the blunting of this

rule an attractive prospect. Like most insurrections, the plot against John was activated by a zealous minority; the myth that the King was confronted by a general uprising of rightfully indignant peers was concocted by his enemies, who enjoyed a substantial monopoly of the chronicles of communication for the following generation. John was able in fact to count on substantial support in the south and west and might well have outlasted his foes but for two turns of fate: the augmenting of the opposition by the Church authorities, and the betrayal of London itself to the rebels.

Stephen Langton was another in a long line of exceptionally able clerics who, as Archbishops of Canterbury, were able to exert substantial influence upon the course of secular affairs in the thirteenth century. He was, indeed, a man of vision and principle well ahead of his own age, and his concern in this developing crisis was to elevate the issues above the sordid level of John's concept of the royal prerogative as well as the totally selfish ambitions of his foes, to a principle of government as a process of insured justice. A devoted spiritual leader and a deeply read student of canon and civil law, there is quite plausible argument for the proposition that Stephen may have been the moving spirit behind the document known subsequently as the Unknown Charter of Liberties. It was he who had opened the barons' eyes to the generalized or abstract principles implicit in the charter of Henry I, at the meeting in August 1214, and in the fall and early winter of that year he had been in continual touch with them, seeking to guide the mounting flood of vengeance into a broad new channel of political conviction. The higher ethical tone of the Unknown Charter, in contrast to the immediately self-serving demands set out later in the Articles of the Barons, further established the belief that a writer seeking to expostulate the concept of a higher law had a hand in preparing the earlier document.

Thus the Unknown Charter opened with a statement of a general principle that the king neither would seize any man without justice, nor would sell justice, nor do injustice. The Articles of the Barons were to begin by demanding attention for their greatest concern—reliefs of heirs and wardships of tenants' estates. On the whole the tenor of the Unknown Charter was in

terms of fundamental principles which were inherent obligations
of good kingship; if Langton did not draft it, nonetheless it was
characteristic of the moral plane on which the Archbishop sought
to maintain the final argument. It was on such a plane, the Primate of All England indicated, that the Church would support
demands to be presented to John, and the acceptance of the
broader propositions made stronger the appeal of the rebel
minority to the larger body of uncommitted tenants throughout
the kingdom.

And now, with the coming of the year 1215, events moved
steadily toward the final issue. Having held court at Winchester
on Christmas of 1214, King John proceeded to London, where
early in the new year a number of the rebel leaders came to him,
accompanied by a large body of armed followers, and demanded
of him three things. The first was a confirmation of the "good
laws" of Edward the Confessor; the second, the reissue of the
charter of liberties granted by Henry I; and the third, the keeping
of the promise he had made at the time of the lifting of the
interdict and his own absolution from excommunication: to
restore all ancient liberties. John, says the chronicler, perceived
that they were in deadly earnest and fully capable of launching
an attack at once; and he "made answer that their demands were
a matter of importance and difficulty." The King asked for a truce
until Easter, that he might "be able to satisfy them as well as the
dignity of his crown." The barons were reluctant; they had
whipped up their own resolution to the pitch necessary to come
to this brink of civil war, and they sensed that time might not be
their friend. Yet the scanty record of this meeting suggests that
Archbishop Langton persuaded them that it was reasonable to
give the King time to frame his answer, and the dissidents at
length acquiesced, having insisted first that the Archbishop, the
Bishop of Ely, and William Marshal should be sureties for the
King's response by that date.

John could act coolly when a major crisis was upon him; he
did not now take precipitate action. Like his foes, he recognized
that the majority of tenants of the realm remained uncommitted—
and he was intelligent enough to realize that few of these felt any
personal loyalty toward him; his first concern must be to avoid

giving them excuse to go over to the rebels, and to build upon their lingering awareness of their feudal obligations. To strengthen this relationship, he sought to exploit another feudal article of faith, that a Crusader should be entitled to a respite from any secular demands upon him; and thus, a few weeks after the confrontation in London, John took the cross. As he hastened to inform Innocent of his commitment, he also told him of the threats of his vassals; it was time to collect the debt the Pope owed him for converting England into a papal fief. Having dispatched his messages to Rome, John then set about putting his castles into a state of defense; this would be his answer when the barons came to him after Easter.

And indeed, upon completion of the octave of Easter, a great array of nobles and men at arms began assembling at Stamford, and the King and his party—unwisely, as it later turned out—left London and established themselves at Oxford. From here John sent his two sureties, William Marshal and Archbishop Langton (the Bishop of Ely having died in the meantime), to learn the specific demands of the barons. The rebels were determined to delay the reckoning no longer; they realized that John had enhanced his moral position with his Crusader's vow, and in addition to garrisoning and provisioning his castles, he had aroused them by bringing to his aid a substantial army of Poitevins—mercenaries perhaps, but not the alien host his enemies claimed them to be, since they came from the remnants of the Angevin fiefs in France. Moreover, John's appeal to Rome had brought results in the form of letters to all parties urging them to avoid recourse to arms and observe their respective feudal obligations. If the rebellion was to succeed, it must be forced through swiftly.

So it fell out that John's emissaries returned to Oxford with a substantial list of demands—in all likelihood, the antecedent draft of the Articles of the Barons to be presented at Runnymede —and an ultimatum that the King immediately grant the same. It was quite possibly the tone of the demands as much as their letter which incensed John, as Marshal and Langton read them to him "one by one throughout." Then the King, when he had heard the paper read, cried out bitterly, "Why, amongst these unjust demands, did not the barons ask for my kingdom also? Their demands are vain and visionary, and are unsupported by any plea of reason whatsoever." Ultimatums in the nature of the case are intended to confirm deadlocks rather than to resolve them. John felt, as he wrote to Innocent a few weeks later, that the refusal of his foes to submit the issues to arbitration underlined their willfulness and exonerated him. Thus he established the base for his subsequent request that the Pope quash the agreement reached under duress at Runnymede.

And now both sides finally were committed to arms, and at the first the advantage seemed to lie with the King; a Crusader and a vassal of the Holy See, with an army not significantly inferior to the rebels, with castles alerted, John was indeed a formidable opponent. In the opening attack, launched at the royal castle at Northampton, the rebels were to be impressed with this strength; after only fifteen days, they were forced to abandon the attempt. But now fell one of those blows of fortune which so often in his career had frustrated John's prospects. When the army of God and Holy Church arrived at the less important royal stronghold of Bedford and were readily admitted by the King's officers, secret messengers came to inform the rebels that it would be possible to deliver London itself into their hands.

On the Sunday next before Ascension Day—the fateful date which two years earlier had been prophesied by Peter the Hermit as the time of John's deposition—the rebels streamed through the open gates of the city "whilst the inhabitants were performing divine service; for the rich citizens were favorable to the barons, and the poor ones were afraid to murmur against them." Now the advantages had been reversed, for with the resources and defenses of the greatest town in the realm now in their possession, the insurgents were all but impregnable. And they understood well the magnitude of their bloodless victory, for now the uncommitted majority of freeholders were to be urged by threats to come over. Letters went out quickly from London to all who had not yet declared against John, calling upon them "as they regarded the safety of all their property and possessions, to abandon a king who was perjured and who warred against his barons, and together with them to stand firm and fight against the king for their rights and for peace; and that, if they refused to do this, they, the barons, would make war against them all."

John, now shut out from the city, could ponder its perfidy; only a few weeks earlier he had granted it a substantial new charter, one of several with which he had favored it since his accession. On the whole, the merchants of the cities and boroughs had suffered substantially less than the landholders from the incessant demands of the Plantagenet kings, and in times of prosperity the levies upon them had been relatively easier to pay. But gratitude, or loyalty, as the case might be, was a rare and perishable commodity in medieval society; it might be said that it was a luxury which could ill be afforded in the crush of contending magnates with equally crass motives. If both vassals and towns which had formerly withheld from the struggle now responded to the rebels' call, it was less a matter of deserting John than of insuring to themselves a voice in the final settlement of the present issue.

The King perceived that his best course of action was now to come to terms with the foe, in the confidence that his case for repudiation would be upheld by the Pope at the proper time. By such an agreement the enemy would be deprived of a just reason for continuing the insurrection and would in due course be forced to give up his stronghold. Under such circumstances, it was to the King's advantage now to accede to the demands presented at Easter, and so, in early June of 1215, John sent word to the barons in arms that he was prepared to meet with them. The jubilant rebels answered with a stipulation of the time and place —on Monday, the fifteenth of June, on the south bank of the Thames between Staines and Windsor, in a meadow called Runnymede.

III

Restatement of the Feudal Law

TWO charters in one were to be drafted when the barons and the party of the King came together at last. The one, which had in it the list of complaints which had finally driven the lords to their rebellion, would not outlive the passions of the present hour; the other, which restated in detail the essentials of an orderly society as it was understood at the time, would be preserved after John's day and would in the distant future become a symbol of government under law. As always, the magnates spoke and thought only of their immediate interests; it remained for a man of vision and dedication like Stephen Langton to seek the elixir, to trace amid these earthly considerations the nexus of the just society. In the end, the issues of the present confrontation would die with John, and the foresight of Langton and the steadfast loyalty of the elder William Marshal would go unrecognized in their own age. If the skies over Runnymede had parted long enough to permit a fleeting glimpse of the city of God, no man would have been prepared to seize the opportunity, for his eyes were continually watching his neighbor's hand upon his sword.

John did not come friendless to the meeting, despite the claim of hostile chroniclers that he had now scarce seven knights to serve him. In the preamble to the agreement as it was drafted, John spoke of the great men upon whose advice he was now granting the charter "for the reform of our realm."* Among those named were Langton himself and the Archbishop of Dublin—the

---

* The text of Magna Carta, with a concise commentary on each chapter, appears in Part II.

80

spiritual overlords of England and Ireland—and seven bishops; there was also Pandulph, the papal legate, and the master of the Knights of the Temple in England. Thus the leading prelates of the realm, many of them having been presented for consecration by John himself and all of them under Stephen's influence and Pandulph's admonition that John was a vassal of Innocent, stood as a buffer between the rapacious rebels and their monarch. To these men were added some of the most powerful temporal lords of southern and western England: the Earls of Arundel, Pembroke, Salisbury, and Surrey, the Constable of Scotland and the Seneschal of Poitou, and a number of others who had served John consistently since he had been crowned. Many of them had had their loyalty repaid shabbily enough: among John's many seductions had been the sister of William de Warren of Surrey, and there was a cryptic suggestion in the records that Hugh de Neville had on occasion to pay his master for the right to bring his wife from the King's bed to his own.

Yet these vassals were held in John's host by various ties which outweighed their scattered grievances; many were his kin, some had been lucky enough to be spared the full force of his rapacity and cruelty, and a few were firmer than most in their sense of feudal obligation. In any event, it is evident that they were literally present, in this hour; for had they not been, the King would indeed have been a prisoner of men who would not have scrupled, now that they had driven the issue this far, to destroy him altogether. The tenor of the agreement now being drawn up, also, indicated that the barons did not have a completely free hand; the difference between the Articles of the Barons, which was the statement of things as the rebels wished them to be, and the concord as it was finally written is one of moderation and amelioration. A charter dictated by bitter and unscrupulous men at swordpoints would never have had significance in the eyes of succeeding generations.

John had the further advantage of knowing that his castles throughout the land were fully garrisoned and ready for action; accordingly, while he was tactically overpowered in the present circumstances, the situation was a temporary one. Both sides recognized this, and the barons, while insisting on full redress of their specific complaints, were careful not to overreach themselves. They received John's assent, ultimately, to all but one of their forty-nine demands; the fact that these were supplemented with some twenty other headings reflected in part the opportunism of other groups—the towns and boroughs, the churches, and some of the erstwhile neutrals who had come to see that their own interests were expressed in the agreement—and in part the determination of Archbishop Langton that this charter should speak in broader terms than a bill of complaint. The Articles were agreed upon and sealed by the King on June 15; three days would now be spent in rephrasing the laconic stipulations into the more formal detail of a state paper. From all evidence, Stephen of Canterbury was the moving spirit, if not the actual draftsman; the document in its finished form breathed his exalted concept of justice within the framework of feudal law. Thus it was that on Friday, June 19, the royal party and the rebel host came together once more, attended the reading of the agreement, and, with the sealing of the copies, made their peace.

The document which had evolved was remarkable for the age and the circumstances. Most of the important elements of English life in the early thirteenth century had been touched upon, and both barons and the King, if they pondered all the implications as the chapters were read, may have sensed, however vaguely, that this went far beyond the stereotype of earlier charters, the general promises to observe good laws and abolish bad ones. It was much more than the enumeration of elemental rights as set up in the charter of Henry I, on which Archbishop Langton had enlightened the gathering rebels the previous August; it reflected the rudimentary development of a common law and of stable political institutions under Henry II, and the rationale of Glanville and his disciples. That the concord signed this day transcended the issues which had led to Runnymede would be demonstrated by the events of the coming year; when the chief counsellors for the young Henry III were able to sift the grain from the chaff, by discarding the ephemeral provisions of 1215, the reissued charter of 1216 and 1217 emerged in its organic form—a restatement of the whole body of feudal law.

Langton it doubtless was who determined not only that the

opening provision of the Charter should render unto God the things which were God's, but in the process should set the high ethical tone he so earnestly intended for the entire document, by the phrase granting "to all freemen of our kingdom, for us and our heirs forever, all the liberties underwritten." Innocent had benefited England and John more than any of them knew when he had selected Stephen for the See of Canterbury, and despite the prolonged vehemence of John's opposition to his Archbishop, the King had him now to thank for the document—both in the present need and for the long view of history. From the outset, Stephen's reaction to his own forced exile at Pontigny and to the expulsion of the monks from Canterbury had been one of compassion in the same instance that he was firm in adherence to principle. When he had at last been received in England, he proceeded without delay to grant his sovereign absolution, to celebrate Mass in his presence, and to give him the kiss of peace. His pastoral acceptance of John's good faith did not diminish his determination to be, as the Primate of All England, the keeper of the King's conscience; it was through his stern intervention at Nottingham in 1213 that John was dissuaded from wreaking vengeance upon the lords who were refusing to follow him to France, and he had insisted that they were entitled to a fair trial of the issue.

Even now, John's situation with London in rebel hands would have been much graver, had not the Tower been placed in Stephen's custody. Yet John's hatred of all who had a part in the confrontation at Runnymede—and particularly of the chief architect of the settlement—bore bitter fruit for the Archbishop. Like most peacemakers, who might be the children of God, his portion among men was often to be ashes. John, in his heated denunciation of the Charter to the Pope, would charge Stephen with the utmost complicity in abetting the rebellion itself. Stephen's hesitation at pronouncing the papal sentence of excommunication the following August against the "disturbers of King and kingdom" seemed to confirm John's charges, and the prelate would be summoned to Rome and once more exiled from his see until peace was restored. He was not to return in John's lifetime or Innocent's; but he had already bestowed his legacy in the latent proposition of the Great Charter.

The document itself, having established a general principle in its opening chapter, now took up the particulars of the Barons' Articles. Foremost was the matter of reliefs, those feudal payments to the lord of a fee by which the heir of a tenant secured the continuance on the grant of the estate to him. These should be limited, declared the chapter, to the "ancient custom of the Fees" —traditional amounts which could be traced by common memory to the Conqueror's time, when he had first established the stipulation that the holder of such and such an estate would owe so many knights' fees to the grantor. It was clear in men's minds, and in their recollection of their fathers' experience, that the Plantagenets had been accustomed to calculate relief in enormous sums—tenfold or a hundredfold greater than what, they insisted, the "old relief" had been. As a practical matter, if not in justice, several monarchs before John had settled a doubtful inheritance by putting it up for bidding, so that the heir who had the most money would be held to have the best claim. It was quite foreseeable that such a practice, or the arbitrary fixing of a relief, or perhaps the coupling of it with a fine or payment to end (*finis*) a claim against the estate, could well bankrupt the feudal system.

This was one thing; but if the heir was under age, the next provision was that he should receive his inheritance without relief or fine when he reached "full age." This was for the very good reason, obvious to the thirteenth century, that the lord of the fee had the right to the use and enjoyment of the minor's estate; he was not entitled to more at the end of this period. And coupled with this chapter was the next, which sought to safeguard the estate while it was in ward (custody). Many a tenant had received back his land from a guardian only to find it substantially wasted, the buildings in ruin, the stock driven off, the inheritance an empty one. All agreed to the guardian's right to "reasonable produce, reasonable customs, and reasonable services"—that is, to the crops or other issues of the land, the duties levied upon goods brought into, out of, or through the estate, and the labor owed to the estate by the husbandmen bound to it. The guardian must not waste either men, by enfranchising villeins and thus reducing the labor owed the estate, or goods, by neglecting to conserve them.

The chapter also spoke of another evil custom, practiced by John but not original with him, of selling or giving the wardship of a particularly valuable estate to a royal favorite or one to whom the king owed something. If the original lord of the fee was the guardian, he presumably would be impelled by self-interest to conserve it; but if it passed into the hands of a stranger, the inclination to neglect it or to strip it of all that was of value was so much the greater. The next chapter made this more explicit: the custodian was to keep up the land specifically by maintaining the buildings, parks (private forests), warrens (preserves for a variety of livestock), ponds, and mills. For the medieval estate had to be self-sustaining, and many of the structures and articles of husbandry, if destroyed, could hardly be replaced at any price.

Having settled in this series of provisions the primary concern of feudal landholding, the Charter next took up the equally important matter of marriage and the protection of widows. Heirs, it was provided, were to be married "without disparagement"— that is, without forcing them into a union with someone beneath their social station. Fathers presumably would be zealous to make the best possible matches for their sons or daughters, but guardians might be all too willing to give a wealthy ward in marriage to a vassal of lowlier degree. It was proposed that one safeguard would be to give notice of the proposed union to the heir's nearest kin, who would be likely to insist upon a betrothal suitable to the family's station in life and desired alliances with other feudal powers.

The protection of widows of landholders was another fundamental concern; while it was seldom that a woman was able to assert the military leadership of her knights that was essential to a system of continual preparedness for fighting, and hence the lord of the fee held it vital to see that an adult male was quickly placed in command of the estate, this had led all too readily to a thrusting aside of a widow before her rightful share of the estate could be settled. John, in his chronic search for money, had accentuated an abuse which obtained all too generally throughout the Middle Ages; in the case of widows of crown tenants, he would demand staggering sums of money in order to settle the claims in the form of reliefs or fines by which the widow could secure her property. Under the feudal doctrine of primer seisin, the king was in any event entitled to an entire year's profits from a tenant's holdings upon his death, and John was not one to take any less than was his due under the law.

Women were entitled to their marriage portion, or the property which they had brought from their own family to the union with their husbands. They might also be entitled to the inheritance of certain property which descended to them, after marriage, from certain of their relatives. Finally, there was the dower, or the portion of the husband's land which was customarily set aside to support the widow after the death of the tenant. Traditionally, the bride was endowed with the dower as she came from the altar at her wedding and received it at the door of the church; Henry's charter of 1217 would insure this to her upon her husband's death "unless she were endowed of less at the church-door."

Finally, in a supplementary chapter, the concord stipulated that a widow should not be distrained (compelled under penalty of fine) to marry again if she preferred to live alone, and that the lord of the fee would only require that she give security that she would not marry without his consent. The obsession with the necessity of preserving the land in the tenure of one loyal to the grantor made this security a highly important one; in the rapid shifting of loyalties among the barons, the remarriage of a widow in control of important lands might well tip a precarious balance of power.

Having settled the primary question of the rights of heirs and surviving spouses, the barons' next concern was with the orderly settlement of debts owed to the crown. John was almost always eager for money, but ready cash was often hard to come by in medieval England, and a lord could not always provide the funds demanded by the king's collectors when they arrived to take payment. Chapter 9 of Magna Carta, accordingly, set out a fundamental rule—to continue down to modern law—that if the debtor was willing to satisfy the debt and his personal property and chattels were sufficient to cover it, the king could not seize his land in payment. The hunger of the Plantagenets, and other great lords whose rapacity was equally consuming, for power as well as revenue had all too often led to a dispossession of estates far in excess of the value of the debt itself. Or if the impecunious tenant had been fortunate enough to have wealthy friends who had provided the surety for his debts, the document sought to halt the practice of turning upon them, so long as the debtor's chattels were available, and distraining the sureties.

Such detailed stipulations in John's charter were the key to its importance in the eyes of contemporaries; it was a thoroughly practical document, spelling out the fundamental safeguards of everyday life among landholders. Indeed, this would prove the secret of its survival in the centuries following the Plantagenets, when the constitutional propositions in Magna Carta would be shunted into semiforgetfulness in the long years of rivalry between Lancaster and York, and in their stead the fundamental private law provisions of the document would keep it alive and functioning. In the reissues under Henry III, indeed, the principal additions to the Charter would be the further details of legal procedure affecting property holding and the rights of individuals affected thereby.

Among the chapters of the 1215 concord which would be deleted in the revisions under Henry, the three on varying debtor and creditor relationships were included. The barons had considered them opportune; one suspended interest payments on the debts of an estate owed to Jewish moneylenders, during the period of an heir's minority, the second extended the protection absolutely to the widow, so that a debt claim against her in such case would be extinguished as far as her dower was concerned; while the medieval uses of a scutage were defined according to immemorial practice: it was to be levied only upon the approval of the common council of the realm, except where its purpose was to ransom the king's person, to make his eldest son a knight, or to provide a wedding portion for his eldest daughter.

As the interest of the Church had been inserted in the opening of the concord, so now, having met the most urgent demands of the barons, the Charter inserted the interest of the towns. The "ancient liberties and free customs, as well by land as by water," were guaranteed to the city of London by Chapter 13, which extended the general confirmation of their prior charters to all other towns and boroughs to whom the Plantagenets and the Normans before them had made grants. The crown found it economically and politically practicable to encourage autonomy in the urban areas which had gradually grown up in the kingdom; not only were they the centers of commerce and crafts, but their interests were often distinguishable from those of the landed warriors—and their available funds were more abundant when an emergency levy was required. An ancient city or borough formed a governmental unit independent of the shires and hence could be played off against them on occasion; a royal castle or a castle of an important crown tenant normally dominated the area, so that with an adequate garrison and a stoutly defended walled city, it represented a strategic center for control of a substantial area.

The irony of the special reference to London's privileges lay in the fact that, only a few weeks before, John had offered the very grant which was now being demanded. This had been timed, of course, to keep the city out of rebel hands; and the betrayal of the city to the barons had been the final straw in the mounting challenge to the King's authority.

Chapter 14—which was to be deleted by the revisors of the Charter—reflected in part the barons' intention to keep the throne under continuing surveillance, and in part Stephen Langton's hope for an orderly system of government. It proposed a method for the convening of the common council of the realm, eliminating the indefinite and often capricious procedures by which an impulsive and continually moving monarch might summon his lords for a "parley." The chapter required adequate advance notice—forty days—and a definite statement of time and place, and a statement of the reason for the summons. Then, ran the article, when the appointed day had come, those present were to proceed with the business at hand, not permitting the king to dismiss those who, often at considerable inconvenience and hardship, had made the effort to attend when some of the others so summoned had wilfully or otherwise turned up absent.

Henry's advisers deleted this chapter, perhaps reasoning that in the time of emergency confronting them after John's death it would be impractical to postpone decisions of state until all the lords could be assembled. There was also the question of who could be counted among the loyal tenants to whom a summons could be directed—or who might indeed switch his loyalty in the forty-day interval. More importantly, the logic of royal administration during the decade of Henry's minority encouraged the development of a petty council of permanent advisers to handle the day-to-day business of the government, in place of the infrequent convocations of the great council of all the lords. Langton, whose brain child this chapter might have been, was under detention in Rome when it was deleted; the germ of the idea of a regular national assembly was already in ferment, however, and half a century after Runnymede the rudiment of Parliament would take form.

The concord between the King and his barons, hammered out under stress that June, was not a model of draftsmanship; its subject matter was distributed piecemeal, so that related topics did not always fall into companion chapters. From the perspective of aftercenturies, this discontinuity may preserve some of the emotion of the time, when men disputed with each other as to what were the propositions of greatest urgency to be set down, and each new clause was dictated to the copyists by that spokesman who would refuse to be put off any longer. It was perhaps some such circumstance which led now to another series of chapters, concerning the machinery of justice and the particular writs of procedure which were available to the dispensing of this justice.

As a fundamental proposition in this portion of the Charter, Chapter 16 stipulated that no man was to be compelled to render greater feudal service than his freehold required. The barons, in this matter, doubtless had in mind the demands for foreign military service which had been made by John. Increasingly, the landholders in England had an antipathy, or at least an apathy, toward the problem of fighting to preserve the royal interests on the Continent. The Angevin provinces had largely become the domain of the king himself and his vassals in that part of the former empire; men with estates centered entirely in England had no enthusiasm for crossing the Channel to defend or recover dominions with which they no longer had ties. The terms of knight service as they were universally understood in medieval Europe limited the vassal's liability to the overlord's requirements within the realm, to defense against invasion, and perhaps to pursuit of an enemy into his territory. The Crusades were manned by persons who had assumed the vow or were in the pay of the lord who had; kings like Henry II and the later Edwards might dream of building great kingdoms by conquest, but the tenants of the crown were increasingly concerned with power bases closer home.

With Chapter 17, the Charter turned to the machinery of justice and the writs of orderly procedure which had had their inception in the heyday of Henry II. "Common pleas shall not follow our court, but shall be held in some place certain," ran the stipulation, a testimonial to the accepted role of the royal courts in the England of the thirteenth century. Rather than enduring the indefinite delays in litigation which were necessitated by the uncertain schedule of a peripatetic royal entourage, including its traveling justices, the tenants now asked that a permanent judicial center be established, with the assumption that Westminster would be the logical place. Here, with permanent repositories for records, and adjacent to the congregating groups of savants in the law and those who sought to study under them, suits between private parties (common pleas) could be systematically conducted.

The establishment of these courts at Westminster would, it was conceded, work hardship on lesser freeholders who could not afford to make the trip to obtain justice there. The King's justices would continue to travel about the land, and in certain types of disputes the ancient county courts would be directed to summon juries of the knights of the shire to administer the law. This was particularly true of the now well-established writs of *novel disseisin*, and *mort d'ancestor*, which dealt with the continual disputes over tenants who had been dispossessed of their freeholds by usurpers who had come onto their land. These, said John's charter, were to be the business of the county courts; but Henry's advisers added the provision that "those causes which for difficulty of some articles" could not be settled there should be referred to the Bench of Common Pleas. In the case of *darrein presentment*, which often involved ecclesiastical interests or the special knowledge of canon law, the charter of Henry vested exclusive jurisdiction in Westminster.

Three chapters in the concord reflected a peculiar liability of the feudal age; they spoke of amercements which might be levied upon offenders of all types, clerical and lay, freeholder and villein. In the elaborately circumscribed society of the Middle Ages, virtually every act of every individual was subject to some accountability; the offense might be great or small, but one could not pass many days without being chargeable with some failure in duty. A merchant might, innocently or not, have failed to sell goods of an accepted quality; a priest might have neglected to say Masses for which he had received a payment; a laborer might neglect to give his proper service in the fields which were the demesne of his lord. Such a man would be found by the manorial courts or other appropriate tribunals to be "in mercy," and would be amerced, or penalized, according to the nature of his offense. But, said the Charter, the penalty must not be greater than the offense, and in any case it must not deprive the clerk of his ecclesiastical benefice or the merchant of his goods or the husbandman of his wainage (tools of husbandry).

In many of these chapters, John himself could readily acquiesce; whatever his own age or the folklore of subsequent ages might say of him, it was not to be denied that he had an intelligent grasp of the needs for orderly procedures in the daily life of his kingdom. He appreciated the developing institutions of common law which his father's great justiciars had founded, and his own sporadic statecraft had tended to strengthen many of the procedures which were the subject of specific portions of the concord. He could have little quarrel with the principles expressed in the matter of common-law writs and the preservation of previously established rights of towns and tenants. Men could assume that, had fate not intervened in other ways, John and the more principled men among the rebels could well have found a common ground in these important areas of the Charter.

The primary objective of the concord, however, was to place strictures upon John's own worst habits, as Chapter 23 was to demonstrate. "No town or freeman shall be distrained to make bridges at riverbanks, except those who were obliged to do so of old," it read; and to this Henry's charter added a supplementary chapter stipulating that the meadows alongside the rivers were not to be placed "in defense" except as they had been in the time of Henry I. While the maintenance of roads and bridges was a responsibility of local communities, the concern of these chapters was with John's callous disregard for the convenience or even the needs of his subjects when his desire for hunting and falconry was in the ascendant.

To place a riverbank "in defense" was to deny its use (Fr. *defense*) to any but the king's party for so long as it was his pleasure or intent to engage in the hunt in that area. Feudal kings and barons alike divided their activities among war, the quasi war of the tournament, and the chase. It had been so since the time of the Conqueror, and one of the sorest burdens William placed upon his kingdom was the appropriation of great tracts of forest into the royal dominion. In addition, the king might notify a particular part of his realm where hunting was especially appealing at the season when he chanced to be near that for a space of several weeks he intended to close off or put "in defense" an extent of riverbank or meadowland for his exclusive use. For such space of time, lesser men could not seek game for their own tables therein, and if it happened that the fields were ready for harvest, the year's crop might be lost because the king and his party were at sport there.

John above all pleasures—except possibly women—loved falconry; it was said that in 1203, with Normandy slipping from his grasp, he was chiefly concerned that his favorite hunting birds should be sent to him from England so that he might indulge his passion. Back in his own realm, as time wore on, he became ever more extravagant in his demands; not merely the area in which he was coming was placed out of the bound of his subjects, but the banks in defense might extend for miles and might be kept inaccessible for great lengths of time. A king so arrogantly concerned with his own sport would be indifferent to the hardships which this might work upon his subjects.

The subjects, in turn, complained to their lords, and it was the lords, whose produce from their lands thus closed to subtenants was correspondingly reduced, who wrote this prohibition into the charter. They followed with another complaint of their own, on a different matter; no royal officers in the shires, it was stipulated, were to hold pleas of the crown. The argument in favor of placing all criminal causes, and other issues in which the king had a public concern, in the jurisdiction of the special justices who would constitute the Court of King's Bench had been that justice in such instances should be uniform and in keeping with the king's peace. To permit local representatives of the crown—the sheriff, the coroner, or the constable in charge of royal castles—to try such causes was not only to revive the variations in punishment of crimes, but to place in the hands of ambitious local representatives an autocratic power which often fell heavily upon the mesne lords and lesser freeholders. It was only to be the king's justices, at whose coming there should be gaol delivery of all accused persons to be judged, who were to hear such cases.

The depredations wrought by sheriffs in their own jurisdiction, out of sight of the king's officers placed above them, were indicated in Chapter 26, where the Charter required that upon the death of the king's tenant the sheriff was required to show the royal letters patent (open) empowering them to attach the chattels of the estate to satisfy any debts owed to the crown. But the sheriffs, with or without the king's connivance, seldom stopped with part of the goods; all were seized and carried off, with little prospect indeed that the widow or heirs would ever obtain possession of them again. The proposal in this chapter was that only so much of the personal goods as would satisfy the debt were to be taken, and this was to be done "in the view of lawful men" who knew the amount of the debt and the value of the assets being attached. It was upon such guarantees of right that numerous private actions on the Great Charter would be maintained in the fourteenth and fifteenth centuries.

John's charter spoke also of a right in which the Church had a fundamental concern, to "prove" the will of the deceased, or if he died intestate, to distribute his goods through the action of his relatives and friends, with a due regard to the shares reserved for his widow and heirs and the private claims against his estate.

The right of canon law to administer property left by dying tenants would continue into modern times in England.

Next the agreement turned to another basic problem of the feudal system: the purveying or requisitioning of goods for royal use. An itinerant court required continually to be supplied with all manner of foods and materials to accommodate the party accompanying the king; when such a party arrived at a royal castle, its needs would far exceed the normal requirements of the garrison in residence. Thus, the king's men would ride into the countryside and collect grain, timber, and other chattels, and often would demand a cart or two to carry the goods with them. Purveyances were an accepted manner of supply, but the issue was always whether the compensation for the goods taken was adequate—or whether it was even paid. The Charter sought to remedy a manifest abuse; it stipulated that payment should be on the spot unless the seller accepted a postponement, and that a fixed sum, set in 1217 "at the old established price" for a cart and two horses at ten pennies per day, should be paid for goods and services.

The provisions concerning the royal castles reminded the barons of another matter, interspersed among the chapters on purveyances. Since the day of William I, castle ward, or guard, had been a fixed duty of a tenant, so that a continuing garrison for the fortress could be assured by requiring a customary amount of service each year from all tenants within the demesne. In due course, many men preferred to give a money payment in lieu of actually attending the castle, and still later, when mercenaries were frequently in full-time station at a castle, the constable would prefer the tenant's money to his personal service. If money was hard to come by, a tenant insisted that he be permitted to discharge his duty by actual service, and Chapter 29 undertook to confirm this right.

In the matter of criminal justice, Chapter 32 dealt with an abuse which all the Plantagenets had practiced—seizing the lands of a convicted felon and holding them beyond the lawful period recognized by feudal custom. It was said that the king had the right to take such lands and lay waste to their produce if he desired, for a year and a day, after which the land was to return to the lord of the fee. John was seldom disposed to pay scrupulous attention to the end of a period in which he could enjoy the income from estates of an exiled or outlawed vassal.

The miscellany of concerns in the Charter was reflected in Chapter 33, which stipulated that the Thames and Medway, the great watercourses serving London and Rochester, should be cleared of "kydells," or fishweirs. This problem had been brought to John's attention earlier, and he had ordered that such obstructions to river transportation be destroyed. Since the great rivers were of primary importance to the trading centers in the towns, their interest clashed with those of the lesser people who sought means of gathering fish for their livelihood and sustenance.

Another economic issue was met in Chapter 35, where the earlier efforts at legislating on the matter of weights and measures were now reiterated. "There shall be one measure of wine throughout our kingdom," John conceded, as also one measure of ale and of grain. This was to be "the quarter of London," a standard measure approximating eight bushels. Woven cloth was to be of one width—two yards within the selvedges, whether this was the gaily dyed fabric to which men of quality were entitled or the somber russets worn by humble folk or the rough halberjects worn under armor. And "of weights," added the charter, "it shall be as of measures." The stipulations were of substantial importance to the growing economy of the thirteenth century; and the standards established at this time, amid the greater affairs of legal procedure and constitutional limitations, were to endure for many generations.

Now the Charter returned to the fundamental issues of law; Chapters 34 and 36 to 46 spoke of procedures which were to be reformed and others which were to be guaranteed. "The writ called *praecipe* shall from henceforth be granted to no person of any freehold, whereby any freeman may lose his court," declared Chapter 34; it marked the reaction of the barons against a process which had set in under Henry II, whereby cases could be diverted from the local courts which had been conducted, from time out of mind, by lords of the manors to settle the disputes of their own subtenants. There was much at stake; since the lords had granted the subtenancy, it was argued that they alone should have the right to dispose of issues arising in the course of that tenure. Not so, Henry's justiciars had answered; it was the obligation of the crown to see that objective justice was afforded to all its subjects, and at the least the king's justice would be present in the manorial proceedings in the writ of right. By this document, the barons were enjoined to do justice to the claimants in their own courts, lest the tenancy involved be taken into the king's hand.

From this procedure it was a short step to the writ of *praecipe*, by which the lord was directed to take the issue into the royal court itself for adjudication. The barons were thus in danger of losing all control over their own tenants in the matter of property disputes, as they had lost it in the matter of criminal proceedings. The control of their own vassals, which went with the right to maintain local courts, was thus vastly lessened, and the throne's control correspondingly increased. While it was a matter of the grantor's interest, the barons phrased it as though it were in the interest of their tenants; they wished the writ abandoned, they said, lest such a tenant might lose his court (which was to say, the right to have his cause heard in the baronial court).

In an issue so vital, the barons insisted upon this essentially retrogressive step; like all political settlements, the Charter was a matter of mutual concessions. The succeeding chapters dealt more liberally with the guarantees of justice: certain writs relating to rights of accused persons were to be issued freely and not for fees; accusations were not to be the basis of prosecution without the presence of "faithful witnesses"; and—in the most famous and legend-circled passage in the entire charter—"no freeman shall be taken or imprisoned, or disseised . . . but by the lawful judgment of his peers, or by the law of the land."

Chapter 39 (which would become Chapter 29 in the definitive form of Magna Carta) would outlive all else in the details of the document; it would be enshrined permanently in the modern law and ideals of England and commonwealths yet unborn. But to each age it would mean something different; to the men gathered at Runnymede, it stated a universal principle only in that it applied to all freemen—and a *liber homo* of 1215 was a freeholder, one entitled to enfranchisement with a tenancy however modest it might be. Thus, the class to whom this chapter applied in the early thirteenth century was little larger than the feudal class of the time of William I, possibly 10 per cent of the total population in England. Yet the proportion of men to be benefited by this provision would grow, even in the turmoil of the three hundred years immediately to follow, as the courts of the land consistently accepted pleas based on the general or specific rights of the charter itself. Four centuries hence, the English Revolution would terminate the great body of feudal tenures which this charter was presumed to undergird, and at the same time would vastly enlarge the classes of English society which would give a modern meaning to the term "free men" and the benefits this chapter would preserve.

So, too, the "judgment of his peers" had its own meaning for the draftsmen of John's charter; simply (perhaps oversimply) put, it acknowledged that a baron should be permitted to lay his case before members of his own class. It was, indeed, a class privilege limited to the great lords and was intended in 1215 to guarantee that when a dispute arose between them, or with the crown itself, it would be submitted to a body of crown tenants, perhaps the great council of the realm itself, for determination as to the issues to be tried; for this was the traditional function of the medieval jury. It would not have occurred to undertenants or mesne lords of the thirteenth century to have expected or particularly desired such an option; they had gained a substantial measure of justice with the accessibility of the royal courts for their claims, and they were content to rely upon the king's justice and the familiar service of a jury of recognition (confirmation of the facts at issue) in their litigation. A jury to try the facts and render a verdict was unknown to the thirteenth century and would in any case have been unacceptable to all tenants, great or small. Chapter 39 embodied the guarantees which they sought and insured them to all who had standing within the feudal concept.

The significance of this chapter, for its own day and after, lay in its context; the chapters before and after it dealt with other dimensions of the same subject matter. Thus, said Chapter

36, all should be entitled to a writ of inquisition by which the
accused party might secure an inquest of the charges by men
who knew the circumstances and who could determine whether
the accusations were made *de odio et atia,* of hatred and ill-will.
The chief issue in this portion of the charter was the tendency to
make such a popular writ a lucrative source of revenue; it was
henceforth to be issued out of the chancery freely with "nothing
. . . given or taken" for it.

There was also Chapter 38, just preceding the "golden
passage" as Coke described it, which provided that bailiffs
(royal officers charged with a certain jurisdiction or bailiwick)
were not to subject a man to any judicial test upon their own
initiative, but upon testimony of proper witnesses. The chapter
hinted at, rather than specified, the abuses of justice which were
involved, but from its place among the series of prohibitions of
malpractices attributed to John, it was clear that the King's arbitrary prosecution of charges against certain tenants was the crux
of the matter.

There was also Chapter 40, which Henry's revisors considered
to be essentially a supplement to Chapter 39 and accordingly combined both chapters; it caused the King to promise: "We will sell
to no man, neither will we deny nor defer to any man, either
justice or right." The practice of charging for the issuance of a
writ as a legitimate means of royal revenue, as well as meeting
the administrative costs of the functions of chancellor's office, had
been taken for granted from the earliest days of Henry I. John's
habit of increasing the charges in proportion to the value of the
cause or the wealth of the applicant was the root of the offense;
but in the ensuing reign it became a settled practice of the chancellor's office that certain writs, essential to obtaining elemental
justice, were to be issued without charge, while those involving a
question of the right to an estate would require a nominal fee.
Those concerning collection of debts might still command a substantial price. With these distinctions, the barons had no fundamental quarrel; for themselves and their tenants, they sought
protection against unreasonable exploitation of the instruments
by which they could obtain their day in the royal courts.

Other chapters dealt with other encroachments upon the

rights of tenants: the assumption of custody over productive estates when the king's claim to wardship was actually subordinate to that of another (as when the former tenant had held of the king by a promise of money payments but had held of a crown tenant by knight service); or when a barony would escheat to the crown, the demand of the king for full feudal service by those whose estates were held of this barony. These were peculiar but fundamental technical issues of feudalism; as they were to be understood in terms of the formulae of their own day, so were the companion chapters on fundamental law which would be interpreted in different frames of reference in later ages.

Finally, the Charter turned its attention to the immediate political and military concessions which the rebels insisted upon having from King John. Hostages and confiscated charters of English, Scots, and Welsh tenants and vassals were to be released; certain specifically named foreign advisers of the King were to be sent from the land; the mercenary troops (presumably the Poitevins included) were to depart; and all who had been dispossessed "without legal judgment of his peers"—including disseisins traced back to Richard I and Henry II—were to be afforded restitution. And now came the *forma securitatis*, the procedure by which the concord was to be carried out: twenty-five of the barons themselves were to be elected a permanent committee of overseers, "who ought with all their power to observe, hold, and cause to be observed, the peace and liberties which we have granted to them." If complaint were to be made against John or his officers and not redressed within forty days, "let these twenty-five barons with the whole community of the country distress and injure us in every way they can; that is to say, by the seizure of our castles, lands, possessions, and in such other ways as they can until it shall have been corrected according to their judgment."

This perpetual right to rebellion, set out in elaborate detail, no man could have expected John to abide by or the Pope to ratify; it was the undoing of the Charter as a whole and the parties who had joined in it. If Stephen Langton acquiesced in this proviso, it must have been either because he hoped to keep the machinery under his own control and thus avoid the anarchy

which it could precipitate, or because he was unable to restrain
the rebels who, as they completed the series of clauses in the
charter, insisted that John should not be permitted to quit the
gathering without being placed under continual surveillance. The
device was crude, but the circumstances were, after all, totally
without precedent; if the lords were to be disappointed in their
plan to subject John to their will, a similar proposition would be
put into operation to subjugate Henry III after the Barons' War
half a century later.

Thus was concluded "the agreement between King John and
the barons for the granting of the liberties of the Church and
realm of England," as the contemporary age described it. John was
disposed to honor the agreement, except in such cases as imperiled
his sovereignty and in any event until such time as he could regain
the upper hand. The same day the concord was sealed he sent
letters to the sheriffs in every county to notify them that peace had
been established and the people were to swear allegiance to the
twenty-five sureties. But the rebels, who were now without a
cause, were having second thoughts. If John had been so ready to
grant their demands, why, they now asked themselves, had they
not asked for more? With so much won by dictation, could not
the entire kingdom be won by force? Quite possibly, many of
those who hated John so intensely had hoped originally that he
would refuse their demands altogether and would have thus given
them a semblance of an excuse to overthrow him completely.
The summer wore on, with no sign that the rebels now intended
to live up to their part of the agreement; having set up a strong
surety program to compel the King to abide by his promises, they
refused to give him the security they had promised to guarantee
their own performance, and in a few weeks this was formally
protested by the bishops. Many of the rebels had returned to their
own estates and were putting their castles into a state of war-
readiness. To excuse their continuing to keep fully armed
retainers about them, they decreed that tournaments were to be
held, one being at Staines where the prize was to be "a bear which
a certain lady will send."

Now, on August 24, came word from Rome. Innocent was

indignant at the circumstances which had led to the confrontation of June 15; they violated the fundamental precept of feudal loyalty to a paramount lord, and when that lord was a vassal of the Holy See, it was a rebellion against the Church itself. Under such circumstances, declared the Pope, the agreement that was sealed was vile and wicked; Magna Carta was thereupon quashed and any actions by any party in observance of it were held to be null and void. Violators of the decree were to be subject to excommunication. The Great Charter of Liberties had lasted sixty-six days.

The rebels were now desperate men; they had lost the concessions they had treated with such contempt after winning them, and their continued stay in London was now proving to be a strategic disadvantage. In September, they had sallied out and by treachery had captured the castle of Rochester, thus seeking to open a line of communication to the French forces of Philip's son, Prince Louis, whom they were now entreating to invade the land to help them in a complete revolution. Louis did not come, and the barons lay helplessly in London while John's forces gave siege to the castle and at the end of November forced its surrender. Now John began his move to regain control of his kingdom; with some of his forces guarding the escape route from London, the King himself moved into the northern and eastern areas of disaffection. It was an itinerary of retribution, for John intended to visit punishment on all who had violated their oaths of fealty. On the other hand, he was not vindictive; the worst offenders might have their lands laid waste, but many were permitted to pay a fine to save their estates, and even the bitterest of his enemies the King offered to restore to their former honors if they would give good and faithful service.

By the end of the winter John had reconquered most of the country except London, and now he was preparing for an attack on the rebels cornered there. But once more, as so often in the story of his strange career, John's expectation of success was to be frustrated. After long hesitation, Prince Louis of France was launched upon his invasion. John's fleet, which might have turned it back, was scattered in a storm, and the French, under a renegade and pirate named Eustace the Monk, landed without challenge. Now the tide had shifted again; Louis made contact with the rebels in London, and the royal forces retreated to the west. The insurgent cause once more was centered in much of the area John had so recently reconquered, and there was no disputing the determination of the rebels now, with their foreign allies, to overthrow the King altogether.

The French were in the island on the flimsiest of excuses; to justify their action they had resurrected the old charge that John was guilty of the murder of his nephew, Arthur of Brittany, and for this had been condemned to the loss of his throne. The story of a formal trial on the matter had been manufactured out of whole cloth, but it was enough to rationalize the expedition in the eyes of Philip and his son. The French landed in May, and by the end of August they had reached the high point of their invasion. But the zeal for the barons' cause was rapidly evaporating; too many in England recognized their bad faith and their total lack of principle. If John was no better, he was at least the lawful sovereign, and men could contrast the continued effectiveness of royal government, wherever it functioned, to the anarchy and spoliation of the rebels and the invaders. By September, as John prepared to counterattack, the cause of the insurgents began to decline.

But the story of the violent reign was now almost at an end. The King was stricken with dysentery in early October, and as he continued in the field, seeking to press the attack upon his foes, his condition became steadily worse. Ill fortune continued to strike whenever his plans seemed almost at a climax; his entire baggage train was destroyed as it attempted to cross the treacherous tidal flats toward Lincolnshire. John himself was carried on a litter to his last abode, the castle of Newark, where, on October 19, he expired, commending his soul to God and his body to St. Wulfstan. For his harsh and stormy reign, he was not to be remembered kindly; one rhyme, in fact, was composed at the news of his death, and ran,

> With John's foul deeds, England's whole realm is stinking,
> As is also Hell, wherein he now is sinking.

But there were others who understood that, in an age when few could measure up to the ideals of a Stephen Langton, John's memory did not need to be entirely vilified. The epitaph on his grave was to read in part:

> In this tomb reposes the likeness of a king
> Who, dying, brought to an end much tumult in the world. . . .

IV

Reissue and Confirmation

THE death of King John did indeed seem to remove the
cause if not the fact of the civil war; the barons, after
all, had wanted nothing so much as to be rid of him as their
sovereign, and now they had no legitimate ground for continuing
the conflict. There were, of course, many imponderables in the
condition of the realm as it was now to be: a nine-year-old prince,
Henry III, was the heir to the throne, and the eastern portion of
the land was largely under the control of the invading French
army. Archbishop Langton was in exile, so that there was serious
question whether Henry could be validly crowned; there was
no exchequer, no crown, no seal, no council of government in
being at the moment. But the loyal party did not dare to leave
the throne empty when Louis of France was claiming it. Indeed,
the French prince was even now besieging Dover, the great
fortress dominating the invasion coast, and seeking to persuade
the King's loyal constable, Hubert de Burgh, to surrender and
come over to him now that John had died. Louis let it be known
that he considered the kingdom to be in his power as of right,
and unless Henry's supporters could seize the initiative, psycho-
logically as well as militarily, all might indeed be lost.

The first step was to arrange for Henry's coronation, which
took place at Gloucester on October 28, nine days after John's
death, with Bishop Peter of Winchester as the celebrant and the
new papal legate, Gualo, present to receive the new monarch's
homage to Rome. The kingdom was placed under the guardianship of William Marshal as *rector regis et regni;* this faithful earl
had now served four Plantagenets, and although he was well
stricken in years, he was the most respected of the lords in the
royal party. With him also were several of those whose names

had been inscribed in the preamble to John's charter of sixteen months before; it was logical enough that their thoughts should return to this grant of fundamental feudal rights, and the decision to revive, revise and reissue the document doubtless occurred to them as a means of swinging the majority of the country back to the King's cause. What had been condemned by the Holy See because it had been imposed upon John by disloyal vassals would now be offered freely by the sovereign.

Thus was Magna Carta resurrected, its fundamental principles to be separated from the dross of the specific impediments placed upon John, and all men would know that the liberties of the realm were assured under the new regime. This was done on November 12, sealed by Gualo the legate and the regent Earl of Pembroke, and it went out with the Earl's proclamation of Henry's coronation and a call to all English lords to renew their allegiance to the King as the King had renewed the grant of their liberties to them. It was a powerful appeal, for though the revision had stricken twenty-two chapters from John's charter, most of these had been *ad hoc* provisions concerning the specific demands made upon the King at Runnymede; and, it was argued, the young King should not be burdened with the strictures placed upon his father. There was some murmuring; the chapters ensuring certain privileges to crown tenants, and for convening a council of the realm to consider how well the charter was being observed, had been dropped out, and certain other feudal rights were not mentioned. But the King's friends pointed to the new chapter which had been added and which promised that when peace was restored another revision would be made in which any desirable propositions which had been omitted would be inserted at that time.

A new Pope ratified this charter; Innocent had died this same year, and Honorius III sat on the throne of St. Peter. The Holy Father continued the excommunication of those who had revolted against John and extended this to the French invaders as well. Disaffection was spreading in the rebel camp, and the French held in contempt many of the English who, though they had invited the invasion, had done so by being unfaithful to their own sovereign. Robert fitz Walter, the so-called marshal of the insurgents, Louis treated with particular disdain, especially as Fitz Walter importuned him for new grants of estates continually. There was also grumbling at the tendency of the English rebels to keep snug in London while the French did much of the fighting. But Louis's control had not yet been seriously threatened, although his father, concerned at the vehemence of the papal condemnation, was disavowing the adventure. There was also the accusation of the Viscount of Melun, when he lay dying in London, that Louis had sworn that when he ascended the English throne he would "condemn to perpetual banishment all those who are now fighting with him and persecuting [their own king], as traitors against their lord, and will destroy the whole race of them from the kingdom." The rebels heard the deathbed testimony glumly; they had already seen much of their land given to French tenants, and they knew the hatred in which many of their countrymen also held them; and on every Sunday and holy day now they realized that their names were repeatedly cursed.

Now, as 1217 came on, the desperation of both rebels and invaders increased; Louis, on receiving word that the Pope would confirm his own excommunication unless he quit England, signed a Lenten truce with the young Henry and hurried back to France. In his absence several English earls quit his cause and made their peace with the new occupant of the throne. When Louis returned after Easter, he found Henry's counsellors rallying a growing number of English to the King's cause, and he set out for Lincoln to seek battle with them. A confused struggle ensued; royalists in the castle were under siege by rebels in the city, who were joined by Louis's forces under Fitz Walter and the youthful Count of Perche. Now William Marshal's army came up and caught the enemy between itself and the royal party in the castle. It proved to be a rout: the English crossbowmen mowed down the horses of the French knights, and the foot soldiers, attacking the fallen and overweighted riders, took prisoner more than half of the army. The remnant of the rebels and the invaders fled in wild disorder; at last, the loyal cause had prevailed.

One more attack, this time by sea, was attempted by Louis's forces, but it too ended in disaster; by throwing hot lime into their enemy's faces, the English navy blinded the host and rammed their overcrowded galleys. The Battle of the Sandwich Islands, like the land engagement at Lincoln, ended the French dream of another conquest, and at the Treaty of Lambeth, Louis agreed to give up all his specious claims. An honorable peace— better than either rebels or invaders had cause to expect—was concluded on September 11. The aged Earl of Pembroke, grand marshal that he had proved himself to be in the years of trouble in the realm, conducted the French to the seacoast and saw to their departure. Now, after so many grievous turns of fortune, England could look to a day of peace.

It was now time to attend to the promise of the previous fall that when the realm was again in order, the King would further amend and reissue the document which, in the eyes of many, had become a grant of great value. Now was to evolve the text of Magna Carta which, except for minor changes in 1225, would be the definitive form of the document. As it turned out, little that had been deleted from John's charter in the tentative reissue of 1216 was actually restored; the revisions of 1217 were intended to make more detailed the provisions for legal procedure, as in the petty assizes and in the control over alienation of land. One of the beneficial policies introduced into the regency by William Marshal had been the principle of preserving the royal estates intact and prohibiting a progressive dimunition of them by fresh grants to tenants in chief. The reissue now stipulated that no tenant in turn should distribute so much of his land that the residue could not ensure the services to the overlord which had been provided in the original grant. The germ of the idea of conservation of interests in land, rather than the irresponsible largesses of Henry II and Richard I, was coming into being.

The new issue of the Charter, now called *Carta de libertatibus*, sought also to revive and strengthen the system of local government administration in England, further suggesting that the Charter already was being treated as a summary of the whole legal system. In a new chapter, the Charter addressed itself to a process of law and administration which affected a large body of humble folk, below the levels of freehold tenures which were the primary concern of the feudal law. The county courts, the courts of the hundreds, and the annual "view of frankpledge" were foundation stones for the system which concerned by far the majority of the population. These were Saxon institutions which had been taken over by the Normans and now were bulwarked by generations of usage. To preserve the peace and organize the local population in primitive times, the custom had developed of requiring each adult male to find security for himself and serve as security for a neighbor, to ensure their respective appearances to answer for any breach of the peace, a form of peace bond known as frankpledge. Every fall the sheriff would view the frankpledge, or inspect the records of securities, to satisfy himself that every man in the community was part of his mutual bond. This viewing was customarily held at the full-attendance session of the hundred courts, composed of all men of the hundred, or the subdivision of the county made up of some hundred families. From the hundreds of the entire county, the sheriff on occasion would convene a county court—in both cases the courts of hundreds or of counties being administrative as well as judicial bodies. The people chronically complained of the frequency with which they were compelled to do "suit of court," and Henry's revision sought to limit the frequency of court sessions and at the same time ensure their greater regularity.

Another innovation was a prohibition of fraudulent gifts in *mortmain,* a problem that was a recurring one within the feudal system, where tenants continually searched for ways of evading some of the obligations which attached to their freeholds. Commonly in the thirteenth century, a tenant of a lay fief would convey his land to a religious house, where it would automatically become a spiritual fief, and the obligations of tenure would thereafter be of a spiritual or charitable nature. The religious house would then convey this land back to the tenant, subject only to the spiritual or charitable obligations; the feudal rights of a temporal lord would thus be extinguished by this "dead hand" (*mortmain*). Chapter 36 of Henry's reissue tried to prohibit the practice, but it still was a subject of legislation in the time of Edward I.

As if to signal the closing of the great rebellion, the final chapter of the reissue provided that all adulterine castles erected or enlarged during the civil war should be razed. Quaintly the grant concluded: "Whereas we do not yet have a seal, we have caused this charter to be sealed by the seals of the aforesaid legate [Gualo] and Earl William Marshal, protector of us and our realm."

The Charter had been issued upon the advice of the king's council, a body which was to undergo significant development in this period of Henry's minority. From ancient times, the royal court had been itinerant, and when the monarch had needed to hold "deep speech" with his most influential lords, he had called them together into a great council. Now, with a boy wearing the crown, it was essential that a smaller council should be maintained to look after his interests at all times. At the beginning, when the issue of the war was still in much doubt, the closest advisers of the son were the most faithful vassals of the father: the Earls of Pembroke, Chester, and Derby, the Master of the Templars, the Bishops of Chichester, Winchester, and Worcester among them. The nucleus would attract to it other influential lords, with whom the responsibility of government would be shared in the coming decade. For both king and realm, a maturer character of government was to develop from these emergency measures; no longer would royal administration be the king as a private person, but an institution of the king in council. The decade in which young Henry would rule through his advisers would be one of general recovery from the generation of upheaval which had fomented and erupted just before. Stephen Langton returned to Canterbury, and at Westminster on Whitsunday of 1220 he recrowned Henry with full ceremony, to erase any irregularity which had been incurred on that tense coronation four years before.

The land was blessed in this time with great counsellors: Marshal, who died in 1219; Langton, who lived nine years longer; and Hubert de Burgh, Chief Justiciar, who lived until 1236. Twenty years of peace helped the institutions of government take firm root, and the great charter of which Archbishop Stephen had dreamed became a symbol in his own day of a once and future rule of law. A general eyre in 1218 had provided the realm with an up-to-date description of the lands held by various ten-

ants; and since for many generations after the written records of
Domesday, documentary proof of the right of the present occupant to his freehold had become lost or nonexistent, Henry's
reign would see a great upsurge of issuing of charters and related
patents to show the validity of a tenure. The insistence upon
orderly proof of such rights would grow throughout the century,
until Edward I would enshrine it in the great constitutional
statute *Quo Warranto:* by what warrant, his government would
ask, did a tenant hold his property? The formal evidence of such
rights was becoming an essential element of property early in
Henry's time with the drawing up of "final concords" in three
parts—one to each party and one, the bottom of the document or
"the foot of the fine," which was deposited in the treasury. Legal
memory would be traced to the rolls of "feet of fines" as well as
to the great rolls of charters, closed (sealed) letters, open (patent) letters, and other records which began to be kept with
regularity under Richard I.

Yet, with returning peace came returning ambitions of great
barons. In 1221 the Earl of Albemarle gathered together a number of malcontents and set upon a brief career of pillage and
plunder, in which he seized a number of villages and subjected
their inhabitants to tortures until they gave him all their possessions. He stormed and took the Castle of Fotheringay when its
lord was absent, and sacked a neighboring town under its protection. In due course, Henry and his council summoned a host
and apprehended the Earl, but upon Gualo's recommendation the
King pardoned him and all his knights in remembrance of his
former loyalty. This, said Roger of Wendover, "gave a bad example to others to rebel against him with confidence in a like case."

Two years later came a letter from Pope Honorius declaring
Henry, now nearly seventeen, to be of age for certain legal purposes, and the following year the King announced that he would
take into his own hands the royal castles and lands which had so
long been held in ward. This was ill news to the custodians who
had thus far enjoyed the revenues from these estates, and some
of them refused or neglected to turn over the properties. One,
Falcasius, seized one of the royal justiciars who was riding on
circuit near his castle of Bedford and threw him into the castle

dungeon. This time Henry acted with more determination; while he laid siege to the castle, he ordered all other properties of Falcasius to be seized, and when the stronghold had been stormed, he hanged two dozen of the bloodiest offenders. Falcasius himself was placed under the custody of the Bishop of London, and Bedford Castle was reduced to a heap of stones. Henry was beginning to manifest some of the familiar characteristics of a Plantagenet, although his vacillations were always to give his career a color of irresoluteness. Throughout his long reign, he would steer an uncertain course; when he was served by able counsellors and was disposed to recognize the fact, all was well; but the steady growth of national institutions and the flowering of national culture in his day was the result of others' laborings.

The vacillating course of an adolescent monarch led to a critical situation in 1223, when Henry ordered sheriffs of all the counties to hold an inquest to determine what rights and liberties had existed in each shire prior to 1215. There was general alarm at this order. Did it mean a rescission of the general concord which had come to be known as the Great Charter of Liberties? Men reminded themselves that, in truth, the lords in many parts of the kingdom had little regard for the charter of 1217. Stephen Langton, whose life work had been epitomized in the Great Charter, was among many who were deeply moved by the events of this period, and at Epiphany in 1224 he urged the King "to confirm to them the rights and free customs, to obtain which the war had been entered on against his father." The attitude of some of Henry's overzealous lords—possibly colored by the obligations which were visited on the tenants as well as the King by this grant—was epitomized by William Briwere, who replied to the Archbishop by blurting out, "The liberties which you demand, since they were extorted by force, ought not by right to be observed."

More agitated than ever by this reply, Langton answered sternly, "William, if you loved the king, you would not disturb the peace of the kingdom." Then Henry spoke up for himself; seeing that his prelate was so deeply affected, he assured him and admonished the rest of the council, "We have sworn to observe all these liberties, and what we have sworn we are bound to abide by." All his life, Henry bore the scars of John's disgrace; he was prepared to make any concessions if there seemed to be serious threat of a like confrontation. In the matter of reasserting the grant of liberties he would prove as good as his word—although there would be a considerable number of times in future years when he would have to be reminded of it and would be asked to reconfirm the charters as a proof of good faith. In spite of himself, he strengthened the standing of the Great Charter by these reaffirmations of its points, as would his son and grandson, until it had become indelible in the record of the fundamental law of the land.

The occasion for the final revision of Magna Carta was presented in February of 1225. A great council had been summoned to consider the King's request for a general levy upon all freeholders. The immediate need was for funds to deal with a plot which Louis of France was making against the lingering Angevin provinces on the Continent. Now, with Henry declared to be of age, was the time to request of him the *quid pro quo*—a final reissue of the grant which had been made in his name in 1216 and 1217. The Charter of Liberties was once more subjected to editing —from John's sixty-three chapters it had gradually been tightened up into thirty-seven—and on February 11 it was solemnly confirmed. By its terms, said Henry, "neither we nor our heirs shall procure or do anything whereby the liberties in this charter contained shall be infringed or broken, and if anything be procured by any person contrary to the premises, it shall be had of no force nor effect." Ten years after Runnymede, Magna Carta had settled into the foundations of English government, a cornerstone later to be covered over and forgotten in the rubble of fifteenth- and sixteenth-century strife, but to be uncovered again in the making of the modern nation.

Henry's grant spoke of two charters, for in 1217 his council had drafted a companion Charter of the Forest, which would enjoy equal importance in the view of Englishmen throughout the late Middle Ages. To distinguish *Carta de Foresta* from its parent concord, the latter had come to be described as *Magna Carta de Libertatibus*, the Great Charter of (general) Liberties,

Magna Carta because of its length and detail; to the feudal mind, both charters were great in a qualitative sense. For the forests of medieval England played a fundamental role in the economy; thousands of persons lived within their boundaries, and every element therein was subject to a body of law quite distinguishable from the common law and often arbitrarily enforced.

The issues which had grown to a point where a separate, detailed statement of forest law was necessary had begun with William I, whose generally benevolent policy toward his subjects had stopped sharply at the greenwood, which he and the kings following him regarded as the natural preserve of royalty and the great nobles. Under Henry II, a process of adding to these preserves had been accelerated; great areas were "afforested," or returned to their natural state, to increase the pleasure grounds for the king and his favorites. Often this afforestation meant the uprooting of entire villages, driving occupants and their livestock from their homesteads, with no thought of a responsibility for compensation or resettlement. For the thousands of persons who continued to dwell within the boundaries of the forest, life was harshly circumscribed; certain beasts of the forest could not be slain at all, for they were the king's or his nobles'. Not even timber or foliage or the ground covering could be used by the peasants without regular payments collected by royal officers who were subject to all the temptations of petty officials beyond the eye of superiors. Forest courts, for considering and assessing punishments for infractions of the forest laws, were maintained by a body of justiciars who had no responsibility to the elements of objective justice which were slowly crystallizing in the common law.

So it was that several chapters of John's charter, which had dealt with the general abuses of the forest, had been excised and made the nucleus of a detailed Charter of the Forest in 1217. The reforms it attempted were far-reaching. Indeed, where Magna Carta was in large part a restatement and return to accepted practices, *Carta de Foresta* was intended to give a new understanding altogether to the regulations of the greenwood. Two chapters provided categorically for the "disafforestation" of all lands taken into the king's hands since the time of Henry II.

A companion chapter sought to relieve the people of the grim
liability of being brought within the jurisdiction of the forest
courts upon a general summons; unless they were charged specifically with a breach of the forest laws or were securities for
men who were so charged, they were not to be liable to forest
justice.

But the king, in any case, would have his beasts of the chase
protected; for those who dwelt in the forest it was required that
they must attend to the "lawing" of their dogs. It was necessary,
wrote an early authority on the subject, "for the safety of men's
goods and houses who lived within the boundaries thereof, that
certain dogs are suffered to be kept." Where these dogs were
capable of chasing the king's deer, such as mastiffs, it was required that "three claws of the forefoot shall be cut off by the
skin." This expeditation was to be done in view of the king's
rangers.

The forestry officers were varied in duty and even more in
their disposition to administer fairly the areas over which they
held jurisdiction. One chapter of the Forest Charter recognized
the extent of exploitation and corruption that existed in the depths
of the greenwood: no forester, it declared, "shall make scotal, or
gather garb, or oats, or any corn, lamb or pig, nor shall take any
gathering." Scotal, said the law writer, "is where any officer of
the forest keeps an ale-house, and by color of his office causeth
men to come to that ale-house in the forest, there to spend their
money for fear of his displeasure." Even cruder forms of exploitation were the outright taking of the goods, produce, or animals
of a terrified peasant who might otherwise be threatened with
investigation at the forest courts for some crime real or imaginary.

The legitimate collections of the forest officers were burdensome enough. At the *swanimotes*, or *swain-moots*, the denizens
of the forest and the royal officers gathered for *agestment*, or the
counting of the number of each man's livestock which were being
pastured in the forest for grazing, and the collection of payments
for this privilege. In the winter the payments were specially designated for *pawnage*, a reference to the mast or ground covering
on which the animals fed. A third gathering of the dwellers in

the forest was in midsummer, when all livestock was to be expelled during the fawning of the king's deer.

The deer were the chief cause of contention; the king pronounced most of them to be his exclusive property, while many
great lords had their own forests (game preserves) or woods
(timber areas), parks (unenclosed areas for small game), or warrens (livestock grounds). To know which was a royal beast, a
stag or a roe, and which was, under rare circumstances, permissible game was not a distinction to be made by the hungry man,
or one who felt he would not be seen. Royal officers were regularly coming upon carcasses of illegally slain animals in the course
of their range through the greenwood; it was customary on finding such evidence of lawbreaking to summon men from the three
nearest hamlets to view the same, and presumably to betray a
neighbor who had recently enjoyed some venison. If a specific
culprit could not be found, one or all of the villages themselves
might be placed under penalty. It was not to be wondered at
that many men fled to the deepest parts of the forest to become
outlaws. By Henry's day, it was recognized that capital punishment for taking the deer was an impractical threat, and indeed
one chapter offered a general amnesty for "all that be outlawed
for the forest only." And for tenants on the king's business, it was
even permitted that they might slay one or two deer for their use
while abroad in the land, if they summoned an officer of the
forest to watch while they did it and thus protected themselves
from the appearance of wrongful taking.

But life was hard, on the thin edge of subsistence which life
in the greenwood afforded the peasants. Such men could only
take *vert* (vegetation or brush) under certain conditions, were
liable for any excessive clearing of *coverts* (undergrowth), and
had to pay *chiminage*, or duties, for the brush they carried to
town to sell. However, the charter sought to make their lot somewhat less burdensome; dwellers in the forest were permitted to
drive their swine or cattle through the king's domain to some
distant pasturage, and even stay overnight in the greenwood,
without penalty; and freemen were further permitted to improve
their land which lay within the forest and to keep aviaries for

birds' eggs and game fowl. Meager as the concessions were in
the final analysis, they were regarded as much a charter of freedom for the humble folk and small tenants as Magna Carta was
prized by the powerful classes. For generations to follow, the two
charters would be taken together as symbols of the breadth of
the privileges granted to the subjects in this era.

The realm over which Henry III assumed jurisdiction at his
majority had changed significantly from the feudalism of the
twelfth century; if the four issues of Magna Carta did not directly
account for these changes, they were symptomatic of them in
part at least. The story of Henry's kingship would be one of continual struggle between barons and crown as it had been in the
past, but the struggle was gradually transformed from a personal
to an institutional or corporate relationship. The established
agencies of national government—the courts, the Chancery, and
the Exchequer—had survived the upheavals of the civil war and
French invasion; the functions of the petty council of close advisers to Henry gradually were changed into or replaced by the
officers of a new agency which came to be known as the king's
wardrobe, an administrative secretariat which would assume
responsibility for the multiplying business affairs of the realm
demanding petty seals rather than the great seal.

There was also the shifting economic basis of royal administration, as the grant of the fifteenth of the tenants' moveables in
1225 was to show. Not only did such a levy—closer to a modern
tax than a feudal aid—bring in vastly more money because it
reached all property in the realm, but it, too, had become institutionalized. Thus, it fell upon everyone equally and was treated
as something owed the state rather than a gracious concession
of individual vassals. In another economic area, too, the period
after the charters began to orient itself toward modern concepts:
with the passing of the royal demesne from the sheriffs' wardships
in 1223 and 1224, the Exchequer began systematically to review
the annual accounts of the sheriffs themselves. From early times,
a sheriff had acquired his office for a substantial payment and
had been permitted to hold large tracts of land within the shire
"at farm" (rents); the balance between the farm and the amount
by which he might exploit the holdings made many a renter

wealthy beyond all reason. Now the surveillance by the king's finance officers was to make the sheriff, within a generation, a salaried officer who would collect and account for the revenues from these holdings.

Although Henry III lacked the forcefulness of his grandfather and the orderly and efficient mind of his son, the England of his day flowered in many fields. The great university centers at Oxford and Cambridge, stimulated by the cutting off of study opportunities in Paris during the years of the papal interdict, acquired formal organization in the thirteenth century. The Church was nearing its zenith of influence in western Europe, and orders of wandering friars were welcomed to England to impart their fresh stores of knowledge in science, arts, and jurisprudence, as well as to raise the moral tone of parish church administration. Bracton, the great student of the common law as it had evolved since Glanville in the past century, would prepare a classic treatise on the subject which would be published after his death. The growth of trade and maritime commerce, stimulated and influenced by the Five Ports, which had provided such sturdy support to the royal institutions in the times of troubles, laid the foundation for a body of commercial law which would survive into the modern age.

The old struggles of individual lords for advantage within the realm continued, as they would until Tudor times, but the barons were, more often than not, inclined to demand a judgment of peers instead of resorting to arms. In 1227 and again in 1232 the insistence upon such a judgment, while made for purposes of self-interest and in a confusion of circumstances, was tacit evidence of the impact of the charters upon barons as well as crown. Plantagenet kings after John were conscious of the limitations, which, small by modern standards, had brought to an end the primitive assumption of absolute royal right. But the quarrels between the crown and the barons went on, and accounted for the ultimate fall from power of Henry's first justiciar, Hubert de Burgh, and the development of a strong administrative system under Peter des Rivaux. Because the King was willing to convene the great council of his lords and invest in them certain responsibility for upholding the law of the land, progress in government was made in spite of many of the crosscurrents of personal and family rivalry which seethed continually below the surface.

In October 1234 a formal interpretation of Chapter 35 of the Great Charter was requested and handed down by the council; because the chapter had sought to relieve freeholders from attendance at a full session of the hundred courts, except twice a year, it had been argued that these courts could be held no oftener than that. A request for a ruling on the issue was made to the king's council; to endure a six-month interval for the settlement of many routine issues was an unconscionable hardship on small tenants and poor men, all of whom were entitled to their hearing. The ordinance issuing from the council required the courts to be held every three weeks. The practical desire for the definition of rights secured by Magna Carta had thus been demonstrated.

In the winter of 1235 and 1236, an even more momentous step in government was taken, when, following the wedding of Henry to the beautiful Eleanor of Provence and her coronation as Queen, the great council met at Merton to consider other issues growing out of rights asserted in the Great Charter, which experience had shown to need clarification. With this statute, the rule of legislative formulation of law, as distinguished from royal decrees and the dialectic of the assizes, began to assume definition. The statute itself, with its elaboration on widows' rights, the enforcement of judgment by successful litigants, the strengthening of the safeguards of heirs' estates, and certain limitations on the use of writs, was a fundamental step in strengthening the force and effect of Magna Carta itself.

Things never progress smoothly toward an ideal state, however, and now Henry, concerned at the obvious limitations upon the crown which the reliance on the charter rights implied, requested the Pope to send a legate to counsel him in the event of a conflict of authority. The King himself, with the succession of important alliances he had recently effected on the Continent—his bride was the sister of the Queen of France, and his own sister, Isabella, was married to the Holy Roman Emperor Frederick—felt that he was entitled to the degree of power that had been enjoyed by Henry II and Richard I, before the loss of the

Angevin empire. Now, alarmed at the possibility that the King might seek to repudiate his obligations under the charters, a council was convened in January 1237. The occasion was Henry's request for a new tax to meet the expense of his own marriage and that of his sister, but this gave the lords the same opportunity they had had in 1225; in return for the granting of the tax, they required a confirmation of the charters. Thus came the ultimate proof of the importance the great document had attained in the eyes of all freemen, and the repeated confirmation of these rights, generation after generation, was to place them finally beyond any challenge. The use of the tax-granting power to secure this concession also established the economic control of the realm which, long after, Parliament would use to confirm its own ultimate supremacy.

The confirmation of 1237, called *parva carta* since its only subject was the formal confirmation, was an epochal stage in the process of embodiment of Magna Carta in the framework of law. The solemn decree of excommunication to be visited upon any who should violate the charters, king or commoner, was read in the Chapel of St. Katherine in Westminster Abbey, and then read with the confirmation in every shire court in the kingdom in the spring term. Yet, it was well that it was repeatedly to be confirmed over the years, for Plantagenet memories were notoriously short, and new issues continually arose which required definition with reference to specific charter rights. One never knew what a king would do when the lords departed after a confrontation; but each new settlement advanced further the responsibility of the lords themselves for the welfare of the realm.

The very next year precipitated another crisis of sorts; a fateful union was celebrated between Henry's sister, Eleanor, and a brilliant and ambitious young Frenchman, Simon de Montfort, who had been invested as Earl of Leicester in 1231. Since Eleanor had taken a vow of chastity upon the death of her first husband, the spiritual and temporal lords alike were shocked and angry at the present sacrilege. There was much talk of enlarging upon the charter and reviving the system of sureties or conservators to see that the King adhered to the spirit of the law, in this case, the preservation of the law of the Church. No specific clause in

Magna Carta had applicability to the problem presented, but the Charter as a principle of good faith was already becoming something more than the sum of its parts. A rudimentary theory of social contract—the proposition that the overlord had obligations to the realm which arose out of the circumstances of the case and transcended specific details of the formal statutes—could be the more readily applied to an ambivalent and generally conciliatory king like Henry III; but it was an idea which would grow in the face of later challenges from stronger monarchs.

Although Henry often dreamed of asserting the mastery of his realm that his grandfather had enjoyed, he was never to achieve it. While his loyal counsellors had brought stability to the kingdom during the decade of his minority, they also had permitted the barons to entrench themselves in their estates; and in the challenges to crown prerogatives which arose in 1225 and 1237, the magnates had perceived that Henry would yield to a concerted demand pressed upon him. Like his father, this king was suspicious of the motives of his most loyal servants, and while he lacked John's vicious cruelty, he also lacked his capacity for subduing his opponents by vigorous, albeit often violent, applications of force. The insistence of the great lords upon gathering into council, that they might be permitted to deal as a body with the self-serving policies formulated by Henry, reduced progressively the freedom of movement available to an indecisive man like the fourth Plantagenet. In the end, the situation invited insurrection by a gifted and aggressive man like Simon de Montfort, and his challenge would be met not by the King, but by his son, the future Edward I.

Henry, who so painfully tried to avoid his father's mistakes at home, was to court his father's disasters abroad. In foreign affairs, all English monarchs of the thirteenth century were influenced by two obsessions, the continuing fervor of the Crusades and the obligation to try to recover the Angevin empire in France. Henry had already had one profitless campaign in 1230, which had ensured the final loss of Brittany; now, in 1242, he undertook to recover Poitou, which Louis, in his brief reign of three years, had captured two decades earlier; but the even greater ineptitude of Henry's generalship on this occasion aroused his

brother-in-law Simon to passionate scorn and criticism, which was
the beginning of a steadily widening schism between the two.
Simon, like many men with confidence in their own known abil-
ities, was contemptuous of the ineptitudes of less able persons;
but his condemnation of the conduct of the war was echoed by
many in England itself. The barons, who had taken the measure
of the King, were going so far as to question whether such foreign adventures should be permitted when they jeopardized the
national interest. From here it would be but a short step to the
proposal that a council of conservators of the realm be appointed
to keep the King from making a fool of himself and the country.

As with John, however, the final uprising had to wait until
the royal foreign policy had clearly become bankrupt; this time
it would be less a matter of ignominious loss on the battlefield
than a clear case of the King of England being used by the
French monarch, the German Emperor, and the Pope for their
own purposes. Having failed in his French campaigns, Henry now
turned his efforts to the Crusade; but the Popes, first Innocent IV
and then Urban IV, had other uses for him. Innocent was intent
on undermining Frederick II and his son in Germany, and to do
so invited Henry to put his young son Edmund upon the throne
of Sicily, that restless fief of the German Emperor, which had been
the start of Richard's troubles. Other involved schemes followed,
with the result that Henry was engaged in a series of futile enterprises, each of which left him further in debt and lower in prestige. He was unable to deliver either troops or money to the
Sicilian business, and ignominiously had to give way to the
French, who could do both. Edmund was discarded in the candi-
dacy for the crown, and ultimately, in a shuffling of political
forces, the illegitimate son of Frederick was crowned in his stead.
To top it all, under papal encouragement, Henry was persuaded
to treat with the French King, Saint Louis, in a series of negotiations which, by the Treaty of Paris in 1259, extinguished all
English claims to Anjou, Brittany, Maine, Normandy, and Poitou.

Thus, a general movement to take over the inept administration of affairs was generated throughout the realm by the time
Henry returned from sixteen years of foreign misadventure. Almost his only significant accomplishment had been the marriage

of his eldest son, Edward, to Eleanor of Castile and the investment of him in the remnant of Angevin authority in Gascony.
Henry's years away from England had made him unfamiliar with
the temper of the time, but men at home were demanding that
government henceforth be a matter of joint responsibility between
the throne and the leading subjects of the realm. Doubtless
unaware of the opportunity he was giving his subjects to put the
proposition into effect, Henry convened a council in Easter of
1258 to ask new aids for his foreign enterprises. Instead, this
became the occasion for the barons to review the long list of complaints that had been accumulated as indictments of Henry's
policies. A fervent nationalism was abroad in the land, accentuated by the general awareness that England had no longer any
significant ties with the Continent; this reacted vigorously against
Henry's insistence upon drawing his own wardrobe officers from
his Poitevin relatives, and the equating of foreign officeholders
with oppressive or inefficient performance was confirmed in
many minds.

The King's ruinous overcommitment to papal diplomacy,
which now reflected a debt to the Holy See which would drain
off a third of the country's entire wealth if it were paid, was an
even stronger charge against him. The kingdom had been, without the consent or approval of its greatest lords, involved in a
Sicilian enterprise which had no remote connection with English
interests. Meantime, the chronic restlessness of the Welsh chieftains had erupted into a new border war, in which Henry's
assumption of leadership had virtually ensured his own defeat.
Finally, the negotiation with Louis IX of France, which the barons would have to take over, released them from any technical
claim of support the crown might henceforth seek to revive to
raise new armies for attack on the Continent. By ineptitude and
vagueness of purpose, Henry had reduced the throne to an object
of contempt.

Thus, at Oxford a body of totally disaffected tenants came
together to take over the affairs of the realm. They had their own
ends to accommodate, but unlike the rebels of 1214 and 1215,
they also had the salvation of the state in view, and they had
the support of the country at large. It was in the name of the

Great Charter that they prepared their program, and Henry, who blanched at any intimation that the document might be invoked against him, agreed to abide by such reforms as might be drafted. The nation was entering upon a five-year period of rule by a council, while the King chose for most of this time to reside in France. The Provisions of Oxford, in preliminary form, were drafted before the end of that year. A supplementary set was added in 1259 at Westminster, and these propositions split the opposition into factions. Watching events from France, Henry sought and obtained papal relief from his oath to abide by the Provisions, but upon his return to England the barons reunited in a military uprising. It was now forty-five years since Runnymede.

The Provisions of Oxford were too ambitious for the age, but they accelerated the movement toward more representative government and the reform of common-law institutions which gave them new life. A council of fifteen members had been proposed, with plenary authority to advise the king on all matters of state and to select the chief ministers in charge of the great departments of government. A slightly smaller council of twelve was eventually agreed upon to supervise the king's actions and ensure that the policies they dictated were carried out. All officeholders, including the sheriff and justiciars, were to be appointed annually. England, had the times permitted it, might have become in effect a commonwealth four centuries ahead of its time; but the great scheme was not capable of sustaining itself. Parliament, after all, was just in the process of being born.

The baronial uprising foundered in the following twelve months as it became clear that it rested upon an unstable coalition of interests. Three parties began to emerge: the older barons, who sought to return to and strengthen their system of hereditary rights in the spirit of the rebels of 1215; the younger lords, united with the commercial interests of London and other towns, who sought a bona fide reorganization of government which would liquidate any features of the feudal system; and Simon de Montfort, who observed the indecisive flux of political affairs with sardonic disdain. The conservative party preferred to support Henry as a prototype of the feudal tradition, while the progressives turned to young Prince Edward. In the end Simon would dispose of both of them, if only for a brief and spectacular interval.

Simon de Montfort was one of those men who gravitated naturally into positions of leadership—and who were foredoomed to ultimate failure because they moved too fast for their own time. Impatient of more pedestrian followers, he thrust them aside for their own good; he knew what was required to improve the government when it was placed in his charge, but his contempt of the men he governed speeded his own overthrow. So it had been in Gascony, where Henry had sent him fifteen years earlier, and so it would be when he had his brief tenure in England after the denouement of the Oxford experiment. A dashing Frenchman, with something of Richard's flair on the battlefield and the political insight of Henry II, he had become a devoted follower of Robert Grosseteste, Bishop of Lincoln and a champion of ecclesiastical and political reform. The Provisions of Oxford he viewed as the culmination of the ideals embodied in the Great Charter, and he determined that neither king nor feudal lord should be permitted to hold back the future. He had joined wholeheartedly in swearing to uphold the Provisions; it would be characteristic of him that he would refuse to permit Henry to recede from them.

After desultory fighting in 1263, both the King and his barons had agreed to submit their dispute to St. Louis of France for decision: Should the King, absolved of his oath to abide by the Provisions of 1258 and 1259, return to his throne with his powers the same as they had been before the drafting of the reform? In January 1264 Louis gave his answers in the *Mise* of Amiens—in the affirmative. The Provisions of Oxford were to be quashed, as Innocent III had quashed Magna Carta.

But the movement to subjugate the throne had gone too far to be halted, short of general civil war. Simon had already raised the standard of revolt the previous summer, and by the time Henry had his judgment from Louis, the Earl of Leicester was in control of most of southern England. The predictable support of Louis for the traditional rights of monarchy, and the threat of French invasion to give the judgment force, united still more of the kingdom behind Simon. In this crisis of events, Henry recognized that a stronger leader than himself would have to rally the royalists, and he turned to his son, now raised to the dignity of the Lord Edward. Fate would have it that the son would achieve in the art of government what the father could not comprehend and De Montfort could not survive to inaugurate; but in this hour Edward was cast in the role of champion of the antireform forces. The gathering armies maneuvered toward a decisive encounter, which came in May 1264 in the Battle of Lewes. Simon's army, persuaded of the justice of its cause, had donned the Crusaders' cross; it also took advantage of the overconfidence of the larger forces under Edward, and in a short, swirling battle both Henry and his son were taken prisoner.

For fourteen short months, Simon would seek to reshape the government to the program drawn up at Oxford and Westminster, as it was modified by the practical demands of the moment. The Lord Edward was to be kept under guard, for Simon understood that Henry was not the man he needed to watch. A triumvirate composed of De Montfort, Gilbert de Clare, and the Bishop of Chichester was to be in attendance upon the King at all times, and the daily business of government was to be under the guidance of an administrative council of nine. Simon took the initiative in proclaiming the confirmation of the Great Charter and the Charter of the Forest, and laid plans for the summoning of a new council; it would mark the formal beginning of Parliament and would convene in January 1265. It was the ancient shire-moot, or county court, projected onto the national stage; knights of the shire and burgesses of the town would be represented for the first time in a joint national assembly. This was Simon's *beau geste*, but in its practical contribution to the development of government it came to nothing. The first national council in which the several estates were represented lacked the boldness of the barons at Oxford seven years before, and with the prospect of a renewed civil war no one was disposed to advocate vigorous action of any sort.

Henry did what he always did in a confrontation: he capitulated, at least for the moment. On this particular occasion his action had more impact than usual, for with Simon's continued protestation that he was actually a royalist, not a dictator, he had

no choice but to take the King at his word. His whole basis for
martial action had been to compel acceptance of the Provisions
of Oxford and Westminster; the King now had declared he would
abide by them. The Parliament, which had settled into the role
of a peace conference, worked out the terms of settlement between the King and his barons. The Lord Edward was delivered
into his father's custody and required to swear that he would
not leave the realm for the next three years. Both father and son
took separate oaths reconfirming the great charters of liberties in
their own name. Now the Earl of Leicester found his control of
the situation beginning to slip; his instinctive dislike for men who
did not respond on an instant to his concept of policy offended
the other members of the triumvirate and council. When he could
find no ministers to do his work adequately, he appointed his own
sons, which opened wider the schism between him and his erstwhile companions in reform.

In May, the Lord Edward escaped, and immediately the
realm was in wild confusion. Simon, riding out of London to try
to put down a general uprising called by Edward, found his way
barred by baronial forces which suddenly rose from all sides.
Seeking to join his son at the castle of Kenilworth, he was inter-
cepted by Edward's army near Evesham, surrounded, and slain.
Now it was the Prince, rather than the Earl, who was the strong
man of the realm; Henry, like all of England, was in a state of
bewilderment at the swift progress of events, but it was clear
that for his remaining years he would be no more than a puppet
on the throne. Edward had marked well his father's weaknesses
and sympathized in general with Simon's dreams; he had learned
thoroughly the lesson of changing times, and he would be prepared when the crown passed to him to carry into law the changes
which were dimly perceived and fumblingly attempted by the
barons and by Simon. The Earl had seen the end of the feudal
era and had tried in vain to bring about the new day in a flash.
It would be Edward who would give his name to the measures
that would make the vision nearer a reality.

For another twelve months the resistance to Edward continued, centered in the stronghold of Kenilworth where Simon
the younger had established his forces while he sought help

from Normandy. Then, in the fall of 1266, a proposal for honorable capitulation was agreed upon, drawn up by Ottobuono, the papal legate, with the Prince's aquiescence. Known as the Dictum of Kenilworth, it forecast the great fundamental laws which would add lustre to the early years of Edward's reign, and it confirmed, beyond anyone's doubt, that the government of England had become a process of joint responsibility between the crown and its leading subjects.

The Dictum offered a process for rehabilitation of those who had rebelled against the crown and were willing to seek pardon. Civil disabilities were limited to the specific dates of war, which Edward later defined as having begun on April 4, 1264, and having ended on September 16, 1265, when peace was proclaimed. It also sought to nullify certain of the precipitate reforms of Simon de Montfort and at the same time confirmed again the two charters of liberties.

The following year Parliament supplemented the Dictum with the Statute of Marlborough, which confirmed the charters yet once again and incorporated the provisions drawn at Westminster in 1259 and the generalized policy pronouncements of the Dictum of Kenilworth in 1266. It still further enhanced the rights of Magna Carta by enlarging upon them.*

"The Great Charter shall be observed in all its articles," ran Article V of the Statute, "as well as such as pertain to the king as to the other." The royal rights as well as the subjects' rights were to be honored; this was the tenor of the general struggle between the several elements of government at this point in time. The Statute then elaborated upon subjects growing out of Magna Carta—distress for services, wardship, suits of court, amercements, and the possessory writs concerning property.

At last the struggle of adjustment in the new political framework of the latter thirteenth century achieved a certain stability. It was reflected in the Parliament of 1270, composed of "nearly all the bishops, earls, barons, knights and free tenants of the whole of England," which took up a tax request which had already been fully scrutinized at the Parliament of the previous

---

* See the annotations to the Great Charter in Part II.

fall, summoned at the time of the dedication of Westminster Abbey. The tax was approved in due course; both King and tenants had learned that the age required such an approach to matters in which all had a concern. Edward could depart on his Crusade in the knowledge that the realm was secure; the very fact that a general levy had been approved for a military pilgrimage to the Holy Land reflected a national unity which was rapidly healing the wounds of the past two decades. When, four years later, he returned as King, he would be ready to draft the great legislation which would earn him the soubriquet of "the English Justinian."

Edward Plantagenet was cast in the heroic mould of Henry II and Richard the Lionheart. He looked like a king, tall and commanding in bearing, straightforward in speech, judicious in discussion of affairs of state. Like his great uncle, he rejoiced in the physical competition of tournament and the sport of hunting on horseback under wide skies. But he also had his great-grandfather's sense of obligation to the demands of statecraft, and he had marked thoroughly the failures of politics and policy on the part of his father. He was conditioned by the changing environment of an exciting intellectual era: Henry de Bracton's new rationale of the law and custom of England, Roger Bacon's disquisitions on science, as well as the more indirect influence of Duns Scotus, St. Thomas Aquinas, and Dante, all of whom had their impacts on his time. The first college at Oxford had been chartered in 1264 and the first at Cambridge in 1284; fresh winds of theological doctrine had been blowing in Europe since the First Lateran Council, in the very year of John's charter, which had signaled an end to ecclesiastical superstition in many areas of national life, and the same spirit was reflected in the new architecture; the great cathedrals as well as many secular edifices began now to be constructed of stone skillfully fashioned by wandering artisans. Even the Barons' War had not seriously interrupted the general peace that had prevailed throughout much of the century, and Edward found a congenial climate for his plan of statecraft when he came to the throne in 1274.

For more than a century now, many rolls of state proceedings had been preserved in the royal depositories in Westminster.

By this time the Court of King's Bench had joined the Court of Common Pleas and Exchequer in a permanent trio of judicial administration in the same place. Early in Edward's own reign, the Year Books of court records would be inaugurated, and the Inns of Court formally established for the training of a skilled professional class of attorneys. Thus, the time was ripe for the laying of the final foundation stones, the great organic statutes which would earn the King his renown in history. It was characteristic of his pent-up legislative instinct that Edward would summon a Parliament twice in 1275, and that the first of the great constitutional Statutes of Westminster should date from this year. The Statute undertook to recapitulate and modernize a number of customs and privileges: fifty-one chapters covered the changes in the law wrought by the century of strengthening national institutions; trial by petty jury in criminal cases was made a required proceeding, over the misgiving of the defendants at having to rely on such a new idea; defamation of magnates, whereby discord might be sown, was specified as a crime; the first limit was set on the length of time allowed to a claim of seisin; and new procedures for vouchers of titles to property were introduced.

Three years later, in 1278, the Statute of Gloucester was enacted, stipulating new procedures in the matters of waste, dower, and curtesy (widowers' rights to estates of their deceased wives). In 1279 came the Statute of Mortmain, seeking to add force to Chapter 36 of the Great Charter of 1225 by discouraging, if not actually prohibiting, the transfer of secular estates to ecclesiastical corporations to hold in trust for their tenants. By the Statute of Acton Burnell in 1283, supplemented by the Statute of Merchants two years later, which systematized the recording of debts and made it possible for the creditors to reach the land of a defaulting debtor in spite of intervening feudal obligations, the law was further modernized.

Westminster II was enacted by Parliament in 1285, giving to the legal profession of later centuries the guidelines of its famous first chapter, *De Donis Conditionalibus*, which brought into being modern, as distinguished from feudal, concepts of real estate rights and liabilities, even though its language technically spoke of the old modes of holding land. Like the first constitutional statute of ten years before, Westminster II covered the spectrum of English life, establishing a wide range of judicial remedies and a supplementary system of *nisi prius* justices to relieve the pressure of work on the courts in Westminster.

The matter of alienation of property, which had been dealt with in rudimentary form in Chapter 32 of Henry's Charter, was taken up in the Statute *Quia Emptores*. The Statute of Winchester sought to introduce the principles of local police administration into town government, though with indifferent success. Finally, at the climax of the swift series of statutory pronouncements in 1290, came the Statute *Quo Warranto*.

The legislation of Edward trimmed deadwood from the feudal law as it had been restated and crystallized in the Great Charter, and amended feudal practice in such a manner as would preserve its effectiveness for another two centuries; at the same time, his generic statutes also provided a legislative framework for the transition to the modern age. Edward foresaw the modern age only as he discerned the abuses and obsolescences which threatened a breakdown in the feudal system; like the charter rights themselves, his legislation would derive its continuing validity from its own capacity for adaptation to modern modes.

The grand progress of Edward's plan of government was the happy result of a remarkable insight into the directions of domestic economic and political affairs of the day. His own practical experience with the crises which had led to Simon de Montfort's rise and fall, and his firsthand acquaintance with the leaders and interests of western Europe during his four years going to and coming from the Crusade, gave Edward an invaluable perspective for the legislative programs he set for himself. The business might have continued uninterruptedly for the rest of his reign, had it not been for the challenge of resurgent nationalism in Wales and Scotland, which decelerated, although it did not terminate, his statutory program. Indeed, the foundation of a national constitution which was laid with the great statutes enacted between 1275 and 1290 made it possible to devise the legislation of his remaining years in terms of the fundamental principles he had set down earlier, and thus preserved them from the flaws of improvisation.

From the early eighties until 1295, Edward's military efforts were primarily engaged in Wales, where a succession of outbreaks led to ever more vigorous countermeasures and at last to the subjugation of the stubbornly independent kingdom. Now Scotland, which had for a time considered a union with England through the marriage of the future Edward II and a granddaughter of the late King Alexander, rose in arms against Edward I and his steadily expanding control of the island. The Scots made a treaty with France which was intended to present an offensive-defensive front to England and indeed for years to come would affect the internal as well as foreign policies of the kingdom.

The Welsh and Scottish wars aggravated the needs for revenue, and one of the major functions of the Parliaments of the early nineties was to consider the King's request for new taxes. A combination of crises, economic and military, foreign and internal, brought a stalemate by 1297 and led to a final series of pronouncements on charter rights which, in the course of four years, would put the final statutory touches to the struggle for documentary guarantees of economic and political liberties which had begun at Runnymede. At this time, Edward was beset by a succession of problems which called for settlement all at once. In France, the sporadic, century-long undermining of the last Angevin province in Gascony had impelled him to undertake a punitive expedition to the Continent, and for this purpose he had concluded an alliance with the Count of Flanders. Simultaneously, the throne found itself in another dispute with the Holy See, over a papal bull forbidding clerical grants in the form of taxes to the crown; the previous year, accordingly, Edward had withdrawn the protection of the royal courts from ecclesiastical tenants. While his ultimate victory in the struggle with the Church was already forseeable, given the temper of England by now, this was presently a time when the spiritual lords might be able to obtain new understanding with the state before they yielded altogether. Finally, the rapid growth of commerce and the dominance of wool exports as a factor in English economy had led to restlessness on the part of the trading classes in the towns as they pressed for greater commercial privileges.

Two years earlier, the legislative development under Edward

had reached a high point in the "great and model Parliament" to which all classes of society were summoned: bishops, abbots, earls, barons among the Lords; and knights, burgesses, and parish chapter representatives among the Commons. The writ of summons had contained the phrase, "Let that which toucheth all be by all approved"; the King did not apparently intend this to be taken as a permanent principle of future legislation but as an indication of the all-encompassing need which confronted the kingdom at the moment. This need was bred by the conditions which would lead to the crisis of 1297, and in this crisis the Parliamentary groups which he had called together found an opportunity to make common cause. Edward had proved a powerful overlord, although sometimes he evidenced a mystic concept of kingship. He was devoted to the Arthurian legends of a lost age of chivalry which he sought to revive by his own occasional round tables, and he it was who captured and brought to London the Stone of Scone. The only opportunity to gain from him a reassurance of his intention to preserve the ultimate liberties of the realm was in times of crisis.

Now the assembled lords and commons demanded, in return for the substantial taxes he required to advance the military programs in Scotland and Flanders, a confirmation of the great charters. It had, indeed, been nearly a generation since Magna Carta and *Carta de Foresta* had been explicitly renewed, although virtually all of the great statutory enactments of the past two decades had been implementations and extensions of the particular subject matter in the charters themselves. It was time, said the magnates, to have the original guarantees confirmed; and once more an Archbishop of Canterbury, Robert Winchelsey, led the coalition of lords spiritual and temporal, and the mercantile interests and commons, in the effort to secure the confirmation. Edward, his mind occupied with his Flanders engagement, responded readily enough, although his first accommodation merely took the form of a Charter of Inspeximus: "We have seen the Great Charter of the Lord Henry, sometime King of England, our father, of the Liberties of England," ran Edward's grant. The charter then recited word for word, with a few minor omissions, the issue of 1225, following which it concluded: "We, ratifying and approving these gifts and grants aforesaid, confirm and make strong all the same for us and our heirs forever."

This was in August; but the legalists among the lords asked themselves whether this kind of grant actually bound Edward as specifically as if he reissued Magna Carta in his own name. The King had by now left for Flanders, and the regent was his thirteen-year-old heir, Edward of Carnarvon. In October the petitioners came to Prince Edward with a draft of a new charter which not only confirmed the great documents in explicit terms, but added several supplementary chapters covering more recent and specific complaints for which redress was sought. In due course Prince Edward acquiesced to the Charter of Confirmation, and it was sent to the King in Flanders, where at Ghent on November 25, 1297, Edward I set his own seal to the new document.

Of the seven chapters in the confirmation, the first four made explicit the commitment of the present generation of royalty to the great charters of liberties; contrary judgments were nullified, the documents were to be read in cathedral churches throughout the realm as grants in Edward's name, and the sentence of excommunication was to be pronounced against all violators. Two other issues of the day were then disposed of in the three remaining chapters: the special *prises*, or requisitions and appropriations of goods for the national emergency, were not to be understood as becoming a precedent; and the seizure of wool exports for extra duties, which Edward had recently ordered, was to be rescinded. The *maltolte*, or extra duty on wool, struck at the heart of mercantile prosperity, and Edward was willing to rescind it when it became evident that it also was jeopardizing the entire economics of customs duties which had been developing since the late years of his father's reign.

But there remained other causes of complaint which, now that Edward was clearly enmeshed in diplomatic and military affairs which were slowly wearing down even his great energies, the barons now sought to press for relief. As the major national offices of Exchequer and Chancery had been loosened from the royal control in the long struggle with Henry III, the new institution of the royal Wardrobe developed to settle a new form of crown control over these affairs. Under Edward, these household officers had developed into a government within a government, with the king's steward and marshal assuming ever broader jurisdiction over all manner of subjects. There were also flaws in the court system and in the arbitrary assumption of authority by certain other crown officers, while in the increasingly important matter of coinage and metalworking, a substantial addition to the weights and measures chapter of Magna Carta cried for attention.

In 1300 the lords in Parliament found their opportunity and insisted on Edward's acquiescence to an addition of twenty Articles on the Charters. The Articles spoke of a number of abuses; to the problems of purveyancing which Magna Carta had recognized were now added the practices of the king's household officers of seizing the finest goods at the fairs, the great towns, or the ports, for which the lords and merchants demanded receipts which could be presented to the steward for payment. There was the practice of prosecuting, before the household courts, any offenses "within the verge," a twelve-mile radius of the spot where the king and his party might be situated; not only were these cases tried before special courts unfamiliar to the parties, but if the royal party moved on the prisoners might move with them, still further adding to the difficulty of their obtaining justice.

Other Articles prohibited the issuing of writs under petty seals which might be used by any number of officials, or the hearing of common pleas in the Court of Exchequer—a sign of the rivalry of the ancient "tax court" with the younger but now larger and more important bench. And, said the Articles, the Chancellor and the Court of King's Bench should travel with the king, "so that he may have at all times near him some sages of the law, who be able duly to order all such matters as shall come unto the court." Although the three great courts had now established themselves at Westminster, many tenants objected to being limited solely to an expensive trip from their own part of the land to have their cases heard there; if the king was coming into that part of his realm, his justice should, as of old, attend him, and better still, the cause might actually be heard before the king (*coram rege*).

Local election of sheriffs was proposed; a reiteration of John's charter, that only good men be appointed to this and other offices, was inserted as a policy matter; and sheriffs were directed to desist from the practice set out in Chapter 18 of Magna Carta, of taking more of a debtor's chattels than was necessary to satisfy the debt. Finally, the Articles concluded with a lengthy provision on the safeguards of quality of gold and silver work; since much of the personal wealth of great men was represented by precious metals worked into articles of many types, it was essential that these goods not be debased and the owners' wealth diminished correspondingly. Three remedies were proposed: one, that silver, for which a sterling standard had already been devised and applied by certain guilds of coinmakers, was to be protected by the stipulation that no smith should "work worse silver than money." A second provided that for gold a certain "touch" was required, the "touch of Paris" being the standard, based upon the secrets of the craftsmen in that city, in the use of a touchstone (quartz or jasper) to produce a distinctive mark when rubbed with metal of a known degree of refinement. Finally, a hallmark was to be stamped on the finished piece—a leopard's head, the provision said—when the warden of the craft was satisfied that it was of proper quality.

Edward I, like John eighty-five years before, could accept some of the Articles in good part, but others only in bad. Like John, he would protest to the Pope that his oath to support them was obtained under duress. But the times had changed; the demands of 1300, at the beginning of another century, were made in the context of a substantial, permanent structure of government, undergirded by legislation for which the King himself had been the architect in the great adventure of his early reign. The Articles on the Charters were based fundamentally upon the accepted fact that the charters themselves were an integral part of that structure; the time had passed when the king by unilateral action could recall his approval once given. The essential elements in that particular device, the English common law, had been joined together in the years between the first Richard and the first Edward; the three centuries to follow would anneal and strengthen the device.

V

The Annealing Centuries

ONE of the last legislative enactments of Edward I, the
Statute of Carlisle, stated that it was made "by the
advice of the barons, earls, magnates, great men and other nobles,
and of the commons of the realm in Parliament." The assertion
of Parliamentary authority was to grow in intensity throughout
the two centuries now beginning. It would in fact provide the
consistent, and often the dominant, theme of national government
during the unstable reigns of the second Edward, the second and
third Richards, and the occasionally insane Henry VI. Parliament,
in this period, was groping toward an understanding of its own
definition; more often than not, it acted as little more than an
institutionalized form of the barons in arms at Runnymede, and
only under wise kings was it subject to a disciplined function as
a partner in national government. It would be during the Tudor
regime, when the warrior barons were giving place to the gentlemen adventurers in the new world of commerce and colonization, that the concept of a balanced division of the power of
government would crystallize; then, in the seventeenth century,
when the Stuarts sought to turn the kingdom back to times when
kings ruled supreme if they ruled at all, the Parliamentary revolution would destroy them.

Under Edward I, Parliament had had its first unwelcome
taste of discipline. It did not intend to give a similar opportunity
to his son, but rather to reassert its role of conservator of the
throne as it had done in the days of Henry III. Yet, in spite of
itself, with each successive occasion in which circumstances or
the personality of the king compelled crown and Parliament to
join in the responsibility for lawmaking, the result of Parliament's
own actions was an irreducible addition to the very slow accre-

tion of law which made less possible a subsequent return to the past. The great legislative complex established in the early years of Edward I would provide a stability which not even the desperate events of the coming centuries would upset. Both kings and Parliaments would justify their policies with appeals to the Great Charters and to the statutes which had been enacted in extension of the rights therein; while this was more often than not a matter of lip service, it nevertheless revealed an awareness that new principles had been written into law which ought to be observed, and the country was reassured that they would be observed.

Edward II was a pale shadow of his father; twenty-three years of age when he came to the throne, he had shown less interest in statecraft than in the pleasures of an uncomplicated life. He was no fool, although his enemies represented him as such. He doubtless perceived at the time of his accession that there were many who intended to thrust him into the position of his grandfather rather than permit him to attempt the role of his father. As matters turned out, he lacked the character to undertake the latter, but he had more character than to be able to accept the former. In one respect, at least, Henry III had been more fortunate, for in the first twenty years of his reign he had had the benefit of dedicated ministers of great ability. Edward II had the misfortune to rely, in the great crises of his own reign, upon men whose ability was unhappily in direct proportion to their capacity for enraging the King's already bitter opponents. First there was Piers Gaveston, whose appointment furnished the excuse for the Earl of Lancaster to prepare his rebellion; after that, there was Hugh le Despenser and his son, who at length drove Edward's own Queen into war against him.

The baronial party had long memories; if they did not consider a return to Runnymede, they had given much thought to the Committee of Conservators and the Provisions of Oxford, half a century before. They viewed the Parliamentary function as an alternative of power rather than a balance: either the crown would be supreme or Parliament would be. It would take nearly four centuries to show the fallacy of the proposition, as well as to make clear the terms upon which Parliament could merit a permanent share of the power of government; for in the late Middle Ages and the early modern era, a powerful king was usually more beneficial to the realm than a powerful Parliament. A powerful king who was wise could compel Parliament to act in the best interest of the state; a Parliament which dominated a weak king or was an accessory to a wicked one had no capacity for controlling itself.

Ninety-five years after Runnymede, the militants in Parliament, calling themselves the Lords Ordainers, prepared their program for subjugating Edward II. In the winter of 1310-11, they drew up a list of more than forty "New Ordinances," by which the present King was to be curbed and some of the work of his father was to be undone. A number of the Ordinances were indictments of specific members of the royal household, like Gaveston, whom Edward already had been compelled to send away, upon the demand of Earl Thomas of Lancaster. The remainder of the list represented the reforms proposed by the Ordainers: reduction of crown expenditures to fit the revenues available to the royal establishment, without reference to *prises* or *maltoltes;* prohibition of the king's right to leave the realm or engage in a foreign war without the approval of the Parliament; review by the Ordainers of his appointments to his household, and a continuing committee of Parliament to hear complaints against any of these officers; invalidation of any statute or act of government, by the king or his judges, contrary to the Great Charters, with interpretation of any passage in the charters to be the responsibility of the Ordainers.

Many of the provisions in the Ordinances were reiterations of the chief Articles on the Charters which Edward I had grudgingly accepted; but the arrogance of the present demands was more conscious, as though the lords dared the new King to resist them. In some other context, many of the propositions would have been fairly urged; but Edward II acquiesced in them now only as means of gaining time and seeking a better balance of the odds. This was apparent to all parties, and although a conflict was now inevitable, the baronial opponents of the crown had the advantage of appearing to be advocates of measures beneficial to the people at large. Popular feeling was against Edward, as a song of that time revealed:

> Our Prince of England, by his own people's consent,
>   At Westminster after the fair made a great Parliament.
> The great charter he made was of wax, so they say,
>   And held too near the fire, so it melted away.

Although the Ordainers sought to keep all the machinery of government out of his hands, Edward II proved himself more resourceful and cunning than Henry III; by backstage persuasion he managed to have certain clerks in the Chancery bring into his hands the great seal. Since, by their own decree, the Ordainers had made known that no writs would be valid without the seal, the King was now able to control the basic governmental affairs of the kingdom. Commissions under his seal went swiftly out to insure royal control of various strong points, including the city of London. Prematurely convinced that he had thwarted the opposition, Edward presented them with the supreme affront of restoring Gaveston to his former honors and authority. In the spring of 1312, the Ordainers were abroad in an armed offensive and captured the French favorite; shortly thereafter, upon the impulse of the more hotheaded Lancastrians, Gaveston was executed on the highway near Kenilworth.

The unbridled ferocity of this action robbed the barons of many of their supporters and enabled Edward to propose terms of peace. After long haggling over details—a public plea for the King's mercy and a restoration of public order without reference to the Ordinances—the peace was accepted in the fall of 1313. It was a victory for the King, but it was also the end to six wasted years of his reign; his own biographer had to confess: "He had achieved nothing laudable or memorable, save that he had married royally and had begotten an heir to his crown." Isabella of France, sister of Charles IV, had been betrothed to him as a child and had married him soon after his accession; the future Edward III was one of four children to be born of the union. The marriage was generally a happy one, but for the fact that Edward was usually an indolent king and Isabella was an ambitious princess; in time to come, this ill-starred combination would destroy the regime.

Indeed, the tragedy of Edward II and his barons was the inability of either side to use its triumphs wisely when it was in the ascendant. The peace of 1313 was little more than a truce dictated by the overshadowing peril of a Scottish uprising. Under the great Robert Bruce, the Scots had already overrun a number of English border outposts, and all of northern England was in a state of alarm. King and lords had to put aside their own quarrel to meet the challenge of the brilliant Earl of Carrick, and thus it was that Edward and a number of his barons—although not the recalcitrant Lancaster—marched north to meet Bruce. At Bannockburn, in 1314, the hosts came together, with the disciplined Scottish pikemen overthrowing and slaughtering the English mounted knights. The day was soon lost, and Edward and his surviving troops fled the field; for many generations after that, Scotland would make good its insistence upon its independence.

Discredited by the enemy's victory, Edward had to come to terms with Thomas of Lancaster, leader of the now resurgent Ordainers. The opposition met the King at York and convened a Parliament, at which Edward once more confirmed the Great Charters and accepted the Ordinances back into full force. Out of this meeting, and one at Lincoln the following February 1315, the Earl emerged as the "Protector" of the throne itself; but in the harsh months to follow, political and natural ills seemed to vie with each other. A general failure of crops that summer spread famine through the land, while the continuing and increasingly bold border raids of the Scots aroused new dissensions in Ireland and Wales. Edward over the next seven years slowly recovered the military resources for a fresh blow at his enemies, relying on a new and abler group of ministers, in the father and son Hugh Despenser. Able, but ambitious to the point of greed, the Despensers gave new life to the Lancastrian opposition by the severity of their own demands in the King's name; but Earl Thomas on his part by his own autocratic behaviour outdid the royalist ministers in breeding enemies. Near York—where his wife had fled to rid herself of him—Lancaster's party was overcome and the Earl himself beheaded. For the second time in his reign, Edward had defeated the Conservators, and at a Parliament at York that same year, 1322, the new Ordinances were specifically separated from Magna Carta, with which the Ordainers had sought to merge them, and revoked.

The Statute of York was enacted by a Parliament which was the first in more than a decade to have a semblance of general representation of all groups. Like the "Model Parliament" of 1295, commons as well as lords spiritual and temporal were present, and whether this was a conscious effort to confine constitutional issues to fully representative assemblies in the future, the formality of a parliamentary enactment was clearly intended to place the full weight of government behind the expunging of the Ordinances. The late Middle Ages groped in vain for a talisman of permanence for the laws they enacted; repetitious confirmations, as in the case of the Great Charters, were as much a confession of the evanescent quality of sovereign guarantees as they were a means of engraving the proposition ever deeper into the national consciousness. Until the full dimensions of a national constitution were determined, and Parliament assumed the responsibility which its supremacy then implied, the factors which kept Magna Carta alive and effective were less its constitutional theory than its practical usefulness in effecting the fundamental rights of private persons. So it was with the other great statutes; their ultimate contribution to the growth of the English constitution derived from their present stabilizing effect upon English society in its private interest, which demonstrated to later generations the benefits of a public system of relationships equally subject to an abiding rule of law.

The claims of later times for the Parliament of York as a progenitor of orderly government were offset by the savage punishment which the royalists at this time visited upon their enemies. Half a dozen earls were hanged, and a greater number of their followers publicly disemboweled. Throughout the realm, estates of Edward's enemies were forfeited, to be turned over to royal favorites. The elder Hugh Despenser was invested Earl of Winchester, and both the father and son were placed high in the King's household. Out of the welter of retribution, certain

administrative changes were also developed, and some of the
reforms proposed in 1300 in the Articles on the Charter put into
effect. Edward, for all his shortcomings, was no chauvinist, and
the Despensers, for all their avarice and arrogance, had a genius
for organization.

But the Plantagenets, like the House of Atreus and the
Medici, had a primordial curse upon them; even the most brilliant
were fated, like Henry II, to have great tragedies in the course
of their histories, while the lesser ones brought ruin ultimately
not only to themselves but to the generations to follow. The total
dishonor of Richard II, indeed, would sound the knell for the
long story of this fantastic family at the end of this century. For
Edward II, also, the end was soon to come, in the guise of epic
tragedy which might have been reserved for a greater king. Isabella, his Queen, was the leader of the final rebellion; she also
was repelled by the excesses of the Despensers and seduced by
the Lord Roger Mortimer, one of the party of Ordainers who
soon escaped from his imprisonment and made his way to France.
Crossing to her brother's domain with her own household, and
soon followed by her eldest son, the young Prince Edward, Isabella found herself maneuvered by circumstances into the leadership of a new movement against Edward.

In the fall of 1326, Isabella and Mortimer led a swift invasion of England, quickly winning London and a number of
important ports. The King and his party fled. The Despensers
were caught and slain, and Edward himself was run to ground
in Wales. The final triumph of his enemies was complete; a
Parliament was convened—on dubious authority, since the summons was sealed by the invaders without the King—and Edward
was deposed. "A foolish king shall ruin his people," was the
text of a contemporary sermon by the Bishop of Hereford; more
formally, the lords of the land, led by the once more resurgent
Lancastrians, charged Edward with incompetence, the loss of
Scotland and Ireland, and the constant violation of his oaths to
uphold the Charter and the companion statutes. The bitterness
of the hatred which had been engendered in the long struggle
with the Ordainers, and the violence of Edward's own vengeance

after the defeat of Earl Thomas, was now coming home to the defeated monarch.

Edward consented to resign the throne if it would go to his son, and on January 17, 1327, the Lancastrian leader, Sir William Trussell, claiming to act on behalf of the whole realm, renounced his homage to his sovereign. Edward's steward broke his staff of office and pronounced the royal household dissolved. The whole land, as it were, held its breath in this dreadful moment; not since Stephen's day, two centuries before, had a king been deposed, and this had been long before the obligation of the Great Charter had been accepted by all parties. The slowly emerging constitution had been stained with a treason that John's enemies might have emulated but never had the ultimate opportunity to attempt. At Kenilworth, the ends of the roads upon which Simon de Montfort and Piers Gaveston had both been slain, the deposed King, while living, was both a reproach and a threat to the men— and the Queen—who had betrayed him. In some unknown dungeon, and manifestly at the instigation of Roger Mortimer, Edward II was eventually murdered.

A fourteen-year-old king was now crowned as Edward III; Henry of Lancaster became chief of the council of the young monarch's advisers and promptly sought parliamentary action for a *post-mortem* acquittal of his brother Thomas, charged with treason during a time of peace. The principle of the argument, although advanced as means of restoring to Henry the forfeited earldom of Thomas, was a fundamental one, and in short course Parliament acted formally upon it. While the Lancastrian claim had some color of legitimacy, since the realm in 1322 had indeed technically been at peace, the single-minded program of self-aggrandizement pursued by Isabella and her paramour, Lord Mortimer, had no concern with questions of legitimacy. Mortimer appropriated to himself the estates of the late Despensers and sponsored a number of lavish tournaments and round tables by which he fostered the legend that he himself was a descendant of King Arthur. While Mortimer, acting through Isabella, persuaded Edward to negotiate a peace treaty with the Scots in 1328—with the proviso of the marriage of the infant David Bruce and the

King's young sister, Joan of the Tower, to seal it—the terms of
the treaty were unpopular in England and provided the excuse
for a plot to dispose of the opportunistic Earl of March.

Mortimer, it was clear, intended to be such a power in the
kingdom that the Earl of Lancaster could only regard him as a
threat to his own ambitions. Lancaster played upon Edward's
growing restlessness under the dominance of his mother and her
lover; and in the fall of 1330, at Nottingham, yeomen of the royal
household broke into the bedchamber where Isabella and Mortimer had locked themselves, and deaf to the Queen's tearful
entreaties, dragged the Earl from the castle. He was hanged as
a traitor to the crown—and as the suspected murderer of Edward
II—in London; Isabella, whose own political and marital infidel-
ities were equally notorious, was retired to a semi-imprisonment
with a lavish annual pension, and after some years of meditation
on her past life, she was moved to take the habit of a nun, and
at the last was buried in the Franciscan Church at Newgate.

The courtly treatment of his mother, after Mortimer's execution, awakened the realm to a new age of chivalry which was
coming in with Edward's majority. Another Lionheart, or at least
a king worthy of his grandfather, had come to the throne, and
after the first unhappy thirty years of the century, men yearned
to have a leader to whom the heart could respond thrillingly. The
national honor received a bolstering three years later, with a
victory over the Scots at Halidon Hill which established a pretender, Edward Balliol, on the Scottish throne and erased many
of the concessions won by Scotland after Bannockburn nineteen
years earlier. And yet, the re-establishment of English overlordship in Scotland only heightened the tension between England
and France, where Philip VI had already annexed the Angevin
province of Gascony and now let it be known that no proposal
for a peaceful settlement of this dispute could be entertained
without inclusion of the Scottish question. After this impasse,
matters hung fire for a space, but the kingdoms moved steadily
farther apart; Philip VI would not retreat from his position under
the French-Scottish alliance, and Edward III became steadily
more eager to resort to arms in an effort to topple France from
its dominant position in western Europe, and if possible—seeking

again that will-o'-the-wisp of the last Plantagenet rulers—to recover the now long-lost empire.

In 1337 the issues were joined, in what men thereafter would
call the Hundred Years' War. Philip issued the ultimate challenge
by declaring Gascony to be confiscated to France; Edward returned the affront by averring that he, rather than Philip, had the
superior claim to the French crown, since he was the son of the
last Capetian royalty, Isabella. The claim was only technical; the
nobles of France had already turned to the house of Valois for
its rulers, and Edward made the claim less in the expectation that
it would be seriously entertained than that it would establish the
legitimacy of his own military objectives in the face of the Treaty
of Paris some eighty years before. The claim was put forth with
a different face when it was used to gather behind the King the
support of his own realm; the throne of England, declared Parliament in 1340, could not be made subordinate to that of France.
In a companion statute in which Edward solemnly confirmed the
Great Charters—as he was to do more than twenty times during
his reign—Parliament voted the new levies needed to challenge
Philip.

Thus strengthened—the feudal lords still gave their allegiance most readily to a gallant leader on the battlefield—Edward
sought combat with his foes. It was six years before the first great
clash of the hosts occurred, at a village called Crécy in Flanders.
Beneath the fluttering pennons of chivalry at the zenith of its
glory, the English army assembled. Sir John Froissart, the warrior
turned chronicler, recalled in heroic lines the battalions of dis-
mounted knights drawn up on the slopes of a valley, and above
them, "in the manner of a portcullis," the English longbowmen
who this day would rain disaster upon the heavily armoured
French cavalry. One wing of Edward's army was under the command of his eldest son, already renowned as the Black Prince;
and Edward himself commanded the reserve force which would,
under his superb generalship amid the confused fighting, throw
its weight upon the reeling enemy at the crucial moment. The
battle was desperately fought in the setting sun and through a
valley where fallen French nobles spread a thick carpet of bodies.
It was said by enthusiasts for Edward that cannon were used for

the first time in this battle, and that the noise terrified the enemy cavalry to add further to the slaughter. The hissing longbows were equally terrifying; once within their range, men fell beneath the rain of arrows whether they sought to advance or retreat.

Edward emerged from Crécy as more than a victor, more than a hero; he was leader of men unsurpassed since the founder of the Plantagenet dynasty. His brilliant campaign against superior numbers of French and their allies fired the imagination of all Europe; here was another Henry II, who for three decades would raise in its final great cadence the saga of the House of Anjou. When his own sun set, the end would come quickly. The King's skilful management of the seige of Calais and its honorable surrender the following spring, and the earlier naval victory at Sluys, gave English arms a luster that had not been equalled for almost two centuries. Still more dazzling triumphs could be told: a Scottish army under David II, seeking to present Edward with a war on two fronts, had been routed at Neville's Cross near Durham, and David himself was now a prisoner in the Tower of London. There was much cause for men to sing the praises of a great king.

The swift series of triumphs on several battlefields brought to an end the first passage of arms between the rulers of England and France, and now for a space a common scourge would settle over both countries. The Black Death came, by all accounts, from the East—"in the land occupied by the Saracens," said some contemporary chronicler, while others put it still farther distant and told stories of a "terrible mist emitting a fearful stench and infecting the air," which visited pestilence upon the shores of the Adriatic and hence, carried by terrified victims as they fled their own doomed cities, through all of Italy. By the time of the great war between the western powers, whole villages of central Europe were reported to be deserted, corpses lay unburied, as Boccaccio reported in the plague of Florence, for men feared contamination from handling even the bed linens where the victims had died. The science of later times would identify this, and the great pestilence of Restoration England, as bubonic and pneumonic; to the men of 1348, however, it was a horror of unknown character and appearance; it struck without warning, and "many of those who were attacked in the morning it carried out of human affairs by noon." Sudden lumps in the joints, then black and blue splotches on the skin, then bloody vomit, then death—so the cycle ran; and so numerous were the dead, said Robert of Avesbury, that in London by Easter 1349 there were two hundred bodies daily placed in mass graves.

So terrible was the plague that fighting itself became impracticable; horses for farm or for war died as fast as men, and a great silence fell over many hamlets left empty of human and animal habitants alike. Manors found themselves stripped of villeins, so that only a handful of husbandmen remained to till the fields, and a practice which had begun before the plague now became common as a matter of necessity: lords leased their demesne lands to any who would work them, and for the labor they had to hire the wages mounted disastrously. To seek control of the inflation of wages and prices, the King's counsellors in 1349 passed an ordinance, and Parliament two years later passed a statute called the Statute of Laborers, providing that "every man and woman in our realm of England, of what condition he be, free or bond, able in body, and within the age of sixty years," was required to "take only the wages, livery, . . . or salary which were accustomed to be given" in 1347.

The legislative effort to maintain the old order was foredoomed; with more than half the population, perhaps two million persons, slain by the Black Death in its fearful course, a statute of Parliament or an ordinance in council could not reverse the torrent of change. Indeed, change had been gathering for a generation before, and the disaster of the mid-fourteenth century only accelerated it. But the Parliament of 1351-52 nevertheless marked a high point in its own development; it had been summoned to consider a whole body of legislation, and before it was dismissed it had given its assent to seven statutes, a vast amount of business for a medieval assembly. Among its enactments were the Statute of Provisors, challenging the papal effort to perpetuate control of ecclesiastical offices in England by appointing provisional successors before the offices were vacant; a companion statute confirmed the old privileges of the clergy, but reasserted the king's right to presentment of candidates for benefices. Most

important of the legislation of this Parliament was the fifth statute (25 Edward III), which sought to modernize many of the
fundamental provisions in Magna Carta.

This statute, a century and a half after Runnymede, would
be cited repeatedly by the Parliamentary reformers of Stuart times
as evidence that the Great Charter was deliberately revised and
updated to preserve it from obsolescence. Like the legislation of
the first Edward, this legislation undertook to trim away deadwood and prepare a seedbed for new growth; and from this
circumstance Sir Edward Coke could take his eloquent argument
that Magna Carta and its supplementary statutes were the origin
of the concepts of due process, trial by jury, and *habeas corpus*.
While Coke would claim too much, it was not to be denied that
the enactments of Edward III, at this transition stage between
the late Middle Ages and the faint traces of the dawn of the
modern age, fundamentally strengthened and extended the effectiveness of Chapter 29 of the Charter, upon which Coke's
rationale of the English constitution would be constructed. Thus
Chapter 4 of the Statute of 1352 admonished the king and council
to maintain their own criminal proceedings within the orderly
processes of the common law courts:

> Whereas it is contained in the Great Charter of the
> Franchises of England, that none shall be imprisoned
> nor put out of his Freehold, unless it be by the Law of
> the Land; it is accorded, assented, and stablished, that
> from henceforth none shall be taken by Petition or Sug-
> gestion made to our Lord the King, or to his Council,
> unless it be by Indictment or Presentment of good and
> lawful People of the same neighborhood where such
> Deeds be done, in due Manner, or by Process made by
> Writ original at the Common Law; nor shall none be
> put out of his Franchises, nor of his Freeholds, unless
> he be duly brought into answer, and forejudged of the
> same by the Course of the Law; and if anything be done
> against the same, it shall be redressed and holden for
> none.

The following year, 1353, another important legislative step
was taken in the Statutes of Staples, which sought to regularize

a process of taxing wool exports which had begun in the time of Edward I. Staple towns, or stipulated centers of export where the tax could be levied, were identified, and companion chapters set out new standards of monetary exchange, regulation of foreign merchants, and related questions of acceptable weights and measures. By now, wool had become the dominant agricultural product of the kingdom, and indeed the decimation of the Black Death hastened the change of many peasant farmers as well as manors from grain crops to sheep raising; there was meat as well as wool to be sold in this commodity. Both the first and third Edwards, pressed for revenues to spur on their war efforts, saw in the wool exports a quick and substantial source of revenue. In the end it was to force them to extend successively the guarantees in the charters—the Confirmation of 1297 was emulated by the Confirmations of 1354 and 1357—and finally to replace the export trade with a native cloth industry.

Edward's economic legislation in the fifties was balanced by new triumphs on the battlefield. At Poitiers in 1356 another great victory over the French culminated in the capture of their king, John the Good (who was not); he joined King David of Scotland in the Tower. With the sovereigns of both nations in captivity, Edward could dictate his own terms. In 1357 the Treaty of Berwick placed David on his throne under strong restraints from Edward, and in 1360 a peace was effected with the French at Calais. Under the terms of this peace, Aquitaine was formally returned to England, the first major retrieval of Angevin territory since the military disasters suffered by King John. Edward III now stood at the pinnacle of his great career; the remaining seventeen years would be an accelerating decline from glory. For most of the sixties, peace abroad and a temporal rule at home continued to sustain his popularity, however; a cultural and intellectual independence of a sort was effected in the Statute of 1362 providing that pleading of cases henceforth should be in English, while six years later came the most vigorous of a number of efforts to insure due process of law within the meaning of Magna Carta's Chapter 29: "That no Man be put to answer without Presentment before Justices, or Matter of Record, or by due Process and Writ original, according to the old Law of the Land."

While it would be many generations more before the spirit of this proposal would become the practice, the statutory interest in specific chapters of Magna Carta° was paralleled by the steady volume of private court actions or petitions to Parliament which claimed a right protected by the Great Charter. Relying on Chapter 31, the widow of a certain tenant in 1306 had sought the guardianship of her eldest son, a minor, since, she averred, the estate of her husband had been held at fee farm (rents) and not by knight's fees. During the reign of Edward II, a number of claims had been made for restoration of land, redress for unlawful uses of weights and measures, or an end to the delays of justice in the name of the Charter. Moderation of amercements (*de moderata misericordia*) as required by Chapter 14 was implemented by a special writ devised early in the fourteenth century. Widows relied on Chapter 18 to obtain their proper rights from executors, and heirs on reaching majority brought action for waste under Chapter 4. The Charter was often cited with one of the great organic statutes which had developed in the last half of the thirteenth century, and after, to extend and modernize the rights on which the action was based. Indeed, the continuing influence of Magna Carta could be discerned, after it ceased to be included among the authorities in the pleadings, in the subsequent legislation which dealt with the same principles of feudal law which it had summarized and restated.

Thus the Confirmation in succeeding Parliaments might tend to become perfunctory, but the daily business of the courts of the land, applying the statutes to a multiplicity of practical private questions, subtly strengthened the rule of law while dynasties rose and fell. Edward's fortunes were now declining; after 1369, when the French renewed hostilities, the tide of battle gradually turned against the great warrior king. Edward was growing feeble, and the Black Prince, who had disappointed the expectations of many when he turned from military affairs to those of administration, was also in suddenly declining health. John of Gaunt, the sixth of the King's twelve children, wed Blanche of Lancaster and by his progeny would found the Lancastrian line

° See annotation to the document, Part II.

of kings in the coming century; meantime, he joined the disgruntled barons whose numbers began to multiply after the defeats in France.

Now, on all sides, men of brief loyalty plotted against the King who had led their land to such spectacular heights two decades before. The Commons, who had now come to be represented regularly in Parliament, organized themselves into a separate house in 1373 and demanded to be consulted on matters of state instead of waiting to be informed of what the magnates and the crown had decided. A new committee of control, to direct the business of the throne, was established; various ministers of the king's household—favorite targets when the king himself could not be attacked—were charged with corruption, and their removal from office left the throne without effective staff to deal with the very business which Parliament demanded be expedited. Dark days were looming for the realm, as both the King and his eldest son were manifestly in rapid decline; the Duke of Lancaster was suspected of secret plans for doing away with his nephew Richard, son of the Black Prince, as the final obstacle to his own claim to the throne; or, failing that, to seek a papal declaration that Richard was illegitimate.

The Black Prince died in 1376, and the King in 1377; the ten-year-old Richard had already been recognized by Parliament as the heir apparent, in an effort to forestall Lancaster, but it was nevertheless a grim prospect that confronted the land as he was crowned. On all fronts facing France, the island was under harassment, and the taxes which Parliament had reluctantly but inevitably found it necessary to grant to the regency to meet the attacks climbed to staggering sums by 1380. An explosion of fearful magnitude was building up, beside which the superficial outbursts of the magnates in their constant struggles with the royalists would pale to insignificance. The Peasants' Revolt was a product of age-long bitterness which the political and economic crisis of the current time had finally galvanized into full fury. There had been various tremors of new thinking before this; in Edward's last year the fiery John Wyclif had seized upon an inchoate protestantism to demand a sweeping reform of the established Church. The Lollards, who followed Wyclif's doctrine, were bred of many forces: the weakened and corrupted papacy during most of the fourteenth century when the popes resided at Avignon in French "captivity," the resistance of Parliament reflected in the Statute of Provisors in 1351 and the supplementary Statutes of Praemunire (forewarning or notice) in 1353 and 1365, and the following year's act repudiating the annual tributes to the Holy See which John had established.

To the stirring of new theological forces was added the economic shifting of barriers in the last century of the Middle Ages. The Black Death had hastened a trend that was already well advanced by the forties, as tenants of estates found it less and less practicable to rely on villein service to maintain their lands. The harsher efforts of the landholders to compel labor from those who remained bound to the land, and the hatred of the wealthy from whose opportunities the villeins were forever dis-qualified by the feudal law, needed only the final burden of the supertax to lead to the revolt of the disenfranchised. In the spring of 1381 the taxgatherers in eastern England were stoned; a few weeks later the government forces sent to subdue the outbreaks were attacked, and by early June a mob of thousands was on the march toward London. It was led by the type of rabble-rousers who always come forth on such occasions—Wat Tyler, John Ball, Jack Straw. At Canterbury the uprising destroyed the palace of the Archbishop, then swept into London itself, where it opened the prisons, pillaged shops, and burned John of Gaunt's palace. Richard and his council had fled to the Tower, and it was only when the main assault on the city had spent itself that a party from that fortress sought to contact Tyler and ask his terms.

After venting its passion against some of the people and places which symbolized the entire system of servitude—Arch-bishop Simon Sudbury was seized in the Tower after the King and his party came out, and hacked to pieces—the peasants made known their demands. The immemorial desire of the landless was the crux of the matter—all villeinage was to be abolished and any man was to have a right to rent land at a reasonable price. Richard accepted this petition, although he had no intention of granting it; the next day, Tyler was emboldened to make new demands, including a charter of liberties for all yeomen and peasants, but the royal forces were sufficiently rallied by now to seize control of the situation from the mob, and the rabble leader was slain on the spot. His head, stuck on a pole upon London Bridge, spoke the end of the main uprising, although a number of royal officers were to be murdered as the government sought to beat down the rebellion throughout the other parts of the kingdom. Richard displayed a firm attitude, once order was restored; he refused to permit mass reprisals, but required trials of all known leaders and permitted their punishment only after conviction before a court.

The few weeks of fury gave much cause for reflection on the state of England as the fourteenth century moved toward its close, but the thoughts that assailed the governing classes were hardly to be objective. Richard had been gratified to find that the symbol of the crown had been a major factor in re-establishing order, but he was too readily persuaded to identify this as personal veneration. As for the lords of the realm, they saw the situation as requiring a return to the system of conservators to guide the King in the directions they considered best. The new group called themselves the Lords Appellants, and they followed the now standard procedure of striking indirectly at the royal power by "appealing" (charging) the King's officers of evil-doings. By 1388 they dominated the "Merciless Parliament" which trumped up accusations against the chief ministers of the crown and sentenced them to death. The Lords Appellant themselves now became the ministers.

Richard was resolved to rid himself of the restraints imposed upon him during his minority, but he was a victim of his own shortcomings, the continuing decline in the military balance abroad, and the reaction of the barons to the Peasants' Revolt. He held a mystical view of his own royalty, and his awareness of the similarity of his position to that of Edward II perhaps prompted his efforts to have that long discredited prince canonized as a saint. He had been hastily married to a Bohemian princess, Anne, but the union produced no issue; when she died a few years later, he conceived of a means of establishing peace between England and France by marrying Isabella, daughter of Charles VI. But Isabella was only seven years of age, and it would be long before an heir to the throne would be possible from this union. If the control of the kingdom were to be recovered, Richard concluded that he must act unilaterally and vigorously.

The final three years of his reign were a confusion of motives and misplaced trust. He perceived that, unless he had legitimate issue of his own, his cousin Henry of Bolingbroke would be next in line of succession, and he sought to hide from himself, rather than to remove this prospect, by banishing Henry from the kingdom for life. Then he roused Henry to personal hatred by seizing his patrimony when his father, John of Gaunt, Earl of Lancaster, died. Rumor had it that Richard was going mad, and his increasingly wide shifts of policy gave force to the story. No man could count on his support or know when his enmity might change to sweet words. In the winter of 1397-98, Richard led his court aimlessly about the Midlands and the West Country, exacting "blank charters" from the representatives of counties which had harbored his enemies a decade earlier and which, it was said, he now would strip of their privileges by writing in his own terms upon the charters. However, nothing came of this, or of many other acts which he began and then failed to finish.

Now Bolingbroke, learning that all men of England were in dread of their own sovereign and that Richard himself had imprudently left the realm to go to Ireland, returned from exile and appeared among the Lancastrians. The northern lords, who had been close friends of his father, quickly summoned their followers and came to his banner. In alarm, the royal party left London and moved westward toward Wallingford, where Queen Isabella was secluded. But the invaders moved parallel to them, and when Richard himself returned from Ireland, he was soon driven to earth and made prisoner. His premonitions of the fate of Edward II were to be borne out, for as the century expired, so did the line of Plantagenets. In February 1400, the King was found dead in Pontefract Castle; by whose hand, no man ever knew.

Henry IV was foredoomed by the circumstances of his own conquest; he owed his throne to the Percy family of Northumberland, whose initial support had raised the revolt against Richard, and they were not men to be shunted aside in the new regime they had helped to found. The taint of usurpation lay upon the house of Lancaster; for a century it had been a chronic opponent of the throne, and for the new century it would be even more beset by rivalries. Scotland was restless once more, although in 1402 the young Prince James was captured and brought to the Tower as a hostage. Wales also rose in fresh rebellion under a vigorous leader, Owen Glendower, but by 1408 the King's son, the future Henry V, had restored order in much of the land. The Percy family, which had sided with the Welsh, was destroyed, including the Earl of Northumberland and his son, Henry Hotspur.

The King sought to restore order to the chaos left by Richard's last years, and half a dozen times during his fifteen-year reign he affirmed the Great Charters. But after his son's triumph on the battlefield, the control of Henry IV became less and less effective in the kingdom, and he abandoned the effort of his earlier reign to re-establish a balance between throne and Parliament. He did not permit his lords an opportunity to reassert a Conservators' role; he simply ruled without them, borrowing from merchants and ecclesiastical authorities friendly to him. His health deteriorated rapidly, and in the late winter of 1413 he died; had it not been for the evil circumstances by which he had attained the crown, he might have been better remembered by his own age. As it was, he had at least prepared the way for a brighter reign by his son.

Henry V came to the throne at twenty-five and died at thirty-four; in the meteoric interval he was to raise to brief new brilliance—and for the last time—the English star of empire on the Continent. At Agincourt he won a fabled victory over the French, and by the treaty two years later the ancient Duchy of Normandy returned, after more than two centuries, to the English Crown. With Henry's marriage to the French princess, Katharine, in the winter of 1420-21 and the birth of an heir shortly before his own death, England after his days might have hoped for a better heritage. Henry had sought, by a combination of military skill and firm diplomatic alliances, to settle the Anglo-French question which Edward III had left unanswered. By the treaty of peace dictated to Charles VI, Henry was to succeed to the throne of France after Charles's death, and the fact that the ailing and half-mad French ruler outlived the vigorous young conqueror by a few months was symptomatic of the transitory nature of Henry's entire policy; had he himself survived, his forceful personality might have preserved more of his dreams than would have been possible under the long minority which now began. In Henry V's gallant career, a supreme singlehanded effort was made to restore the golden age of Henry II, or at least the advances made by Edward III in his heyday. The dream died with this Henry.

The fifteen-year minority of Henry VI was generally a time of political disintegration at home and abroad, so that the material patrimony which had been provided at his father's death was all but gone when he came of age. The custody of England's French possessions was left to the able Duke John of Bedford, but the continual rivalries at home, among those who spoke or wished to speak for the infant ruler, choked off the vital economic support needed for an effective administration in Paris. The lords in Parliament legislated much during this time, but substantially in their own interests; the meeting of 1423 was the last to enroll a confirmation of the charters on the statute books, until the Petition of Right in 1628. The brief career of Jeanne d'Arc inspired new patriotism in the forces behind the callow Dauphin whom she crowned Charles VII; but it was Bedford's death in 1437 that robbed the English King, just as he was approaching an age when he could speak in his own name, of his most effective servant in the Continental possessions. Henry VI was not a warrior like his father, and his was a bitter inheritance when he attained majority. His marriage to Margaret of Anjou put him under the domination of a woman considerably his superior in intelligence and aggressiveness.

The Hundred Years' War ended in 1448, with the loss of Normandy for the last time and, by 1450, the slipping away of all the rest of the conquests of Edward III and Henry V. The familiar pattern of retribution developed; the King was attacked through his ministers, and the House of Lancaster, which was to end its possession of the throne under Henry VI, became the symbol of national frustration in the field of foreign affairs. As it later became evident that the King was succumbing to the insanity of his French grandfather, a sense of desperation gripped the kingdom. The long minority, now followed by an ineffective and subsequently mad monarchy, the popular feeling against the French queen, and the developing sense of opportunism in the opposition party centered in Duke Richard of York—all were elements gathering for an explosion of the first magnitude. From 1422 to 1485, when the first of the Tudors came to the throne, England was virtually in a state of anarchy at the highest level of its government; stability derived only from the steady growth in the strength of Parliament in this period.

The White Rose of York seemed to be the logical successor to the Red Rose of Lancaster until, somewhat to general surprise, Queen Margaret gave birth to a son in 1453. The disappointment of the Yorkists, the dread prospect of another long-drawn-out minority, and the somewhat sudden confinement of the Queen before the birth led rapidly to the rumor that the baby was a bastard, and hence barred from the succession. Whether or not it was Margaret's child, it was loudly whispered not to be Henry's. When the following year the King was declared to be insane, the Duke of York was named Lord Protector and promptly arrested his most serious adult rival for the throne. This rival was the Duke of Somerset, scion of the Lancastrians; and from this affront in 1454 and Somerset's release in 1455 when the King temporarily regained his senses, the sporadic Wars of the Roses began.

In the course of the following five years, Somerset and York both fell in battle, and Queen Margaret, with her young son, Prince Edward, retreated to Wales to organize a new Lancastrian effort. A blood bath engulfing the flower of English aristocracy was to follow; Duke Richard's son, the Earl of March, captured King Henry after the Battle of Towton on Palm Sunday, 1461, and upon shutting him in the Tower of London, proclaimed himself Edward IV of England. Margaret continued to lead a sporadic opposition, which was climaxed in 1468 by the Yorkists' defeat at Edgcott and Edward's own capture. The usurper king soon escaped, and for two more years an indecisive campaign raged until, with Henry released from the Tower, the hosts met for a final battle at Tewkesbury. Here the Lancastrian cause perished; Henry was recaptured, his son slain, and Queen Margaret made prisoner. In a few months it would be reported that Henry had died, apparently by the same means that had been used to dispose of earlier incompetent monarchs. Edward ruled fifteen more years unchallenged by rivals, who were dead, or by Parliament, which he could do without by living off French largesses and the funds of wealthy mistresses. He died of such living, men said, at the age of forty.

Another Edward, the fifth of that name, was now the successor to the throne, and since he was only twelve years old, it was obvious that a council of advisers would once more have to be given charge of the government during the minority. Lord Hastings, Lord Stanley, the Archbishop of York, and the Bishop of Ely were the logical members of the council, since they had been close friends of the late King and were known to be loyal to his son. There was also another important personage to enter the picture—Richard Crookback, Duke of Gloucester, the uncle of the new Edward V. Gloucester was especially solicitous of his nephew and placed him in the Tower for maximum security until his coronation, which was set for June 22, 1483. Meantime, the uncle discovered treason aborning in the council, arrested its leading members, and ordered Hastings' execution. His other nephew, Edward's brother, the ten-year-old Duke of York, was also sent to the Tower to protect him from alleged dangers.

Now came Richard's own bid for the throne. He charged that all of his brother's children were illegitimate, a not altogether unreasonable argument in view of Edward's long line of mistresses. But there were too many in the late King's court who could swear that the children in this case were by the Queen, Elizabeth Woodville. No matter; Richard persuaded a number of clergy to preach sermons on the illegitimacy of Edward himself, alleging that Edward's marriage to Elizabeth had been invalid because of a prior engagement he had made. A carefully selected council of magnates was assembled on June 25—the coronation of Edward V having been postponed by his uncle while the charges could be considered—and petitioned the Duke of Gloucester, whose creatures they were, to accept the crown. Richard III was formally crowned on July 6 in the presence of a vast number of armed followers who had come to the city for the occasion; he professed himself gratified that he could not be charged, like his brother, with having usurped the throne.

What had become of the princes in the Tower was only partly known. That they were murdered was hardly disputed, but when and by whom was never settled; Richard's ruthless bid for the throne, and his systematic elimination of all opponents and members of his late brother's party, cried out his own duplicity, but its extent was never documented. The times were too confused; the mockery of the splendid coronation drove men to revolt, and by the same circumstance many of the great lords of the land had fled to exile as Richard tried to extend his slaughter of opponents. The King pretended an interest in—and, indeed, sought to introduce—a number of reforms of the government which had fallen to such a low estate during the long years of regicides and civil conflict. But events did not wait for any redemptive efforts which the King might have envisioned; in August 1485, Richard was met on the field at Bosworth and slain. The fallen crown was plucked from a hawthorn bush and placed upon the head of the new King, Henry of Richmond. Thus began the age of the Tudors, and thus ended the feudal aftermath, in a characteristic storm of primordial savagery.

In a century of minor kings, ursurping kings, and murdered kings, government progressed only as fast as occasional respites in passion would permit. Election of knights, burgesses and even yeomen to Commons, and the growing importance of the Speaker of the House, marked some progress in political affairs, while the special equity jurisdiction of chancery courts, as a catalyst for the common-law courts, made some headway in this era. But the incipient doctrine of a constitutional order was of necessity kicked aside in the clash of candidates for the crown; since 1423, Parliament had not enacted any specific guarantee of the liberties in the Charter and the great organic statutes of the earlier age. However, legislation continued to be passed to extend and modernize the statutory principles which in turn had developed from the Charter rights, and the citing of specific chapters in Magna Carta in the law courts gave way to more reliance on the successor statutes; in part this was evidence that the old feudal obligations were ceasing to be causes of action, and that the private law heritage of the Great Charter was to be sought in the more contemporary provisions of Parliament.*

The modern age was now dawning; only seven years after Henry VII came to the throne, Columbus discovered the New World, and the sixteenth century would be an age of throwing off political, economic, and religious doctrines of the past. Parliament was kept busy under both of the early Tudor kings, legislating to keep pace with changing times; in the early sessions under Henry VII, there were still legislative concerns with such matters as hunting in the royal forests and the reasonable price of longbows, but under Henry VIII the most significant statutes, aside from Church establishment, were those on uses (trusts) and on wills.

The changes had cast a few shadows before; despite the ruthlessness and violence of the ruling powers in the fifteenth century, Richard III's brief legislative activity had made provision for the new special courts of "pie powder" (Fr. *pie poudre,* or dust on the feet) which were established at the great trading fairs to settle conflicts of commercial law. Although constitutionalism, like treaties, was silent beneath the clash of arms, the dying medievalism of the past century had rather ironically produced a classic on the subject—Sir John Fortescue's work *In Praise of the Laws of England,* written about 1471 for the edification of Edward IV—a fruitless objective which at least left the legal profession richer for a comparative analysis of the principles of English and French public law of that day. Greatest of all had been the summary of the body of property law by Thomas Littleton; his treatise *Of Tenures* would be edited (somewhat arbitrarily) by Sir Edward Coke and in that form would provide not only for the abolition of feudal tenure in 1660 but for the growth of English and American property law into the early twentieth century. The legal heritage of medievalism was the more remarkable because of the odds against which the common law had contended; due process, the inviolability of contracts, the recordation of rights in property, the freedom of the subject under ever-

---

* See annotations on this subject in Part II.

broadening conditions of government, indeed were to be interpreted in new terms in the new age, but their continuity from the Middle Ages was undeniable.

Under Henry VIII and Elizabeth I, the intellectual thunderclaps of the Renaissance, the Reformation, and the Reception (i.e. of the Roman law) were to clear the political atmosphere. Edward IV had anticipated the cultural consequences of the new learning spreading from Italy of his day, and some of the refinements of the arts and literature were introduced into the rough garrison atmosphere of his court. Henry VIII brought splendor to his own court, and the peers of the realm began to pride themselves on their individual learning. The meeting of the Kings of France and England on the Field of the Cloth of Gold in 1520 symbolized the wealth and the culture (albeit occasionally superficial) which the new economic orientation of the sixteenth century was to offer. The excitement of the Renaissance, with its new discoveries of ancient cultures and of fresh scientific and artistic principles, accelerated the decline of medieval belief; Machiavelli may have made his name an ultimate synonym for cynicism, but he performed a historic service to political science by challenging men to question the basis of law and government itself. From him it was a relatively short step to Martin Luther, John Knox, and Thomas Cranmer. The new knowledge led to disputes with established theological doctrine; the intellectual independence bred in this process led naturally to an emphasis upon private conviction rather than traditional dogma.

For the rule of law, the Tudor declaration of freedom from Rome was reflected in the refusal to rely further on ecclesiastics for the expert administration of the legal system. Administrators were selected by Henry VIII from laymen outside the formalized regimes of medieval legal learning; and as men argued that religious principles must be revitalized by seeking the pristine ideas of the early fathers of Christianity and applying them to new times, so also they argued with equal conviction for a revival of the original principles of Roman jurisprudence and their application to the new common law that the age demanded. A competence in both Roman and canon law (the two "laws" for which bachelors were trained in the later law centers) was the essence of the Reception which completed the trilogy established by the Renaissance and Reformation. It was Henry VIII who founded the Roman law Regius professorships at Oxford and Cambridge; it would be two hundred years before a professorship on the common law would be added, and the training for the practice of the common law would fall meantime upon the Inns of Court.

From 1514, when treaties of peace were concluded with France and Scotland, until 1588, when the Spanish Armada was defeated, England enjoyed a reign of peace and prosperity unparalleled in men's memories. The overturn of papal authority was effected with relatively little domestic upheaval, and even the business over Lady Jane Grey and Mary I and the execution of Mary Queen of Scots did not seriously threaten the firm Tudor grip. It was economics rather than religion which was the great moving force of sixteenth-century England, and the absolute break with Rome was only a logical component of the Tudors' instinctive realization that there had to be an absolute break with medievalism in all its dimensions. If Henry VIII had little patience with the great legislative advances of earlier days, it was primarily because he understood that the past had to be trimmed of its deadwood in order to serve the future. He led Parliament rather than subjugating it, and his legislative program aimed at laying the foundation for a modern administrative state. The Acts of Supremacy in religion and government were not intended to establish a tyranny but to ensure greater freedom of movement for the state as an entity; with many strong-willed leaders of this and subsequent generations, Henry sought this freedom for expeditious action because he knew the executive function was only thus to be made effective.

The great Tudors had their way with Parliament because they articulated what the majority of Englishmen sensed; the times were Protestant not only in religion but in politics and economics. Mary I represented a proposal of retrogression in the religious phase, James I briefly considered it as a possible course of action in the political, and Charles I in political and economic. These monarchs Parliament abandoned or overwhelmed; almost as strong-willed, in their ways, as Henry VIII and Elizabeth, they never accepted the changes which the Parliamentary majority demanded and the great Tudors identified. Henry's Statute of Proclamations of 1539 was a case in point; the Act provided that in cases of emergency the King and council could issue proclamations having the force of an Act of Parliament. Later critics of Tudor absolutism would point to this statute, failing to note that the very subject of the statute was a recognition of the legislative power of Parliament, and further that the statute had within it a number of safeguards against its misuse. The enormous output of legislation under Henry VIII attested to his readiness to accord Parliament its full share of responsibility in the affairs of government.

Under the Tudors, a number of special courts were developed, either by the monarchy or by Parliament, to cope with the increasingly complex needs of modern times. A special Court of Augmentations was created in 1536, primarily to administer lands expropriated from the monasteries, but in the process to complement the auditing and accounting procedures of the Exchequer. Courts of Wards and of Surveyors were established as early administrative agencies to systematize the feudal revenues due the crown from guardianships and from estates escheating to the king. But more important was the realization that new judicial machinery was required to render the law more efficient in its traditional functions. Since feudal law had based its most important actions upon rights in land, new courts were developed to apply remedies to other issues. Modern times brought questions of contract liability, personal injuries which called for new methods of satisfaction, and new types of evidence needed to establish proof in such matters.

From earliest times, a subject seeking a new remedy would petition the king and his council; and the chancellor, as a member of the council, for many years had issued writs under which the common-law courts could assume jurisdiction of the subjects of the petitions. It was a logical step from this to the devising of a separate court under the chancellor, which would have the responsibility for "doing equity" where existing common-law procedures did not fit the case. To this substantial advance under the Tudors were added a number of special or prerogative courts, of which two were destined to become instruments of Stuart tyranny. One—the Court of Star Chamber—originally was established by Parliament to do for criminal law what Chancery was doing for civil (noncriminal) law; it was only after Elizabeth and the early Stuarts came to use it as a means of prosecuting those who could not be reached through the common-law courts that it found its name becoming a synonym for arbitrary judicial process. The same was true of the Court of High Commission, which took over the criminal cases formerly assigned to papal jurisdiction. Both courts were abolished by Parliament in 1641.

Amid the swift developments of the modern age of the sixteenth century, there was a concern for the continuity between the older institutions and the new, and a succession of brilliant law reporters and writers developed, in the congenial intellectual atmosphere, to perform the task. Their labors laid foundations for the political and legal issues of the Parliamentary struggle of the next century; the new editions of compiled statutes uniformly began with the Great Charter—suggesting to the careless of that day and later ages that the law began with the Charter of 1225 (as confirmed in 1297)—and thus refreshed legal memory which had not, for a century now, had the formal reminder of a Parliamentary confirmation. The introduction of printing into England had been one of the cultural innovations of Edward IV, and by the time of Henry VII a number of lawbooks had come from the presses. *Antiqua Statuta* was a collection which appeared very early in the era, and appeared in a number of editions under its more familiar (and larger) title of *The Booke of Magna Carta with Divers Old Statutes.* A dozen such compilations were produced in the sixteenth century to serve the growing legal profession. To these were added the early treatises—St. Germain's *Doctor and Student,* Fitzherbert's *Grand Abridgment,* Lombard's *New Natura Brevium*—which further indoctrinated the readers in the Inns of Court with the precedents proceeding from Magna Carta to their own day.

Men in later times would look back to the Tudor era, and particularly to the years of Elizabeth, as a golden age in almost every element of life. In part the recollection was, inevitably, a distortion of reality, and in part a rationalization of motives which often were even more materialistic than in the feudal era. But the age sparkled even under the most objective scrutiny, and the more so because it represented a triumph over two preceding centuries of almost continual strife and decline. The feckless aristocracy of medievalism became the peers of the realm, and the provincial commoners the new gentry, in the stimulating climate of Tudor mercantilism; before the end of the century, England was laying plans for New World colonization which would in turn create an empire incomparably greater than the Angevin power at its height. From 1307, when Edward I died, to 1607, when the first permanent English colony was planted in the territory claimed a generation earlier for the Virgin Queen, the world had been transformed in every intellectual dimension. What emerged from that transition, annealed and burnished, was a constitutional and jurisprudential system which would now be shaped on the anvils of two revolutions.

Coke and the English Revolution

WHEN James VI of Scotland became James I of England in 1603, Sir Edward Coke was in the second of his three careers. In 1600 he had been appointed to the Court of Common Pleas in repayment for his long service in the interests of Elizabeth I, beginning with his first term in Parliament in 1589. After more than a decade as an ardent supporter of the rights of the crown, his fifteen years on the bench would give him a new perspective of the nascent modern constitution, and at the close of his long public life he would return to Parliament as an even more zealous advocate of rights against the crown. His great rival, Sir Francis Bacon, would correctly complain that there was often too much of Coke in Coke's jurisprudence, for, steeped in legal lore as he was, the great jurist not infrequently would read into his sources what meanings he concluded they should have; he was not a critical and objective scholar like his contemporaries John Selden and Sir Robert Cotton. Yet he always spoke with vigorous conviction, inundating his opponents with citations from Year Books and other reported cases which led men to accept his often empirical propositions on the strength of his prestige as lawyer, parliamentarian, judge, and reporter of the courts. Ultimately, when he confronted James's son, Charles I, in the parliamentary crisis of the twenties, his apologetic for the constitutional implications of Magna Carta would provide the legal talisman for the English Revolution.

The revival of the Great Charter as a fundamental of modern constitutional argument was not the singlehanded accomplishment of Coke, nor did the concept appear full grown in the troubles of the seventeenth century. The preceding generations had kept the private law elements of Magna Carta alive and flourishing, through the adjudication of the common-law courts, and by its own enactments in extension of the chief principles of the Charter in successive statutes, Parliament had preserved it as a starting point of government process. For more than a century now the printing press had supplied all lawyers and lawmakers with collections of statutes, which uniformly began with the grant of liberties in the ninth year of Henry III. In 1527 John Rastell had published his *Great Abridgement* of the English law, grouping the main areas of jurisprudence under appropriate subject headings, and including a detailed discussion of twenty-four of the chapters in Magna Carta, "bycause the moste parte of them retayne theyr force, and bynde the kyng's subjects unto this day." Two years later Rastell wrote *The Pastyme of People,* a popular history which described with fair accuracy the evolution of the Great Charter from 1215 to 1225; this was one of numerous recapitulations of history which had a wide appeal to the Tudor public and made laymen as well as lawyers aware of the role of the Great Charter and the subsequent organic statutes in the evolution of their nation. Indeed, it was from the chronicles of Roger of Wendover and Matthew Paris, printed in this era, as well as from the manuscripts of the ancient Year Books, that Coke and his contemporaries gained most of their knowledge of Magna Carta.

But the most significant factor of all in the gathering forces of the seventeenth-century upheaval was the steady strengthening of Parliament itself, and particularly of the House of Commons, in the last twenty years of Elizabeth's reign. While the great Queen had managed to the end to keep the assembly under her control—Sir Edward himself had been her Speaker in 1592-93 and her Attorney-General the following year—there were adamant independents among the members, and their numbers grew with each year. William Cecil, Lord Burghley, was one of many who guided the House between the challenges of a high-strung genius on the throne and an increasingly self-conscious middle class in Commons. By the last of Elizabeth's Parliaments, it had become commonplace for the Queen to assure the members of their immunities: "For freedom of speech, her Majesty willingly consenteth thereunto, with this caution: that the time be not spent in idle and vain matters, painting the same out with froth and volubility of words."

There had been men like Peter Wentworth, who had sought every possible means of offering a challenge to the royal prerogative and ultimately would die a martyr's death in the Tower in support of Parliament's right to debate all business placed before it. There had been the frustrated Puritan minority, continually fretting that under Elizabeth the Protestant Reformation had seemed to do little more than move the ritual of churchmanship from Rome to Canterbury. And there had been also friends of the crown like Coke and Francis Drake and Walter Raleigh. These were the elements in Commons as the old century passed; but the composition of the House was inexorably changing in this same period. The country gentlemen, the wealthy lawyers, and the great merchants all acquired landed estates and qualified for seats; they took it as their right to have a voice—nay, a deciding role—in matters of state, and they did not intend to be thrust into any lesser position. This was a harsh fact which James I at length came to accept, but Charles I never did.

James, after all, had wanted the English crown badly enough to speak softly when his mother, the Queen of Scots, had been executed by Elizabeth's ministers in 1587. At that time he had already been King of Scotland for twenty-five years, having been crowned when he was but eleven months old; and he had had to wait another twenty-five years before he finally was summoned to London. He had reason to expect a long and successful reign, even though he followed, somewhat colorlessly, the vibrant and beloved Queen; he had shown his ability to steer a straight course between the extremes of Presbyterian Puritanism and the older Highlands Catholicism in Scotland, and had deftly thwarted a succession of plots against himself. The new monarch assumed that, as a matter of course, he would enjoy the obedience accorded his predecessor, since he offered his subjects a continuation of the policies which had brought wealth and prestige to the realm in the immediate, glowing past. If anything, in James's view, he could offer much more: his wife, the Danish princess Anne, had presented him with several children, including two sons, thus insuring a continuity to the Stuart line which the three children of Henry VIII had not been able to do for the Tudors. He was a philosopher-king, or so his courtiers described him; his education in youth had been broad, and his interest in the arts and opportunities of the new century was equally broad. While he found no new Shakespeare to dazzle the intellectual scene, he would give his name, in 1611, to a translation of the Bible which would rank equally with the Bard's plays as the supreme creation of the mother tongue.

The reign had begun auspiciously enough; at a conference at Hampton Court in 1604, the project for the translation of the Scriptures had been approved, and in the spring of 1606 the Virginia Company of London was formally chartered to attempt the colonization of a part of the New World where England, after a generation of war with Spain, now hoped to establish itself permanently after Elizabeth's efforts under Raleigh had failed. Yet, with the calling of his first Parliament, James found himself brusquely challenged on both philosophical and legal grounds. The King, who himself had a few years before written a book, *The Trew Law of Free Monarchies,* an expostulation on the divine right of kings, found the Commons determined to put an end to certain obsolete feudalisms which were now merely an invitation to abuse. These included the old practice of purveyancing, which had ceased to have practical justification now that the court was no longer itinerant and Parliament was expected to provide a royal income, and wardships, which at least required modernization in the light of the developing law of trusts.

James was thoroughly upset by the boldness of the House in raising these issues and sent word that he considered these matters to be outside the scope of subjects properly to be considered by Commons. "I would wish you to take care," he was to say on repeated occasions, "that you do not meddle with the main points of government; that is my craft." He received back a blunt reply from the House: It was no part of their thoughts to impugn his Majesty's prerogative, said the petition; but the old laws and customs were to be followed: "Since Magna Carta in Henry III's

time, a part of every king's glory" had been to make laws progressively diminishing purveyances. Having cited the King to
Chapters 19 and 21 of the Great Charter, and to the amending
legislation on the subject set out in the statute books,* the petition
urged his Majesty to "be pleased to receive public information
from your Commons as to the civil estate and government." The
debate, with renewed references to the Charter, continued for
another session of Parliament, but failed to produce any legislation—apparently because the House of Lords was not enthusias-
tic. But James had had his first confrontation with the limiting
principles of Magna Carta.

The readiness of the leaders of the Lower House to cite the
Charter—a phenomenon quite rare in Elizabeth's Parliament—
demonstrated the general knowledge of its place as the original
statute of the realm which had been fostered by the lawbooks and
historical chronicles so widely read in the Tudor age. It was a
ready-made instrument for a Parliament bent on asserting its
rights against a sovereign who was manifestly incapable of controlling it as the great Queen had done; the arguments might
be somewhat strained on occasion, as when Sir Edwin Sandys, a
veteran of Elizabeth's Parliament, opposed the King's proposal for
a permanent English-Scottish union because common citizenship
would invest the newcomers with all the rights guaranteed to
Englishmen by the Charter. A more apt application of the
Charter's Chapter 30 as a challenge to the King's prerogatives
arose when one Bate, a London merchant, refused to pay an
"imposition," or surtax, levied by executive action of the crown.
The Court of Exchequer found Bate liable to a fine for resisting
what they held to be absolute right of the King; but Parliament
in 1610-11 hotly disputed the ruling, citing a number of fourteenth-century statutes which had proceeded from Chapter 30 to
a progressive limitation of the practice. The issue died with this
Parliament, but James was too intelligent to have failed to discern
the limits to which he could expect his claims of prerogatives to
extend.

Two new lawbooks had appeared in this space as well: in

---

* See annotation to these chapters of the Great Charter in Part II.

1607, the *Interpreter* of John Cowell, an Anti-Parliamentarian of Cambridge, who nevertheless was at pains to stress that Magna Carta "is of such extent [that] all the lawe wee have, is thought in some part to depend on it." Then, in 1610, John Selden's historical survey, *England's Epinomis,* reprinted in detail the charter of 1225; it would be the basis, eighteen years later, of his vigorous advocacy of rights against the Crown in the case of the debate on Coke's great Petition to Charles II. Coke himself was steadily assuming a greater authority in the law; from his first year on the bench he had begun the editing and publishing of reports of cases he considered significant—made more significant after his oftentimes gratuitous comments upon them. As instinctive a politician as he was a devotee of his "lady of the common law," he doubtless was aware of the arguments raised in Parliament in challenge to James's initial efforts to assert his prerogatives, but it was not until 1616 that his own time came to challenge James's pretensions, and the challenge brought about his removal from the bench.

Coke (the name was often written, and more often pronounced, Cooke) had come of reputable stock. His father was described as "a gentleman of Lincoln's Inn" and he himself, after study at Cambridge, was entered "a student of municipiel law" at the Inner Temple. He had made his name famous at the bar of his own day, as well as to generations of lawyers to follow, by his pleading in Shelley's case with its fundamental rule as to the establishment of a fee simple in land. He had married well, not once but twice—first to an heiress who brought him thirty thousand pounds and substantial properties, and after her death, to Lady Elizabeth Hatton, granddaughter of Elizabeth's Parliamentary leader and his own political patron, Lord Burghley. Coke's lucrative law practice and his eminence in public affairs had brought him to the attention of the Queen herself, and among her last acts was the appointment of the brilliant attorney at the age of forty-eight to the Bench of Common Pleas, where he became Chief Justice soon after James's accession. He was reputed to be a ferocious, even brutal judge, no more objective in the trying of cases than he would be in his analysis of constitutional history. He had presided at the trial of Sir Walter Raleigh in 1603, describing him as "a spider of hell" and assuring him that he would "make it appear to the world that there never lived a viler viper upon the face of the earth than thou."

Sir Edward had undergone a revelation, upon his elevation to the chief justiceship of the Common Pleas, as Thomas à Becket had experienced when he had been consecrated Archbishop. Both men had been, prior to this transfiguration, vigorous supporters of a dominating monarchy; both had then had a complete change in the perspective with which they viewed the royal prerogatives. In his career as crown attorney for Elizabeth, Coke had been an uncompromising defender of the Crown's pre-eminence in governmental power; on the bench, he transferred this loyalty to the law itself, and to King James he could quote Bracton: "The King ought to be under no man, but under God and the law." He could have said the same of Parliament, for in his view no individual or institution could escape subjection to the distilled wisdom of the centuries to be found in the common law. His quotation to James had not been kindly received; neither was his opinion in the case of Dr. Bonham in 1610, in which he contended that an Act of Parliament or of the Crown could be limited or set aside if it ran counter to the sum of the common law itself. James suggested to the Chief Justice that he "correct" this report, but this came to naught.

Coke was as vehement and uncompromising in his defense of the law against the Crown's encroachment as he had been in his prejudicial trial of Raleigh. All the prerogative courts of Tudor times he now saw, in his altered perspective, as challenges to the primary jurisdiction of the Court of Common Pleas. They did not proceed, he complained, "according to the course of the common law." Casting about in the ancient records of jurisprudence, Coke seized upon and revived for modern use two long-neglected writs: the writ of prohibition, by which inferior courts could be ordered to refrain from hearing a case deemed beyond their jurisdiction; and *habeas corpus*, which lawyers of the sixteenth century had begun to use as a means of testing the legality of an imprisonment. By the writ of prohibition, Coke crippled the functions of such prerogative tribunals as the Court of Requests and the Court of High Commission. The effective use of the writ of *habeas corpus*, with its manifest threat of an equal degree of curtailment of the Crown's own authority, had to await Parliamentary implementation half a century later; but the inspiration would be Coke's, and a further contribution of his genius to the English constitution which was evolving.

Following a fruitless session—the "Addled Parliament"—of 1614, James resorted to the tactics of Lancastrian kings and undertook to rule as long as possible without having to call another Parliament. Having thwarted the early House efforts, which relied on Magna Carta and other basic laws to control his powers, and having consistently won cases on the issues in his courts, James assumed that his judges could be counted on to support any action he might propose if he could base it on his concept of his prerogatives. The test came in 1615-16; the King had ordered his judges through his chancellor to recognize the royal right to grant *commendams,* the commending to a custodian of the care of an ecclesiastical vacancy until it could be permanently filled. In a letter to Coke and the other eleven judges, the King directed a stay in the proceedings in a case involving a benefice held by the Bishop of Coventry *in commendam;* at Coke's direction, the judges disregarded the King's injunction as an infringement upon the jurisdiction of their court. Thereupon James summoned them to his chambers, tore up the letter they had prepared stating their position, and demanded a promise of their obedience in the future. Eleven capitulated; Coke did not, but told James he would do what an honest and just judge ought to do.

Coke's dismissal from judicial office which in due course followed was regarded as a triumph for his long-time rival, Sir Francis Bacon, the ardent royalist. The conflict between Coke and Bacon was personal, professional, and ideological—an unhappy confluence of circumstances which placed two such brilliant men in positions never to be reconciled. They had been rivals for Lady Hatton's hand, and Coke had won; they had competed for high political office, and in terms of eminence, Bacon had won. In the matter of pedigrees, Bacon's was better; his mother was related by marriage to the powerful Cecil family. His rapid rise in law and public affairs had paralleled Coke's, and he was the author of an equally long and equally distinguished list of works in science and philosophy as well as some excellent monographs in law. But it was in the function of the Chancery, or equity court—that greatest counterbalance to the common-law courts—that Bacon and Coke came to their fundamental conflict. Under Elizabeth's great chancellors the ancient office had assumed new eminence as the keeper of the royal conscience and the trier of issues under more flexible rules of investigation where, as Bacon himself wrote, "a man will not be prejudiced by mispleading or defect of form, but only by the truths of the matter." The early ancestor of scientific jurisprudence, Bacon saw the Chancery process as one which "resorts to whatever means there are whereby the truth may be known." These were proposals to slap Coke in the face, for they suggested a diluting of the impeccable (but sometimes mechanistic) process of jurisprudence which he had conceived as the characteristic of the common law. The Chancery was the one court which had a power—the injunction—to match or excel the common-law writs of prohibition and *habeas corpus*; in the short view of the matter, Bacon's triumph over Coke in the issue of 1616—James himself decided in favor of Chancery because he thus could establish that he was "judge over his judges"—was a blow to the legal structure which was being built up to challenge the prerogatives.

Coke's dismissal from the bench was to be the factor that finally directed his own great learning into the course of Parliamentarianism; having experienced in his own career the consequence of the return to absolutism in the crown, Sir Edward had now come full circle from his days as an Elizabethan devotee of the prerogatives. He was now well advanced in years—sixty-four when he departed the bench—and many men would have granted him the privilege of retiring honorably to rest on his laurels. After all, his eminence as an authority on law was unchallenged; even Bacon complimented him on particular points. The legal profession, after the publishing of his reports, accepted them as the ultimate statement of the subject and declined to go farther back than his writings to establish any point of law which might arise. So massive—if also so often superficial—had been his assembly of cases from the first Year Books to his own age that no one was disposed to work over the same ground. Until the late nineteenth century, the common law of England would be substantially what Sir Edward had said it was.

In 1620, the issue between the King and Parliament again was joined. James called the new session because he needed funds; the members eagerly sought election because, for a full decade, there had been no opportunity to debate reforms and new laws which had been crying for attention since the turn of the century. Obsolete statutes in profusion had been found choking the growth of the law; various prerogative courts established under the Tudors were in need of amending if not abolishing; coinage was devalued and trade in decline, to such an extent that Commons chafed to legislate somewhat in aid of both; there was also the business of accelerating the Puritanizing of the Church of England, which a new generation of Protestants demanded. The King watched with misgiving as the turbulence of reform mounted in the new House. Reviving a "judgment which hath been asleep these three hundred years," Commons impeached the Lord Chancellor for bribery and compelled his removal from office. Thus, Sir Francis Bacon, the Chancellor, was to be humbled by Sir Edward Coke, who had returned to Parliament with this session as a member from Liskeard.

One of the most sensitive issues in dispute between crown and Commons was the practice of granting trade and industrial patents to the King's favorites; it had become the modern equivalent of the lavish grants of estates by which medieval kings had bolstered their following of barons. The patents had begun under Elizabeth, as a means of encouraging the new merchant lords to develop local manufactures or to expand import and export trade. Two types of abuses followed from the practice: monopoly was encouraged, to the severe burden of many middle and poorer classes; and the power of patentees to arrest and imprison persons charged with infringing upon their rights was easily extended to any parties held in enmity by the patent holder. The House had in mind a recent flagrant case where a patent for the manufacture of gold and silver thread had driven many independent goldsmiths to ruin; men under the Attorney-General had sought to enforce the patent rights by breaking into private houses to seize evidence of infringement and to force the suspects to stand trial or post heavy bonds. All London had been in an uproar by 1618 over the matter, and both Houses of Parliament hastened into debate on the patent process when they convened.

Coke spoke at length against the imprisonments effected under this and other patents, and elaborated upon Magna Carta as the basis of English freedom; it was at this time that he made the assertion that the Charter had been "confirm'd 32 Times" in the course of history, and exhorted the House to reassert the freedom from arbitrary seizures set out in Chapter 29, for "if this is suffered, no man can live in safety." A Magna Carta Bill, to prohibit imprisonments under private patent and to have retroactive effect upon Bacon and his fellow officers, was debated at length in Commons, but was cut off from enactment by the determined effort of James I at this point to bring an end to the Parliamentary assault upon his government.

Seeking to keep the members attendant to their proper business, the King informed them that they were not to question the conduct of officers of the Crown, but to vote him the funds he needed to advance the nation's interests abroad. The House responded with the renowned Protestation of the Commons, insisting that "the liberties, franchises, privileges, and jurisdictions of Parliament are the ancient and undoubted birthright and inheritance of the subjects of England," and that "the Commons in Parliament have the liberty and freedom to treat of these matters in such order as in their judgment seems fittest; and that every member of the said House hath like freedom from all impeachment, imprisonment and molestation . . . for or concerning any speech, reasoning or declaring of any matter or matters touching the Parliament or Parliament's business." James had had enough; he personally tore the Protestation from the official journal, dissolved the Parliament, and placed Coke and various other leaders of the opposition under arrest. By this action, he committed Parliament to a course of no return, but fate was to reserve the retribution for his son; James himself died three years after the session of 1620-21.

In seizing Coke and others of the 1620-21 Parliament, the Crown also took possession of a number of the manuscripts on which Sir Edward had been at work since his dismissal as Chief Justice in 1616. The jurist scholar was already well advanced in his monumental work on the laws of England, which would climax his life-long study and suggest the logical continuity of the common law from the feudal to the modern age. "I was committed to the Tower," Sir Edward wrote, "and all my bookes and studdie searched and 37 manuscripts were taken away." In due course, thirty-four of these were returned, although Coke declared he would have given three hundred pounds for the other three. These may have been the drafts of the last three volumes of his *Institutes;* the first, renowned to history as *Coke on Littleton,* was published in 1627, but the others, completed in the following years, were considered by the Crown to be too dangerous to be printed, and were seized again before his death in 1634. The second *Institute,* on Magna Carta and the great organic statutes, would not be published until the outbreak of the Civil War in 1642. Coke's legacy on the Great Charter would thus be a means to justify the Parliamentary uprising; but it was germinated in the Parliament of the twenties.

Some discussion of Magna Carta, indicating its general impression on legislative consciousness, occurred in the Parliament of 1624, but tempers had momentarily cooled by then, and James himself was inclined to be more conciliatory. The contemplated marriage of the heir apparent, Prince Charles, to a Spanish Catholic princess had fallen through, and now negotiations were under way to arrange a marriage with the French Princess, Henrietta Maria. Although she also was a child of Rome, she was from a land presently hostile to Spain, England's greatest colonial rival in the New World, and the English public was less able to oppose the contemplated union with the daughter of a presently friendly king. In any event, James was nearing the end of his life, and a certain mellowness settled over his relationship with his subjects at the last. While he had proved less able than Elizabeth to keep the upper hand in all his dealings with them, he had postponed by a generation the final challenge to the lingering medieval powers of the monarchy, and in so doing he had kept faith with the past which he had inherited.

The Stuarts had been chosen by destiny to make the final

assertion of the concept of the ultimate prerogatives of the crown
in confrontation with the economic realities of the modern age.
If Charles I was temperamentally unsuited for the task, there was
also the fact that time itself had run out; the Reformation was an
accomplished fact, the emphasis upon trade and industry was
rendering daily more meaningless the hereditary posture of
prerogatives, and Parliament had demonstrated its capacity to
control affairs when the economic pinch upon the government
became severe enough. Charles's troubles began immediately, for
the economic pinch was indeed painful when the first of his
Parliaments convened in 1625. The King shared his father's conviction that matters of war, peace, and diplomacy were exclusively
the concern of the Crown and distinctly beyond the right of
Parliament to question; but Parliament was resolved to assert its
interest in these subjects in its own terms.

The sessions in June 1625 began under inauspicious circumstances; Westminster was infested with plague, and by early July
Parliament would be compelled to adjourn to Oxford. Charles
had just celebrated his marriage to the Princess, and Puritan
passions flared at the news that he had agreed to the new
Queen's continued observance of her own faith, which was
reported to be pointing to the suspension of the stringent Reformation laws against English Catholics. Finally, the King was
already committed to an expensive war of attrition against Spain
and had placed the war effort under the direction of his father's
favorite—and one of Commons' favorite targets—the Duke of
Buckingham. Already there were military reverses to report, and
the King's requests for the traditional "subsidies" of the Crown,
augmented by the usual lifetime assurance of customs revenues,
were harshly met. A one-year term of "tonnage and poundage"
(customs) was voted, and two subsidies instead of the requested
seven; and the House proceeded to the drafting of a new Protestation of its right "to discover and reform the abuses and
grievances of the realm and state." To show his outrage at this
meager financial accommodation, and to choke off action on the
Protestation, Charles dissolved the Parliament less than two
months after it had been summoned.

In February 1626 Charles attempted a new tactic. Before

issuing a call for another Parliament, he appointed Coke and a number of other critics to offices of sheriff, thus rendering them ineligible for membership in the House. But others remained, and new opponents arose; indeed, with each successive convening of the House there appeared to be a greater volume of protest against the government. In this session it was to be an attempted impeachment of Buckingham, whose incompetence as a military commander had been demonstrated in a disastrous attack upon Cadiz. One of the charges alleged that the Duke had obtained judicial appointments of friends for money, and this abuse of his powers "doth as much as in him lies to make the King breach his Word with his People," as set out in the prohibition in Magna Carta against the sale of justice. As the impeachment proceedings dragged on, and the antigovernment critics waxed more vehement, the Crown made matters infinitely worse; two of the managers of the impeachment proceedings, Sir Dudley Digges and Sir John Eliot, were arrested and sent to the Tower. Thereupon the Commons rested and resolved that "there be no business till we are righted in our liberties."

For a week the House and the King were deadlocked, the House declaring through one of its members that its rights rested "upon the good Charter of our great inheritance" and that no man was to be committed to prison except upon a lawful judgment as prescribed in the Charter. In due course, Digges and Eliot were released, and by taking the impeachment proceedings into the prerogative Court of Star Chamber, the Crown managed to get Buckingham acquitted. On June 15, with a long message justifying his action, Charles dissolved this Parliament, having obtained even less from it than he had from the first. The conflict between Crown and subjects was looming even greater; in his announcement of the dissolution, Charles asserted that "he well knoweth, that the calling, adjourning, proroging and dissolving of Parliaments . . . do particularly belong unto himself, by an undoubted prerogative, inseparately united to his imperial crown; of which, as of his other royal actions, he is not bound to give an account to any but to God only, whose immediate lieutenant and vice regent he is in these realms and dominions, by the divine Providence committed to his charge and government."

Commons sought to meet the King's message with a Remonstrance of its own, pointing out its disapproval of the attempt to
weaken the opposition of the House by appointing certain of its
erstwhile members as sheriffs, and insisting that its first obligation
had been "to search into the causes of those mischiefs which
this your kingdom suffereth, and divers of the grievances that
overburden your subjects: without doing of which, we could
neither be faithful to your Majesty nor to the country which doth
trust and employ us." It protested the commitment of Digges and
Eliot, and contended that its own action had been misinterpreted
to the King himself by Buckingham, whom it prayed Charles to
dismiss. Charles's reply was as peremptory as James's to the
Protestation of 1621; he ordered that the Remonstrance be publicly burned and sought once more to manage his affairs without
calling another Parliament.

Matters were rapidly going from bad to worse; in an effort
to raise money, Charles in the fall of 1626 ordered a "forced
loan," or a payment to the royal treasury equivalent to what might
have been raised had Parliament granted the original request for
subsidies. Chief Justice Carew warned the King that the loans
were illegal, whereupon he was dismissed. A number of men were
arrested in the next several months upon refusal to pay the loan,
and when, early in 1628, most of these were released, it was said
that more than seventy gentlemen had been seized in the course
of the dispute. But the basic constitutional issue was tested in a
case involving five knights—Sir John Corbet, Sir Thomas Darnel,
Sir Walter Earl, Sir Edmond Hampden, and Sir John Hevening-
ham, all leaders of the Parliamentary challenge—who sought a
writ of *habeas corpus* upon their committal to the Fleet Prison.
The warden returned a brief for each of the men stating that "he
was and is committed by the special command of his Majesty."
Serjeant Bramston, counsel for Corbet, then argued:

> . . . if the law be, that upon this return this gentleman
> should be remanded, I will not dispute whether or no a
> man may be imprisoned before he be convicted accord-
> ing to law; but if this return shall be good, then his
> imprisonment shall not continue on for a time, but for-

ever; and the subjects of this kingdom may be restrained
of their liberties perpetually, and by law there can be
no remedy for the subject; and therefore this return
cannot stand within the laws of the realm, or that of
Magna Carta . . . which are the inheritance of the
subject.

John Selden, counsel for Hampden, elaborated upon the
technical meaning of Chapter 29 of the Great Charter, and traced
its legislative history to Elizabeth's time. The words, "We will not
commit him to prison," said Selden, referred to the King himself;
by this Charter and subsequent statutes, he argued, "no freeman
whatsoever ought to be imprisoned but according to the laws of
the land; and . . . the liberty of the subject is the highest inheritance that he hath." Others of the defense counsel spoke in similar
vein; but Attorney General Robert Heath, on behalf of the
Crown, argued that since the first Statute of Westminster it had
been clear that a person could not be admitted to bail in cases
where the King or his law enforcement agencies committed him.
"The difference," said Heath, is that "the king is head" of the
system of justice, and hence it is an absolute prerogative which
cannot be invoked by a writ intended for a lesser accusation.
Prophetically—although unknowingly—the Crown counsel suggested the alternative which, under Coke, Parliament would
devise:

By the Statute of Magna Carta, no man shall be put
out of his freehold, &c. But if the king will do it, must not
the party that is so put out go to the king, by petition?
. . . it is a petition of right. . . .

The King's Bench upheld the crown argument; due process,
the court held, did not require that a cause of imprisonment be
stated when the King in his judgment considered that the circumstances warranted a commitment. Until a cause for imprisonment
was stated in the King's good time, said Chief Justice Hyde, a
habeas corpus could not issue, for it concerned only detention in
prison after the cause of the detention was known. Charles had
won a spectacular victory over Charter rights in his court, but

it was to be short-lived. The continued worsening of the war
with Spain, and now with France, made it imperative that a new
Parliament be summoned; and in January 1628 the writs went
out. Since the King had neglected to anticipate this call in November, when sheriffs were appointed, it was too late to use such
appointments to disqualify the opposition leaders; and since the
new Parliament was expected to act on the financial issue which
had occasioned the forced loans, the imprisonments of those who
had resisted the loans were terminated, and, it was reported,
"those gentlemen who suffered for the loan were elected in many
places."

It was evident that the time had come to halt the trend toward a new absolutism in the throne; the readiness of the King's
courts to accept the King's interpretation of his own prerogatives
was a threat to a return to the Middle Ages. Although there
were a number of the members of Commons who sought to revive
the attack on the Duke of Buckingham, a meeting of the leaders
at the home of Sir Robert Cotton prior to the opening of the
session agreed that the issue could only be settled by carrying it
directly to the King; "the violated rights of the subjects must first
be vindicated," and an end be put to the claim that the king's
needs or desires could go beyond the judgment of Parliament (in
the matter of forced loans) or beyond the fundamental law (in
the matter of arbitrary arrests). Fate had brought together a
body of advocates far worthier than the barons at Runnymede
to plead the cause of a constitution: Coke, now in his seventy-
sixth year, was to lead them, but with him were men of such
power of argument and conviction as Selden, Eliot, Sir Thomas
Wentworth, and John Pym.

"This is the crisis of Parliament," observed one member as
the session opened. It was indeed to be so, for both sides were
determined not to yield their ground. The case of the five knights
was in everyone's thoughts; as Sir Thomas Wentworth put it:
"projectors," he said, had "extended the prerogative of the king
beyond the just symmetry" of crown and Parliament working in
harmony; these "projectors," he went on "were the men guilty of
imprisoning us without either bail or bond." "By one and the
same . . . have king and people been hurt," said Wentworth, and

the cure could only be had "by reinforcing the ancient laws made by our ancestors, by setting forth such a character of them, as no licentious spirit shall dare to enter upon them."

This was a strange man who spoke these words. He had entered Parliament in 1621 at the age of twenty-eight, considered to be a supporter of the King. He soon found himself in opposition, upon James's denial that the privileges demanded by the House were their ancient right. Throughout his career in Parliament, he sought an honorable middle course, and when Charles's intransigence drove him to support the Parliamentary opposition, he did so reluctantly. He was the prototype of the men of the middle, caught in the fury of extremes which bred the civil wars and the Revolution. He held a mystic view of the obligations which went with the prerogatives, and if it was a question of whether the ultimate executive power should be vested in King or Parliament, he would at the last support the King. Fate, rather than Charles's acumen, confirmed Wentworth as a royalist after the Petition of Right; accepting the King's Answer to the Petition at face value, he was made a baron in the same year, and became the crown's administrator for the Council of the North. From that time forward, he would serve his monarch faithfully, never losing the hope that Charles would be able to lead Parliament by a great example in the grand manner of the Tudors. In 1640 he was to be created Earl of Strafford, and as the Earl of Strafford a year later was executed by Parliament.

Coke saw that the forced loans constituted the fundamental issue, for the arbitrary imprisonment of the knights had been based upon the original wrong of the loans themselves. He asked, "Who will give subsidies, if the king may impose what he will— and if, after Parliament, the king may enhance what he pleaseth? . . . Will any give a subsidy that will be taxed after Parliament at pleasure? The king cannot tax any by way of loans. . . . The lord may tax his villein high or low, but it is against the franchises of the land for freemen to be taxed but by their consent in Parliament." It was reported that Sir Edward had drafted a bill—which was never introduced—which would set out at length the definition of Magna Carta as it prohibited loans and arbitrary imprisonments; but in due course both Houses, upon extensive conferring, hit upon the alternative suggested by Attorney General Heath in the five knights' case—a Petition of Right.

The liberty of the subject, as the great surviving principle of Magna Carta, was extensively debated in both Houses as they moved toward agreement on the Petition. Men were guided by Coke's learning, but the arguments were voiced by many, all addressed to the proposition that the Great Charter and "six statutes" in implementation of its Chapter 29 had made clear beyond any doubt that the liberty of Englishmen was not to be breached by arbitrary action of the government. Sir Edward Littleton emphasized the public or constitutional law of the Charter; Chapter 29, he declared, expressly defined the procedure which must be followed when a subject was charged by the King—it must be by judgment of his peers. John Selden traced the descent of the chapter through the reigns of Edward III to Henry VIII and declared that it was the settled law of the realm that a writ of *habeas corpus* or of *corpus cum causa* "is the chiefest remedy in law for any man that is imprisoned, and the only remedy in law for him that is imprisoned by the special command of the king, or by the lords in council, without showing cause of commitment."*

In the course of the conference with the House of Lords, the judges in the five knights' case were summoned to explain their ruling. All agreed that Magna Carta was binding law, but Chief Justice Hyde was firm in his conviction that there was no "statute that goeth so far that the king may not commit" without cause shown if his judgment found such action warranted. Littleton replied that Parliament did not question the authority of the King to commit a man to prison, but claimed the right and responsibility under the Charter to define and regulate the authority. John Glanville, a brilliant lawyer from Plymouth, also cited the "good old statute called Magna Carta, which declareth and confirmeth the ancient Common Law of the Liberties of England." Thus it proceeded through the long debate, from April to June. Many men spoke of the heritage of the Great Charter which they now held out as an inviolable right of all subjects; it was not, as

* For the details of the statutes implementing Magna Carta throughout the centuries, see the annotations in Part II.

many in later times would agree, an exaggeration of Coke but a general conviction that held it now to be part of the constitution.

To be sure, the great jurist became carried away with himself as the bill progressed toward final adoption; rejecting a proposal of the Lords that the Petition of Right add a clause recognizing the sovereignty of the crown, Coke made his famous peroration:

> I know that prerogative is part of the law, but sovereign power is no Parliamentary word; in my opinion, it weakens Magna Carta and all our statutes; for they are absolute without any saving of sovereign power. And shall we now add to it, we shall weaken the foundation of Law, and then the building must needs fall; take we heed what we yield unto—Magna Carta is such a Fellow, he will have no Sovereign.

So at length, despite efforts by Charles's ministers to keep it from a vote, the Petition of Right was perfected; unable to get Commons to act upon his desperately needed subsidies until it had carried its point, the King at length had to receive the bill. He then inquired of his learned—and compliant—judges what legal effect his consent to the Petition might have; they told him that it would amount to an admission of the illegality of his former action and a concession that the prerogative was limited. Charles then sent an artfully ambiguous reply to the House that he "willeth that right be done according to the laws and customs of the realm," adding that in the matter of liberty of the subject and its preservation "he holds himself as well obliged as of his prerogative." It was a legalistic answer, and the lawyers in Parliament saw through it and refused to accept it. Finally, as the Commons remained insistent, Charles at length called them before him and gave a formal Answer with the ritualistic Norman French formula: *Soit droit fait come est desire*.

The Petition of Right was to be developed by subsequent circumstances into one of the building blocks of the modern constitution; and despite its prompt derogation by the King in practice, it was the greatest advancement of the ancient constitution since the Articles on the Charters in 1300. Like them, the Petition enlarged upon the principles of Magna Carta, whereas the other fundamental statutes cited by the Parliamentarians were essentially reiterations of the original restatement of the law. The form of the Petition was as novel for its day as the Charter of Liberties of 1215 had been; the latter had taken the form of a grant of an estate in land—which, to the thirteenth century, was one of the most important forms of documentary guarantee—while the present bill was an adaptation of a private prayer to the King, now used as a statement of public policy, for the benefit of a law which had been held superseded by the royal prerogative. Its most important feature was the fact that by his Answer Charles I ratified Parliament's (and Coke's) interpretation of the Great Charter as a constitutional limitation upon the modern age, however this interpretation may have departed from the understanding of Magna Carta to its own age. It was also, as the King's own jurists had warned him, a concession that the prerogative was limited, although civil war, execution, and revolution would be required to give the proposition permanence.

The petition in its opening chapters recited laws of Edward I prohibiting arbitrary or forced loans and averred that from the imposition of such loans had flowed the other evils now to be redressed:

> And where also by the statute called *The Great Charter of the Liberties of England,* it is declared and enacted, That no freeman may be taken or imprisoned, or be disseised of his freehold or liberties, or his free customs, or be outlawed or exiled, or in any manner destroyed, but by the lawful judgment of his peers, or by the law of the land;
>
> And in the eight and twentieth year of the reign of King Edward the Third, it was declared and enacted by authority of Parliament, That no man of what estate or condition that he be, should be put out of his land or tenements, nor taken, nor imprisoned, nor disherited, nor put to death without being brought to answer by due process of law;
>
> Nevertheless, against the tenor of the said statutes, and other good laws and statutes of your realm to that end provided, divers of your subjects have of late been imprisoned without any cause showed; and when for

their deliverance they were brought before your justices by your Majesty's writs of *habeas corpus,* there to undergo and receive as the court should order, and their keepers commanded to certify the causes of their detainer, no cause was certified, but that they were detained by your Majesty's special command, signified by the lords of your privy council, and yet were returned back to several prisons, without being charged with anything to which they might make answer according to the law.

Having then protested the quartering of troops in private homes and the imposition of martial law, the Petition concluded with a stipulation that these specific ill practices be terminated and a guarantee against their renewal be granted to the people "as their rights and liberties, according to the laws and statutes of this realm."

Charles undertook to have the last word on the matter; when Parliament met in January 1629, a committee of the House led by John Selden found that, although the King's printer had received the Petition and the King's acceptable Answer of June 7, the Attorney-General after the prorogation on June 26 had called in the printed copies and substituted the unacceptable answer of June 3. There was also a complaint by one Rolles, a merchant member of the House, that he had been seized and arbitrarily imprisoned, subsequent to the acceptance of the Petition, on a refusal to pay the forced loans which Charles was continuing. The House might have debated what further action it could take in the matter, but an even more insistent issue was now being pressed upon them. Puritan groups were becoming ever louder in their complaints against the King's progressive relaxation of strictures upon the English Catholics and were demanding that Parliament press the throne for a more vigorous Protestant policy. Men like Eliot and Selden were not religious zealots; they belonged to a secular generation which was disposed to use the Puritanical excitement to amplify their own political protestations. Now the outcry against high church ceremonials, and outright "Popery," drowned out the other themes; Charles had recently made a unilateral declaration of peace and unity in ecclesiastical affairs which the Puritans insisted opened the way for a possible return to Catholicism.

On this occasion one new member spoke out that he had been informed that one Dr. Alabaster "had preached flat Popery at St. Paul's Cross," upon the order of his bishop, while another cleric, Dr. Manwaring, already censored by the House for his sermons, had been rewarded for his recusant attitude by a rich Church preferment. The speaker was a large man of commanding bearing; a contemporary recalled that his clothes were drab, his linen plain "and not very clean," his face ruddy, and his voice "sharpe and untunable." Hearing him, one member who knew him whispered to another that, "if we should ever come to a breach with the king . . . that sloven in such case will be one of the greatest men in England." The speaker's name was Oliver Cromwell. He represented a new generation of militants who were coming to prominence, men who had grown impatient with the slow progress of the religious and political struggle and were prepared to take the next step beyond the protestations, petitions, and remonstrances of the twenties. It was Cromwell's maiden speech; in the Parliamentary uprising of the forties, he would be heard from again.

The end of this Parliament was now rapidly approaching; seeing that the King was unrepentant and their efforts on the Petition unavailing, the members now determined to read a succession of statements into the record of their own House. When, on March 2, the Speaker delivered to the House a message from the throne commanding adjournment until the following week, the House replied that it had the full determination of its own adjournment. Sir John Eliot then read a proposed remonstrance on the demands of the King for "poundage and tonnage," which, when "not granted by Parliament, is a breach of the fundamental liberties of this kingdom, and contrary to your Majesty's royal Answer to the Petition of Right." The Speaker sought to leave his chair before a question could be put to the House on the remonstrance, but was physically restrained by several members, while the rest of the membership quickly passed three resolutions, against "innovation in religion," against the levying of subsidies of "tonnage and poundage, not being granted by Parliament," and against the voluntary payment of such new levies by any merchant.

Charles came personally to the House of Lords on March 10 to dissolve the Parliament, basing his action upon "the disobedient carriage of the lower House." He then followed the dissolution with a public declaration of some length, defending his actions and giving his own interpretation of the final answer to the Petition of Right. It was not true, Charles insisted, that by his acceptance of the Petition he had abandoned his own right to impose executive levies upon imports and exports—although this was precisely the aim of the Petition as debated in Parliament. The misinterpretations of the Petition and Answer, said Charles, "were raised by men not well distinguishing between well-ordered liberty and licentiousness, as if by our Answer to that Petition we had let loose the reins of our Government." It would be eleven years before another Parliament was summoned. By his Declaration Charles had made clear that he had in no sense changed his view of his prerogatives, and by his actions in the coming decade he would demonstrate that he would not be bound by the Petition.

The King moved swiftly to deal with those responsible for the "disobedient carriage" of the Commons; Selden, Eliot, and several others were singled out for arrest by the Privy Council and proceedings in the Star Chamber readied. After a prolonged legal struggle, the men were sentenced to imprisonment for as long as the King pleased, and it was reported some died in prison unable or unwilling to pay the fines imposed upon them. Others were released upon giving sureties that they would come no nearer the court than ten miles. This quarantine Charles found only partially effective, and he soon felt compelled to issue a Proclamation against the spread of "false rumors" throughout the kingdom that he was "for destroying the liberties of the people."

Sir Edward Coke was not in the final session of Parliament; he had retired to his estate at Stoke Poges to attend the details of the publishing of the first volume of his *Institutes* and to perfect the manuscript for the remaining volumes. He could watch the vigor of the Parliamentary challenge of 1629 with satisfaction, for it demonstrated his own prescription for the proper behaviour

of a Commons man: "every member . . . should have three properties of the elephant: first, that he hath no gall; secondly, that
he is inflexible and cannot bow; thirdly, that he is of a most ripe
and perfect memory." For better or worse, Coke in his own lifetime had observed the last two admonitions to the fullest; there
would be substantial qualification among his critics and friends
as to the first. Parliament, in its session, had paid him the tribute
of insisting upon the full force of his Petition of Right; and in
1631 Charles I would pay a tribute of another sort. Hearing that
Coke was preparing to publish another book—in all likelihood
the second *Institute* with its detailed analysis of Magna Carta
and the great constitutional statutes to which he had always
referred—the King ordered that all Coke's manuscripts once more
be seized. He was, said Charles, "too great an oracle amongst the
people." The fiery old jurist died three years later, but his words
would be heard again and again through the voices of the Revolution; the opening of the first Civil War would be heralded by the
long delayed publishing of the second *Institute*.

With Coke in his grave and Parliament in limbo, Charles I
could congratulate himself that the right (presumably divine
right) had triumphed at last. Eliot died in the Tower; Archbishop
William Laud of Canterbury developed the prerogative courts
of Star Chamber and High Commission to a new level of administrative effectiveness; peace was concluded with France and
Spain; and money continued to be raised by executive levies on
imports and exports as though the Petition had never been. To
be sure, one John Hampden in 1637 challenged the right of the
crown to support the fleet by a levy of "ship money" in various
ports and inland towns, but a divided Court of Exchequer found
in favor of the government. Charles had underestimated, however, the enduring character of both the Puritan movement and
the political and economic aims of the English middle classes;
his attempts to govern without Parliament, without accommodation of the English Puritanical demands, and without an understanding of the even more insistent Protestantism in Scotland,
all were culminating in a fateful and tragic decade to follow.

The Parliament of 1640, like that of 1620, was called after
a long period of unsettled business; Charles, like his father, re-

fused to recognize that there was anything which might concern the members more than the affairs for which he had summoned them. An ill-advised series of punitive expeditions to Scotland had not only met with reverses but had exhausted the extraordinary revenues on which he had relied for independence from Parliament; and a series of brutal punishments directed against Puritan preachers and publicists had outraged the citizens of London and the growing areas of Protestant disaffection in various parts of England. When Parliament convened, it demonstrated at once that it had not abandoned the objectives of the twenties; no subsidies could be considered, declared the veteran John Pym in a lengthy speech, until the abuses of the past decade were redressed. Another member enumerated specific complaints received from half a dozen counties—against ship money, patent monopolies, and prerogative courts. Finally, the long-dead Coke spoke afresh in the words of another member, whose boldness sent a tremor through the very foundation of the throne:

> The case is this: the Charter of our Liberties, called Magna Carta, . . . was but a renovation and restitution of the ancient laws of this kingdom . . . and in the third year of his Majesty's reign that now is, we had more than a confirmation of it; for we had an act declaratory passed, and then, to put it out of all question and dispute for the future, his Majesty by his gracious Answer . . . invested it with the title of Petition of Right. What expositions contrary to that law of right have some men given to the undermining the liberty of the subject with new-invented subtle distinctions, and assuming to themselves a power, . . . out of Parliament to supersede, annihilate and make void the laws of the kingdom?

The speech concluded with the asking of the ominous questions: "What hath been done [in] any way to impeach the liberties of the subject, contrary to the Petition of Right?" and "Who have been the authors and causes of it?" This Parliament and the succeeding one would begin with the traditional practice of indirectly attacking the King by impeaching his ministers; but when Charles then elected to assume all direction of government into his own hands, he himself at last would be the target.

The Parliament of 1640 was dismissed in two months; it was "the Short Parliament." And yet, with no improvement in the military or financial situation, the King within the year had to summon another one—the fateful "Long Parliament" which would continue until Cromwell dismissed it in 1653. On November 7, the veteran Pym once more prepared to intone the grievances which would be heard before the matter of the King's business. The grievances were threefold, he said: against the privileges of Parliament itself, against religion, and against the liberty of the subject. Under the first heading, he cited the disregard of the rights guaranteed to the House, of free speech and of freedom from prosecution afterwards, and of arbitrary dissolution of the session; Parliament, said Pym, "receives a being by the summons, and a civil death by dissolution, not only thereby to die, but to be made *intestabiles*, unable to make their wills." Under the second heading, Popery he found encouraged, contrary to the law, and he recited a variety of Puritanical complaints and added instances of "the encroachment of ecclesiastical jurisdiction."

Under the third heading, Pym enumerated in detail the secular complaints which revealed the variety of royal actions which had bred such bitterness in the realm; the continued practice of patent monopolies for the benefit of favorites and the impoverishment of the buying public; the imposition and continued expansion of the ship-money levies, beyond the needs or uses of national defense and without the consent of Parliament; the revival of the feudal practice of imposing a fine for refusal to accept a knighthood and its attendant obligations, a new device Charles had seized upon to add to his revenues; and another revenue stratagem, the enlarging of the forests in defiance of the first and third chapters of Carta de Foresta, to drive out of lucrative holdings tenants who had enjoyed them under "three or four hundred years of quiet possession." The bill of complaint went on, protesting the "extra judicial declarations of judges, without hearing of counsel or argument" in many criminal matters; the abuses of the prerogative courts which, Pym said, had originated in Parliament's need to have special agencies to which to refer special questions, but which under Charles had become "an instrument of erecting and defending monopolies, to set a face of public good upon things pernicious."

Others echoed Pym's words; the people of the kingdom, said one speaker, "must have ease and justice; ease in their consciences . . . from the intolerable burden of innovation in religion" (by which the Puritan militants always meant a return to old rituals in derogation of their own innovations), and justice in being free "from all illegal arrests and imprisonments against Magna Carta, being our greatest liberties." Ominously the speaker concluded: "But if the people have all these easements, yet if they have not justice, they cannot subsist; justice is to the civil body as food to the natural; if the streams of justice be, by unrighteousness, turned into gall and wormwood, . . . they who drink of these brooks must needs die and perish."

Excitement mounted with the catalogue of protests, and by December—a month after it had convened—the House responded to the Protestant pressure by impeaching Archbishop Laud as "the most advanced of all our Popish bishops." It was the first of a series of proceedings by which Parliament would strike at the King's ministers: Sir Francis Windebank, Secretary of State; Lord Finch, Keeper of the Great Seal; Sir George Ratcliffe, commander of royal armies in Ireland, who was reported planning to move troops to England to support Charles. A torrent of bills now poured from the members in the following weeks: one to ensure regular Parliaments at no greater intervals than three years, disqualification of members who held patent monopolies, proposals to abolish the prerogative courts, and to make executive imposts illegal. A revolution was under way—as yet confined to vehement Parliamentary action, but grimly warning the royalists of the fury behind it. The Earl of Strafford, a onetime Parliamentary critic who had replaced Lord Buckingham as the King's chief adviser, was impeached and eventually executed. London itself was virtually under mob rule, and in Commons the most extreme of the Puritans, led by Cromwell, were out for the blood of Anglican bishops.

The summer months were taken up with the impeachments of various ministers of state and religion; but in the early fall a general rebellion in Ireland presented the question of dispatching an army to restore order in that Catholic stronghold. To raise a military force and place it in the King's hands would be to invite an armed reprisal against Parliament itself, which had now for almost a year held control of the government. The alternative was to stipulate that Parliament should control the militia and approve the officers to be appointed to the army. To effectuate this, and to recapitulate the whole body of grievances which the revolutionists intended to have accommodated, Commons by a narrow vote in November 1641 passed the Grand Remonstrance, which was presented to Charles on December 1. The document restated all the complaints of the earlier sessions, vigorously condemned the failure to honor the Petition of Right and the effort to circumvent the ancient Charter rights, and insisted upon the abolition of all special courts, executive powers of levying duties, and other actions on matters of state independent of Parliament.

Charles recognized that by this extreme summary of demands the revolutionaries intended to destroy the prerogatives entirely; and he realized that the time had come to make a stand. His first attempt was a failure; he sought to break into the House and arrest Pym and other ringleaders, but friends among the Parliamentarians had sent warning ahead, and these men escaped into the seething and hostile mass of London itself. The King and his party thereupon departed the city and prepared for war; so did Parliament, but the spring and early summer were taken up with the drawing of battle lines, as men quickly moved from one camp to the other. In June 1642 the Puritan core of the House sent a "Humble Petition" and nineteen propositions to the King; they were essentially a rephrasing of the Grand Remonstrance, with a more explicit demand that all appointments of ministers be approved by both houses, that "great affairs of the kingdom . . . as concerned the public . . . are proper for the high court of Parliament" to debate, and that all members of the government must take an oath prescribed by Parliament to uphold the Petition of Right.

The legacy of Sir Edward Coke was manifest in the stubborn insistence upon upholding the great constitutional statement of 1628, and now, on the eve of the appeal to arms, his voice spoke again. The Long Parliament was aware of the impounded manuscripts and the pertinence of the "comment on Magna Carta" represented in the second of his *Institutes*. In December 1640 a motion was made in the House "to recover Sir Edward Coke's . . . bookes . . . taken from him during his last illness." Several weeks later Commons was informed that the King had agreed to deliver the papers to one of Coke's executors. It was early in the session, and Charles may have felt that this was a small concession which might improve the temper of the House. In May 1641 Coke's heir was authorized by Parliament to publish the second *Institute*, and it appeared early in 1642. The commentary on Magna Carta, like much of Coke's earlier work on feudal law, had a number of erroneous or exaggerated statements in it; he was writing to prove that the Great Charter had binding force in his own time, and in the course of his effort he often overstated his own case. It was obvious that he had written what the revolutionaries wanted to read, for he assured them repeatedly that there was not to be found in the Great Charter, "any saving at all for the king, his heirs, or Successors."

Parliament took the initiative in asserting the constitutional force of Magna Carta in publications supplementary to the second *Institute;* in 1643 it authorized printing of William Prynne's *Soveraigne Power of Parliament and Kingdom;* a student of law and religion, Prynne already had attracted wide notice—and stern punishment—for his pamphleteering in favor of Puritan and Parliament. He had already lost both ears in the pillory as corporeal retribution for his journalistic activities, and had twice received life sentences of imprisonment, each subsequently commuted. He bore on his body the evidence of royalist reprisal, and in his personality the fanatic convictions of the revolutionary.

The *Soveraigne Power* began with an acknowledgment of its debt to Coke for demonstrating that the Great Charter and Charter of the Forest "are both fundamental, perpetual & unalterable." It then went on to argue that the ultimate authority of government rested in the high court (legislative, administrative, and judicial) of Parliament and that the king could not constitutionally withhold approval of a bill which passed both Houses "because it is point blanke against the very letter of Magna Carta (the ancient fundamental Law of the Realm, confirmed in at least sixty [!] Parliaments) Chapter 29 *We shall deny, we shall deferre* (both in future tense) *to no man* (much less to the whole Parliament and Kingdome, in denying or deferring to passe such necessary publike Bills) *justice or right,* a law which *in terminis* takes cleane away the King's pretended absolute negative voyce to these Bills we now dispute of."

Prynne's was manifestly a propaganda piece; he had virtually doubled Coke's generalized comment that some thirty parliamentary confirmations—an underestimate—had been accorded Magna Carta. His argument clearly revealed the ultimate Parliamentary objectives in this House: nothing less than the sovereign power in its own right. The Parliamentary revolutionaries were becoming more aggressive with each passing month; in March 1642 they had enacted their first ordinances (calling for raising a militia) "without the king's name and authority," and they had earlier abolished the system of prerogative courts and initiated impeachment proceedings against a number of the royal judges. A loan of £100,000 for the national defense had already been negotiated with the citizens of London, and a series of skirmishes had been fought between royalists and Parliamentary forces. Oliver Cromwell had been one of the first to enlist in a cavalry detachment guarding eastern England in the fall of 1642. In the summer of 1643, after an alliance with the Scottish Presbyterians, Parliament ordered its own Great Seal. From Bridewell Prison, in this same year, came an anonymous book, *Briefe Collections Out of Magna Carta; or, The Knowne Good Old Laws of England;* its theme was the one made familiar by Prynne: the king by the Charter was prevented from denying freedom from arbitrary arrests to his subjects or altering the meaning of laws enacted by Parliament.

This was the argument steadfastly maintained by the Parliamentarians throughout the four years of the first Civil War, to the capture of Charles I in June 1646. When, with the King as prisoner, Parliament laid its terms before him in the proposition of New Castle, it was in effect a demand for complete surrender of his prerogatives. Charles rejected the proposition. He was now counting on the widening divisions in Parliament and the restlessness of the Puritan army to destroy his enemies while he bided his own time. Cromwell, who had risen to the command of the army, watched the political and sectarian differences multiply in Parliament and also bided his time; he perceived that the disciplined, triumphant, and morally persuaded force represented in the army was quickly acquiring, if only by default, the balance of power in the realm. "It is our duty," he had written to a fellow Puritan leader in the midst of the Civil War, "to sympathize in all mercies; that we praise the Lord together in chastisements or trials, so that we may sorrow together." Now, in the summer of 1647, Cromwell and his son-in-law, Henry Ireton, undertook to mediate between the extremes.

Parliament rejected Cromwell's overtures because they seemed to concede too much to the King; and in any event the Houses were still arguing amongst themselves as to whether the entire episcopal structure of the Church of England should be abolished, and what form of theocracy they would have in its place. The radical element in the army were calling for complete democracy—older leaders called it anarchy—in secular as in religious affairs. Confusion mounted daily, and in December Charles found his chance and escaped to the Isle of Wight. There he struck a bargain with the Scots; if they would provide him with an army and restore his throne, he would decree England to be a Presbyterian state. Royalists flew to arms again, and by the spring of 1648 the second Civil War was in full force. Charles and the Scots made headway throughout the north; the Puritan army proved its fighting prowess, but had no political confirmation for what it undertook; and Parliament, fearing the army as much as it feared the Scots, sought to make it own terms with the King.

Between the ambivalent policies of Charles, the unpopular Presbyterianism of the Scots, and the now witless inaction of Parliament, a military dictatorship was coming into being as of necessity. Cromwell's troops had driven clear to Edinburgh on the one front and were at the gates of London on the other; the hand of the Lord, said the Puritans, had guided them to this hour and would deliver their enemies into their hands. In November the army served a long remonstrance on Parliament, demanding that the King now be brought to trial for having made war on his own people. With Charles recaptured, on January 27, 1649, the High Court of Justice summoned for this occasion passed sentence of death on the sovereign; its charges were reminiscent of a quarter of a century of Parliamentary complaints: Charles, being "trusted with a limited power to govern by and according to the law of the land and not otherwise," had been guilty of asserting "an unlimited and tyrannical power to rule according to his will, and to overthrow the rights and liberties of the people . . . which by the fundamental constitutions of this kingdom were reserved on the people's behalf in the right and power of frequent and successive parliaments or national meetings in council."

It could only have come to this, for Charles Stuart could not conceive of a royal government in which the king was not beyond accountability to any other power in the realm. As for his enemies, their motives and their concepts of government and polity were mixed; men like Cromwell had the vehement intolerance of all liturgical religions and institutional precedents that made them contemptuous of the royalists, the Anglicans and the Parliamentary sectarians alike. They saw government as a divine responsibility for a Puritan elect, who ruled on the people's behalf; the concept of a Protectorate was already taking form. Charles they considered "a tyrant, traitor and murderer, a public enemy of the commonwealth." Their own vindictiveness would consume them in the end, and already the way was being prepared by Charles himself, as he proceeded with final dignity to the last drama on the scaffold. For many in England already were repulsed at the Puritan intransigence and looked upon him as a martyr, perhaps even as a saint; something noble in the heritage of the kingdom, if not in the King, was dying with him—and he seemed at the end to sense that men would sicken at the drab pietism of his conquerors and look back to the monarchy as a symbol of their own peculiar destiny. He prepared for the axeman by removing his cloak and his medal of St. George, handing them to his priest with a single admonition: "Remember."

The Puritans sought to slay the kingdom with the King; on May 19, 1649, the House of Commons, having abolished the monarchy and the House of Lords, proclaimed that England "should thenceforth be governed as a commonwealth and free state by the supreme authority of this nation, the representatives of the people in Parliament." Behind the truncated Parliament stood the army, and at the head of the army stood Cromwell. Secure in England, the General now took his forces to Ireland, and with a succession of victories followed by a slaughter of prisoners as a warning, the country was subdued by the following year. Cromwell then crossed back to England and marched on Scotland, where Charles II, recognized as his father's successor, was to be crowned King of the Scots on New Year's Day, 1651. Cromwell eventually made contact with the new royalist armies and at Worcester that spring surrounded and destroyed them. The new King managed to escape and in the course of many adventures reached France; Scotland was put under military occupation, with General George Monck in command.

Having beaten down their enemies, the Puritans now turned to the organizing of a new constitution. Cromwell dismissed the old Parliament in 1653, and a hand-picked Puritan "Parliament of Saints" was returned that same summer. The Protestant Commonwealth had operated, with little to show for itself, for four years; for another four it would be under the Protectorate of Cromwell, taking its authority from the Instrument of Government drafted by this new Parliament. The Lord Protector was accorded the executive power of the state; triennial Parliaments were provided for; and religious freedom was granted to all but Roman Catholics and Anglicans. Militant theocrats had no intention of giving their old enemies any quarter; men spoke fair words about a republic, but the manifest control of the state was under the mouths of Roundheads' muskets. Cromwell kept busy stamping out real or alleged insurrection, dissolving uncooperative Parliaments in 1655 and 1658 with as much exasperation as the King he had executed; and in September of that year, worn out from his twenty years of war and state experiments, the Lord Protector died.

Although Oliver Cromwell had undertaken to preserve the continuity of his government by making his son Richard his successor, the arid Puritan constitution was rapidly shriveling into oblivion. Richard was, like the many English kings who succeeded strong fathers, unequal to the task thrust upon him, and the Parliament which met in January 1659 was to preside at the liquidation of the Protectorate. Extreme sectarians sought to seize control of the House of Commons and substitute a rigorous Protestant dictatorship; the army rose in defiance and recalled the old Rump Parliament of the Commonwealth; but these men brought back into power with them the old Parliamentary dread of military despotism and called upon General Monck in Scotland to restore some kind of order to the state. It was evident that the republic was intellectually bankrupt; Monck would be one of its liquidators, and Charles II would be recalled to a chastened monarchy.

The third Stuart king recognized that absolutism had died with his father; at Breda in Holland in the early spring of 1660 he published a Declaration that he sought a means whereby God might "put us into a quiet and peaceable possession of that our right, with as little blood and damage to our people as possible. Nor do we desire more to enjoy what is ours, than that all our subjects may enjoy what by law is theirs, by a full and entire administration of justice throughout the land." The weary Parliament, already restored to two houses in the confused changes of the previous year, resolved "that they do own and declare that according to the ancient and fundamental laws of this kingdom, the government is and ought to be by king, Lords and Commons." In May Charles crossed to Dover and was escorted to Westminster by General Monck, soon to become the Earl of Albemarle.

In its eleven years of existence the Interregnum had contributed little to the art of government, and whatever the quality of the Restoration under Charles II, men felt that it could not but improve on the gloomy life under the theocracy. A general revulsion of the regicide heritage swept over the land; Parliament ordered that "the carcasses" of Cromwell, Ireton, and the other powers of the dictatorship "be with all expedition taken up and drawn upon a hurdle to Tyburn, and there hanged up in their coffins for some time, and after that buried under the said gallows." In their efforts to purge themselves of the dark past, men hoped to merit a better life in the new monarchy.

Charles spent his twenty-five years on the throne in cautious revival of royalist institutions; he dreaded to suffer his father's fate, as Henry III had lived all his life in the shadow of John's.

Circumstances thus combined to nurture a balance between "king, Lords and Commons" in which the seedbed for a constitutional monarchy was being prepared. The principles of the Petition of Right were ratified, after forty years in which the heat of the sessions in which they were forged had cooled; an act for convening of Parliament "once in three years at the least" was adopted in 1664; an Act of Indemnity and Oblivion had sought to remove civil disabilities from former royalists and to restore the ecclesiastical organization of the traditional Church of England. Even the Plague of 1665 and the Fire of 1666, which ravaged London, offered a kind of purge of the past.

As if to acknowledge that the feudal age, with its vestigial rules of land tenure as well as prerogatives, had been expunged with the Restoration, Charles's first Parliament in 1660 abolished a vast catalogue of ancient property laws, including most of the provisions on wardship, marriage, and military tenure as these applied to landholding. In the generation of civil disturbance just ended, new and complex forms of conveying or preserving titles to property had been devised as a safeguard against decrees of forfeiture or foreclosure while the real owners were in prison, in arms, or in exile. From the problems of restoring estates to rightful owners in the first years of the new monarchy, it became evident, as it had to Edward I, that certain claims could only be determined if the individuals themselves took the pains to secure an enduring record of their rights. In 1677, accordingly, Parliament devised an Act for the Prevention of Frauds and Purgeries, which was to affect all future contract law under the generic title of the Statute of Frauds. By its terms, promises affecting a wide variety of goods were required to be put in writing and properly signed and witnessed, if an individual intended to claim them as a right to be protected by the law. In particular this referred to the law of real property.

Two years later, Parliament contributed the second great constitutional proposition of the century, in the *Habeas Corpus* Act of 1679. It climaxed a long series of efforts over many generations to enlarge upon the old common-law writ, evolved first in the struggle of the royal courts of the fourteenth century to remove cases from the local courts to their own bench. When the struggle for jurisdiction had been won over the inferior courts, the writ had then been used to combat the competition of Chancery and later of prerogative courts. Only when Elizabeth and the early Stuarts began committing political recalcitrants without formal process did *habeas corpus* become recognized as the chief safeguard of personal liberty. The last Parliament of Charles I had enacted a statute on the subject in 1649, but the Interregnum had unsettled the conditions to such an extent that it had never had any significant effect; under a series of prosecutions by which the disruptions of the Civil Wars were being punished and the expropriated estates of old royalists and ecclesiastics were being restored, the threat of renewed arbitrary commitments loomed again upon the realm and accounted for the action of 1679.

Because "great delays had been used" by those to whose custody accused persons had been committed, ran the Act, "and by other shifts to avoid their yielding obedience to such writs [as *habeas corpus*], contrary to their duty and the known laws of the land, whereby many of the king's subjects had been and hereafter may be long detained in prison, in such cases where by law they are bailable," it was to be provided henceforth that any judge was to issue the writ in any case where the prisoner had not been committed by lawful means. All who were shown the writ were promptly to produce the person named therein, and the courts were to set him at liberty, pending his formal trial, unless the court itself ordered his recommittal.

The last ten years of Charles II's reign saw another dimension of government develop in the groups which came soon to be known as the Whig and Tory parties. The Cavalier Parliament elected at the accession to the throne was royalist and Anglican, a reaction to the Puritan excesses of the past twenty years. The diminishing passions of anti-Catholicism were fanned back to life by a succession of statutes enacted in the first fifteen years of the Restoration which gradually removed more and more of the former disabilities laid on the old order. The King's brother, James, was converted to the Roman faith, and since Charles himself was childless, the old Puritan party was aghast at the prospect that a Catholic king would some time mount the throne again. Then, in 1678, burst the bomb of the "Popish plot," a malignant fraud concocted by an unfrocked cleric, Titus Oates, which fed the mounting Protestant hysteria. It was said that the conspirators would kill Charles himself and re-establish a papal government under his brother, the Duke of York. Cromwellian veterans boasted drunkenly in London taverns of the coming of a third Civil War, and a number of recently restored Roman Catholic leaders were seized and persecuted. The rabid Puritans, delegating to themselves the role of patriots, called themselves the "Country Party" or Whigs. The royalists, cast temporarily into a defensive role, came to be called the Tories.

In the mounting excitement of the eighties, three successive Parliaments were dissolved for attempting to enact legislation to exclude a Roman Catholic from the succession. Having made great capital out of the Oates fabrication of a Jesuit conspiracy, the Whigs now concocted a conspiracy of their own; an illegitimate son of Charles II—James Scot, Duke of Monmouth—was put forward as the rightful heir to the throne. A Protestant bastard, the extremists argued, was preferable to a legitimate Catholic as the successor to the second Charles. Predominantly Protestant though the country had become, it was not ready to accept this alternative; the last years of the reign experienced a gradual subsiding and an acceptance of the fact that the Duke of York would be the next king. In 1685 Charles died, and the fourth and last of the Stuarts came to the throne. While Englishmen generally felt that the late reign had justified the Restoration, they understood that the King himself had not distinguished the age. An epitaph written in jest at an earlier period of the regime was now recalled:

> Here lies a great and mighty king,
>   Whose promise none rely'd on;
> He never said a foolish thing,
>   Nor ever did a wise one.

Much less could be said for James II; he did nothing wise, and most of what he said and did was foolish or foolhardy. The Puritan extremists had momentarily overreached themselves with their loud ranting against a Roman Catholic monarch. James was fifty-one when he was crowned, and his only children, both daughters, were married to Protestant stalwarts: Mary, the elder, was the wife of William of Orange, and Anne, the younger, had married Prince George of Denmark. Had the new King been more intelligent in these circumstances, he would have given the disgruntled Whig minority no opportunity to raise a new tumult. But James was neither astute nor capable of overriding even a prostrate opposition; at his only Parliament, which by his own estimate had ten royalists for every dissenter, he arrogantly asserted his intention to stamp out the last vestige of Puritan reform.

Following the practice of long-dead kings—whose own fate might have been a warning—James vested the offices of Chief Justice and Chancellor in a single man, the notorious George Jeffreys, whose wholesale extirpation of insurrectionists in the realm became known as the "bloody assizes." Jeffreys also became head of an ecclesiastical commission to reorganize the discipline of the Church of England, thereby accomplishing for James II what Charles I, for all his ineptitude in the religious crisis, had not been able to do: he drove the Anglicans into the Protestant camp. Issuing a Declaration of Indulgence, by which he purported to offer religious freedom to all groups, James ordered it to be read in all churches of the realm in the spring of 1688; but seven bishops of the Church of England, led by the Archbishop of Canterbury, refused to carry out the command, citing the Parliamentary Act which barred such a declaration. The fundamental question was not the substance of the Declaration itself, but whether the King by his own action could nullify a statute of Parliament. At the trial of the seven bishops, all London—which once had held all Anglicans as bad as Roman Catholics—turned their acquittal into a holiday, and the outbreak of rejoicing spread like wildfire across the kingdom.

It was an unmistakable sign that James by his own arrogance and shortsightedness had thrown away the support which his people had been willing to offer him. William of Orange, now intensely interested in the events which might hasten the day when his wife, the Princess Mary, might come to the throne, made plans to cross to England, and sent a declaration of his desire to offer genuine religious and political freedom. James played his last card, a characteristically crude one; it was announced in July that the Queen had given birth to a son, thus insuring a Catholic successor to the throne. No one believed it who did not wish to believe it. The reported pregnancy was of remarkably short duration; the Princess Anne was not present to examine her mother; and Archbishop William Sancroft, who was required to be present at the birth of an heir to the throne to certify its validity, was still under restraint in the Tower for his role in the case of the seven bishops.

Things moved rapidly to the denouement. At the joint invitation of leading Whigs and Tories, the Prince of Orange landed in Devonshire in November, and on every side, as predicted, men flocked to him. James sought to summon a host, but officers charged with putting the realm into a state of defense deserted to William; the Princess Anne joined her sister's cause, and the spurious baby prince—doomed to wander ineffectually through history as the "Old Pretender"—was not even seriously considered. James sought to flee, remembering his father's fate, but even in this he was inept. He was caught—to the embarrassment of his son-in-law, who refused to see him and arranged for his deportation to France in a fishing boat. It was the final ludicrous episode in his brief and inconsistent reign, and a comic relief to the bloodless but Glorious Revolution.

Men sensed that a fateful transition was approaching its climax; at the moment, another Interregnum was in being, but no one relished the proposition that the Restoration should be replaced by another Commonwealth or Protectorate. Rather, on December 21, sixty lords gathered in council with William and proposed a convention to settle a form of government. It was evident that this government would continue to be monarchical, and it was evident that William and his wife would be offered the crown; but all were concerned that a constitutional framework at last be devised out of the disparate efforts of the past generations. The convention Parliament opened on January 22, 1689, and heard a letter from the Prince of Orange, who was acting as administrator of national affairs. "It now lieth with you," wrote William, "to lay the foundation of a firm security for your religion, your laws and your liberties." The first business was to determine the status of the throne itself, and members cited the cases of Edward IV, Henry VI, and Richard II to support the conclusion that "King James II, having voluntarily forsaken the government, it is a voluntary demise [laying down] in him." It was eventually voted to declare the throne vacant; but before electing the new occupant, it was necessary to draft a fundamental statement of the constitution, for, said one member, "all the world will laugh at us, if we make half a settlement." It was time, said another, "to make a new Magna Carta."

And thus it came about that on February 13, 1689, at Whitehall, the Prince and Princess of Orange were escorted to the step under the canopy of state, and in the presence of Parliament a Declaration of Rights was read to them. Upon the Prince's acquiescence in the Declaration, on behalf of himself and his wife, they were proclaimed William III and Mary II. The coronation took place on April 11, and by the end of the year, after Parliament again went into convention, the Declaration was perfected into a statutory Bill of Rights. Together with the Petition of Right, including its chapter restating and preserving the constitutional principle of Magna Carta, and with the *Habeas Corpus* Act of 1679 and the final Act of Settlement to come in 1701, the English constitution had been perfected. The Bill of Rights began with a recital of the grievances for which James II had lost his throne— an enumeration which would serve as a model for men in a distant city in England's New World colony of Pennsylvania eighty-six years later—and having then declared a number of specific rights "as their ancestors in like case have usually done," the Bill declared these to be "the true, ancient and indubitable rights and liberties of the people of this kingdom."

So they were, because Parliament, now the supreme political and legal authority of the realm, had said they were; because William in his earlier actions and by his acceptance of the Declaration the previous February had ratified the proposition; because Sir Edward Coke by his eloquent and overpowering advocate's brief for Magna Carta and its heritage had persuaded the seventeenth century that the ancient constitution had had an unbroken continuity to their own day; and above all, because the constitution which now was asserted reflected the genius and conviction of a far larger proportion of the people of England. If a charter of liberties, drafted by and for a small elite of the thirteenth century, could be accepted and adapted by a much broader body of men in this age, who was to say that it could not in the future be extended to all men?

The great struggle toward a limited monarchy as well as a "mixed kingdom" had reached its climax. In his grave at Stoke Poges, Sir Edward Coke could now sleep peacefully.

VII

"The Rights of Englishmen"

WILLIAM PENN, who accepted from Charles II his vast proprietary grant of New World properties as the opportunity for a "Holy Experiment" in political and religious freedom, was at pains to make clear to all prospective colonists the obligations they carried with them to the new Quaker commonwealth. In 1682, in the preface to his first Frame of Government, he described the twofold mission of "the divine right of government" (in contrast to the divine right of kings, a doctrine which presumably had died on the block with Charles I more than thirty years before): "first, to terrify evil-doers; secondly, to cherish those that do well, which gives government a life beyond corruption and makes it as durable in the world as good men shall be." Good laws and good men were both necessary elements in a good society, Penn concluded, for "though good laws do well, good men do better."

He spoke from the harsh lessons of his own experience, from the welter of political and religious contention through which England had passed in this century of civil wars, regicide, restoration, and revolution, and from the perennial hope which New World colonization held out to men despairing of witnessing, in their own lifetimes, the full realization of their various reforms in the land of their birth. The seventeenth century had been an age of violent breaking with the past and at the same time one of persistent attempts to reclaim from their past what men believed was a heritage of fundamental rights. The first charter of the Virginia Company, issued in April of 1606, had assured the settlers that they took with them "all liberties, franchises, and immunities" to which they were entitled at home; but this meant

208

one thing to James I and quite another to some of the Parliamentarians, already opposing the King's claims for his prerogative, who signed their names to the list of "adventurers" who would help to plant the colony.

James, as well as his son and grandsons, had viewed the settlements in English North America in various lights as their own shifting circumstances made necessary; at the outset, it was a matter of chartering trading companies which would assume all of the risks and return some of the profits anticipated to the crown. Later, it was a case of granting enormous tracts of wilderness to favorite followers (or, as in the case of Penn's father, to those to whom great debts were owed) which they could rule in the manner of feudal baronies if they were so disposed. Ultimately, most of the colonies would become proprietaries of the crown, with the consequent question of whether their rights of local self-government were a matter of benevolence from the king or an inherent privilege traceable to the most fundamental laws of the national history.

This, of course, was the basic issue which was threshed out in England itself in the course of the seventeenth-century struggle between Parliament and the Stuarts. In the same year that the Jamestown colony had been founded, John Cowell's *Interpreter* had been published in London, tracing the legal heritage back to Magna Carta on which all law was "thought in some part to depend." The Pilgrim Fathers—although they of course were not aware of it—sailed from Plymouth the year before the Protestation of the House of Commons reminded the King that "the liberties, franchises, privileges, and jurisdictions of Parliament are the ancient and undoubted birthright and inheritance of the subjects of England." In 1629, when the Charter of the Massachusetts Bay Company was drafted, the Commons under Sir Edward Coke's leadership had forced upon Charles I the acquiescence in the Petition of Right. The Massachusetts Body of Liberties was drawn up in 1641, the same year that Parliament abolished the prerogative Court of Star Chamber and the year before the Long Parliament began the English Civil War. Rhode Island and Providence Plantations obtained a charter from Charles II three years after the Restoration laid the foundation for a limited monarchy; and three years before Penn wrote his Frame of Government, Parliament had passed the *Habeas Corpus* Act.

Not that any of these had a direct bearing on royal policy as it concerned the American colonies; indeed, the Stuart kings both before and after the civil wars had come increasingly to assume that the New World possessions were if anything the last preserve of the prerogative. Charles II paid tribute to Virginia's resistance to the Commonwealth, reputedly, by calling it his "Old Dominion"—and promptly made huge grants of the colony's lands to the men who had been most faithful to him during his exile. To his brother, the Duke of York and the unhappy James II to be, he gave a territory between the Hudson and the Delaware Rivers almost as vast in area as England itself. Until the colonies became independent, the English crown assumed the right to disallow acts of provincial assemblies long after the Bill of Rights of 1689 had taken such power out of the royal hands in respect of acts of Parliament.

But in the long view of political history, what counted was the convictions of the colonists themselves, born of the conflicts and experiments of seventeenth-century England and the hopes and objectives they themselves planted in the New World. The right to create a government where none existed might be born of necessity, as in the case of the Mayflower Compact, drafted by men who found their landfall had been beyond the limits of the Virginia Company and who covenanted with themselves "into a Civil Body Politick, for our better ordering and preservation . . . and by virtue hereof to enact, constitute and frame such just and equal Laws, Ordinances, Acts, Constitutions and Offices, from time to time, as shall be thought most meet and convenient for the general good of the Colony." But in any event, from the earliest times the settlers insisted upon the rights they believed belonged to all Englishmen: the privilege of petitioning for redress of grievances, freedom from arrest and imprisonment except for cause shown and by due process of law, and the right to limit taxation to the levies authorized by elected representative assemblies. From the first colonial legislature, which met at Jamestown in 1619, to the first Continental Congress at Philadelphia in 1774, the theme was consistent.

Several of the earliest colonial spokesmen on the subject were men thoroughly indoctrinated in English legal principles, although not all of them were prescient advocates of democracy. John Winthrop, a product of the Inns of Court, articulated the authoritarian posture of the New England theocracy when he wrote, in 1645, of the distinction between natural and civil liberty; the one, he maintained, "is common to man and beasts," and "is a liberty to evil as well as to good," while the other "is the proper end and object of authority and cannot subsist without it." This authority, interpreted and applied by the Puritan oligarchy, was repudiated by Roger Williams, who in his youth had been a protégé of the great Coke himself; in a book published the year before Winthrop's, with the forbidding title of *The Bloudy Tenent, of Persecution, for cause of Conscience,* he enunciated the proposition "that the sovereign, original and foundation of civil power lies in the people," and that "a people may erect and establish what form of government seems to them most meet for their civil condition."

Coke's teaching manifestly made a profound impact upon the men most intimately concerned with the planting of the New World colonies, as it did upon legal and political theorists attempting to reshape the government of England itself. In 1642 Parliament had at last effected the posthumous publication of his second *Institute,* with its detailed and occasionally imaginative exposition of the Great Charter and the subsequent organic statutes of earlier times. Although William Penn disclaimed any formal legal knowledge, he was able to quote the author of the second *Institute* with great effect in his defense at the Old Bailey in 1670, following his indictment for tumultuous assembly after a meeting of the Society of Friends. He reminded the court that "lord Coke . . . tells us, That Common-Law is common right, and that Common Right is the Great Charter-Privileges," and went on to cite "the 14th and 29th chapters of the Great Charter of England, which say, 'No freeman ought to be amerced but by the oath of good and lawful men of the vicinage.'"

Penn, who had suffered so much for his religious nonconformity, and who ardently supported George Fox in his dreams of Quaker colonization in America, saw in Magna Carta as Coke had revealed it an invaluable guide to the great society he now had the chance to fashion. In 1687, five years after he had drafted his Frame of Government for Pennsylvania, he arranged for the publication in Philadelphia of a documentary tract entitled, *The Excellent Privilege of Liberty & Property; Being the Birth-Right of the Free-Born Subjects of England.* In an introduction signed "Philopolites," he advised that it was written "for the information and understanding (what is their natural Right and Liberties) of such who may not have Liesure from their Plantations to read large Volumes," but for whom "it may raise up noble Resolutions . . . not to give away anything of Liberty and Property that at present they do (or of right as Loyal English Subjects, ought to) enjoy, but take up the good Example of our Ancestors, and understand, that it is easy to part with or give away great Privileges, but hard to gain, if once lost."

Five documents, with commentary upon the first three, were reprinted in the little volume: Magna Carta, in the definitive reissue by Henry III in 1225; the Charter of Confirmation of Edward I in 1297; the Statute *De Tallagio non Concedendo,* or restraints upon taxation, of the same year; the Patent issued to Penn in 1681; and the grant of the Charter of Liberties to Pennsylvania— an adaptation of the Great Charter itself to the needs of his own colony. The commentary reflected a number of years of lay advocacy in reliance on Magna Carta according to Coke; in 1675 Penn had written his conclusion that the rights and privileges of Englishmen preserved by the Great Charter were of three kinds: "I. *Ownership,* consisting of liberty and property. In that it supposes *Englishmen* to be *free,* there is *liberty;* next, that they have *freeholds,* there is property. II. That they have the *voting of their own laws;* for that was an ancient free custom, . . . and all such customs are expressly confirmed by this *Great Charter;* besides, the people helped to make it. III. An influence upon, and a real *share in, the judiciary power,* in the execution and application thereof."

If Penn accepted Coke as uncritically as his contemporaries did, there were the same extenuating circumstances; the revolutionaries of the seventeenth century had long since persuaded themselves that their liberties derived from an ancient constitution—and had not asked themselves whether the words of such a constitution, embodied in Magna Carta and the great organic statutes, had meant the same thing to the Middle Ages as they now wished them to mean to their own time. There was also the fact that Charles I in his Answer to the Petition of Right, and Charles II in accepting the terms of his own restoration, had ratified the new meanings expressed in the second *Institute*. James II was in the midst of his brief and dissension-wracked reign, and the Glorious Revolution was in the immediate offing, when Penn published *The Excellent Privilege*. Good ancient laws, rather than present autocratic kings, were the hope of the realm; Penn quoted Coke to this point: "A greater inheritance is deriv'd to every one of us from our Laws than from our Parents; For without the former, what would the latter signifie?"

In commending Magna Carta to "the Free-men, Planters and Inhabitants in this Country," Penn paraphrased the second *Institute:*

> This excellent Law holds first place in our Statute Books; 'tis called *Magna Carta,* or the great Charter, not in respect of its bulk, but in regard to the great importance and weight of the matters therein contained; it is also stiled, *Carta Libertatum Regni,* The Charter of the Liberties of the Kingdom; . . . because it makes and preserves the People Free. . . .
>
> Likewise, though it be said here, *That the King hath given and granted these Liberties,* yet they must not be understood as mere emanations of Royal Favour, or new Bounties granted, which the People could not justly challenge, or had a right unto before; for the Lord Cook in divers places asserts, and all Lawyers know, that this Charter is for the most part only Declaratory of the principal ground of the Fundamental Laws and Liberties of England; no new Freedom is hereby granted, but a Restitution of such as lawfully they had before.

Penn then called his readers' attention to "the 29th Chapter. NO FREEMAN SHALL BE TAKEN, &c. Deserves to be written in Letters of Gold; and I have often wondered the Words thereof are not Inscribed in Capitals on all our Courts of Judicature,

Town-Halls, and most publick Edifices; they are the *Elixir* of our *English Freedoms,* the Store-House of all our Liberties."

The Proprietor sought to match these high-sounding words to practice; more than most grantees of New World colonies, he took a deep interest in the welfare of his colony, and twice made two-year visits to it, in 1681-83 and again in 1699-1701. On his second trip, he urged his freeholders to express themselves on any improvement in the several frames of government which had been proposed: ". . . if in the constitution by charter there is anything that jars, change it," he admonished them. The Charter of Privileges which resulted was to content the colony until the coming of the Revolution. It was a sweeping, Americanized version of the English Bill of Rights, and in several points went boldly beyond the common law; both the right to counsel, which would not be universally guaranteed in England for more than a century, and the right of defendants to summon witnesses in criminal cases, which was currently under debate in Parliament, were written into the Pennsylvania Charter. The fundamental rule of Magna Carta, on due process of law, was also reiterated with reference to "the ordinary course of justice."

The Pennsylvania Charter of 1701 thus climaxed a century in which the New World colonies devised their own native constitutional systems, colored by the issues which had agitated the mother country at the time of their own settlement. None had as benevolent and conciliatory a patron as William Penn; most of them had to wrest concessions from a distant crown minister or from a governor or lieutenant-governor bringing with him his own instructions from Westminster, which often were at variance with local custom and understanding. But virtually every colony, within a century of the Jamestown settlement, had drafted its own statement of its fundamental liberties in deliberate emulation of the contemporary political arguments in the mother country, and in firm commitment to Magna Carta's Chapter 29 which Penn had so lavishly endorsed.

"No mans life shall be taken away, no mans honour or good name shall be stayned, no mans person shall be arrested, restrayned, banished, dismembred, nor any ways punished, . . . no mans goods or estaite shall be taken away from him nor any way indammaged under colour of law or Countenance of Authoritie, unless it be by vertue or equitie of some express law of the Country waranting the same," ran the first article of the Massachusetts Body of Liberties in 1641. Many of the feudal provisions of Magna Carta itself were abolished in this document, twenty years before the first Parliament of Charles II would take a similar step, while the writ of *habeas corpus,* guaranteed by the Petition of Right but honored almost entirely in the breach in England until the Restoration, was firmly insisted upon. Two copies of "Sir Edward Cooke upon Magna Carta" had been ordered purchased by the General Court to aid in drafting the Body of Liberties, and when in 1646 the Court sent an address to the Long Parliament, it was able to show in parallel columns that Massachusetts had preserved (and, in fact, had improved upon) "the fundamental and common laws of England."

The Connecticut Code of 1650 incorporated substantial parts of the Body of Liberties, including the paraphrase of the chapters of Magna Carta. So did the New York Charter of Liberties of 1683, which quoted the Great Charter almost verbatim: "That no freeman shall be taken and imprisoned or be disseized of his freehold or liberty or free customs, or be outlawed or exiled, or any other ways destroyed, nor shall be passed upon, adjudged or condemned but by the lawful judgment of his peers and by the law of this province. Justice nor right shall neither be sold, denied, or deferred to any man within this province."*

It was logical enough, therefore, for the average colonial in the eighteenth century to assume that he lived under a system of legal and political institutions which had been brought with his forebears from England, confirmed in the charters which the colonies received at their founding and made more explicit in the statements of fundamental rights which his local assemblies from time to time had drafted. His most vivid knowledge of English history had to do with the circumstances under which he or his ancestors had come to the New World, and the battles which had been won in the mother country in the seventeenth century in the name of fundamental liberties of the subject he assumed had con-

---

* See annotations to the Charter in Part II.

ferred the fruits of victory upon himself as well. To be sure, Charles II had disallowed the New York Charter of Privileges as limiting the royal prerogative, but the prerogative itself had been all but abolished by the English Bill of Rights in 1689. The acts of 1712 and 1715 in the Carolinas had incorporated not only Magna Carta but the Petition of Right, the *Habeas Corpus* Act, and the fundamentals of the Bill of Rights—thus specifically making the organic law of the English constitution a part of the local law of that colony.

The three-quarters of a century which elapsed between the Glorious Revolution which established the limited monarchy in the mother country and the decade of growing friction after the French and Indian War between the British government and its American colonies had further confirmed the conviction of colonial leaders that they enjoyed the rights of Englishmen as a matter of course. Parliamentarians could point to the Navigation Acts of 1660 and 1696, and the Molasses Act of 1733, as evidence that colonial control was vested in Westminster; but these were after all statutes affecting matters of external trade and did not suggest that personal liberties or the autonomy of local courts and legislatures was in question. It was not until the Stamp Act of 1765 that Americans rudely awakened to the fact that Parliament did not recognize that the English constitution necessarily followed the flag.

The Stamp Act, an internal tax levied by Parliament on the several colonies, seemed to Americans to strike at the heart of the freedom set out in the opening clause of the Petition of Right, "That they should not be compelled to contribute to any tax . . . not set by common consent in Parliament." Patrick Henry, in the Stamp Act Resolves submitted to the Virginia House of Burgesses, translated this to the colonial government; "the first adventurers or settlers" of the colony brought with them "all the liberties, franchises, privileges and immunities, that have at any time been held, enjoyed and possessed, by the people of Great Britain." This included, said Henry, the right of local taxation as "the only security against a burthensome taxation, and the distinguishing characteristick of British freedom, without which the ancient constitution cannot exist." The General Assembly of

Virginia "have the only and sole exclusive right and power to lay taxes and impositions upon the inhabitants of this Colony," and any such effort by another government "has a manifest tendency to destroy British as well as American freedom."

In Massachusetts, John Adams echoed the same sentiment in drafting the Instructions of the Town of Braintree, a document which marked his entry into politics and into the constitutional struggle with the mother country. The stamp duties were unconstitutional, said Adams, because it was "a grand and fundamental principle of the constitution, that no freeman would be subject to any tax to which he had not given his own consent, in person or by proxy." As to the law's conferring of jurisdiction upon the vice-admiralty courts and thus taking it away from the colonial tribunals, he found this "directly repugnant to the Great Charter itself; for, by that charter, 'no amerciament shall be assessed, but by the oath of lawful and honest men of the vicinage'"; and, he warned, "this act will make 'such a distinction, and create such a difference between' the subjects in Great Britain and those in America, as we could not have expected from the guardians of liberty in 'both.'"

The Stamp Act Congress that fall reiterated the sentiments of both Henry and Adams, insisting that the local control of taxation and the right to trial by local juries were inherent liberties of Englishmen, whether in the colonies or in England itself. For the colonists in particular, Adams was to write in a letter to Benjamin Franklin, these rights must continually be insisted upon lest a distant Parliament assume that silence indicated an acceptance of the violation. To the contrary, he said on another occasion, it must be made clear that there never was a people "more strongly attached to their natural and constitutional rights and liberties than the British Colonists of the American Continent."

The law books and tracts upon which the English revolutionaries of the previous century had relied were much harder to come by in America, but men like Adams and Thomas Jefferson had almost all of the great classics in their personal libraries. In the same year as the Stamp Act, Adams had written a *Dissertation on the Canon and Feudal Law* setting out the theory that British liberties were original rights and had their foundation in human nature itself; he listed among his authorities a roster of seventeenth-century writers ranging from John Seldon, Coke's great contemporary, to John Locke, whose essays *On Government,* written before but published after the Glorious Revolution, were to become a veritable Bible for the American revolutionary spokesmen. As for Jefferson, his vast law library included most of the authorities from Glanville and Bracton of the twelfth and thirteenth centuries and all of the works of Coke and Blackstone, including Blackstone's definitive tract on *The Great Charter and Charter of the Forest,* published in 1759.

Adams's letter to Franklin may have supported him, if any support was needed, in his testimony before a committee of the House of Commons in 1766; as commissioner for the colonies, Franklin was in London at the time the House was conducting hearings on the effect of the Stamp Act. There is reason to believe that sympathetic members of the committee asked him questions which permitted him to expound at length on the American position. The colonial assemblies, Franklin maintained, had the sole right to levy internal taxes, and "the Petition of Right expressly says, [taxation] is to be by common consent in Parliament, and the people of America have no representatives in Parliament, to make a part of that common consent."

As the King's ministers, the royal courts, and Parliament itself continued to insist upon their paramount authority in matters of the overseas dominions, the colonials in their turn became equally insistent upon the protection afforded by the common law and the constitution against invasion of local affairs. James Otis, the famed Boston attorney, challenged the constitutionality of the writs of assistance issued in 1761 by the Court of Exchequer in London, upon the request of a royal port official in Boston. To issue such a writ, in effect drafting colonials to aid in royal administration, was to infringe upon the right of Massachusetts to administer the local affairs of its own port, Otis argued; and since the constitution and "natural equity" prohibited such invasion, the constitution would bar such arbitrary judicial action in the colony as it would in England.

To this reasoning Samuel Adams, the firebrand of the family, would add his own argument against the Townshend Acts in

1768. "Champagne Charlie" Townshend had become Chancellor of the Exchequer two years before and died a year later; but in this short period, it was said, "English government in America [became] little more than a series of deplorable blunders," and in any event his Parliamentary bills continued after him. One act suspended New York's legislative function until that colony complied with an earlier Parliamentary enactment; two others undertook to organize royal customs commissioners and strengthen the tax-collecting process in the colonies. Adams drafted the letters from the Massachusetts House to the British Ministry contending that the acts were contrary to the fundamental law of the British constitution. "If, then, the constitution of Great Britain is the fundamental right of all British subjects," said Adams, "it is humbly referred to your Lordship's judgment, whether the supreme legislative of the empire [Parliament] may lightly leap the bounds of it, in the exercise of power over the subjects in America, any more than over those in Britain."

The limitation upon royal control over colonial rights to local government was stressed in 1768 by Thomas Pownall, former Governor of Massachusetts, in his *Administration of the Colonies, Wherein the Rights and Constitutions are Discussed and Stated,* published on his return to London. Pownall concluded that the instructions given royal governors upon their departure for the New World, authorizing them to convene local legislatures, were "declaratory and not creative" law; the governor in such case was merely being "directed to act conformably to a right actually and already existing in the people. The crown cannot establish any colony upon—or contract it within a narrower scale than the subject is entitled to, by the great Charter of England."

So the debate mounted, culminating in the "intolerable acts" of 1774—the Boston Port Bill, closing the port in retaliation for the Tea Party, and two acts for "the better regulating of the government of the Province of Massachusetts Bay" by a provision to "purge the constitution of all its crudities" and for the removal of certain cases to other colonies or to Great Britain. By this action, Parliament served final notice that constitutional principles recognized in England did not extend to the colonies. The colonies promptly accepted the challenge, and from the resolutions of several assemblies convened the first Continental Congress. At Philadelphia on October 4, 1774, in language which in part deliberately echoed the wording of the English Bill of Rights, the Congress issued a Declaration "as Englishmen their ancestors in like cases have usually done, for asserting and vindicating their rights and liberties." The Resolves embodied in the Declaration reiterated the fundamental colonial insistence that the colonies brought with them in their original charters the freedoms and privileges of native English subjects, including the common law and its fundamental guarantee in Magna Carta (as understood by the seventeenth-century revolutionists in the mother country) of local trial by jury. The 1765 act for quartering troops—the resistance to which had first cost New York its legislative privileges—violated the specific prohibitions of the Petition of Right; this and other enumerated acts of George III's Parliaments were protested in the subsequent Resolves.

The Revolution would transform these theories into confirmed principles, just as the English Revolution had ratified the restatement of the ancient constitution in modern terms. But the fact remained that, until the Treaty of Peace in 1783, colonial theory was diametrically opposite to prevailing legal conviction in the mother country. Early in the eighteenth century there had been some difference of opinion between counsel for the Board of Trade and for the Privy Council as to whether colonists going to America took with them the common law and Parliamentary enactments up to the date of their migration; but they consistently agreed that no acts of Parliament subsequent to settlement extended to any colony unless the act specifically named the colony. Further, the Privy Council on several occasions advised the King to disallow a colonial statute which sought to incorporate a Parliamentary act into local law. In 1775, on the eve of the Revolution, the widely read Blackstone in the seventh edition of his *Commentaries* stated flatly:

> Our American plantations [were] . . . obtained in the last century either by right of conquest and driving out the natives (with what natural justice I shall not at present enquire) or by treaties. And therefore the common law of England, as such, has no allowance or authority there;

they being no part of the mother country, but distinct (though dependent) dominions; though . . . not bound by any acts of Parliament, unless particularly named.

Reaching such an impasse on the legal front, the colonists still had one supreme authority, hardly refutable in England, to support their case. John Locke, philosopher and scientist turned political theorist for a space, had published his study of the origins of government as a summary of the meanings of the revolutionary processes of the seventeenth century. Although much of what Locke said had been said by others before and after him, the time and circumstances of his essay as well as its clarity of analysis gave his work an almost universal authority among Englishmen of the eighteenth century. Before governments began, Locke contended, man in a state of nature was perfectly free and all men were equal to each other; political societies were organized to provide corporate protection for and more effective enjoyment of the rights and liberties which were natural to the human race. It followed, in Locke's view, that governments could only rest upon the consent of the governed.

But though men, when they enter into society, give up the equality, liberty and executive power they had in the state of nature, into the hands of the society, to be so far disposed of by the legislative as the good of the society shall require, yet it being only with an intention in everyone the better to preserve himself, his liberty and property (for no rational creature can be supposed to change his condition with an intention to be worse), the power of the society or the legislature constituted by them can never be supposed to extend farther than the common good.

The purpose of government and of law being to effectuate the greater public good, Locke defined the prerogative as the power to act "according to discretion for the public good"; to use the power otherwise was tyranny. As for determining which was which, there might need to be an "appeal to Heaven," but a more practical test was whether "a long train of abuses, prevarications and artifices, all tending the same way" made it clear that the governing power was committed to a course which would destroy the end for which it was itself created. In such an eventuality, men could exercise their inherent right of revolution, for as society was created with their consent, it could not continue without their consent. Locke was the highest of all the authorities relied upon by those who led the colonies progressively closer to the exercise of that ultimate right; Jefferson, who knew him by heart, incorporated whole Lockean phrases into the Declaration of Independence.

Among the most discerning of the spokesmen for the American position in the final years of crisis was an immigrant Scotsman who would one day become one of the most astute Justices of the early Supreme Court of the United States. A graduate of St. Andrews and a successful young practitioner at the Pennsylvania bar (he had read law under John Dickinson, who penned the eloquent *Letters from an American Farmer,* another of the leading arguments of the colonial case), James Wilson, on the eve of the second Continental Congress, to which he would come as a delegate, published his *Considerations on the Nature and Extent of the Legislative Authority of the British Parliament,* a revision of an earlier pamphlet he had written after a careful comparison of the constitutions of Great Britain and Pennsylvania. Wilson focused his attack upon the cardinal principle of the great Blackstone himself, that while the benefits of Parliamentary legislation did not extend to the American colonies except as Parliament willed it, the colonies themselves were subject to the control of Parliament.

Wilson's thesis relied on Locke's doctrine of the legitimacy of government turning upon the consent of the governed, and on the rule enunciated by the Swiss political theorist Burlamaqui that "the happiness of the society is the *first* law of every government." In the nature of the case, said Wilson, Americans could not be subject to the control of a distant Parliament not familiar with their interests and without representation from the American constituents, for "a regard to justice is by no means the ruling principle in human nature." How, he asked, could a far-off House of Commons attain "a natural right to make laws, by which we may be deprived of our properties, of our liberties, of our lives?" And again: "What act of ours has rendered us subject to those, to whom we were formerly equal? . . . Do those, who embark, free-men, in Great-Britain, disembark, slaves in America?" No, Wilson concluded; "it is repugnant to the essential maxims of jurispru-dence, to the ultimate end of all governments, to the genius of the British constitution, and to the liberty and happiness of the Colonies, that they should be bound by the legislative authority of the Parliament of Great-Britain."

It was not to Parliament, the author declared in his climax, that the allegiance of the British subjects in America was owed, for Parliament had "no dominion over their equals and fellow-sub-jects in America." It was rather to the crown—the unifying sym-bol by which the dominion concept of the later British Empire would actually be effected—that the colonies held firm to the mother country. Wilson had thus, in the process of refuting the Parliamentary power over America, provided the rationale for the final rebellion; for when the crown deserted the colonies' interests (in American opinion), there remained no obligation of allegiance.

So it was that in the Declaration at Philadelphia in 1776, the catalog of grievances against the crown would reiterate many of the fundamental provisions of the Petition of Right and the Bill of Rights which, it was alleged, George III through his ministers had denied to his overseas subjects. The King was charged with several of the same offenses attributed in 1689 to James II: dis-pensing with and suspending laws, maintaining a standing army and quartering troops without legislative consent, imposing arbitrary taxation, encouraging illegal prosecutions in strange courts, and corrupting the jury process. For abdicating his govern-ment in the colonies and waging war upon his subjects—offenses once charged to King John and to Charles I—as well as for "taking away our Charters, abolishing our most valuable laws, and alter-ing fundamentally the Forms of our Government," the Declara-tion held the "Free and Independent States . . . Absolved from all allegiance to the British Crown."

It now remained for the revolutionists to restate, in positive rather than negative terms, the rights of Englishmen which they now proposed to certify as rights of Americans. In the state constitutions which in most instances now were drafted to replace the forfeited colonial charters, the volubly venerated principles of the ancient and modern constitutions of Great Britain were written into the law of the new nation. Magna Carta, in the "golden passage" apotheosized by Coke, received its proper place in the new fundamental laws of nine of the thirteen new states; Connecticut copied Chapter 29 from its 1650 code, where it had been taken almost verbatim from the Great Charter. Maryland's constitution rephrased the chapter in suitably republican terms: "That every freeman, for any injury done him in his person or property, ought to have remedy, by the course of the law of the land, and ought to have justice and right freely without sale, freely without any denial, and speedily without delay, according to the law of the land."

Massachusetts, New Hampshire, North and South Carolina, Pennsylvania, Vermont, and Virginia reiterated the chapter in essence. Georgia courts would ultimately receive the whole body of Magna Carta into the state law. Rhode Island, which elected to retain its colonial charter, could point to the guarantee therein of all rights and liberties of Englishmen which also included all of Magna Carta; and New York in its constitution retained "such parts of the common law of England, and of the statute law of England and Great Britain," as were in force at the time of independence. This "reception" of the common law and of British fundamental statutes would be reiterated in Virginia in the early years of the new Commonwealth, and from Virginia would be adapted to the constitutions or codes of states to be created progressively over the next century and a half, until the Great Charter of Liberties would finally extend its influence halfway around the world from Runnymede.

After founding their whole case for freedom upon the guarantees set out in the English Bill of Rights, it appeared to many Americans, when the issue of ratifying the new Constitution of the United States came before them in the winter of 1787-88, that the absence of such a list of guarantees from their own national charter was ludicrous. North Carolina, for one, delayed its ratification for several months after the necessary majority of states had put the new Constitution into effect; James Iredell, who would become one of the Justices of the Supreme Court provided for by the new charter, told the ratifying convention that "a declaration of rights, asserting and securing from encroachment the great principles of civil and religious liberty, and the unalienable rights of the people," should be a condition of North Carolina's ratification.

Alexander Hamilton, writing in *The Federalist* (in one of the numbers published after the Constitution had been ratified, but in criticism of the flood of amendments which had been proposed), sought to defend the omission. "It has been several times truly remarked," Hamilton observed, "that bills of rights are in their origin, stipulations between kings and their subjects, abridgments of prerogative in favor of privilege, reservations of rights not surrendered to the prince. Such was MAGNA CARTA, obtained by the Barons, sword in hand, from King John. Such were the subsequent confirmations of that charter by subsequent princes. Such was the *Petition of Right* assented to by Charles the First, in the beginning of his reign. Such also was the declaration of right presented by the lords and commons to the Prince of Orange in 1688, and afterwards thrown into the form of an act of Parliament, called the Bill of Rights. It is evident, therefore, that according to their primitive signification, they have no application to constitutions professedly founded upon the power of the people, and executed by their immediate representatives and servants."

A people who had just completed a lengthy struggle against a central government they considered too dangerous because too strong, however, was not reassured by words like Hamilton's. The new Constitution, men argued, created an equally strong government, its form already sharply distinguishable from the loose and ineffective Confederation. James Madison, whose reputation as the Father of the Constitution was already assuming its classic proportions, took the initiative in introducing a number of proposals for amendment into the first federal Congress in 1789, from which those which would become in time the American Bill of Rights were to emerge. While certain state leaders opposed the Constitution for the more powerful position it gave the national government, Madison told the House of Representatives at its first session that he was persuaded "the great mass of the people who opposed it, disliked it because it did not contain effectual provisions against the encroachments on particular rights, and those safeguards which they have been long accustomed to have interposed between them and the magistrate who exercises the sovereign power."

Chapter 29 of Magna Carta—as well as the principle that private property should not be taken for public use without just compensation (the ancient issue of purveyances of requisitions for the crown)—would thus be enshrined in the due process clause of the Fifth Amendment, and in the right to a local trial in criminal cases set out in the Sixth. That these several Charter rights had been interpreted in terms of an erroneous historical interpretation by Sir Edward Coke did not affect their ultimate validity; as the people of the United States ratified the Amendments, they ratified the contemporary understanding of what the Charter's words meant. The same was true of the Second and Eighth Amendments, which reiterated specific provisions of the English Bill of Rights concerning the right to bear arms and the protection against excessive bail or fines. The Third Amendment, outlawing the practice of the British Quartering Act of 1765, echoed the sixth chapter of the Petition of Right.

Thus the legend of Magna Carta would be perpetuated in American law, until almost a century later when new historical research would reveal the extent of Coke's misconception of the original meaning of the Great Charter. Then, as the patina was stripped off, the legacy of the Charter—the capacity of the common law to adapt its letter to changing ages and broadening franchises—would be revealed. Coke had assumed that the words of the Charter first written in 1215 had the same meaning in 1628, when he was completing his commentary, and as the Parliamentarians assumed in 1642 when they published his *Institute* as an apologetic of the English Civil War. To the men of the Revolution of 1688 the words had assumed a yet broader meaning— and to the men of 1776 and 1789 a still broader. Yet the process was essentially valid, for the fundamental feature of the confrontation of King and barons at Runnymede—the insistence that the governor as well as the governed is ultimately subject to the rule of law—was in fact the same when Charles I acceded to the Petition of Right, when William III and Mary II accepted the

Declaration of Rights, and when George III was served with the Declaration of Independence.

The colonials of the seventeenth century drew up their bodies of fundamental privileges in the full awareness of what was being insisted upon in the mother country. Many, like William Penn, anticipated that in the New World, if anything, the rights of Englishmen would be more widely enjoyed than in England itself. If Coke had misled them in his own misconception of the literal significance of the thirteenth-century Magna Carta, he had done them the greater service of converting the Great Charter into an abstract proposition of enduring worth. This was the proposition that personal liberty of the subject or the citizen is the highest function of law itself.

VIII

The Enduring Proposition

IN an excess of democratic fervor, John Adams wrote, in
1779, in defense of the new constitutional theory of the
United States: "[W]here the public interest governs, it is a government of laws, and not of men; the interest of a king, or of a
party, is another thing—it is a private interest; and where private
interest governs, it is a government of men, and not of laws. If,
in England, there has ever been such a thing as a government of
laws, was it not *magna charta?* and have not our kings broken
magna charta thirty times? Did the law govern when the law was
broken? or was that a government of men? On the contrary, hath
not *magna charta* been as often repaired by the people? and, the
law being so restored, was it not a government of laws, and not
of men?"

Fervent antimonarchist that he was, Adams may be forgiven
for not documenting his "thirty times" that English kings had
flouted the Great Charter; he may have had in mind Coke's statement that on more than thirty occasions, Magna Carta had been
confirmed, presumably to remedy a similar number of violations.
In any event, in Adams's mind the Charter itself had already
become a symbol, a generic term, which he was using on this
occasion to establish, in answer to foreign criticisms that the new
American constitutions created an institutionalized mobocracy,
his conception of true government as a political system in which
"the public interest governs."

Already the young nation, which had justified its Revolution
in terms of the rights of Englishmen to which it was itself entitled,
was beginning to develop its own constitutional legend. The
debates over ratification of the federal Constitution, to replace the
ineffective Articles of Confederation with a charter for a stronger

228

central government, had already defined the fundamental poles of opposition between the supporters of greater and the advocates of lesser federal authority. If "the law of the land," the catch phrase from Magna Carta, was to govern, which land was meant —the several states or the union as a whole? Alexander Hamilton, James Madison, and James Wilson, at the Constitutional Convention of 1787 and in the ratification argument of the following winter, had insisted that, if only in the interest of uniformity, the answer had to be in favor of the whole nation. The states' rights advocates, momentarily put on the defensive by the obvious failure of the Confederation and the ratification of the new Constitution, found their new leader in Thomas Jefferson and in the antifederalist writers, chiefly from Virginia and the southern states, who recapitulated his philosophy.

Hamilton, it is true, had undertaken to explain away the need for a Bill of Rights in the Constitution, arguing that Magna Carta had been a concession between king and subjects which had no function in a republic; but he had been making a lawyer's defense of his client's fundamentally weak position, and once the Constitution was ratified and the Bill of Rights added, he could argue with much more conviction. "The power which can create a supreme law of the land," he declared, "is doubtless sovereign, as to such case." The Virginians, Jefferson, John Taylor of Caroline and St. George Tucker, author of the first important commentary of the Constitution, were to dispute him vigorously. James Wilson, now an Associate Justice of the Supreme Court of the United States, substantiated the Hamiltonian argument that the people of the nation, in establishing their union, had brought into being a sovereignty superior to that of the states in any question of national jurisdiction.

In any event, the slowly crystallizing concept of government did not depart too far from the arguments which the revolutionists had employed a generation before. Mr. Justice Wilson was essentially paraphrasing, in his Supreme Court opinion, what he had earlier said, in 1776, in his Address to the Inhabitants of the Colonies: *That all power was originally in the People—that all the powers of Government are derived from them—that all power, which they have not disposed of, still continues theirs*—are maxims of the *English* Constitution, which, we presume, will not be disputed." These Lockean propositions were an important gloss upon the due process concept attributed to Magna Carta, for they marked the point of departure of American constitutional theory from the English. The political fact which had emerged from the seventeenth-century revolution was the supremacy of Parliament; even the great constitutional principles set out in the Petition of Right, *Habeas Corpus* Act, and the Bill of Rights were, in the final anaylsis, only statutes depending for their permanence upon the consensus of Parliament. For the majority of American legal and political exponents, the law of the land was a "higher law" laying a restraint upon legislatures as well.

"The common law of England is a system of rules, supported by precedents, handed down from remote antiquity. These precedents have . . . been held in too great veneration," wrote Nathaniel Chipman of the new state of Vermont in 1793, adding that "when the reason for a law ceases, the law itself ceases." Thus the American view was that neither the common law expounded by the courts, nor the statutory law (which either reiterated or modified the common law) of the legislatures was to be beyond the reach of the "higher law"—the "public interest" principle of John Adams. On this principle, both the federalist and antifederalist leaders were virtually at one; and in the implementation of the principle, the application of the standard to common-law, statutory, or constitutional questions, there arose the peculiarly American process known as judicial review.

St. George Tucker, author of the first American annotations to the *Commentaries* of Blackstone and an ardent supporter of Jefferson's concept of a strictly circumscribed area of federal authority, saw a fundamental danger in the acceptance of the common law as national law. In such a case, he was convinced, the federal courts would assume an unlimited jurisdiction over all questions brought before them for review. The preferred—and in his view the only thinkable—alternative was to limit the jurisdiction of the federal courts to the subject matter set out in the Constitution. The common-law jurisdiction of courts, Tucker insisted, must be permitted only to the states. Common-law rules and procedures would be applied by the federal courts in cases

where the federal Constitution and Congressional enactments had
failed to provide guidelines for decision, but the cases actually
to come before them for decision were to be explicitly limited.

To identify the proper spheres of federal and state judicial
power led logically to the function of judicial review, a function
which Tucker himself, as judge of the Virginia General Court in
1788, had vigorously asserted with reference to the state constitution. He could not but have been gratified when, in 1812, the
Supreme Court of the United States denied to the federal courts
a common-law jurisdiction over criminal cases. But Tucker's
advocacy of a literal interpretation of federal constitutional
powers in general was to be rejected by John Marshall's court; in
a famous opinion in 1819, the great Chief Justice was to observe:

> This . . . is . . . a constitution intended to endure for
> ages to come, and, consequently, to be adapted to the
> various *crises* of human affairs. To have prescribed the
> means by which government should, in all future time,
> execute its powers, would have been to change, entirely,
> the character of the [Constitution], and give it the
> properties of a legal code. It would have been an unwise
> attempt to provide, by immutable rules, for exigencies
> which, if foreseen at all, must have been seen dimly, and
> which can best be provided for as they occur.

"As to the words from Magna Carta, after volumes spoken
and written with a view to their exposition, the good sense of man-
kind has at length settled down to this: that they were intended
to secure the individual from the arbitrary exercise of the powers
of government, unrestrained by the established principles of
private right and distributive justice," wrote Justice William
Johnson, a leading member of the Court, in the same year. Thus
American constitutional law developed its fundamental doctrine:
the guarantee of due process, taken in England to be a limitation
upon the crown and the judiciary but not upon the legislature, is
in America a limitation upon any branch of government, and the
test of whether the limitation has been exceeded is the peculiar
function of the judiciary.

As the events of the seventeenth century ratified a more
libertarian interpretation of the Great Charter, and the revolu-

tionary generation of the eighteenth century ratified the proposition that its benefits were the natural right of the colonists who
formed the new United States, so the developing constitutionalism
of the nineteenth and twentieth centuries continued to broaden
and diversify the application of the due process doctrine. The
first generations of constitutionalists, being children of the
American Revolution, interpreted it in terms of personal liberties;
this doctrine reached its apogee in the *Commentaries* of Justice
Joseph Story, first published in 1833, and continued through many
faithfully read editions during the rest of the century.

By the end of the Civil War decade, however, a new America
was coming to maturity. The accomplished political fact of an
indissoluble union necessarily put an end to the early compact
theory of federalism, which had clung to the proposition that
national sovereignty rested upon the consent and suffrance of the
paramount state sovereignties. The limitations upon the powers of
government, which the Bill of Rights through the Fifth Amendment had fixed upon the federal agencies, was now fixed also
upon the states through the Fourteenth. This famous constitutional proposition, intended originally to insure civil justice for
the newly freed Negro slaves, was to undergo a succession of
judicial interpretations which in due course led the due process
concept to a functional status unimagined by the advocates of
the English or American Revolutions.

In Victorian England, the trend of jurisprudence had been
steadily away from the theory of the eighteenth-century Enlight-
enment, that natural law and natural justice placed a limit upon
the powers of government. Even at the height of this theory,
Blackstone was teaching that Parliament was beyond the reach
of any inhibitory principles, although Parliament by its own
acts recognized the three "absolute rights of every Englishman,"
which he defined as security from personal injury, physical freedom, and the complete freedom to use, enjoy, and dispose of his
property. Nearly a century later the reformer Jeremy Bentham
wrote that, while the power of Parliament was absolute, it was
directed in its legislative function by the proposition that the
ultimate objective of legislation is the greatest benefit to the
greatest number.

That English courts rejected any element of the American doctrine of judicial review was set out by the judiciary itself in a case in 1871, in which it was firmly declared that enactments of Parliament "are the law of the land; and we do not sit here as a court of appeal from Parliament." Yet, in the same year as this decision, a leader of the English bar was writing: "A statute which is contrary to the reason of the common law or purports to take away a prerogative of the crown is none the less valid, but it will, so far as is possible, be applied in such a way as to leave the prerogative or the common-law rights of the subject intact. To this extent the reason of the common law prevails: we cannot say that Parliament cannot do any of these things, but we can still say that there is a presumption against its doing them."

This capacity for restating the effect of a fundamental constitutional principle in terms of a changing society, while preserving an essential consistency or continuity, has been the ultimate secret of democratic government in the Anglo-American context. The barons in arms at Runnymede had viewed Magna Carta as a summary of *feudal* rights and obligations beyond impairment by the crown; the parliamentarians of the seventeenth century had largely abolished the feudal provisions of the Charter and reasserted that it was a summary of *personal* rights beyond impairment by the crown. This had been the proposition accepted by the American revolutionaries of the following century, and the early constitutional theorists of the young republic. Now was to come another fundamental change in the rationale of the Charter rights, from persons to property, inaugurated with the interpretation of the Fourteenth Amendment.

In the emotionally surcharged atmosphere of the post-Civil War era, there developed a theory that the Amendment, aside from and under the guise of accommodating the civil rights of the freedmen, was intended to convert the rights of all state citizens into rights of United States citizens and to give the federal courts the power to override any and all state laws which might be held to infringe upon these rights. This "conspiracy theory" was a vigorous revival of the Tucker doctrine of the inherent danger in a federal common law, and led the Supreme Court of the United States, by a five-to-four division in 1873, to construe the privileges and immunities in virtually the same terms as before the amendment was ratified. Thus, in acceding to a deep-seated dread of centralized power, the courts nullified, for several generations, the effective functioning of the amendment in the field of personal liberties.

On the other hand, the Supreme Court of the latter part of the nineteenth century was concerned with the efforts of the states to infringe upon the indiscriminate uses of property rights in the flush of a rapidly industrializing era. State legislative efforts at regulation and control in response to the rapid social changes being effected by industrialism were now discerned by the Court as substantial denials of due process. In this turn of events, the Court extended the concept of due process from the historical one of the enforcement of law, to the radically new one of enactment of law. It was at this point that the American doctrine reached its farthest departure from the English, in insisting that legislative as well as executive and judicial acts were subject to constitutional surveillance.

"But are we all . . . at the mercy of the legislative majorities?" asked Justice Rufus Peckham in 1905, answering his own question in the negative by holding, with the majority, that New York's power to regulate the length of working hours in the baking industry violated constitutional freedom of contract. In dissent, Justice Oliver Wendell Holmes averred that "a constitution is not intended to embody a particular economic theory. . . . It is made for people of fundamentally differing views, and the accident of our finding certain opinions natural and familiar or novel and even shocking ought not to conclude our judgment upon the question whether statutes embodying them conflict with the Constitution."

This converting of the fundamental principle of Magna Carta —freedom of individual subjects from arbitrary acts of government—into an economic dogma congenial to the *laissez-faire* ideals of the time reflected the influence of the writings of Thomas M. Cooley in the sixty years following the Civil War. Even the title of his great work, *Constitutional Limitations*, corroborated the author's sympathy with a highly restrictive concept of governmental power, and it was more than ordinarily symbolic that the first of its many editions should have appeared in the year that the Fourteenth Amendment was ratified.

"The maxims of Magna Charta and the common law are the interpreters of constitutional grants of power," Cooley wrote, "and those acts which by those maxims the several departments of government are forbidden to do cannot be considered within any grant or apportionment of power which the people in general terms have made to those departments." But, Cooley added, it did not follow "that in every case the courts, before they can set aside a law as invalid, must be able to find in the Constitution some special inhibition which has been disregarded, or some express command which had been disobeyed." Constitutional limitations, in the context of the Great Charter's chapter on due process, were in Cooley's view to be derived from the convictions of the established orders of society; for

> . . . general rules may sometimes be as obnoxious as special, when in their results they deprive parties of vested rights. While every man has a right to require that his own controversies shall be judged by the same rules which settle those of his neighbors, the whole community is also entitled at all times to demand the protection of the ancient principles which shield private rights against arbitrary interference, even though such interference may be under a rule impartial in its application. It is not the partial character of the rule, so much as its arbitrary and unusual nature, which condemns it as unknown to the law of the land.

Such a doctrine was avidly applied by the courts to the mounting tide of economic legislation through which various state governments, in the last quarter of the nineteenth century and the first decade of the twentieth, undertook to restrain the exploitation of power by the new industrial giants. Where before the courts had looked upon due process as a procedural matter, they now discovered that it was even more important in substantive issues; for, as a New York court observed with remarkable candor in 1884, a law which in any way "interferes with the profitable and free use" of the property of an individual or corpo-

ration "arbitrarily deprives him of his property and some portion
of his personal liberty."

The constitutional interpreters of the turn of the century
were devotees not only of Cooley but of Herbert Spencer, whose
aphorism that "every man has freedom to do aught that he wills,
provided that he infringes not the equal freedom of every other
man" was confidently grounded upon Magna Carta and the English and American Bills of Rights. The courts for the most part
read this as an unassailable guarantee of complete freedom of
contract, never to be infringed by regulatory statutes; and in vain
did Mr. Justice Holmes assert that "the Fourteenth Amendment
does not enact Mr. Herbert Spencer's *Social Statics.*"

Indeed, a cult or political mythology of Magna Carta began
to develop in the period ushering in the present century, as many
apologists for the freedom of corporate enterprise saw in the
Charter an immemorial promise of freedom from government
interference. William D. Guthrie, long-time leader of the New
York bar and the chief counsel in the cases by which a proposed
federal income tax was held invalid in 1895, the assertion of Congressional power over interstate commerce in lotteries was disputed in 1903, and a federal tax on oleomargarine was assailed
as a taking of property without due process, crowned his professional labors in 1916 with a book on the heritage of Magna Carta.
In this volume Guthrie confidently asserted that constitutional
law and the principle of representative government began at
Runnymede and continued unbroken to his own day. This principle, as he interpreted it, permanently and forever insulated property rights from regulation by agencies of the state in the name
of social reform or economic democracy.

Indoctrinated with this concept of due process, the courts in
general during the first three decades of the twentieth century
required the advocates of social reform to assume the burden of
proof of the constitutionality of their legislative program. Then,
with the major crisis which burst upon the free enterprise system
with the great depression, the propriety of government intervention in the national interest compelled a re-examination of the
dogmas of economic jurisprudence which had obtained for the
sixty years after the Civil War. Did not due process require, on

the one hand, a responsible use of private freedom as much as it assumed, on the other, a responsible use of government power? Coercion and curtailment of personal liberty, it was belatedly perceived, could result from arbitrary and irresponsible acts of individuals toward other individuals, as well as from oppressive government.

As the Supreme Court of the United States, first under Chief Justice Charles Evans Hughes and later under Chief Justice Harlan F. Stone, re-examined the social and economic issues of their time in the light of the due process clauses of the Fifth and Fourteenth Amendments, the effective force of due process came to be stated once more in terms of personal rather than property values. The clauses, in the words of Justice Felix Frankfurter in a 1952 case, once more are understood to epitomize "those canons of decency and fairness which express the notions of justice of English-speaking peoples," and the term itself is "a summarized constitutional guarantee of respect for those personal immunities." As though to dispose of the stereotyped concepts which had been so long accepted by the followers of the Cooley doctrine, Mr. Justice Frankfurter then added a concise essay on the enduring proposition of Anglo-American constitutionalism:

> In dealing not with the machinery of government but with human rights, the absence of formal exactitude, or want of fixity of meaning, is not an unusual or even regrettable attribute of constitutional provisions. Words being symbols do not speak without a gloss. On the one hand the gloss may be the deposit of history, whereby a term gains technical content. . . . On the other hand, the gloss of some of the verbal symbols of the Constitution does not give them a fixed technical content. It exacts a continuing process of application.
>
> When the gloss has thus not been fixed but is a function of the process of judgment, the judgment is bound to fall differently at different times and differently at the same time through different judges.

Frankfurter concurred in the argument of Edmund Burke that the freedom of the subject was preserved rather than jeopardized by this shifting and ever-flexible concept of due process: "To believe that this judicial exercise of judgment could be avoided by freezing 'due process of law' at some fixed stage of time or thought is to suggest that the most important aspect of constitutional adjudication is a function for inanimate machines." He added:

> The faculties of the due process clause may be indefinite and vague, but the mode of their ascertainment is not self-willed. In each case "due process of law" requires an evaluation based on a disinterested inquiry pursued in the spirit of science, on a balanced order of facts exactly and fairly stated, on the detached consideration of conflicting claims. . . . on a judgment not *ad hoc* and episodic but duly mindful of reconciling the needs both of continuity and of change in a progressive society.

This, indeed, is the ultimate contribution to free society of the Anglo-American constitutional rationale—the capacity of its own basic tenets to be interpreted in terms of succeeding and drastically differing social and political needs. Neither Stephen Langton, nor Sir Edward Coke, nor the Founding Fathers at Philadelphia could prophesy the ultimate formula for government under law; each age, of necessity, must define it in its own terms. The Great Charter, like the Constitution of the United States, is in the final analysis a symbol with which each generation must keep its own faith.

PART TWO

THE DOCUMENTS OF THE LEGACY

MAGNA CARTA (1215)

Concordia inter Regem Johannem et barones pro concessione libertatum ecclesie et regni Anglie

MAGNA CARTA (1225)

Carta de libertatibus Regis Henrici III

INTRODUCTION TO DOCUMENTS

"THE agreement between King John and the barons for the grant of liberties to the church and realm of England," runs the title on the back of the copy of the Lincoln Cathedral manuscript of the Great Charter, in precise clerical Latin. The reissues by the advisers of Henry III in 1216 and 1217 were simply described as charters, and the term *magna carta* came into use only after the grants in Henry's name had been divided into two documents—*Carta de Foresta,* or the Charter of the Forest, and the other Charter of [General] Liberties. The adjective "great" doubtless was suggested first by the length and detail of the latter, in comparison with the single subject treated in the Forest Charter; in the matter of intrinsic values, both charters were regarded by the Middle Ages as "great," and they were usually confirmed together. Magna Carta was the fundamental restatement of the common law, while the Forest Charter concerned a special body of jurisprudence outside the common law.

In assessing the legal and political significance of the Great Charter, therefore, it is necessary to keep several charters, and a number of supplementary statutes, in mind—beginning always with the agreement between John and the rebels at Runnymede, for this is indelibly impressed upon the mind of specialist and layman alike by the high drama which centered upon it. Antedating this would be a number of documents, although for practical purposes they must be limited to the coronation charters of the first and second Henrys and (for what they were worth) the two charters of Stephen; and certainly the provisions of the Unknown Charter of Liberties and of the Articles of the Barons must figure fundamentally in any analysis of Magna Carta. Subsequently, there are the two charters which evolved from the reissues of 1216 and 1217, and the definitive issue of 1225. Certainly there must also be considered the Confirmation of 1297 and the Articles upon the Charters in 1300.[1] Beyond these documents, considering the size and purpose of the present volume, the basic materials then become increasingly selective. The great constitutional statutes of Edward I, of which *Confirmatio Cartarum* and *Articuli super Cartas* were logical parts, fundamentally affected the character of the charters themselves, as did his statute *de Tallagio non Concedendo*, or restraints upon tallages (arbitrary levies). Many of the confirmations of the charters through Edward III were the points of departure for elaborate statutes which also refined and modified specific chapters in Magna Carta itself.

Finally, there is the matter of Magna Carta as it was understood by the English and American revolutionaries in the seventeenth and eighteenth centuries, colored by Sir Edward Coke's authoritarian interpretation. The statute of 1660, abolishing many feudal tenures, rendered obsolete at least ten of the thirty-seven chapters of the Great Charter of 1225; so a committee of the House of Commons reported in 1863 in an Act to repeal a large number of "sleeping statutes" including, at that time, all or part of seventeen chapters of Magna Carta. Other Parliamentary enactments from 1863 to 1948 have excised all but ten of the chapters; these—including the renowned Chapter 29 (39 in John's Charter)—it is safe to assume will remain unchallenged as continuing parts of the modern British constitution. As for Coke's interpretation, the fact cannot be overlooked that it was ratified by the Petition of Right and the Bill of Rights in English constitutional law, and by incorporation into state and federal constitutions of the United States.

Coke erred in assuming that the provisions written down in 1215 and 1225 had the same meaning that they did for him in his own time; but he was not alone in this, for the earliest printed lawbooks of the preceding Tudor century suggested the same thing. In any event, the error has been exaggerated; as the narrative in Part I of this study undertakes to illustrate, the very practicality of Magna Carta as a private law document invited progressive alteration in its feudal principles over the centuries, so that its revival as a constitutional document in Stuart times did not do such violence to the past as has occasionally been alleged.[2] If anything, as Chapter 8 of Part I points out, this metamorphosis of the Great Charter from a medieval to a modern proposition is analogous to the evolution of the rationale of the Fourteenth Amendment to the Constitution of the United States, and is symptomatic of the viability of the Anglo-American legal system itself.

To demonstrate this, by way of commentary on the specific passages of Magna Carta, is the burden of Part II. Having related the legend of the Great Charter in the preceding portion of this study, it now remains to give the reader a reasonable appreciation of the legacy of seven and a half centuries. The fundamental documents of the legacy, set out herein, are two: the short-lived grant of 1215 and the definitive reissue of 1225. History has been kind to John in one respect, in that his name is identified in the public mind with the original charter; but history has reserved the ultimate irony, for his name in fact has become synonymous with a charter which survives to the present and which was issued by his successor.

In any case, the material which follows consists of the preamble and headings (*capita* or "chapters" as later editors called them) of both charters, with certain typographic devices employed to differentiate between passages in John's charter which were deleted, passages in Henry's which were added, wording which was preserved from the one into the other, and those specific chapters which have survived to the present. Thus, the text which has remained unchanged since 1215 appears in ordinary Roman type; what was set down in John's charter but omitted thereafter is also in Roman type but enclosed in brackets; what was added in Henry's time appears in italics; and those chapters or parts of chapters which are preserved today are printed in boldface type.

Below the text of each part of the Charter appears a brief commentary which undertakes to clarify the meaning of certain feudal terms and the signification of the passage. The origins of the principle and its subsequent modification or reinterpretation are also briefly discussed, as well as the extension of the principle into the later common law. While the present space and purpose do not permit an exhaustive critical study, it is hoped that this treatment will provide the reader with an adequate understanding of what Magna Carta meant and means.

MAGNA CARTA

JUNE 15, 1215; FEBRUARY 11, 1225

Preamble

[JOHN,] *HENRY,* by the grace of God King of England, Lord of Ireland, Duke of Normandy and Aquitaine, Count of Anjou, to the archbishops, bishops, abbots, *priors,* earls, barons, [justiciars, foresters,] sheriffs, provosts, officers, and all his bailiffs and faithful people, *which shall see this present charter,* Greeting. Know that by the inspiration of God and for the salvation of our soul and [those] *the souls* of [all] our ancestors and successors, to [the honor of God and] the exaltation of Holy Church, and the improvement of our kingdom, [by the advice of our venerable fathers Stephen, archbishop of Canterbury, primate of all England and cardinal of the holy Roman church, Henry, archbishop of Dublin, William of London, Peter of Winchester, Jocelyn of Bath and Glastonbury, Hugh of Lincoln, Walter of Worcester, William of Coventry, and Benedict of Rochester, bishops; of Master Pandulph, sub-deacon and member of the household of the lord Pope, of Brother Aymeric, master of the Knights of the Temple in England; and of the noblemen William Marshal, earl of Pembroke, William, earl of Salisbury, William, earl of Warren, William, earl of Arundel, Alan of Galloway, constable of Scotland, Warren fitz Gerald, Peter fitz Herbert, Hubert de Burgh, steward of Poitou, Hugh de Nevil, Matthew fitz Herbert, Thomas Bassett, Alan Bassett, Philip d'Albini, Robert de Roppelay, John Marshall, John fitz Hugh, and others of our faithful,] *of our mere and free will have given*

244

and granted to the archbishops, bishops, abbots, priors, earls, barons and to all of this our realm, these liberties following to be held in our kingdom of England for ever.

Charters as evidence of promises made by lords to their vassals, and by rulers to their subjects—particularly, as in medieval England, to the small percentage of the population comprising the freeholders—were a common and often ephemeral device. A large number were granted in Anglo-Saxon times;[3] William the Conqueror was familiar with the practice, and while few records of his day have been preserved, a rather casual count of grants of liberties to towns, boroughs, and similar groups shows at least eight important charters of this type issued by kings from William I through John.[4] Similarly, English monarchs of Saxon times took coronation oaths, and the more detailed coronation charters of Henry I, Stephen, and Henry II in the post-Conquest era reflected the slowly elaborating recognition of the obligations owing by the ruler to those ruled. Until John's charter, however, such grants had seldom been explicit and were not framed, as was the preamble to Magna Carta, in terms of a large number of attesting witnesses. Henry I listed three bishops and half a dozen temporal lords; Stephen's Oxford Charter contained a long list of names, but these were sureties as much as supporters; and the brief charter of Henry II was attested only by Richard de Luci.

Of the three coronation charters, that of the first Henry was the most nearly analogous to John's. It was the one interpreted by Archbishop Langton to the barons some months before Runnymede[5] and constitutes a model, while the Unknown Charter of Liberties[6] and the Articles of the Barons[7] constitute the primary source, of the provisions in the Great Charter itself. The other details of 1215, and the added features of the reissue of 1225, derived from generally accepted principles of feudal law set out in the rolls of records begun under Henry II and regularized under Richard I. The form of John's charter was suggested by the form familiar to a grant of an estate in land, the most important document known to the feudal age.

Both John and his son assumed the same titles, claiming the kingdoms of England and Ireland, the duchies of Normandy and

Aquitaine, and the ancestral province of Anjou. At the time—the decade from 1215 to 1225—Angevin rule or overlordship was effective in most of the British Isles, the semiautonomous Aquitaine, and Poitou, Guienne, and Gascony on the vaguely defined northern and western borders of Aquitaine. These titles had little significance for the effective purposes of the grant; it was to England alone that it was intended to be applied.

The Charter was addressed to the principal lords spiritual (archbishops, bishops, abbots, priors) and temporal (earls, barons) as well as to the chief administrative officers of counties (sheriffs) and of certain boroughs (provosts) and other officers and bailiffs. Henry's charter omitted the justiciars and foresters because their concerns were dealt with separately in the Charter of the Forest. John's charter was issued "by the advice of" a number of men who were committed to him for a variety of reasons; twenty-seven of them are named in the preamble of 1215, and "others of our faithful" are implied. The importance of their ecclesiastical and temporal holdings, and the authority with which their names would be received wherever the Charter was read, points to the significance of the grant as a state paper. It also disposes, at least in large part, of the old argument that Magna Carta was imposed upon a virtually defenseless king; the men listed here were not only opposed to the extreme demands of the rebels but were concerned that the document as a whole should be a guarantee of fundamental feudal rights.

There were two archbishoprics in England—at Canterbury and York, with the latter presently unfilled since Geoffrey had recently died in exile—and one in Ireland. Archbishop Henry of Dublin had been faithful to John during his excommunication, despite censure from the Pope. He was present at Runnymede to protect the interests of the papal fief of Ireland, as well as to support his king. Archbishop Langton, from all evidence, was the chief draftsman of the Charter and would be the prime mover in the ultimate reissue of 1225.

Among the bishops listed in the preamble, William de Sainte-Mere-Eglise, a Norman protégé of Hubert Walter and a great favorite of Richard I, had been Bishop of London since John's coronation. Although he had been directed by Innocent to pronounce John's excommunication, and had fled to exile thereafter, he had recovered his high place in the King's favor after matters were patched up, and it was he who had received from John the Crusader's vow a few weeks before. Peter des Roches, of Winchester, and Jocelyn de Welles, of Bath and Glastonbury, had been the King's intermediaries in the settlement of the dispute with Innocent whereby Archbishop Langton was eventually received in England. Hugh de Welles, brother of Jocelyn and Bishop of Lincoln, was a loyal vassal of John; in the King's campaign of 1215-16 to recover the kingdom after the barons' bad faith, he would place his three castles at the disposal of the crown. Walter de Grey, of Worcester, was one of John's favorite courtiers, and shortly after Runnymede was nominated Archbishop of York. William de Cornhill, of Coventry, was Royal Justiciar and custodian of much of the Church property seized by the crown during the dispute with Rome. Benedict of Sausetum, of Rochester, had earlier been nominated as one of a party to carry an earlier peace offer to the Pope. Thus the seven bishops, in company with the two archbishops, placed the weight of the Church on the side of moderation if not of sympathy for the King against the rebels.[8]

Abbots were the chief officers of abbeys, or monastic communities; priors were subordinate officers in abbeys or the heads of priories, or dependencies of an abbey or monastery. None were named in the preamble, although several of the bishops had been abbots prior to their consecration. Inasmuch as many abbeys and priories had been built with baronial grants, and in many instances were heavily in debt to Jewish moneylenders, some of these lesser spiritual lords were undoubtedly sympathetic to the rebels and interested in such provisions as Chapter 10 on usury. On the other hand, the ecclesiastical tenants of barons supporting John would doubtless give their support to the side chosen by their grantor.

The presence of Pandulph, the papal legate who had settled the dispute between the Pope and John and who had received the King's homage for his kingdoms, added further weight to the ecclesiastical authority balancing the rebel forces at Runnymede. For the past four years the cardinal subdeacon had been in contact with John, with Innocent's full authorization to deal with him as necessary to enforce papal decisions and to see that the King lived up to his feudal obligations to Rome. John's record in this circumstance had been unimpeachable, and the Legate could certify to the Holy See that John had indeed become a true son of the Church—a relative matter, at best, but a substantial consideration in terms of the support it gave to the crown in this hour. Pandulph would be the officer to confirm to Innocent that the Great Charter was a violation of feudal obligations, particularly after the barons refused to honor their part of the bargain.[9]

The Knights of the Temple provided a final powerful churchly force on John's side. One Durand, a member of this influential, militant religious order, had been named by Innocent to accompany Pandulph on his original mission to England. Brother Aymeric, master of the order in England, would be a name to reckon with; founded originally in 1119 as a religious order to guard the site of Solomon's Temple in Jerusalem and to protect Christian pilgrims to the Holy Land, Templars were a power throughout Christendom by 1215. Together with the Knights Hospitallers, who had built a hospital in the Holy Land, the Templars had been vested with successive papal authority over the past several generations such that kings and archbishops could not assert jurisdiction over them.

Of the lords temporal named in the preamble, the foremost was William Marshal, Earl of Pembroke and one of the devoted public servants of a selfish age. His loyalty to Henry II in his final tragedy had won the admiration of Richard I, who had endowed him with great estates; he had served John faithfully, and after John's death would be protector of the kingdom and person of the young Henry III. Alan of Galway or Galloway, as Constable of Scotland, and Hubert de Burgh, Seneschal (Steward) of Poitou, assured John of the continued control of these important dominions outside England; as Constable of Dover Castle, de Burgh would defend that pivotal fortress against the force and blandishments of the invading French, and would render equally effective service to Henry III as his Chief Justiciar. William of Salisbury, one of the many illegitimate sons of Henry

II, came to Runnymede from a successful campaign against the rebels in the west country. William, fourth Earl of Surrey and Earl of Warren, was a cousin of John; William d'Albini or d'Aubeney, Earl of Arundel, was later a Royal Justiciar, and his kinsman Philip d'Albini was one of John's chief military leaders. Warren fitz Gerald and Peter and Matthew fitz Herbert had attested the surrender of the kingdom as a papal fief; the brothers Alan and Thomas Basset were leading captains in John's armies; Hugh de Neville held a number of important shrievalties in John's reign; Robert of Ropsley and John fitz Hugh were leading officers of the royal administration; and John Marshal was Earl William's nephew.[10]

For the times, then, these were moderate men; between them and the ecclesiastics, it was hoped that the Charter might have reasonable prospect of having binding force when it was published throughout the realm. Of the group who attested to John's charter, at least nine would be witnesses to the first reissue made in the name of Henry III; Bishop Peter of Winchester, one of these parties, would officiate at the young King's first coronation. Thus the preamble affords strong evidence that the Great Charter was not a unilateral action, but emerged as a reasonable balancing of the interests predominant in the heart of medievalism. Those chapters which represented the most adamant positions of the rebels were the very portions to be deleted from the reissues, and what was revised and preserved in the coming decade—and further modernized and extended by the legislation of later kings and Parliaments—represented the fundamental values of feudal law.

When, in 1225, Henry III at his majority made the definitive reissue of Magna Carta, he declared that it was given "of our mere [i.e., independent and uninfluenced] and free will," and no attesting witnesses were considered necessary. After 1265, when Parliament became an entity within the government of the realm, confirmations of the Charter became integral parts of comprehensive legislative programs, as in the fifth chapter of the Statute of Marlborough in 1267 or the opening chapter of the first general statute of Edward III in 1340. These uniformly referred either to the reissue of 1225 or to the Charter of Inspeximus or the Charter of Confirmation in 1297; and they became, for all practical purposes, Parliamentary confirmations to which the kings assented. More than fifty of these in medieval times,[11] often made as part of a general modernization of the chapters in the charters, helped to make the Great Charter a fixed element of the ancient constitution and persuaded the modern age that it was something of fundamental importance to be preserved in the new constitution.

1 [1]   *Freedom of the Church*

FIRST, *we have granted* to God, and by this our present charter *we have confirmed*, for us and our heirs forever, that the English Church shall be free, and shall have *all* her rights entire and her liberties inviolate; [and we will that it be thus observed; which is apparent from this, that the free-dom of elections, which is considered most important and essential to the English Church, we, of our mere and free will, did grant and confirm by our charter and did obtain ratification of the same from our lord, Pope Innocent III, before the quarrel arose between us and our barons; and this we shall observe, and we will that it be observed in good faith by our heirs forever]. **We have also granted to all freemen of our kingdom, for us and our heirs forever, all the liberties underwritten, to be had and held by them and their heirs, of us and our heirs, *for ever*.**

John's charter provisions began, as did the coronation charter of Henry I, with a grant of liberties to the Church; it is possible that Stephen Langton, Primate of All England, who had cited Henry's charter to the barons prior to the uprising, consciously modeled the opening of the 1215 charter after Henry's document of 1100. Langton, the draftsman of Magna Carta in all probabil-ity, would seek in his opening to set a high moral tone for the grant as a whole; and what better way than to render first unto

God the things that were God's—the precise words used in the opening of the chapter—and to link this to the promise of liberties extended to all freemen?

Henry's opening provision had been an explicit promise to "make free the Church of God," by which he meant that he would "neither sell nor lease its property, nor on the death of an archbishop or a bishop or an abbot . . . take anything from the demesne of the Church or from its vassals during the period which elapses before a successor is installed." John's statement in 1215 was more general and consequently was subject to different interpretations in different reigns. Almost immediately after the chapter was written, it was altered; the first reissue of 1216 dropped the reference to the detailed charter which John had granted, early in 1214, on freedom of elections. Langton was in exile by this latter date, and Henry's advisers may well have sought, in the event that the Archbishop did not live to return, to keep the choice of the successor in the King's hands. Freedom of elections—freedom, that is, from royal interference, for which John had been notorious even before the quarrel with the Holy See over the successor to Hubert Walter—was a major concession to the ecclesiastical powers which, as the chapter indicates, had already been settled before Runnymede; in practice, however, English kings insisted upon their rights to a voice in such matters.[12]

The dispute over the relative authority of temporal as against spiritual jurisdiction in any ecclesiastical office extended from before the Constitutions of Clarendon to after the Reformation measures of Henry VIII. In Saxon times, clerical parties apparently were generally subject to lay jurisdiction in matters of criminal and civil liability, even though certain concessions in rights to proof and in types of penalties might obtain. The Conquest had introduced a policy of dividing jurisdiction between lay and ecclesiastical courts, and by the twelfth century the latter were claiming that all matters touching clerics came under the canon law. The Norman kings, as Henry II, were not prepared to concede so much, however, and the Constitutions in 1164 had sought to recapture the jurisdiction of criminal cases involving ecclesiastics. The spiritual lords insisted upon the "benefit of clergy," and the disastrous quarrel with Thomas à Becket endowed their case with a powerful emotional advantage.

By John's time, the "plea of clergy" usually was effective in removing an accused person from the civil to the clerical court, but the support for the plea steadily declined in the thirteenth century, and Edward III in 1352 was able to make a substantial reform in the system. The change had begun with the practice of charging the cleric in the common-law court, though reserving to him the right to "claim clergy" and have the case removed to the church court at any stage in the proceeding. Then came the requirement that the accused spiritual person should stand trial at common law and only be delivered to the church court if convicted. "Benefit of clergy" has been credited with having an ameliorating effect upon the course of criminal law in general, over the centuries; by its emphasis upon a penal process in keeping with the magnitude of the crime, it may have encouraged a more rational development of criminal jurisprudence after Reformation times. It became increasingly artificial in its operation, however, and was formally abolished in 1827.[13]

Other rights and liberties of the Church as understood by the opening chapter of Magna Carta were suggested in the subsequent chapters, particularly the provision in Chapter 18 (26 John) on distribution of property by will. This probate jurisdiction of ecclesiastical courts continued in England until 1857, although it gradually diminished after the Reformation as common-law courts widened their own claims to jurisdiction.

The companion clause in the chapter, guaranteeing rights and liberties of the subject, related to all of the succeeding chapters (cf. "all the liberties underwritten"), and extended them "to all freemen" (*omnibus liberis hominibus*). Scholars have generally reached agreement on the point that "freemen" of feudal times were freeholders, or tenants of estates of varying degrees of importance. Thus, Magna Carta in this period proceeded from the same premise as the feudal law which it articulated: rights and liberties were a class privilege, properly to be claimed by less than 10 per cent of the population of England in the thirteenth century.[14] Not until the end of the Middle Ages did the concept of a wider category of "free men" come into being, and even after the English Revolution—and the American—free-holder qualifications for political suffrage, limiting the franchise to propertied classes, continued to be common.

It is important to remember that, in the context of Chapter 1 of the Great Charter, the rights and liberties set out in the rest of the document were limited to a very small group and to the particular guarantees covered by the other chapters. Coke and his contemporaries lost sight of this fact and understood Magna Carta to be a general grant of liberties to all English subjects. The seventeenth-century revolutionary movement was to give this effect to the Charter, but only after the numerous feudal peculiarities of the document had been rendered obsolete,[15] and after the residue had become a symbol rather than a self-executing statute. "The so-called liberties of the subject," it has been stated in the twentieth century, "are really implications drawn from the two principles that the subject may say or do what he pleases, provided he does not transgress the substantive law, or infringe the legal rights of others, whereas public authorities (including the crown) may do nothing but what they are authorized to do by some rule of common law or statute."[16]

The contrast between contemporary English and American guarantees of rights and liberties of the individual, both claiming to come from the Great Charter, lies in the fact that the English constitution is a consensus of statutory provisions subject to Parliamentary modification as current public opinion may permit. The American guarantees are embodied in state and federal constitutions which not only are more difficult to amend but often acquire the status of "higher law."[17] As for liberties of the Church, the English legal position is still one of commitment to establishmentarianism, while the First Amendment to the Constitution of the United States is specifically anti-establishmentarian.

2 [2] Reliefs

If any of our earls or barons, or others holding of us in chief by knight's service shall have died, and when he has died *his* heir shall be of full age and owe relief, he shall have his inheritance by the ancient relief; that is to say, the heir or heirs of an earl for the whole barony of an earl a hundred pounds; the heir or heirs of a baron for a whole barony a hundred pounds; the heir or heirs of a knight for a whole knight's fee a hundred shillings at most; and who owes less let him give less according to the ancient custom of fees.

Chapters 2 through 6 of Magna Carta were virtually repealed at the time of the Restoration, with the abolition of feudal tenures in 1660, and were formally repealed in 1863 by the Statute Law Revision Act of that year.[18] As late as 1607, however, Chapter 2 was being cited as authority for the collection of reliefs as a source of royal revenue independent of Parliament.[19] In the feudal age, from its earliest beginnings, the issue of the relief, or amount to be paid to insure a regranting of an estate to the heir of the former tenant, had been a matter of contention between the paramount lord and the freeholders. The exorbitant reliefs demanded by William II became one of the "evil laws" which Henry I in his coronation charter promised to abolish; only "a just and lawful relief" was permissible. What this amounted to had become a matter of "ancient custom" by 1215, and the chapter tried to make it explicit by itemizing the representative payments for the most common types of estates.

This subject had been the first one on the agenda of the barons: "After the death of their forebears, heirs of full age shall have their inheritance by the ancient relief expressed in their charters," ran the opening Article. From the time of the Conquest, and certainly from the Domesday survey, a charter as evidence of the obligations as well as the rights to an estate was of the highest importance; however, it had only been within the memory of men then present at Runnymede that rolls of records of such grants had begun to be kept by the royal treasury, and it would be almost a century before, in the statute *Quo Warranto,* such a record would be required to enforce a payment or protect a title.

In the Conqueror's time, estates were granted in terms of the number of knights' fees a given estate would be required to

support. The military considerations giving rise to this requirement also limited the grant to the lifetime of the present tenant,
in many instances. It was only during the reign of Henry II, when
the realm became more stable, that the renewal of the grant to
the heir changed from a matter of grace to a matter of course.[20]
In any event, the financial consideration or relief for the renewal
was a variable amount, despite what the tenant's charter might
say, and often had become a matter of bargaining between
grantor and freeholder. In the case of the crown, the "earls or
barons, or others holding of us in chief by knights' service" might
be liable for any number of arbitrary additions. A fine (a type
of quitclaim) might be levied in settlement of the sum agreed
upon as the relief; or a hidden levy known as "queen's gold"
(a contribution to the consort's funds) might be demanded.

While the tenor of these and other chapters of Magna
Carta—particularly in its reissues—was that the obligations were
those obtaining between any grantor and grantee, the language
of this particular chapter was concerned directly with John and
his tenants in chief. A century after Runnymede, a petition to
Edward II protested a levy of "queen's gold" in addition to relief
as a violation of this chapter,[21] indicating that it was taken to
be a limitation upon the crown.

3 [3] *Wardships*

IF, however, the heir of any such shall be under age, *his
lord shall not have the ward of him until he has received his
homage; and after such heir* shall be in ward, when he is
come of age, *that is to say, twenty and one years,* he shall
have his inheritance without relief and without fine; *so that
if such heir, being under age, be made knight, nevertheless
his land shall remain in the custody of his lord unto the term
aforesaid.*

This chapter, in 1215, was a verbatim copy of the second of
the Articles of the Barons. The reissue in 1216 added a provision

dictated by the dubious and vacillating loyalties of the war: no
lord of a fee was to have the guardianship of a minor heir until
he had received his homage. Nor, the reissue stated, should a
minor be excused from the custody of his lord even if he were
made a knight. These were concessions calculated to attract
support to the young Henry III in the near anarchy which followed John's death; by the ritual of homage, the guardian held
the knights' fees of the minor's estate for the support of the crown,
and also assured the minor of his rights to his land. Conversely,
since knighthood carried with it the assumption of adult status,
the King through his advisers promised not to cut off the guardian's interests in the wardship by making the heir a knight some
years before he actually reached majority.

The primary objective of Chapter 3 was to eliminate reliefs
and other financial claims upon an estate which might be insisted
upon when the heir came of age. Since the guardian was entitled
to the income from the estate during wardship, it was not equitable for him to attempt to demand at the end of this period any
further payments by the heir in order for him to enter into possession of his land. The language of the chapter in this case was
directed at all lords of fees, although it was assumed to operate
against the crown as well; John, and various kings after him, were
reluctant to give up properties which they might have held for
a number of years in the case of youthful survivors of former
tenants. In 1334 the Earl of Athol petitioned for delivery of his
inheritance by Edward III according to the "Great Charter made
by his progenitors, and confirmed by himself."[22] In later generations the chapter became the basis for regular suits between private persons to compel delivery of estates held in custody.

The provision of homage reflected feudalism's ethical and
practical concepts of the interests in land to be protected. A
fatherless heir, it was argued, must be in ward to someone; it
should not be his mother, lest she remarry and bear other sons
who would covet the estate of their elder half-brother and on this
account might destroy him. The same consideration ruled out
kinsmen, and pointed to the lord of the fee "who can never
inherit that land in demesne." By the ritual of homage, the lord

was assured of the heir's loyalty and in turn committed himself
to warranting the heir's title to the estate and to protecting the
heir's interests by undertaking to "faithfully guard . . . woods and
tenements"[23]—the burden of the next chapter as well.

Feudal obligations outweighed blood ties, and wardship
might be divisible in terms of several estates held by an heir of
different grantors. In such case, according to the Statute of Westminster II, the lord of the oldest tenure was to have the wardship
of the body of the heir, and the several lands were put in ward
to their respective grantors.[24] The final important addition of the
reissue of the Charter was the definition of the age of majority
when the guardians were required to give back the lands—
"twenty and one years." Henry was to assert his majority and
obtain papal ratification of it for certain purposes when he was
seventeen. The stipulation of twenty-one years as the age of full
legal competence has become a standard of Anglo-American law,
although the past quarter-century has heard arguments in favor
of the lower age for certain purposes.

4 [4] *Waste During Wardship, etc.*

THE custodian of the land of such an heir who is under
age shall not take from the land of the heir any except reasonable produce, reasonable customs, and reasonable services,
and this without destruction or waste of men or of goods;
and if we shall have committed the custody of the land of
any such a one to the sheriff or to any other who is to be
responsible to us for the issues *of the land,* and that man
shall have caused destruction or waste from his custody we
will recover damages from him, and the land shall be committed to two lawful and discreet men of that fee, who shall
be responsible for its issues to us or to him to whom we have
assigned them; and if we shall have given or sold to any one
the wardship of any such land, and he has caused destruction
or waste therein, he shall lose that custody, and it shall be

handed over to two lawful and discreet men of that fee who shall be in like manner responsible to us as aforesaid.

Waste, according to contemporary definitions, is any negligent or deliberate action by the present occupant of property which injures the full enjoyment of the property by the person known to be the future occupant or owner.[25] The definition would have sounded familiar to the thirteenth century, for the problem was essentially the same, and indeed far more acute. Chapter 4 of Magna Carta was one of the earliest of many attempts at remedy; provisions in the Statutes of Marlborough, Westminster I, and Gloucester would supplement it. The problem in this case arose out of the matter of wardships and was reflected in the neglect of resources and deterioration or destruction of structures on lands in ward, so that heirs frequently would find their inheritance to be in ruins when they finally came into possession.

Chapter 4 was not immediately effective in meeting the problem; for one thing, it was concerned with preserving the King's interest in the property rather than assuring direct relief to the heirs themselves. The major part of the chapter prescribed procedures for giving the King damages in waste where lands of a deceased crown tenant have been placed in ward of a sheriff or other representative of the crown; the alternative case involves waste where the crown has placed the lands in ward of a private party, for which the penalty is removal of the wardship. This emphasis upon royal rights was used by various private defendants as an avoidance of actions brought directly against them by despoiled heirs. In 1309 such an argument was made: "These tenements are holden in chief of our lord the King . . . and we do not think that . . . anyone but the King ought to have amends for waste."[26]

By this date, however, Chapter 4 of the Great Charter had been clarified and generalized by the fundamental statutes already mentioned—one of many instances in which Magna Carta was kept current by amendment—and the court rejected the defense. Two years later, relying on the provision of treble damages set out in the Statute of Gloucester, the court found liability where the guardian had "felled oaks each appraised at half a mark, one hundred ash trees, each appraised, etc., one hundred apple trees each appraised, etc. . . . to the disinheritance" of the plaintiff.[27] Thus Chapter 4, as amplified by later legislation, ultimately became the starting point for an important element in the Anglo-American law of property.

Guardians, of course, were always entitled to "reasonable produce, reasonable customs, and reasonable services." To the feudal age, this meant the villein services of tillage and harvest, and the income from the crops or from various fees (customs) for bringing goods into, across, or out of the estate. But this was to be done "without waste or destruction of men or goods"; the guardian was not to reduce the amount of labor to which the estate was entitled by enfranchising some or all of the villeins and thus stripping the land of its workers, nor was he to permit loss, breakage, or theft of the tools of husbandry which were essential to an agricultural economy and difficult or sometimes impossible of replacement. This was the burden of the next chapter, which was made more explicit in the reissue.

5 [5] *Sustaining Lands in Wardship*

The custodian moreover, so long as he shall have the custody of the land, shall keep up the houses, parks, warrens, ponds, mills, and other things pertaining to that land, from the proceeds of the land itself; and he must return to the heir, when he has come to full age, all his land, furnished with ploughs [and implements of husbandry according as the time of wainage requires and as the proceeds of the land are able reasonably to sustain] *and all other things, at least as he received it. And all those things shall be observed in the custodies of archbishoprics, bishoprics, abbeys, priories, churches and dignities vacant, which pertain to us; except that such custodies shall not be sold.*

This chapter supplemented the preceding chapter by making explicit the responsibility of him who had land in ward; he was to keep up its premises "from the proceeds of the land itself," and he must return to the heir at his majority the land and all its implements "at least as he received it." A medieval estate had to be kept self-sufficient, and the chapter is at pains to enumerate the particular features to be kept up: the houses or dwellings of the tenants and their men; the parks, or private game preserves which were enclosures within the forests (called *chases* if not enclosed); the warrens or livestock compounds; the ponds for fish, geese, and ducks; and the mills where the grain from the estate was ground.

John's charter was concerned with the wardship and upkeep of lay fiefs; the reissue of Henry III added a similar stipulation respecting those ecclesiastical vacancies "which pertain to us." Chapter 26 (33 John) added the stipulation that vacant abbeys were to be placed in the custody of the lords who had founded them, presumably with the same burden placed upon the custodian. Chapter 5, in this portion, is concerned with abbeys, priories, and churches of royal foundation, while all archbishoprics and bishoprics were under the guardianship of the king as *patronus et protector ecclesiae.* Ecclesiastical fiefs which became vacant upon the death of the incumbent were not the same as lay tenancies, which had minor heirs to be put in ward; it was said that in the case of the spiritual tenement the "spiritualties" became the subject of the dean and chapter of the mother house, while the "temporalties" reverted to the king.[28]

Under the Constitutions of Clarendon each spiritual lord held his crown lands as a barony, and hence it was arguable that such lands could in fact be put in ward during the period of a vacancy. The vacancy could then continue for an indefinite time while the crown enjoyed the revenues from these lands, only limited by the provisions of this chapter that certain of the revenues must go to the upkeep of the premises. Since the reissue of the Charter had omitted, in Chapter 1, the guarantee of free elections to fill ecclesiastical vacancies, the new text in Chapter 5 gave the crown the same degree of control over Church tenancies as Henry II had enjoyed. It was not until 1340, under Edward III, that the dean and chapter were able to obtain a right to pre-empt such wardships at a reasonable price.

The right asserted by the crown over vacant Church lands was not always a matter of greed; the thirteenth-century law had not settled the question of how a spiritual community could hold land and discharge secular obligations when it was without a head. In such cases, the king, as "patron" of the Church, had the obligation of assuming the responsibilities of administration.[29] If Chapter 5 was not effective in disposing of all of the problems of custodians' responsibilities, in either lay or ecclesiastical fiefs, it was in part due to the fact that these problems could not be entirely comprehended until a modern commercial economy had developed.

6 [6]   *Marriage of Heirs*

Heirs shall be married without disparagement, [so nevertheless that before the marriage is contracted, it shall be announced to the relatives by blood of the heir himself.]

This is the last of the group of chapters (2-6) in Magna Carta concerning the arbitrary disposition of property when it passed from a tenant to his heir. Disparagement, or the marriage of one party to another of lower status in the feudal system, could well be a form of injury to the inheritance; a female heir endowed with great estates was a valuable prize in the hand of the custodian and might be married off to a favorite to her detriment if it was to his enrichment. Or an ambitious landholder might be prepared to bid high for the hand of such an heiress, to the enrichment of her guardian as well as himself.

John's charter had contained the further stipulation that the relatives of the heir (or heiress) were to be notified before a contract was settled. This provision sought to safeguard the other tenants from a union with a hostile house; as the Unknown Charter of Liberties put it, the heir should be free to marry as the lord desired, save to the enemies of the king. This clause was omitted from the reissue, quite probably because it was adequately covered in the last sentence of the following chapter.

7 [7, 8]   *Widows' Estates*

A WIDOW, after the death of her husband, shall have her marriage portion and her inheritance immediately and without obstruction, nor shall she give anything for her dower or for her marriage portion, or for her inheritance, which inheritance her husband and she held on the day of the death of her husband; and she may remain in the house of her husband for forty days after his death, within which time her dower shall be assigned to her, *if it were not assigned to her before, or unless the house be a castle; and if she depart from the castle, an adequate house shall be forthwith provided for her, in which she may validly dwell, until her dower be assigned to her, as aforesaid; and she shall have in the meantime her reasonable estovers of the common. And for her dower shall be assigned to her the third part of all the lands of her husband which were his during coverture, unless she had been endowed of less at the church door.* No widow shall be distrained to remarry, [so long as she prefers to live without a husband,] provided she gives security that she will not marry without our consent, if she holds of us, or without the consent of her lord if she holds of another.

With the short life expectancy of the Middle Ages—particularly for men engaged almost continually in war or the dangerous pastimes of the tournament or the hunt—the protection of survivors and their estates was a continuing concern. Following the five chapters on inheritance and its various ramifications, two chapters (combined into one in the reissues and thereafter progressively enlarged) dealt with widows' rights. One of the most obvious, if also crude, methods of providing for the care of a marriageable widow was to expedite another marriage; this also had the advantage of keeping the estate in a condition of constant support of the lord of the fee and of making the new marriage a means of bringing two estates into an advantageous union. Forced marriages of widows, however, were an old abuse which the charter of Henry I had explicitly condemned; and John's Chapter 8 (the last sentence of the present chapter) reiterated the prohibition, suggesting that the abuse had been revived. The record is fairly clear, in fact, that the promise of 1100 had never been kept, and John simply followed in the footsteps of his predecessors in compelling remarriages which were to his advantage.

Indeed, the widow of a tenant was even more at the mercy of the lord of the fee—whether king or baron—than a minor heir. To avoid an unwelcome remarriage, or to acquire what was rightfully hers, or to avoid an indefinite postponement of the delivery of her property, she was beset by a great many pressures to make what might be a highly disadvantageous settlement. The chapter sought to guarantee that the widow should have her estate promptly, without delay or payment, and within the forty-day period in which she should remain in her late husband's house. The one exception, added in 1216, was that if "the house be a castle" (i.e., a fortified residence) she was to be furnished a suitable alternative, the reason being that a male commander of the castle garrison needed to be put in possession as quickly as possible.

The widow's estate might be made up of three parts: her *marriage portion* (the "dowry" as it was later called), or property which her father bestowed upon her at the time of her marriage and which by the terms of the gift might revert to her after the husband's death; any inheritance from her family which she received in her own name during the marriage; and the *dower* or portion of her husband's estate which was set aside at the time of the marriage for her possession in the event of his death. According to feudal custom, the dower was bestowed upon the bride as she came from the altar, and the reissue of 1217 fixed it at one-third of all the lands of which her husband was possessed during the marriage, "unless she were endowed of less at the church door."

During the time in which the specific portion of the lands in dower were being determined, the widow was entitled for her support to "reasonable estovers [food and fuel] of the common [undivided estate]." Finally, the reissue of 1217 added the provision that the dower to which the widow was entitled was to be

one-third of all lands held by her husband during coverture
(period of marriage). Thus, the chapter, in the course of its
several revisions, established a number of important elements of
law—and in the process fundamentally affected the economics of
feudalism. By insuring that the widow had a right to one-third of
her husband's property, the chapter correspondingly reduced by
one-third the resources of the estate to go to the heir, or if the
heir was a minor, the revenues from the estate to be taken into
the hand of the lord of the fee.

In many areas of England, local custom sanctioned the alloca-
tion of more than one-third of the property to dower, and it was
not surprising that in due course (in 1292 and 1313, to cite two
instances) suits should be brought against specific estates by the
lords of the fee to reduce the amount to one-third.[30] The trend of
adjudication after the 1217 revision, however, was generally in
favor of the widow's claims; the language of the chapter supported the argument that the one-third interest extended to properties acquired by the husband after the marriage ceremony—
that is, during his lifetime and not merely at the time of "church
door"—and conversely prevented the reduction of the widow's
interest by any alienation of land during this period. As early as
1221, widows were successfully relying on the chapter to protect
their estates from diminution by any acts by the husband,[31] compelling the courts to develop new safeguards for grantees of land
which might be subject to dower rights. The Statutes of Gloucester and Westminster II[32] strengthened the widow's position and
the provisions of this chapter, so that the economic protection
of women was substantially enhanced throughout the Middle
Ages.

The modernization of the law on widows' estates began with
the Statute of Uses (trusts) in 1536,[33] and the Dower Act of
1833[34] rendered much of the old common law obsolete. It was not
until the comprehensive revision of the statutes on property in
1925, however, that this chapter of Magna Carta was formally
repealed.[35] Two factors accounted for the gradual abandonment,
in modern times, of the common law of dower: the difficulty of
transferring land to a new owner with the cloud of a possible
dower action on the title; and the relatively greater importance of

other forms of property, besides land, which became essential to the widow's full beneficial interest.

In the United States the common-law rule continued for many years, particularly in those jurisdictions which "received" the common law as it was at the time of colonization, or which adopted Magna Carta in whole or in part into the system of local law. This has led to a wide variety of statutory modifications of dower law and has correspondingly complicated this area of real estate law in the United States.

8 [9]   *Crown Debtors and Their Pledges*

NEITHER we nor our bailiffs shall seize any land or rent for any debt, so long as the *present* chattels of the debtor are sufficient for the payment of the debt *and the debtor himself is ready to satisfy therefor.* Nor shall the pledges of a debtor be distrained so long as the principal debtor himself has enough for the payment of the debt; and if the principal debtor fails in the payment of the debt, not having the wherewithal to pay it, *or will not pay if he is able*, the pledges shall answer for the debt; and if they wish, they shall have the lands and the rents of the debtor until they shall have been satisfied for the debt which they have before paid for him, unless the principal debtor shall have shown himself to be quit in that respect towards those pledges.

Having disposed of the problems of inheritances (Chapters 2-6) and of widows' rights (Chapter 7), the next four chapters of John's charter concerned themselves with various financial disabilities laid upon tenants and estates. Only the first of these, as it turned out, was preserved in the reissues, and it should be considered in relation to Chapters 14 (20 John) and 18 (26 John). The problem of debts and their satisfaction where the creditor was the crown could be a serious and certainly chronic threat to the tenants' security and well-being. The incessant levies—aids, amercements, reliefs, scutages, tallages—kept almost everyone under financial obligation to the crown in varying degrees; and to enhance the prospects of payment of the obligation, the crown required pledges or sureties who might find the full burden of the debt falling upon them if the principal debtor was in exile or in such straits that he could not meet the demand.

Land, always the fundamental and vital asset of feudalism, was to be protected at all costs. Medieval kings, as well as the early Tudors and the early Stuarts, frequently yielded to the temptation to repossess tracts which had been granted to tenants who later fell into debt. The repossession usually more than satisfied the debt, but this was so much the worse for the debtor; the revenues from the land relieved the king of financial pinches which developed when Parliament refused the full monetary grants requested by these later kings.

Of the three methods of satisfying a creditor's claim—going against the debtor's body, against his chattels, or against his land —the first had dropped out of use soon after the Conquest, and the third was disliked by the feudal law because it jeopardized the power base of the entire economy. Slavery for indebtedness had been an Anglo-Saxon process; it was to be revived, as imprisonment, in a retrogressive step in the Statute of Westminster II and would persist until the nineteenth century. Dispossession of the debtor's lands had proved too readily susceptible of abuse, and this chapter of Magna Carta sought to limit the remedy and confine the King to an action against the personal property of the debtor. Of the three rules set out in this chapter—protecting land while there were chattels sufficient to satisfy the debt, protecting the surety from suit so long as the principal debtor could be reached, and permitting the surety to succeed to the creditor's rights if the surety was compelled to satisfy the debt—the first, aimed at the crown, is the one which has failed to survive into modern law.

The depredations of estates wrought by the crown or the crown officers in feudal times had several dimensions; two other chapters of Magna Carta (14 and 18) sought to protect from seizure the property essential to the tenant's particular status, and to limit the seizure of chattels to the amount sufficient to satisfy the debt. Eighty-five years later, the Articles upon the Charters undertook to lay fresh restraints upon excessive seizures in debt claims by the crown (Chapter 12) and in cases where the claim was disallowed (Chapter 19). Until the right of arbitrary action was finally taken from the crown by the Bill of Rights and the Act of Settlement, however, statutory safeguards operated only imperfectly.

The Charter provisions on suretyship have continued to the present, and thus Chapter 8 of the 1225 reissue is part of the modern law. The Middle Ages recognized this chapter as a major advance in property law, and various private actions were based upon it.[36] Westminster II (Chapter 18) recognized a process which had developed in the ensuing period of the thirteenth century and was known to common lawyers for more than six hundred years thereafter as "fi. fa." (from *fieri facias,* an order to a sheriff that he "cause to be made up" from the debtor's chattels the amount due on the debt). The statute also recognized the alternative writ of *elegit* (i.e., the creditor "elects" to have a jury place a value on the chattels and deliver the debtor's land to him until the debt is satisfied).

With the growth in permanent records and their importance in establishing legal rights, after the legislation of Edward I, debt claims rapidly became a matter of recording, laying the ground for the modern processes of suit, judgment, and execution. But Chapter 8 of Magna Carta was of fundamental importance in that it provided the starting point for an eminently sophisticated system of protecting the interests of the three parties in a typical debt situation: the creditor (first the king, but soon any private claimant), the debtor, and the surety.[37]

[10]   *Usury*

[If any one has borrowed anything from the Jews, more or less, and dies before that debt is paid, the debt shall not draw interest so long as the heir is under age, from whomso-

ever he holds; and if that debt falls into our hands, we will
take nothing except the principal contained in the bond.]

Another type of debt problem was presented by John's
Chapters 10 and 11—a problem compounded of racial and religious antipathies, of the peculiar and often anomalous status of
the Jewish community in England and other parts of medieval
Christendom as a consequence, and of the two centuries which
were yet to pass before the modern concept of mortgage law
began to take form. In Chapter 10 of the 1215 charter, the inheritance of minors was protected; in Chapter 11, the estates of
widows. In the first instance, the interest on a debt owed the
Jewish creditors was suspended for the period of the minority;
in the second, the debt itself was extinguished. The chapters are
a faithful, almost verbatim copy of Articles 34 and 35 of the
barons, and constituted a bold effort to repudiate a vast number
of obligations which constituted a separate and equally serious
burden on many estates.

Christians were forbidden by medieval church law to lend
money at interest; and the need for such an economic service—
both to king and to tenants—created a natural niche for Jewish
moneylenders. William Rufus had summoned them to England,
and for two centuries they were to be under royal protection—a
sometimes indifferent guarantee, as in the violent persecution of
the Jews at the time of the coronation of Richard I—until their
expulsion from the realm in 1290. The "king's Jews" by the early
thirteenth century had become a major factor in the economy,
holding notes on many lay and ecclesiastical properties; the
chronically precarious nature of their claims compelled them to
demand enormous rates of interest, and such charges against
estates held in ward during a long minority could impair or
destroy the inheritance.

Both this chapter and its companion were deleted from the
reissue of the following year; the advisers of Henry III needed to
encourage rather than alienate moneylenders. The twopence per
pound per week which was the standard rate of interest brought
in an excellent revenue from which the crown could periodically
extract substantial levies, and on occasion the king could take

into his hand the debts owing to his Jews by Gentile tenants. Since the Jews served the king and had only such rights as he chose to enforce in their behalf, their relation to the king was quite similar to the relation of villeins to the lord of an estate.[38] To preserve the sweeping repudiations of 1215 could only have been to the injury of the crown, and although these were doubtless omissions from the reissue of 1216 which were urged by the tenants for reconsideration in 1217, they were never restored to the Charter.[39]

Two decades earlier, in the reign of Richard I, the systematic regulation of moneylending had been inaugurated with the development of a recording process. A body of officers, some Christian and some Jewish, prepared three copies of each deed, or "gage," which set out the terms of a loan; one copy went to either party and the third copy was deposited in a chest, or "ark," which was kept in royal custody. A few years later, a special Exchequer of the Jews was created to administer the financial and judicial matters growing out of the recording process. Thus, by 1215, the grip of the Jewish creditors upon many of the assets of English tenants had become firm and continuing. It would extend to many processes of feudalism in the coming century, as debtors defaulted and Jews succeeded to their estates even though prohibited by law from becoming tenants in reality.

Before the end of Henry's reign, Jews controlled the fees of many tracts of land, with the knight service which went with them; they had the ward of property of minor heirs and arranged their marriages; where they acquired debtors' rights of advowson, they could even present Christian candidates to Christian bishops for installation in Christian churches.[40] The protest of the feudal community resulted in an edict of 1271 that Jews could no longer hold free tenements, and the following two decades witnessed an increasing number of restrictions laid upon them, until their expulsion.

[11]   *Debts of Widows and Minors*

[AND if any one dies leaving a debt owing to the Jews, his wife shall have her dower and shall pay nothing of that debt; and if there remain minor children of the deceased, necessaries shall be provided for them corresponding to the holding of the dead man; and from the remainder shall be paid the debt, the service of the lords being retained. In the same way debts are to be treated which are owed to others than the Jews.]

This chapter, the companion of the preceding one, was stricken from the reissue of 1216 for the same reason: it impaired the crown's use of the Jews as an agency for financing much of the feudal economy. The self-interest of the debtor was evident in the extent of the attempted repudiation—the widow's estate, being freed from the debt, reduced the security for the debt by one-third; all minor children were then entitled to support in keeping with their status in the feudal system; and all services due from the estate to the lord of the fee were to be preserved. Whatever was left, which was usually nothing, was attachable by the creditor.

Remarkable as this repudiation was, the chapter went further, and extended the repudiation to all other creditors in like situations. A financial anarchy would have resulted from the retention and enforcement of this chapter; it reflects as clearly as anything in Magna Carta the greed of the rebels when given the opportunity to state their terms.

[12] *Scutages and Aids*

[NO scutage or aid shall be imposed in our kingdom except by the common council of our kingdom, except for the ransoming of our person, for making our oldest son a knight, and for once marrying our oldest daughter, and for these purposes it shall be only a reasonable aid; in the same way it shall be done concerning the aids of the city of London.]

Three subjects were attacked in this chapter; the excessive number of scutages or payments in lieu of knight service, which

John had levied in the course of his profitless military efforts on the Continent; the restatement of the well-established feudal rule that aids could be demanded for the king's ransom, for the knighting of his oldest son, and "for once marrying our oldest daughter"; and the special levies laid upon the city of London. While this chapter was deleted from the reissues, the first subject was preserved, in more vaguely general terms, in the final Chapter 37 of 1225, and the second subject was considered to be self-evident.[41] If the third was seriously considered, it was in terms of the special charters which, before and after Runnymede, progressively enlarged the privileges of the city of London.[42]

Thus the omission of this chapter from the reissues was essentially a matter of editing rather than an effort to rescind the propositions set out. To be sure, the provision in Chapter 37 of 1225 that *escuages* (another form of scutage) were to be levied according to the custom in the time of Henry II was conveniently broad; yet the problem created by John's levies[43] was well recognized, and under Henry III there was a decided increase in the number of tenants who resumed the practice of performing knight service in person. Chapter 20 (29 John) recognizes that personal service rather than a monetary substitute should be assured to the subject according as the one or the other is less onerous. From the middle of the thirteenth century until the abolition of feudal tenures in 1660,[44] scutages steadily declined in effectiveness as related to their original objective of providing funds for military affairs of the state.

Constitutional writers of the nineteenth and early twentieth centuries read into Chapter 12, limiting certain levies to those approved by "the common council of our kingdom," and into Chapter 14, providing for the convening of such a council, the beginnings of parliamentary government and of control of taxation by that government. Not even Coke went so far in his claims for Magna Carta, and for a very good reason: neither Chapter 12 nor 14 was retained in the reissues. The first Parliament was precisely half a century after Runnymede; and by the latter years of Edward I, Parliament was beginning to perceive that, where feudal incidents were insufficient as a revenue source, it could exact concessions from the crown in return for its grants of funds.

The *Confirmatio Cartarum*, the Statute *de Tallagio,* and the subsequent *Articuli super Cartas* were all obtained under such conditions. But it would require the modern economic understanding of taxation in the sixteenth century, and the political supremacy of Parliament in the seventeenth, to effectuate the constitutional principles which were prematurely attributed to these ephemeral chapters of 1215.

9 [13] *Liberties of Towns*

[And] **the city of London shall have all the ancient liberties and free customs** [as well by land as by water]. **Moreover, we will and grant that all other cities, boroughs, towns *and the barons of the Five Ports,* and *all other* ports, shall have all their liberties and free customs.**

The Normans found London to be a thriving congeries of townships and contiguous communities, which already had a certain unity as a trading port with a special reeve in charge of it. William I had briefly confirmed its liberties and customs won in Anglo-Saxon times, and a succession of charters from Henry I to Henry IV attested to its steady development toward its ultimate world eminence in modern times. Throughout the Middle Ages the city grew in population, wealth, and power; it is not without significance that this should be one of the chapters of Magna Carta to have been preserved over seven and a half centuries to the present. London as a vigorously independent political force, with its artisans and merchants, its powerful defenses complemented by the great Tower, and above all its long-established rights to limited taxation and the election of its own sheriffs— confirmed by a charter of Henry I early in the twelfth century— was literally a law unto itself. It was the most important prototype of the ancient demesne, that irreducible and all but indestructible body of pre-Conquest (and perhaps pre-Anglo-Saxon) customs which survived through all the changing frames of historical reference.

London was not the capital of a nation in 1215, but its focal relationship to Westminster, Winchester, Canterbury, and Rochester made it the economic hub of the realm, and its political dominance would follow as a matter of course. It had taken a decisive part in national affairs on several occasions; in Stephen's day it had claimed the right to elect the paramount lord whom it would recognize as king, just as in the seventeenth century it would take a decisive part in the Revolution, Commonwealth, and Restoration. While Henry II had undertaken to reduce its independence, its leaders had taken advantage of Richard's long absence and the fall of his regent, Longchamp, to win a sweeping reassertion of its privileges. In 1191 John, in Richard's name, had added substantially to its "ancient liberties," and as King he had granted no fewer than five charters, the latest being in May 1215. But London, despite these favors, had betrayed him a few weeks later.

Its mayor, William Hardell, would be among the sureties named in Chapter 61 of the charter of 1215 to enforce its demands. The present chapter preserved the principal privileges the city had claimed from ancient times, or had won in the grants beginning in 1191—including, at that time, the right to elect its mayor and council. The 1215 charter guaranteed these privileges "as well by land as by water," presumably an attempt to assert jurisdiction over all of neighboring Middlesex and the right to levy customs upon traders coming to or going from the city. The reissue deleted this particular phrase, but did not otherwise reduce the broad guarantee contained in the chapter, while other chapters of the Charter further enhanced its metropolitan character. Chapter 11 (17 John) prepared the way for Westminster to become the permanent seat of royal justice; Chapter 23 (33 John) provided for the clearing of obstructions from the city's great watercourses; and Chapter 25 (35 John) would standardize weights and measures essential to its trade and would adopt some of its own standards (e.g., "the quarter of London").

The city long maintained its autonomy; the Court of Hustings at the Guildhall, presided over by the mayor and aldermen, had jurisdiction over most private actions within the walls, while the sheriff's court heard personal and commercial disputes. In criminal matters involving the king's justice, the mayor would be one of the members of the bench and the proceedings would be at

St. Martin-le-Grand, outside the walls.[45] In commercial matters, Londoners had the benefit of their own courts at trade fairs throughout the realm, and claimed exemption from a number of tolls while imposing a succession of restrictions upon foreign merchants doing business within its walls. Chapter 9 of Magna Carta was to be cited, over the next three centuries, as a blanket grant of economic and political liberties against other groups in favor of the city.[46]

The chapter also applied the guarantee to "all other cities, boroughs, towns" which could exhibit a valid charter of privileges. There were a number of these; Henry I had granted a charter, confirming an earlier grant by the Archbishop of York, to the town of Beverley, specifying administrative autonomy for its merchant guild, free burgage (right of its citizens to certain tenurial exemptions and privileges), and "the same law of liberty as the men of York have." Henry II had given Bristol a toll-free grant in 1155; Anselm, Abbot of Bury St. Edmunds, had given a charter to the borough exempting the residents from the jurisdiction of county courts; Cambridge held a charter limiting the amount of its annual "farms" or rents to the exchequer. So ran a number of grants, usually specifying some particular privilege, to towns like Gloucester, Hastings, Leicester, Lincoln, Oxford, and Winchester.[47]

A *borough* was an autonomous area within a county, with its own courts, customs, and guilds; later it would, like urban areas, have the right to its own representation in Parliament. The word *town* was usually a generic term, while a *city* was a fortified urban center, with its own castle and garrison and often the cathedral of an important diocese where public and private documents would be preserved in the cartulary.

Henry's charter extended the full scope of Chapter 9 to "the barons of the Five Ports," the important Channel towns of Dover, Hastings, Hythe, Romney, and Sandwich which held out against the French invasion, harbored the royal navy, and launched the successful Battle of the Sandwich Islands which ended the rebellion of the barons and Prince Louis's adventure in 1216. The castle of Dover was, with the Tower of London and certain fortresses on the Scottish border and the Welsh marches, the key to the control of England; Hubert de Burgh had held it faithfully as Constable for John and Henry, and the baronies represented in these towns had well earned their special concessions. In the thirteenth century, other towns would be brought under the jurisdiction of one or another of these five, and a special administrative officer, the Warden of the Ports, would bring the economy of this area into a virtual league or confederation.

Because of the volume of commerce which was channeled through these ports, as well as their concern with the affairs of the kingdom's navy, they would provide the rudiments for the later law of admiralty. Originally conceived as a special jurisdiction for injuries to persons and property at sea, either of a public or private nature, admiralty in subsequent centuries became almost exclusively a matter of maritime commercial law. Even before the crystallization of this body of jurisprudence, in the fourteenth and fifteenth centuries, the specialized subject matter coming before the courts of Dover led to conflicts between the different courts, a problem which was the subject of Chapter 7 in the Articles upon the Charters in 1300 which nevertheless preserved to the residents "their old franchises confirmed by the Great Charter."

[14]   *Calling a Common Council*

[AND for holding a common council of the kingdom concerning the assessment of an aid otherwise than in the three cases mentioned above, or concerning the assessment of a scutage, we shall cause to be summoned the archbishops, bishops, abbots, earls, and greater barons by our letters under seal; and besides we shall cause to be summoned generally, by our sheriffs and bailiffs all those who hold of us in chief, on a certain day, that is at the end of forty days at least, and at a certain place; and in all the letters of such summons, we shall express the cause of the summons, and when the summons has thus been given the business shall proceed on the appointed day, on the advice of those who shall be present, even if not all of those who were summoned have come.]

Chapter 14 of John's charter was made necessary by Chapter 12; in fact, the division into "chapters" being an artificial device of later times, the provisions in the original draft run continuously. This is evident from a reading of the last sentence of Chapter 12, which is carried directly into Chapter 13; and having elaborated sufficiently upon the rights of towns, the theme of the first part of Chapter 12 is taken up again in Chapter 14. This was the proposition that extraordinary levies should not be demanded "unless by the common council of our kingdom," and a method of summoning such a council accordingly had to be conceived. Although neither 12 nor 14 survived among the chapters of the reissues, they are significant as an expression of the nascent proposition that a regular "parley" of great lords should be an essential ingredient of government.

The medieval monarchy was a one-man government; the legitimacy of any act of government turned upon the assent, and usually upon the sole initiative, of the king. Most of the "good" or "bad" laws of earlier times were actually crystallized customs or the edicts of particular rulers; the most nearly recognizable series of laws in the most rudimentary modern sense were those of King Canute in the eleventh century, and those of Henry II between 1164 and 1176. Thus, Magna Carta, covering the spectrum of medieval jurisprudence as broadly as it did and becoming progressively refined and confirmed in the decade between 1215 and 1225, in a very real sense marked the beginning of statutory expression of law in English history.

Later generations of scholars gave specialized meanings to terms which, in the feudal age, were used interchangeably or synonymously. Thus, Henry's legislation might be described as "constitutions" (from the Roman law *constitutio*, an establishing decree) and thus ideologically similar to the *doms* or "dooms" of Anglo-Saxon kings. Or his law might be described as an *assize*, a term of many meanings, but derived from a Norman French concept of the deliberative processes of a "sitting" for administrative or judicial purposes. The century following Magna

Carta favored the terms *statute* (or "estatute") and *ordinance,* used interchangeably but occasionally distinguishing between an enactment by joint action of the king and a full assembly of magnates, and an enactment by the king in council.

The itinerant court of the Middle Ages carried the government to various parts of the realm, dispensing on the spot such justice, fiscal levies, or administrative decisions as established custom prescribed. In the *curia regis* were the permanent advisers on such matters; periodically—although sometimes after an interval of months or years—all of the great lords of the realm would be summoned to a great council to devise or to ratify a new statement of law on particular subjects. Chapter 14 looked toward the time, still generations away, when such a council would meet regularly and when its acquiescence would be necessary to give any law its effect.

The proposal in Chapter 14 did not go so far as to describe a truly representative assembly; it was to be limited to the crown tenants, the more important of whom ("the archbishops, bishops, abbots, earls and greater barons") were to be summoned directly by the king "by letters under seal," while the lesser tenants in chief were to be notified by sheriffs or other royal officers. Mesne lords, knights, and burgesses were not taken into consideration; hence, this concept was not the same as the first Parliament called by Simon de Montfort in 1265 or the "great and model Parliament" of Edward I thirty years later.[48]

The chapter suggested certain other difficulties in assembling the early councils: there was to be sufficient notice ("forty days at least") and a definite place of meeting. Nor were the lords who had put themselves to the often considerable inconvenience of attending such a council to be sent home because "not all of those who were summoned have come"; those who were present were to constitute the quorum.

The council envisioned in these passages never materialized; the reissue of 1216 omitted the chapters, and for the next half-century Henry III followed the practice of earlier kings. During the minority of Henry III a permanent petty council—the first transitional step from the medieval *curia regis* to the Privy Council of early modern times—developed as a matter of necessity.

Chapters 12 and 14 were deleted, not so much because they envisioned a Parliamentary process (which they did not) ahead of their time, as because they attempted to impede the crown in the matter of arbitrary levies.

[15]　Scutages and Aids of Undertenants

[WE will not grant to any one, moreover, that he shall take an aid from his freemen, except for ransoming his body, for making his oldest son a knight, and for once marrying his oldest daughter; and for these purposes only a reasonable aid shall be taken.]

An important and well-established principle of feudal law was reiterated in this chapter: mesne lords were bound by the same restraints in relation to their subtenants as the crown was in respect of those who held of the king. The principle had been expressed in the coronation charter of Henry I, and was traceable to Norman practices before the Conquest. "Aids were, at first, benevolences of vassals," one writer has said; they were graciously offered on one of the three major occasions affecting the feudal relationship: marriage, knighthood, or ransom. But "what originally flowed from regard, superiors soon changed into a matter of duty, and on a gratuity erected a right."[49] Moreover, it was always a very short step from the three universally acknowledged occasions justifying an aid, to a special levy which could be authorized by a writ purchased from the Exchequer. Thus, a lord could secure a writ permitting him to take contributions from his freeholders to pay off his debts, or an heir could demand aids to pay the required relief for his inheritance.

Thus, the right of recourse to extraordinary levies was considered an essential of feudal economics, and it was for this reason that the reissue of the Great Charter dropped the chapter. The intention of the barons—this was the sixth of their Articles, and was copied verbatim—was to cut off a source of revenue to the crown by prohibiting the sale of writs authorizing aids. The effect was virtually the opposite, for in the course of Henry's reign it became general practice for the undertenant to purchase a writ which he was required to show to the sheriff of the county where he wished to enforce his levy. In part this was a means of continuing the flow of fees into the treasury of the ever money-hungry Plantagenets, but also it was a means of preserving and extending the scope of royal judicial administration; since the sheriffs were only subject to orders from the crown, only a royal writ would effectuate the levy.

Thus, indeed, "the clause expunged from the charter seems practically to have fixed the law."[50] The chief legal concern was to devise some standard of reasonableness; this was first established by the Statute of Westminster I, as to the maximum amounts which tenants could levy. By the century's end, an analogous schedule of maximum levies allowed to the crown was also placed on the books.[51] When this was accomplished, the aid was transformed from a feudal obligation into a revenue measure, to be continued until the general abolition of tenurial processes in 1660.

10 [16] *Distress for Services*

NO ONE shall be distrained to perform any greater service for a knight's fee, or for any other freehold, than is due from it.

The characteristic theory of feudalism, that all freehold estates carried with them certain fixed obligations, was preserved in English law long after the abolition of feudal tenures. It was not until the Statute Law Revision Act of 1948 that this chapter was formally removed from the roll of statutes in force,[52] although its effective provisions had been all but nullified by the general modernization of English property law in 1922 and 1925.[53]

For the thirteenth century, this provision meant that military services which had been the original basis of landholding were to be strictly limited to the dominions where the king's authority was recognized. The Unknown Charter of Liberties defined this as Normandy and Brittany on the Continent, but many crown tenants had refused to follow John even that far, and had objected when he sought to levy a scutage in lieu of their personal service. The Articles of the Barons simply stated that the limit to the services owed was that which was customary for a knight's fee, but in the drafting of the chapter the limitation was extended to services "for any other freehold." This led to the development, in the later Middle Ages, of several writs of relief for freeholders. The earliest, *cessavit per biennium*, extinguished liability for the service after a two-year lapse in performance. The second, *ne injuste vexes*, enjoined a lord not unjustly to vex his tenant; it survived until 1833. The most widely used writ, which survived to the present in some jurisdictions, was replevin, an action to compel the return of personal chattels alleged to have been unlawfully taken (distrained).[54]

The concept of distress, or distraining (Fr. *distraindre*, to draw away from), had its origins in primitive European law, but after Magna Carta it became a formal process, confirmed and also protected from abuse by case law and statutory enactments, as a means of compelling performance of any services due. The medieval law averred that the goods were taken by the distrainor to be held until the owner desisted from his wrongful refusal to perform; it followed, then, that the goods remained the property of the owner rather than the distrainor and could not be sold. The situation was substantially altered in 1690 when the right of sale was conferred upon the distrainor in cases where the service owed was the payment of rent.[55]

Because an action of replevin had to allege that the distraint was unlawful, when in fact the whole thrust of the law of distress was that it *was* lawful, an alternative writ of detinue (Lat. *detinere*, to withhold) was developed, confessing the lawful nature of the taking of the goods, but demanding their return upon settlement of the issue. Replevin has been abolished in many American jurisdictions, in favor of a statutory formula for actions of distress and in preservation of the process of detinue.[56]

11 [17]   *Common Pleas*

COMMON PLEAS shall not follow our court, but shall be held in some place certain.

The statecraft of Henry II in the twelfth century prepared the way for the system of royal courts, centrally located, which was the practical prerequisite to a national government. Early in his reign he began regularly to send justices on eyre (circuit) to various parts of his kingdom where he and his attendant court could not be present. Because these justices usually had plenary authority, and abused it on occasion, the eyres lost a substantial amount of their early popularity. The General Eyre continued until the fourteenth century as a comprehensive administrative session which reviewed debt and tax claims as well as hearing legal disputes; but traveling courts dealing only with specific matters—as the following chapters of the Charter provided—proved more effective.[57]

Henry II also established the first independent department of a national government since Roman times, in the treasury and general accounting processes of the Exchequer. This important agency, charged among other things with examining the records of all sheriffs and bailiffs of the realm, also was recognized as the logical group of royal officers before whom judicial actions could be brought involving revenue actions. The development of a formal court came about rapidly; from cases involving non-payment it was a short step to actions in other subject areas brought by the Exchequer officials themselves. The final step, opening to this court a general jurisdiction, was the one permitting private persons to bring suit before it; this was effected by the writ *quo minus,* a fictitious action in which the plaintiff claimed a right to have his case heard because it involved a wrong to himself "by which he was less [*quo minus*]" able to pay what he owed the king.

The volume of judicial business which grew steadily during the relatively long period of domestic peace and settled government under Henry II not only was more diversified than it was convenient to place before the Exchequer, but was manifestly of two distinguishable types. One involved criminal issues, thus calling into operation the king's justice and centering in a series of actions known as pleas of the crown. The other involved actions between subject and subject, or common pleas. For many years, the criminal cases would be heard before "the justices assigned for the holding of pleas before the king himself," as the ancient description ran; Chapter 5 of *Articuli super Cartas* in 1300 required that both the Chancellor (who could issue writs) and the King's Bench were to follow the court. Major criminal cases for many generations to come were to be held, wherever possible, before the king (*coram rege*), but it was obvious that the great body of criminal charges should be heard, locally and more expeditiously, in the periodic assizes.[58]

Common pleas were another matter; in the nature of the case, they did not require representation of the royal interest before the court, since they concerned private parties. They did require a convenient means of recourse to authoritative records, and these were generally kept in the premises of the "chief courts" meeting regularly at Westminster. Finally, because their business, being private, did not need to await the king's return when Henry or his sons were absent from England, it was logical that they should not "follow our court, but . . . be held in some place certain." The place was not stipulated, but it was obvious that it was intended to be Westminster; and once both Exchequer and "the Bench" (as it was called for many years) were settled at Westminster, a permanent capital for the kingdom would develop there in due course.[59]

The Court of Common Pleas began as an itinerant court established by Henry II about 1178, in response to the complaints against the autocratic actions of the justices in eyre. Within a decade, however, it seems to have settled upon the practice of conducting the major part of its business at Westminster, perhaps because the volume of cases awaiting it in this populous area and the convenience of consulting the records in the Exchequer and adjacent cartularies gave it little opportunity to move.

Glanville's treatise, written in the last years of Henry II, sought to divide civil pleas "into such as are discussed and deter-

mined in the king's court only, and such as fall within the jurisdiction of sheriffs of counties." Under the first heading he placed
questions of baronial tenures, advowsons (rights of presentment
of candidates to fill ecclesiastical vacancies), dower, fines, reliefs,
encroachments upon another's land or public ways, and debts.
Under the second he placed freehold issues appealed from the
baronial courts and actions brought by villeins.[60] Once the bench
became permanently situated at Westminster, however, by far
the greater part of the private or civil actions came to be administered by that court. On the other hand, Chapter 11 contained
the seeds of a long-continued jurisdictional dispute between the
developing courts. In 1300, Chapter 4 of the Articles upon the
Charters undertook to halt a practice which had developed, under
the writ of *quo minus,* whereby common pleas were being heard
in the Court of Exchequer "contrary to the form of the Great
Charter."

The King's Bench, as it crystallized, did not consider itself
bound by the chapter if it wished to assume jurisdiction in a
specific case. For many years it was insisted that the chapter
merely provided that cases involving private disputes ought not
to begin *coram rege,* but could be removed thereto at any
stage.[61] Throughout the Middle Ages and the modern centuries,
until the issue was finally resolved in the Judicature Act of
1873, the three common-law courts vied for autonomy or sought
to invade each other's jurisdiction. In terms of scope and volume
of business, Common Pleas grew steadily; under the *nisi prius*
system, a great number of cases begun at Westminster were continued there on the stipulation that they would be settled "unless
before (*nisi prius*)" they came up for final hearing local justices
or commissioners sent through the locality where the parties were
resident should dispose of the case. This rudimentary system of
trial courts not only relieved Westminster of a backlog of cases
but provided the practical machinery for regular royal justice at
the local level which marked the end of the old manorial courts.

By the late nineteenth century, the variety of royal courts
and the continued struggles over jurisdiction between the old
common-law divisions culminated in the act of abolishing the
older agencies and establishing a Supreme Court of Judicature.

Equity, divorce, probate, bankruptcy, and admiralty courts joined
the list of those whose independent existence was terminated in
favor of a general court with specialized administrative divisions.
In 1875 a revision of the Judicature Act formally repealed Chapter
11 of Magna Carta; and in 1925 the Supreme Court of England
assumed its present five divisions: the dual system of appeals
through the House of Lords and the Court of Appeal, and the
three divisions of first instance: Chancery, King's (now Queen's)
Bench, and the specialized division of Probate, Divorce, and
Admiralty.

12　[18]　*Assizes of Novel Disseisin, Mort d'Ancestor*

ASSIZES of novel disseisin, *and* of mort d'ancestor [and
darrein presentment] shall be held only in their own shires
and in this manner: [we, or] if we are outside of the kingdom
our principal justiciar will send two justiciars through each
shire [four times] *once* a year, who with [four] knights of
the shire [elected by the shire] shall hold [in the shire and
on the day and in the place of the county court] the aforesaid
assizes of the shire. *And those causes which at the coming
of our said justices sent to take the assizes in the shires cannot
be determined shall be settled by them in some other place
in this circuit; and those causes which for difficulty of some
articles cannot be settled by them shall be referred to our
justices of the bench, and there shall be settled.*

Having established, in the preceding chapter, the permanent
location of the Court of Common Pleas, the Charter then turned
to the much-valued possessory assizes, which so fundamentally
affected feudal rights to land, and sought to insure their administration at the local level. The three chapters involved—18, 19,
and 20 in the 1215 charter—and the several procedural changes
wrought within them by the reissues, vividly illuminate the somewhat conflicting or at least competing policies which were striv-
ing for effectuation.

The writs themselves were of comparatively recent origin, and heretofore had been returnable *coram rege;* the first objective of this chapter, therefore, was to make them returnable before the royal justices in assize, i.e., at local sessions of the shire. One of the chronic complaints of freeholders throughout the Middle Ages was the frequency with which various courts were held and the resultant hardship of requiring all freemen to be present and available to serve as jurors.* Chapters 18 and 19 of John's charter made an effort to remedy this situation by stipulating that the royal assizes should be held "on the day and in the place of the county court," and that if the business could not be settled on that day a "sufficient number of knights and freeholders" were to stay over until all the pending cases had been heard.

The reissue made several changes in the procedure; it reduced the circuits from four times to once a year in each shire, and it substituted for the former Chapter 19 the provision which appears as the last sentence of Chapter 12 of 1225: Where the royal traveling justices could not settle all of the possessory suits on the appointed court day, the cases would be continued to some other point on the circuit. In addition, the amended chapter stipulated that cases involving difficult points of law were to be referred to the Bench (i.e., Common Pleas) at Westminster for trial. All of these changes were for the convenience of the royal administration, and the first two worked substantial hardships on the parties to the actions, since they could rely on only one day annually in which the assizes would be held locally and were compelled otherwise to seek out the justices elsewhere on circuit, bringing their papers and witnesses with them.[62]

However this might be, the central fact was that the chapter greatly enhanced the importance of the possessory assizes themselves. Their importance derived from the fundamental premise of feudalism, that land must at all times be in possession of someone responsible for the performance of the services and the discharge of the "incidents" which were attached to the land. The services were commonly military (knight's fees) for temporal lords, or frankalmoin (charities) for spiritual tenants; they might,

* For a discussion of the problems of "suit of court," see the annotation to Chapter 35 of Magna Carta, at pp. 342 ff.

alternatively, consist of stipulated annual payments of rent, goods, or labor (socage), or of a lease with the privilege of subleasing (fee-farm). In the case of crown tenants, they might consist of serjeanty—either a major military command (grand serjeanty) or a token payment (petit serjeanty).* The incidents—reliefs, homage, wardship, and consent to marriages of heirs and widows —were covered in the opening chapters of Magna Carta.

The legal recognition of the person who was actually and literally on the land, claiming the rights of possession and looked to by the lord of the fee (the primary grantor) for the performance of the services due from that estate, was the essence of the feudal concept of seisin. Modern ideas of ownership were not involved, since the underlying theory of feudalism was that all land ultimately came from the crown; possession and enjoyment of the land fundamentally depended upon the readiness of the actual tenant to perform the services attaching to the estate. If another party claimed an older and better seisin, the first remedy devised by the royal courts was the writ of right, whereby the titles of the one in possession and the one claiming possession could be settled.

There were several disadvantages to the writ of right. The party in actual possession could interpose all manner of delays in responding to the demand for a testing of titles, and since the primary concern was that the services attached to the land be performed, the lord of the fee was under no pressure to expedite the matter so long as performance was assured. In addition, the ousted party might be hard put to it to prove that he had the better seisin; documents were often lost and sometimes nonexistent; and if the party in possession had no better evidence, he at least could show that for as long as he had been in possession he had met the obligations attached to the tenancy. Finally, if brought to trial, the party in possession had the right to demand settlement of the issue by battle; since most wrongful entries upon land were by acts of violence, the party in possession in all likelihood was prepared to defend his claim by force, either in person or through a hired champion.[63]

* See the annotation to Chapter 27, pp. 314 ff.

Under Henry II, a more equitable procedure developed in the form of the writ or assize of *novel disseisin*. If the dispossessed party could show that he had formerly been seised of the land in question, and that there had been a recent (*novel*) act of dispossession (*disseisin*) by the present tenant, he was to be put back in possession and the present tenant then would be obliged to rely on the writ of right. In practice, since the plaintiff by showing his former seisin would show his ability to prove a better seisin, the possessory assize usually settled the matter. Hence the action had become highly prized by the time of Magna Carta, and the chapter undertook to insure that it should be administered locally, where local knowledge of the facts could readily be brought to focus upon the issue.

At the Assize of Northampton in 1176, Henry II recognized another possessory action which had gradually been evolving. Termed *mort d'ancestor*, it was designed to establish the proper party to be seised of the land of a tenant after his death (*mort*). The plaintiff had to establish, first, that the late tenant had been "seised as of fee of the tenement" (that is, lawfully invested with the possession of the estate he held) at his death; next, he had to establish that he himself was the next heir of the ancestor, that is, the relative who had held the estate—father, mother, brother, sister, uncle, or aunt. If the plaintiff was not actually in possession at the time he brought this action, he would allege that between the time of the death of the ancestor and the time of the suit, someone else had wrongfully entered upon the land.[64]

The early possessory assizes provided the bases for more effective remedies during the reign of Henry III; various writs of entry were being developed, even in John's day, to aid various types of claimants to enter into enjoyment of rights and estates alleged to be withheld from them. By the middle of the thirteenth century the important writ of trespass had been formulated as one of several actions compelling a party to show cause why he had done injury to a plaintiff, whether in matters of land, goods, or duties owed. The royal courts assumed jurisdiction over all these actions, to the steady derogation of the manorial courts, because the complaint always alleged a breach of the king's peace (*contra pacem*) resulting from the defendant's acts, which might have been carried out with force and arms (*vi et armis*). Freeholders brought trespass actions because the defendant broke into the "close," or inclosure (*quare clausum fregit*), of the plaintiff's estate; lessees came to enjoy a comparable remedy in a special trespass action which came ultimately to be known as ejectment.

Writs of entry have been abolished by statutes in many American jurisdictions, in favor of an elaboration upon the common-law actions of trespass and ejectment. The original possessory assizes had become obsolete even before the end of the Middle Ages; a few colonial jurisdictions gave occasional consideration to *novel disseisin,* but it was subsequently repealed or abolished in the new states. Chapter 12 was formally extinguished in 1879 in England.[65] It was of fundamental importance, however, for having provided a statutory basis for a succession of legal remedies to assist the owner of real or personal property, and thus to afford the security for property rights in general which has been one of the fundamental values of the common law.

[19] *Continuance of Assizes*

[And if the aforesaid assizes cannot be held within the day of the county court, a sufficient number of knights and freeholders shall remain from those who were present at the county court on that day to give the judgments, according as the business is more or less.]

The barons inserted this clause into the charter of 1215 to save their undertenants from the inconvenience of having to follow the justices in assize if their causes were not heard and settled on the local court day. The reissue deleted the chapter and substituted the procedure set out in the last sentence of the preceding chapter. The problem was chronic; the Statute of Westminster II in 1285 sought to transfer the case to the county courts under *nisi prius,* and throughout the fourteenth century there was a vacillating policy on the matter. The problem was alleviated, if not disposed of, with the rise of more effective legal remedies and the maturing of the *nisi prius* system.[66]

13 Assizes of Darrein Presentment

ASSIZES of darrein presentment shall be always taken before our justices of the bench, and there shall be settled.

The charter of 1215 had included this action among those it sought to confine to local court sessions, when these coincided with the coming of the royal justices in assize. The reissue transferred the jurisdiction for this action to the Court of Common Pleas at Westminster. Under the revision of Chapter 12 in the reissue, specific cases under the other petty assizes which contained difficult problems of law were transferable to Westminster, and it seems likely that the whole subject of "last presentation" contained enough difficulties to require complete adjudication before the most learned members of the bench.

The primary issue was simple enough: under the feudal law of advowson, the patron of a local church claimed the right to present a candidate for the benefice whenever it was vacant. When a dispute arose over the right, the plaintiff asserted that as the one, or the heir of the one, who had made the last (*darrein*) presentment, he was seised of the right. To ascertain the factual situation, local knowledge was of as much practical importance in this as in the other possessory actions, and the general practice prior to the reissue had been to send the inquiry to the local sheriff.[67] Advowsons were an important element of feudal law—one of the incidents of an estate—growing out of the medieval assumption that since the parish church was built upon the tenant's land, its rights went with the land. However, a generation before the charters, Pope Alexander III and the savants of the canon law had developed the distinction between the ownership of the church building and the right of patronage, or presentment. This ultimately opened a whole new realm of knotty juristic propositions which indeed required to be "taken before . . . justices of the bench."[68]

For one thing, a nice distinction had to be made between the right of appointment of a candidate to be considered by the bishop, and the right of the bishop to determine the qualifications of the candidate and to invest him: "Jurisdiction in matters of patronage belongeth to this court, but jurisdiction as to parsonage belongeth of Court Christian," declared Chief Justice Bereford in 1311.[69] There was also the fact that the crown, the great lords, and many powerful monasteries (controlled by orders which were often alien) all had fundamental interests in advowsons. After the Reformation, there was the added issue of rights of presentment to Roman Catholic as distinguished from Anglican benefices,[70] and still later to various sectarian chapels.

While it was obvious that the greater part of these complexities were not foreseeable in 1225, there were enough instances of "difficulty of articles" to warrant placing this action under the court at Westminster. From the standpoint of the development of common-law concepts, the greatest challenge was represented by the canon law's recent differentiation between the corporeal right of ownership of a church and the incorporeal right of advowson. The idea of an incorporeal hereditament (an inheritable but intangible right) was completely new to the materialistic feudal land law, and it would be more than a century before it came to be understood and generally accepted. When it attained that stage, the concept logically led to other incorporeal rights, and this in turn would free the common law from its primitive basis of tangible land or chattels, and make it capable of adaptation to a new frame of society after feudalism had passed.

Among the incorporeal rights which developed in the late Middle Ages and in the new commercial context of the modern age, and which were generally recognized in England and America, were rents, easements, franchises, and covenants attached to the land itself. Advowsons apparently were not recognized, even in such Anglican colonies as Virginia,[71] nor were the details of law on commons, even in such an economy as New England. But the other hereditaments were indeed transferred to the New World and became integral parts of the law of the United States.[72] Thus Chapter 13, although it did not directly relate to a legal principle which was recognized in the United States, epitomized an inchoate body of legal concepts which would develop in later times into very important dimensions.

The assize of *darrein presentment* was based on the assumption that the right itself descended to the heirs of the founder or first patron of the benefice. Could it be alienated with the land? Or could it be retained or alienated to another? In answering these questions, the common law evolved other new concepts which would contribute to the later flexibility of the system in changing times. The incorporeal right was held to be severable, a piece of property in itself; but it could also be found, under the circumstances or by its nature, to be appendant (annexed to and fused with) the land, or appurtenant (attached by agreement of the parties). To determine title to such rights, the Court of Common Pleas developed another "show cause" writ (*quare impedit*) by which it could be demanded of a claimant why he impeded another in his asserted right.[73]

Chapter 13 was formally repealed in 1863, although a general revision of the law on real actions had already, in 1833, substantially rendered its procedures obsolete.[74]

14 [20-22] *Amercements*

A FREEMAN shall not be amerced for a small offence, except in proportion to the measure of the offence; and for a great offence he shall be fined in proportion to the magnitude of the offence, saving his countenance; and a merchant in the same way, saving his merchandise; and a villein *other than ours* shall be amerced in the same way, saving his wainage, if he shall be at our mercy; and none of the above fines shall be imposed except by the oaths of honest *and lawful* men of the neighborhood. Earls and barons shall be amerced only by their peers, and only in proportion to their offence. [A clergyman shall be amerced like those before mentioned, only in proportion to his lay tenement, and not according to his ecclesiastical benefice.] *No clergyman shall be amerced according to his ecclesiastical bene-*

fice, but according to his lay tenement, and in proportion to his offense.

This, together with Chapter 29 (39 John), comprises the fundamental constitutional germ which the ensuing centuries of Englishmen have faithfully preserved to this day. Colonial Americans frequently cited the chapters together, and the Founding Fathers wrote their essence into state and federal constitutions.[75] They cut through the feudal verbiage and discerned two basic guarantees—reasonable and proportionate penalties (not cruel or unusual), and liability determined by residents of the neighborhood. The guarantees had essentially the same meaning in the thirteenth century, but the feudal language revealed the differing circumstances: John's three chapters—consolidated into one in the reissue—in each instance stressed the class in feudal society to whom the guarantee applied.

Certainly the provision, inexplicably missing from the Articles of the Barons, that "earls and barons shall be amerced only by their peers" made clear the class privilege envisioned in this process and should temper some of the uncritical eulogy of this phrase in Chapter 29. Still, Chapter 14 did include most of the groups in English society of its day, and to this degree was a more fundamental guarantee than Chapter 8 of the coronation charter of Henry I, which promised: "If any of my barons or of my men shall incur a forfeit, he shall not be compelled to pledge his movable property to an unlimited amount, as was done in the time of my father and my brother; but he shall only make payment according to the extent of his legal forfeiture, as was done before the time of my father and in the time of my earlier predecessors."[76]

If these were some of the "good laws" of Edward the Confessor to which the charter of 1100 was resorting, it was in contrast to the primitive blood feud of the earlier Saxons, as well as to the practice of the early Norman dukes, which William the Conqueror brought to England, and which had it that for any offense a vassal's entire possessions were placed at the king's mercy. To be "in mercy" was a common experience; most Englishmen, of high or low degree, in the thirteenth century took it as a matter of course that they would be in violation of some prohibition in the course of a year.[77] During the reign of Henry II, efforts were made to establish maximum amounts for each type of amercement, and Glanville declared that it had become a general rule that the amount was to be fixed by the oath of "lawful men."[78] Magna Carta, therefore—as in most of its chapters—was essentially declaratory of the established law in this respect.

The purpose of the jury was the familiar one of this period, a recognition or declaration of the goods belonging to the offender. The chattels most essential to his station in life—the "countenance" of the freeman, the merchandise with which the merchant plied his trade, the wainage, or implements, of the villein—were exempt from the penalty. This in itself helped insure that the amercement for most offenses would be nominal, for almost any tenant was permitted to include in his "countenance," or *contenement* (that which comprised the tenement or holding), his arms and armor, his horses, ploughs, and oxen, and food and seed for a year. The merchant or trader would have most of his worldly possessions represented in the goods he offered in towns or fairs and so avoid being reduced to destitution.

Villeins had an ambivalent status; as to the lord to whose lands they were attached, they resembled the Continental serf, but as to the rest of society, they were virtually freemen. They might even acquire a tenure in land, to continue at the pleasure of their lord (copyhold), in which case the menial services they performed were dignified as a feudal obligation of estate (villeinage). The courts held, however, that this was to be distinguished from other tenures as an "unfree" tenure continuing only at the will of the lord.

The value of Chapter 14 was well recognized in its own time and repeatedly enhanced with the passing years. Chapter 6 of Westminster I extended the guarantee to cities, boroughs, and towns—which frequently incurred corporate liability in the Middle Ages—and reiterated that no amercement was to be had without reasonable cause. In 1313-14 the Great Eyre of Kent, a series of instructions to justiciars, directed that the justiciars take note of any who "have been amerced without reasonable cause and beyond the quantity of their trespass, and not by their peers, by whom alone they should be amerced."[79] The latter phrase, echoing words of Westminster I, suggests that "judgment of peers" for this limited purpose is a privilege being extended to all classes. In the fourteenth century the limitation upon amercements was extended to the baronial courts by the development of the writ *de misericordia moderata*, which directed the local court to modify or reduce the amercement it had levied, for "if it exceed the value of the trespass, it is not a moderate amercement."[80]

Indeed, the insistence of succeeding centuries that amercements were to be "affeered," or determined by juries in the local courts, contributed significantly to the development of modern understanding of jury functions; from the fourteenth to the eighteenth centuries, cases appeared in the reports insisting upon this guarantee.[81] The amercement itself, thus subject to the judgment of "suitors" (freemen and villeins attending a term of court for jury service), was an ameliorating force in the area of civil liabilities, and in some American jurisdictions it continued to the present in some form.[82] In the Middle Ages, amercements were sharply distinguishable from fines, which were variable and arbitrary payments to terminate a claim by a tenant or a threatened criminal action by the crown. Indefinite imprisonment was a standard method of compelling payment of a fine, and the matter of its proportion to the subject matter was never considered material. Enforcement of amercements, on the other hand, was by distress, and again only after jury determination of the amount.

Amercements fell into disuse—although still extant in some jurisdictions—with the growth of modern definitions of a fine. But the chapter in Magna Carta has been preserved because of the principle it established, and which developed steadily throughout the ensuing period, of restraint upon arbitrary impositions by governmental authority.

15 [23] *Making of Bridges*

NO town nor freeman shall be distrained to make bridges at riverbanks, except those who were obliged to do so of old and by right.

This chapter has been preserved, together with the one following, as one of the fundamental expressions in Magna Carta against arbitrary and capricious actions of the state which worked unnecessary hardships upon the subject. Its literal stipulation has little practical significance for modern times, and even in the thirteenth century it was not so much the letter of the chapter as the motivations and experiences which lay behind it that prompted the barons to add this to their articles and to draft it into the charter.

The liability of men of a particular locality for keeping bridges in a state of repair, as part of the system of national defense, was an ancient obligation, a companion to the requirement for the maintenance of roads and the stipulation that all men of the hundred, borough, or town had to attend the local militia. But John's reason for insisting upon this duty, and extending it to many more bridges than had formerly been subject to the liability, was not military but personal. His inordinate love of falconry led him and his followers into many parts of the English countryside where the sport was reported to be most rewarding, and for his convenience on these expeditions he would send word ahead to the local sheriffs to put all bridges in repair.

It was not merely that the bridges were to be kept up, but the message that the King was coming to hunt carried with it the understanding that no one else was to indulge in the sport until he had satisfied himself and passed on to other pursuits or other areas. But his schedule was always capricious; his actual arrival in an area placed in readiness might not materialize, and meantime the inhabitants had been placed under several burdens. They were first called from their daily tasks to mend the bridges in question; next, they themselves were denied the right to hunt birds which, for them, was more often than not a means of simple subsistence; finally, since many miles of adjacent land—as the following chapter recognizes—were put "off limits" for hunting, any crops which required tending or harvesting in that zone had to be neglected.[83]

This chapter, accordingly, sought to limit John's orders at least to those freeholders and communities which could be shown to have customarily borne these duties.

16   *"Defense" of Riverbanks*

NO riverbanks shall be defended henceforth, except those which were in defense in the time of King Henry our grandfather, by the same places and in the same bounds as they were wont to be in his time.

This chapter, added to the reissue, preserved the latter part of John's Chapter 47 (*q. v.*) and elaborated upon the problem set out in the preceding chapter. *Defensum* in feudal law referred to an inclosure, a prohibited area of activity, or the act of prohibition (cf. Fr. *defense*), and this chapter specifically condemned John's practice of placing "in defense" great stretches of meadowland along the rivers for his hunting pleasure. The charter of Henry III was content to limit the areas to be so "defended" to those which had been designated in the time of Henry II, which would be as far back as the memory of local residents would extend.

Coke clearly misunderstood the meaning of this chapter, interpreting it as a command to local residents not to deny passage along the rivers or to prevent strangers from fishing from the banks.[84] Although it has long since fallen into disuse, the chapter remains in force as a testimonial to Magna Carta's general effect as a restraint upon arbitrary application of governing authority.

17 [24]   *Pleas of the Crown*

NO sheriff, constable, coroner, or other bailiff of ours shall hold pleas of our crown.

The next ten chapters of 1215 addressed themselves to practices of one or another of the chief agents of the crown whose jurisdiction was the local shire, borough, or town. The oldest of these offices was that of sheriff, which originated in the shire-reeve of Saxon times, who was the king's deputy in the county;

after the Conquest the office was strengthened, although it did not approach the Continental Norman concept of a viscount (cf. Lat. *vicecomes*) with his often plenary authority in his local area. The Normans and Plantagenets kept relatively tight reins on their sheriffs—one of their most effective devices being the annual audit of their records by the barons of the Exchequer—and introduced successive limitations such as annual appointments, transfer from a commission to a salary basis, and (in the Articles upon the Charters) the increase in criminal liability for "false returns."

Of necessity, however, the sheriff was vested with broad authority in the course of discharging the administrative and judicial duties of the shire, and the infrequent visits of superior authority made it possible for many of them to build powerful and lucrative holdings virtually unchallenged. The kings found this objectionable only as it infringed upon their own interests in deriving sufficient revenues from the shire; and to keep watch upon their own interests and conversely to limit the opportunities of the sheriff to enrich himself at the royal expense, in 1194 the new office of coroner was created, "for the guardianship of those things which pertain to the crown (*corona*)." Originally the coroner's duties were virtually coextensive with those of the sheriff, so far as the sheriff's responsibility for royal business was concerned; but in the thirteenth century the coroner was already concerning himself in large part with the investigation of homicides and other crimes of violence, since these were a fundamental concern of the royal courts.

The third agent of the crown who figured prominently in local affairs was the constable in charge of the royal castles which commanded strategic areas throughout the island. As commander of the castle garrison, he represented the most effective force for the keeping of order in the vicinity, and logically many disputes which arose in the course of this responsibility were heard before him. He was often made the warden of the royal forests adjacent to the castle, and thus had still wider jurisdiction.

A fourth class of officials was simply described as bailiffs, a term for any agent charged by the crown with authority over a certain subject, or within a certain area. The shire was the sheriff's bailiwick, but others of the king's bailiffs might have responsibility for distraining the goods of debtors or serving the writs issuing out of the royal household.

The burden of Chapter 17 was that none of these officers were to try the criminal cases over which the king's justiciars asserted jurisdiction. This was significantly modified from the proposal set out in the first part of Article 14 of the Barons, where it had been stated that the sheriffs were not to intermeddle with pleas of the crown without the coroners' participating. The implication was that the coroner was expected to act as a check upon the sheriff; as the chapter was drafted, it altered the wording to the strengthening of the central authority, by taking the trial of criminal cases out of the hands of all nonjudicial officers in the locality.

One may conjecture that this improvement of the crown's position in the course of drafting the chapter reflected the weight of the King's supporters, or perhaps the weight of opposition to the rebels. Possibly Archbishop Langton's philosophy was at work here; the true reform lay not in attempting to set a watchman over the sheriff in the matter of jurisdiction of criminal pleas, but to place the jurisdiction where it belonged—in the hands of trained judges. There is no evidence to corroborate such a supposition, but the fact remains that Chapter 17 did just this, and that it was consistent with the trend of government policy, begun long before Magna Carta and continuing until the establishment of an effective system of local courts in 1846.[85] Throughout English history, the concern of the central government was to prevent the concentration of judicial power in the sheriff; it would be an equal concern *vis-à-vis* the other agents of the crown at the local level.[86]

It should be noted that Chapter 17 prohibited these several agents from trying the cases (holding pleas); it was never understood to relieve them of the responsibility of investigating crimes and keeping rolls of "appeals" (charges) and pleas of the crown. This was part of the business of the sheriff; most royal writs were delivered to him, and he was accountable for serving them and returning them personally to the itinerant justices when they came to the county. In addition, he was the presiding officer at the county courts, which had judicial as well as administrative jurisdiction over much local law; and as a crown tenant in his own right, he might also preside at his court baron over property disputes of his subtenants. It would have been arguable that he was competent to hold pleas of the crown; but this would have increased his power when the continued objective of the royal authority was to decrease it.

Under Chapter 35 of the reissue, the sheriff's local judicial functions were recapitulated, and with the prohibition in Chapter 17, Magna Carta substantially effected his circumscribed jurisdiction. The Sheriff's Act of 1887 repealed most of the provisions in both chapters, and the Statute Law Revision Act of 1892 completed the process.[87]

[25] *Fixing of Feudal Rents*

[ALL counties, hundreds, wapentakes, and trithings shall be at the ancient rents and without any increase, excepting our demesne manors.]

This chapter was deleted from the reissue, in all likelihood because it curtailed the sources of royal revenue as much as it imposed restraints upon self-seeking sheriffs. In any event, the sheriffs were among the leading magnates whom Henry III and his counsellors were eager to win over, and the depredations which were the object of this chapter in John's charter were considered adequately dealt with in other parts of the reissue. That they were not, in fact, is demonstrated by the later statutory efforts to deal with the subject.

The county or shire was the fundamental administrative subdivision of England, from earliest Saxon times to the present. Smaller units within the county were called hundreds, or in certain areas originally subject to the Danelaw, they were called *wapentakes*. The *trithing*, or *riding*, was a circuit followed by county officials in a few of the largest counties.

After the Conquest, it became common for the shire-reeve, or sheriff, to contract with the crown to rent to the sheriff the right to collect all revenues payable within the county, guaranteeing to the crown a fixed amount. This became known as fee-firm (Lat. *firma*) or ferm or farm; it amounted to a license to the sheriff to pass the charges on to the tenants in the county and to levy upon them whatever charges he could to insure that his rent was handsomely recovered. The abuses built into such a system were self-evident, and Plantagenet kings were seldom above the practice of raising the rental charge in the full expectation that the sheriffs could and would pass the cost on to the tenants in the county.

The renting of an administrative district was a not uncommon practice in the Middle Ages, and in the feudal rationale it was readily analogous to the leasing of an estate in land by an individual tenant. By the time of the charters, tenure by fee-farm was virtually synonymous with socage (the performance of fixed services or payment of fixed sums) and by the fourteenth century these had become entirely merged. Tenure by fee-farm was usually perpetual and therefore could be inheritable; Chapter 27 (37 John) deals at some length with the procedures to be observed in this subject area.[88]

The present chapter sought to fix the rentals of counties or their subdivisions and prevent any increase on the part of the king. An exception was made in the case of royal manors which in turn might be held at fee-farm and which might be increased to any amount which the king could recover.

In 1300, Chapter 14 of *Articuli super Cartas* provided that "bailiwicks and hundreds of the crown, nor of other great lords of the land, be not let to farm at over-great sums, whereby the people are overcharged by making contribution to such farms." The problem would remain long after that.

18 [26]　*King's Tenants and their Debts*

IF any person holding a lay fee from us shall die, and our sheriff or bailiff shall show our letters-patent of our summons concerning a debt which the deceased owed to us, it shall be lawful for our sheriff or bailiff to attach and enroll the chattels of the deceased found in the lay fee, to the value of that debt, in the view of lawful men, provided nevertheless that nothing be removed thence until the clear debt to us shall be paid; and the remainder shall be left to the executors for the fulfillment of the will of the deceased; and if nothing is owed to us by him, all the chattels shall go to the deceased, saving to his wife and children their reasonable shares.

This essentially was the text of Article 15 of the Barons; in editing it for inclusion in the Charter, it was improved upon by adding the stipulation on letters patent (open letters) of authorization and the final clause safeguarding the rights of the widow and children. The abuse at which the chapter aimed was obvious: sheriffs who rented their bailiwicks with a view to enjoying the returns from various services owed the crown would with even greater zeal gather up the property of a deceased tenant where it was claimed that a debt had been owed by the tenant to the crown. The chapter stipulated that the sheriff or bailiff was henceforth to proceed only by exhibiting a paper setting out the crown's claim, attaching chattels sufficient in value to satisfy the claim, and doing this by the witness of men of the shire who were in position to know the value of the property.

Once such a debt, if it were shown to exist, had been satisfied—nothing being removed from the estate until the settlement had been recorded in the Exchequer—the chapter then was at pains to insure that all remaining chattels of the deceased tenant, after the apportioning of the survivors' shares, should be used by the executors to carry out the will of the dead owner. The chapter recognizes that the right to dispose of personal property was generally exercised by the thirteenth century. The reverse was true with reference to land; although a tenant might be able to alienate his real property during his lifetime—subject to the safeguard added by Chapter 22 in the reissue—the feudal law insisted that at his death the lands of which he was seised were to descend to his heir.[89]

The distribution of chattels by naming of executors was well established in the time of Henry II; it had been well known in

Roman law, but had come into English practice after the Conquest through the canon law.[90] This part of Magna Carta, therefore, was simply declaratory of existing practice, and the writ *de rationabili parte* (on reasonable parts) frequently relied on the common law rather than the specific chapter of the Charter in the later medieval period.[91] The importance of this part of Chapter 18, in fact, was not so much its insurance of legal shares to the survivors, which was well established, but its emphasis upon the role of executors, who were responsible for seeing that specific chattels went to specific individuals outside the immediate family.

The preparation of wills was a commonplace of the short life expectancy of the Middle Ages; men customarily, after they came of age, were prepared to commend their souls to God, their bodies to a specific church, and their personal goods to various parties. Confession and absolution were the usual accompanying ceremonies; and it was through the offices of the Church, as the Church itself argued successfully under Henry III, that the will was to be "proved." If the will failed to name executors, the Church "ordinary" would perform the function or, in later times, appoint an administrator. If the tenant died intestate, the Church took over the distribution of his goods. The probate or proving of a will—since many were oral or nuncupative (reduced to writing after a dying disposition)—was the subject of much legislation in succeeding centuries, but it was not until 1540, when land had become subject to testamentary disposition, that the law uniformly required that wills of real property be in writing. The Statute of Frauds in 1677 added the requirement of a minimum number of witnesses, but the need for writing, witnesses, and signing was not applied to wills in general until 1837.[92] A lay court of probate was established in 1857,[93] and Chapter 18 was not formally repealed, as obsolete, until 1949.[94]

[27]   *Intestate Succession*

[IF any freeman dies intestate, his chattels shall be distributed by the hands of his near relatives and friends, under the oversight of the church, saving to each one the debts which the deceased owed to him.]

This chapter was the logical complement of the preceding chapter, and scholars are unsure as to the reasons it dropped out of the reissues. The law it stated was long established; the coronation charter of Henry I had provided that tenants' bequests were to be effected as they desired, and that if one died intestate, "his widow or his children or his relatives or one of his true men shall make such division for the sake of his soul, as may seem best to them." This chapter added a rather important clause, that the distribution was to be done "under the oversight of the church," a procedure which became general practice in the thirteenth century.

To die intestate was strongly condemned by the feudal age; it was an irresponsible act which was regarded by the Church almost as a mortal sin, and by the state almost as a crime. The lord of the fee or the king often treated the fact of intestacy as virtually tantamount to forfeit and took all of the dead man's chattels into their own hands. This was too transparent an excuse for outright appropriation of another's property, however, and it was customary, from the time of Henry I at least, to enlist "near relatives and friends" to effect the distribution of the intestate's goods. So far as the Church was concerned, there were worldly interests of its own to be satisfied, and an extra amount of the chattels might be diverted to the spiritual administrators in partial atonement for the sin of dying without a will. This may have accounted for the deletion of the chapter in the reissue.

19 [28] *Purveyances for Castles*

NO constable or [other] *his* bailiff [of ours] shall take anyone's grain or other chattels, *if the man be not of the town where the castle is,* without immediately paying for them in money, unless he is able to obtain a postponement by permission of the seller. *If, however, he be of the same town, he shall receive payment within forty days.*

Purveyances, a medieval form of requisition, were recognized as unavoidable consequences of an itinerant court. A royal castle normally had its own villeins and certain demesne lands which produced enough food and fuel for the normal needs of the garrison; but when the king and his court arrived, the needs for provisions suddenly soared, and it was expected that the constable of the castle or his agent would quickly seek supplies from the nearest sources. The charter of 1215 undertook to protect the parties from whom the goods were taken by requiring prompt payment in currency, unless the owner of the goods was amenable to a delayed payment. The reissue added the provision that payment should be immediate in cases of a stranger, or within forty days if he was a local resident.

From the earliest times, it was customary for certain portions of grain and fuel to be delivered from the surrounding countryside to the castle of a king or crown tenant; the castle, after all, was a fortified center for the preservation of law and order and entitled to the support of the local area it protected. A regular market for the provisioning of the castle was common. It was the abuse of the system, and the often arbitrary taking (*prises*) of goods without any payment, at which the chapter was directed. In the Articles upon the Charters, eighty-five years later, Chapter 2 set out a lengthy procedure for diminishing the abuses, which only served to indicate that they were still prevalent.[95]

The problem was never settled while the crown was compelled to rely on feudal means of maintenance, and while kings continued to treat these as part of their prerogative. A partial attempt at modernization was made by Edward III in 1362; but it was three centuries later, with the general abolition of feudal tenures, that this chapter and the two following were virtually repealed—with the substitution by Parliament of a perpetual guarantee of financial support for the king's household, aided in part by an excise of fifteen pence per barrel of beer or ale sold in the kingdom.[96] The chapter, along with 20 and 21, was formally repealed in 1863.[97]

20 [29] *Castle Ward*

NO constable shall distrain any knight to give money in place of his ward of a castle if he is willing to furnish that ward in his own person or through another sufficient man, if he himself is not able to do it for a reasonable cause; and if we shall lead or send him into the army he shall be free from ward in proportion to the amount of time by which he has been in the army through us, *for which he has done service in our wars.*

The preceding chapter dealt with purveyances of food and chattels for castles, and before completing the specific stipulations on other types of purveyancing, a further provision on services due to the castles was interjected. It is only the later, artificial editorial device of dividing the subject matter of Magna Carta into "chapters" that makes it appear, in cases like this one, that the progression of ideas in the Charter is interrupted.

Next to the hardships of sudden and substantial taking in the name of the lord of the castle, the greatest burden derived from the ancient requirement that local knights should devote a certain amount of each year to manning the garrison. This was the duty of the lesser freeholder which was comparable to the local militia service demanded of yeomen and villeins in general; but over the years it had become customary for many knights to substitute money for their personal performance of castle ward, or "keeping." In due course, with the growth of reliance upon hired fighting men, the king or his local officer came to prefer the money; and at the same time the knight might find occasion when it was easier for him to discharge the obligation in person than by payment.

The chapter preserves to the knight or undertenant the right to do castle duty in person or by substitute and adds the important provision that when he is called to the king's service in an active military campaign he may expect a proportionate reduction of the liability in general.

21 [30, 31]   *Purveyances for Carriage and Timber*

NO sheriff or bailiff of ours or any one else shall take horses or wagons of any freeman to make carriage except [on the permission of that freeman] *he pay the old established price, to wit, for carriage with two horses, x d. per day, and for carriage with three horses, xiv d. per day. No demesne cart of any clerical person or knight or any lord shall be taken by the aforesaid bailiffs.* Neither we nor our bailiffs *or any others* will take the wood of any man for castles, or for anything else which we are doing, except by the permission of him to whom the wood belongs.

This chapter completes the provisions with reference to purveyancing and deals specifically with the use of horses and wagons to carry the goods being gathered for the king, and with the timber which may be sought for fuel or for other use. The reissue combined the two earlier chapters on the subject and added a specific clause on the fair rental price for the use of horses and carts. The problem refused to abate, however, throughout the medieval period, chiefly because it was endemic in the system of a continually moving court living off the land and relying on agents who in the nature of things took more than enough to meet the need.

From the legislation of Edward I—the Statute *de Tallagio,* which undertook to renounce the crown's right to arbitrary taking, and the chapter in *Articuli super Cartas,* prescribing an elaborate procedure for compelling crown agents to give receipts which were redeemable in the king's Wardrobe (warehouse)—to the middle of the fifteenth century, more than a dozen statutes were enacted in a vain effort to settle the problem. When the court settled at Westminster, and Parliament granted funds on obtaining royal assent to specific measures, the practical necessity for purveyancing disappeared. When James I sought to revive the practice as a revenue measure, Parliament protested; and when his agents took timber in violation of Chapter 21, the courts found against the crown.[98]

22 [32] *Lands of Felons*

WE will not hold the lands of those convicted of a felony for more than a year and a day, after which the lands shall be returned to the lords of the fees.

"Year, day and waste" was an immemorial prescription for the action of the crown against the estate of a tenant convicted of felony. Upon conviction, all of the felon's personal property was subject to seizure by the crown; it was forfeited, and any claims of other parties upon such property were extinguished.[99] But the real property—the fundamental value in the feudal system—must ultimately escheat to the lord of the fee after the crown had visited a criminal penalty upon it; customarily, the buildings were leveled and the trees uprooted, the apparent theory being that the corruption of blood ascribed to the felon had tainted his land as well. This, at least, was one view; another held that the waste was an indirect penalty laid upon the original grantor for his bad judgment in choosing his tenant.[100]

In any case, Chapter 22 established that the land was not to be considered as forfeited; it was to return to the grantor after the king's justice was satisfied. An "appeal" (charge) of felony, if it led to a conviction, led thereafter to outlawry and the right to slay the convicted party upon capture; his recourse was to claim sanctuary, abjure the realm, and receive a safe-conduct to a port of exile. In either case, his tenure had died, and his land of right was to escheat to the grantor. The right of sanctuary was abolished in 1624, but the law of escheat for felony continued until 1870, with some of its provisions continuing until 1938.[101]

23 [33] *Weirs*

ALL the fish-weirs in the Thames and the Medway, and throughout all England shall be removed forthwith, except those on the coast.

Like Chapter 9 (13 John), this provision injects a specific interest of the towns—and particularly London, whose two great waterways are specifically mentioned—into the bargaining which went into the composition of Magna Carta. That it has continued to the present is less a testimonial to the importance of the particular subject than to the fact that, together with Chapter 30 (41 John), it complements the proposition set out in Chapter 9, that the ancient privileges granted to the towns are to be kept inviolate from the encroachments of the national government.[102]

In the twelfth and thirteenth centuries, the guarantee was of much more direct significance. Medieval England, as well as many parts of colonial America, found the great rivers the most practical avenues of commercial transportation; they were cheaper to use than roads, and the roads themselves were indifferently maintained. For the great bulk of their economic traffic, London and other English cities came to depend upon their rivers as vital arteries. It was therefore imperative that certain types of fish traps—*kydelli*, or weirs, which formed permanent obstructions in the waterways and presented continual hazards to navigation —be prohibited. The matter had been the subject of several previous charters, from Richard I in 1197 and from John in 1199, and would be the subject of much later legislation. As London, in particular, continued in modern times to develop into a great seaport and center of world trade, the guarantee of 1215 continued to be of fundamental importance.[103]

24 [34] *Writ of Praecipe*

THE writ which is called praecipe shall not be given for the future to any one concerning any tenement by which a freeman can lose his court.

"When anyone complains to the king, or his justices, concerning his fee or his freehold," wrote Ranulph de Glanville, "if the complaint be such as be proper for the determination of the king's court, *or the king is pleased that it should be decided* *there,** then the party complaining shall have the following writ of summons:

> "The king to the sheriff, health. Command *A.* that without delay he render to *B.* one hide of land, in such a vill, of which the said *B.* complains that the aforesaid *A.* hath deforced him; and unless he does so, summon him by good summoners, that he be there before me or my justices, [etc.]."[104]

This was the writ of *praecipe*, or *praecipe quod reddat* (order to return), developed in the time of Henry II as one of the several writs of entry which complemented the possessory actions covered by Chapters 12 and 13 (18 and 19 John). It appears at this point in the Charter (where the continuity of the chapters is more uneven than heretofore) because it deals with the misuse of this and certain other elements of legal procedure set out in Chapters 26 (36 John), 28 (38 John), 29 (39 and 40 John), and 42 (John). These half-dozen chapters bring the Great Charter to a climax—the pinnacle being Chapter 29—upon the issue of the diverting of recognized rules of orderly justice to tyrannous or arbitrary uses. Unfortunately, the group of chapters addressed to this general proposition opens on a fundamentally reactionary note.

The problem began, explained Glanville, with the failure of undertenants to obtain justice in the court baron; the failure was usually due to the fact that the complainant could not compel the opposing party (particularly if he was the lord of the manor holding the court) to answer his suit. In such case, said Glanville, the complainant "shall have a writ of right, directed to the lord of whom he claims to hold." This writ directed the lord to do justice in his court lest the cause be transferred to the king's court.[105]

The writ of *praecipe* went the next step beyond; it was directed to the sheriff—the royal agent—rather than to the lord and required the party charged with the wrongful act to appear before the royal court if he failed to return or restore the property complained of. Since this property was the freehold tenement itself,

* Italics supplied.

the extended use of *praecipe* threatened to remove from the manorial courts the jurisdiction over the estates of their under-tenants and thus destroy the key to the grantors' control over the whole system of incidents and services of tenure. This develop-ment was consistent with the general trend toward centralized administration of justice, but it struck at the very base of feudal-ism. In the barons' view, it meant that a freeman would "lose his court," i.e., his right to have the issues affecting his freehold estate determined in the court of the grantor. In the view of the under-tenant, conversely, the restraint now placed upon this writ meant that he was placed in his former position of disadvantage in this court.

This was not entirely true; Chapter 24 did not seek to restrain the use of the writ of right, which at least in theory preserved to the freeman the privilege of having the cause removed to the royal court if justice were not done in the manorial court. In practice, of course, the complainant's case was fundamentally jeopardized if it involved an action against the very lord whose court would hear the case, and the mere fact that the case had been heard at all might satisfy the requirements of the writ of right, thereby removing the possibility of having it heard in the king's court.[106]

This decidedly retrospective chapter was preserved in the reissues of Magna Carta, attesting to the stubbornness with which the barons, including Henry's supporters, clung to the ancient right of judging the complaints of their own tenants in their own courts. But history was against them; while the Chancery discon-tinued the issuance of writs of *praecipe* in cases involving such tenants, the royal courts simply widened the number of writs of entry by which a complainant could regain possession of his property. All of these writs—whether alleging that property held as security for a debt was now to be returned upon the discharge of the debt, or that there was a defect in the title of the occu-pant—brought the causes into the king's court and contributed to the continuing decline of the manorial administration of justice. In 1267, Chapter 29 of the Statute of Marlborough confirmed the entire rationale of these writs.[107]

The chapter was part of the group in Magna Carta which

was rendered obsolete with the abolition of feudal tenures in 1660; it was virtually repealed in 1833 and formally removed from the statutes in 1863.[108]

25 [35] *Measures and Weights*

THERE shall be one measure of wine throughout our kingdom, and one measure of ale, and one measure of grain, that is the London quarter, and one breadth of dyed cloth and of russets and of halbergets, that is two ells within the lists; of weights, moreover, it shall be as of measures.

Another interjection into the general tenor of the Charter of a fundamental economic interest is represented in this chapter. One may conceive of one logical reason for placing the subject at this point: Chapters 34 to 48 of John's charter are concerned broadly with restating procedural and administrative principles which were to be enforced throughout the kingdom. Some were retrospective, undertaking to preserve feudal tradition, while others, like this chapter, confirmed a development looking toward a newer orientation of the economy. The need for standardized weights and measures had earlier been recognized, in the Assize of Cloth under Richard I in 1197 and in the Assize of Wine under John in 1199. A broadened statement of these standards would benefit all consumers: king, barons, freeholders, and villeins in general.

The need for the restatement derived from the fact that it apparently was not being lived up to; customs varied widely over the realm, and traders and merchants found it practically impossible to conform to standards which were different in each locality.[109] Buyers had even greater complaints; if there was one standard measure used for buying, there might be another for selling. The chapter established no definite standard for liquid measures, although it did for dry—"the quarter of London," a quantity approximately equal to eight bushels. It also attempted to fix the width of woven goods at two yards (ells) between the

selvedges (lists), whether for fine dyed cloth available to persons
of quality, or drab goods (russets) for villeins, or *halberjects* (or
haubergeon or *hauberject*) or the coarse cloth worn under armor.

The chapter did not dispose of the problem; in 1217 the
merchants of London were permitted to pay a fine to be relieved
of the strict conforming to the measures of cloth set out in the
chapter. In 1228 Henry III sought to enforce the provision by
supervising in person the destruction of a number of false weights
and measures. But the problem of false or debased coinage, and
of uniform standards for determining quantities of goods, ante-
dated the Conquest and extended into the reign of the three
Edwards. Parliamentary surveillance began in the fourteenth century, and in the fifteenth the Exchequer was authorized to fix a
standard which should be followed by every borough and town.
As late as the sixteenth century the merchants of London, whose
standard set out in Chapter 25 was still used, were still consistently being found in violation.[110]

It was not until 1824 that a substantial revision of the standards for weights and measures was effected in England, which
rendered most of this chapter obsolete. It was formally repealed
by the Weights and Measures Act of 1878.[111]

26 [36]   *Writs de Odio et Atia*

NOTHING shall henceforth be given or taken for a
writ of inquisition *nor taken of him that prayeth inquisition*
concerning life or limbs, but it shall be given freely and not
denied.

One of the great advances in Magna Carta was this chapter
confirming the availability of a relatively new writ, suggestive of
habeas corpus but not to be confused with it. As late as Glanville's writing, the criminal law maintained an inflexible attitude
toward felonies; if there was an "appeal" (charge) of such a
felony, the trial was still by battle, although in matters other than
criminal the *duellum* was rapidly disappearing. The primitive law
saw no alternative to a direct meeting of the accusation, and no
better means of settling the issue than by battle; but gradually

the canon law introduced to the common law the concept of an indirect defense (*exceptio*) which could itself be referred to a jury "of the country."

The indirect defense was a plea that the criminal charge had been brought "out of malice and hate" (*de odio et atia*) and that such a charge, placing the defendant in jeopardy of life or limb, ought to be the subject of an inquisition by a local jury. If the jury found the facts to be in favor of the plea, the proceeding on the criminal charge was then dropped. Since the facts establishing the good or bad faith of the charge in most instances would go into the nature of the felony charged, the procedure involving this writ advanced criminal justice a long step farther away from trial by battle and at least a short step closer to the modern function of a jury trial.[112]

Popular as it became in a short time, the writ had a relatively short life, giving way to the more general use of bail, by which sureties were given for the appearance of the accused following his release from prison. It continued to be used sporadically in the later development of the criminal law, until formally abolished in 1828.[113] Jury trials were made the sole basis for criminal inquisition by the Statute of Westminster I, although as late as the sixteenth century it was sometimes necessary to subject accused persons to torture to persuade them to accept this method of settlement.[114] In practice, it is obvious, jury trials did not assume the significance of modern times until the concomitant right to counsel, confrontation of accusing witnesses, the right to call witnesses on behalf of the defense, and the use of formal rules of evidence were recognized after the English Revolution.[115]

It was with the realization that these guarantees to fair and impartial trial of criminal matters were only recently won in English law that the first Congress wrote them into the Sixth Amendment of the Bill of Rights. The "speedy and public trial" met the issue which the medieval writ *de odio et atia* had first encountered; the guarantee of an impartial local jury, the informing of the accused of the charges against him, the confrontation of hostile witnesses and the calling of his own witnesses, and the right to counsel, all reflected contemporary objectives of the common law, not entirely won by the last decade of the eighteenth century.[116]

Habeas corpus was by no means unknown to the later thirteenth century, but its primary function was to secure the appearance of a defendant or of jurors rather than to determine the validity of the current imprisonment of a person charged with a state offense. A variation of the writ was used by private parties in civil suits to compel performance by the adversary party; in the fifteenth century *habeas corpus* was being used by royal courts to take parties and their causes out of the jurisdiction of inferior courts, or even by debtors to remove themselves from courts where their creditors sought judgment against them. It did not occur to lawyers of the Middle Ages and the Tudor period, therefore, to apply the writ to the matter of securing the personal liberty of the subject.[117]

It was only with the growing Parliamentary struggle with the crown in the first quarter of the seventeenth century that men like Coke and Selden discerned the possibilities of such a function for *habeas corpus*. Their first efforts were rebuffed, with the ruling of the courts that the writ could not run against a special command of the sovereign; and although the Petition of Right overthrew this rule, it remained for the *Habeas Corpus* Act of 1679 to remove ambiguities as to what court had the right to issue the writ and what subject matter it should cover.[118]

Another important provision in Chapter 26 was elaborated upon in Chapter 40 (John): Justice was not to be sold. Writs involving issues of life and limb were to be given freely, with nothing taken for their procurement. While this was never understood to mean that reasonable charges for costs could not be required for other types of writs, or for securing the trial of the cause in a particular court, the stipulation that writs *de odio et atia* were to be denied to none and to be given without charge was consistently observed after Magna Carta.

27 [37] *Prerogative Wardships*

IF any one holds of us by fee-farm or by socage or by burgage, and of another he holds land by knight service, we will not have the guardianship of the heir or of his land which is of the fee of another, on account of that fee-farm, or socage, or burgage, nor will we have the custody of that fee-farm, or socage, or burgage, unless that fee-farm itself owes knight service. We will not have the guardianship of the heir or of the land of any one, which he holds of another by knight service on account of any petty serjeanty which he holds of us by the service of paying to us knives or arrows, or the like.

This chapter also dealt with a feudal problem on which a general settlement was sought: the priority of various types of services and incidents in the hierarchy of tenures. Medieval tenants held various parcels of land of different grantors and owed to each grantor only the duties which ran with the particular land held of that grantor. The fact that some of the land of an heir was held of the king, by some duty less than knight service, was not henceforth to be used to give the king the benefits of wardship of the body or other lands of the heir. Knight service was the paramount duty, and the wardship of body and land held by such fee went to the lord of that fee, in preference to the duties owed the king in the various forms of rental.

The chapter added a second stipulation: where the only lands of an heir were held of the king by petty serjeanty—the token payment of such things as knives or arrows—none of these lands were to be put in ward of the crown. In no case, in fact, did the chapter recognize that the king should have the custody of lands held by rental processes, unless some of the rental terms involved knight service. Thus, the chapter accomplished a dual purpose, doing away with the crown's seizure of lucrative wardships by prerogative, and insuring the retention of most of an heir's estate in support of his military obligation.

28 [38] *Wager of Law*

NO bailiff henceforth shall put any one to his *open* law *nor to an oath* on his simple affirmation, without credible witnesses brought for this purpose.

Whatever the somewhat conflicting scholarly interpretations of this chapter, it dealt with a fundamental feudal process: the testing of the guilt or innocence of accused parties. The ancient rituals of ordeals, whereby the victim's ability or lack of ability to offset the physical effects of bearing hot irons, enduring scalding water, or being bound and thrown into cold water—the results being ascribed to divine reaction—were condemned by the Lateran Council held in the same year as John's charter, and this action by the Church was recognized by the revisions of the chapter made in 1217.

An alternative to the ordeal was the "wager of law," or compurgation, by which an accused person swore to his innocence and then was required to find a stipulated number of "oathhelpers" to swear that his oath was credible. This was only slightly less esoteric than the ordeal, and only slightly more effective in finding the truth than trial by combat. For a regime groping for a more rational means of inquiry, like that of Henry II in its heyday, some other form of inquisition was essential. Thus, in 1166 in the Assize of Clarendon, evolved the process of review of the evidence preliminary to formal trial which developed into the grand jury.[119]

The essence of the provisions in the Assize of Clarendon was the emphasis upon "credible witnesses brought for this purpose," as Chapter 28 requires. By the first chapter of the Assize, "the twelve most lawful men of every hundred, and the four most lawful men of every vill," were to testify whether there were any suspected felons in their area; and while the second chapter provided for the ordeal of water, the fourth required that the accused be brought before the royal justices "together with two lawful men from the hundred and the vill . . . to bring the record of the county and the hundred as to why they were captured; and there they shall make their law before the justices."[120] The trial was not to be precipitated merely upon the "simple affirmation" of a crown officer.

29 [39, 40] *Due Process of Law*

NO freeman shall be taken or imprisoned or disseised *of any freehold, or liberties, or free customs,* **or outlawed,**

or banished, or in any *other* way destroyed, nor will we go upon him, nor send upon him, except by the legal judgment of his peers or by the law of the land. To no one will we sell, to no one will we deny, or delay right or justice.

This most famous and familiar provision of Magna Carta, in spite of exaggeration and misconception over the years, remains the apogee of the document as a whole. It meant one thing to the early thirteenth century; it was subjected to considerable intellectual and political glosses in the fourteenth; it became all but dormant in the fifteenth and much of the sixteenth centuries; it was revived and interpreted out of context, but what is of first importance, was then ratified in its modern meaning by the English Revolution in the seventeenth century and made the basis of the constitutional argument in favor of the American Revolution in the eighteenth. Today its modern interpretation is a dominant theme of Anglo-American constitutional jurisprudence.[121]

"King John grants that he will not take a man without [prior] judgment, nor will he take anything for justice, nor will he do injustice." So read the opening chapter of the Unknown Charter of Liberties. "The body of a freeman shall not be taken, imprisoned, disseised, outlawed or exiled, or in any other manner destroyed, and the king shall not go or send against him by force, except by the judgment of his peers or by the law of the land." So read Article 26 of the Barons. These provisions, compared with the text as it was eventually drafted, not only illustrate the sources of the chapter but make clear the significance of the chapter to its own age. It is fundamental and elemental that an assessment of Chapter 29 (39 John) begin with this viewpoint.

Modern editors have ascribed to this chapter the title, "Due Process of Law,"[122] and it is not too much to aver that this was in fact the general principle set out in the original document, provided that it is understood as the thirteenth century understood it. Chapter 29 follows upon the "Wager of Law" heading ascribed to Chapter 28, and it is literally in the midst of the series of chapters in the Charter dealing with a succession of procedural safeguards of feudal rights. While it would be a century and a half before one of the confirmations of Edward III would actually use the phrase,[123] it was already almost three centuries since the

Salic law of Conrad II had provided that no man should be deprived of his fief but by the law of the Holy Roman Empire and the judgment of his peers.[124] Moreover, it was well-established English law that judgment should precede execution and should be determined by a group of tenants equal in dignity to the principal.[125]

The word freeman (*liber homo*) appears in this case to include all holders of free tenements, i.e., the guarantee is not limited to the tenants in chief, nor is it extended to villeins or those of unfree tenures. That this is the intended scope of the term is indicated by the additional phrase of the reissue, concerning "freehold, or liberties, or free customs"; *liberum tenementum* was thus used as a generic term in contradistinction from villein tenure, *libertates* referred to the body of intangible rights and usages which were associated with free tenure, and *consuetudines liberes* in all likelihood were concerned with the tolls and other levies which mesne lords as well as tenants in chief could lay upon goods going out of, coming into, or passing through their lands.[126]

If this was, as seems likely, the understanding of the word "freeman" in the charters of 1215 and 1225, it was not so narrow a guarantee as it might have been—although it was restricted enough, considering the small number of freeholders in proportion to the total population of the time. This being the case, the interpretative statutes of Edward III could easily make the ideological transition from a freeman to a man—villein or tenant—as was done in 1331[127] and was made more explicit in 1354.[128] By that date the system of villeinage was breaking down, lands were being leased or worked by hired labor, and the body of freeholders itself was steadily enlarging. Whatever the great barons—the "peerage" of later times—might wish to make of the phrase, the litigants in the common-law courts of the fourteenth and fifteenth centuries proceeded on the assumption that the guarantee of Chapter 29 extended to all who had any standing in the courts.[129]

The guarantee of the 1215 charter was explicit: such freemen were not to be arbitrarily captured and imprisoned, or dispossessed, or set outside the law, or turned out of the country—the executions of a judgment in a criminal trial—until after the judgment. The king was not himself, nor through his agents, to send an armed force against a person charged with a felony until after the judgment. The test of due process was, first, whether the judgment was "the lawful judgment of his equals" (*legale judicium parium suorum*) and "by the law of the land" (*per legem terrae*),[130] as the second condition. The "peers" (*pares*) were not the aristocrats of later ages, but the tenants of equal rank—barons to judge barons, not in a common-law court where a justiciar might be lower in the feudal hierarchy, but in the council of the realm. But the "law of the land" (*lex terrae*) was not the law of the king's court alone (*lex regni*) but all the local customs and variants of law that obtained throughout England; in such case, the justices might be of lower feudal rank but yet the equal (or superior) of the men whose cases they judged.[131]

In the sense that the net effect of these specific stipulations in 1215 was to set a limit to the arbitrary use of the governing power, this chapter is indeed a "golden passage." The mistaken view of the seventeenth century that it established the modern principle of trial by jury and the personal liberty of the individual as the Petition of Right asserted it does not detract from its real importance; as one leading legal historian has observed: "These clauses do embody a protest against arbitrary punishment, and against arbitrary infringements of personal liberty and rights of property; they do assert a right to a free trial, to a pure and unbought measure of justice. They are an attempt, in the language of the thirteenth century, to realize these ideals—just as the demand for the laws of Edward the Confessor was an attempt, in the language of the twelfth century, to realize the same ideals. It is not until these ideals have been expressed in Magna Carta that we cease to hear the demand for the laws of Edward the Confessor."[132]

It was because the Great Charter restated the generally recognized principles of English public and private law, and nowhere in a more universal principle than in Chapter 29, that it came in later ages to be treated for practical purposes as the starting point of English law.

By the end of the thirteenth century, and early in the reign of Edward II in the fourteenth, complainants were relying consistently upon Chapter 29 to preserve their rights in court. In 1299 the widow of a mesne lord undertook to protect her dower lands from reclaiming by the lord of the fee on the ground that she should not "be removed or disseised against the form of the aforesaid Charter." In 1314 another widow similarly relied on "the Great Charter of liberties, which contains that neither the king nor any of his ministers will oust any man of his free tenement without reasonable judgment."[133] From the language of these pleadings, it is evident that the medieval lawyers already were developing a body of jurisprudence which, first, took the "judgment of peers" and "the law of the land" to guarantee trial by lawful procedure; and, second, during the coming century equated "law of the land" with the common law.[134]

In 1331 Parliament enacted one of six fundamental laws expanding upon Magna Carta, and particularly upon Chapter 29, which the advocates of the English Revolution would call the "six statutes." The legislation was a restatement of the guarantees in this chapter and in Chapter 26 as well:

> It is enacted that no man from henceforth be attached by any accusation, nor forejudged of life or limb, nor his lands, tenements, goods nor chattels seised into the king's hands against the form of the Great Charter and the law of the land.[135]

Twenty years later the second of the series of statutes provided a valuable insight into the understanding of the Middle Ages of the nature of the rights preserved in Magna Carta:

> Whereas it is contained in the Great Charter of the Liberties of England that none shall be imprisoned nor put out of his freehold, nor of his liberties or free customs, unless it be by the law of the land; it is accorded, assented and stablished, that from henceforth none shall be taken by petition or suggestion made to our lord the king, or to his council, unless it be by indictment of good and lawful people of the same neighborhood where such deeds be done, in due manner, or by process made by writ original at the common law; nor that none be put out of his liberties nor of his freeholds, unless he be duly

brought in to answer, and forejudged of the same by the course of the law; and if anything be done against the same, it shall be redressed and holden for none.[136]

Three years later the third statute reiterated "that no man of what estate or condition he be"—an extension of the guarantee to all persons, villein or tenants—"shall be put out of land or tenement nor taken, nor imprisoned, nor disinherited, nor put to death, without being brought in answer by due process of law."[137] The fourth and fifth statutes, in 1362 and 1363 respectively,[138] were of less significance; but the sixth, in 1368, illustrates the stage to which the jurisprudence of Chapter 29 had evolved, with its stipulation that "no man be put to answer without presentment before justices, or matter of record, or by due process and writ original."[139] The King's answer to the Parliamentary action stated that "because this Article is an Article of the Great Charter, the king wills it. . . ."[140]

The reiteration of these propositions, continuing into the early fifteenth century, served to broaden the meaning and make more universal the awareness of the Great Charter, not only to the late Middle Ages but to the first printers of the English statutes in the Tudor period. Perceiving that Magna Carta indeed summarized the feudal law as it stood at the "beginning of legal memory," and that it was treated as such a fundamental principle of jurisprudence by succeeding Parliaments, the compilers of the laws of the realm placed it first in their lists and impressed further upon the mind of the sixteenth and early seventeenth century the status of the Great Charter as a cornerstone of English government. The conversion of the status into a constitutional principle, relied upon, ratified, and extended by the English and American revolutions, is the theme of Chapters 6 and 7 of Part I of this volume.

30 [41] Foreign Merchants

ALL merchants, *if they were not publicly prohibited before*, shall be safe and secure in going out from England and coming into England and in remaining and going

through England, as well by land as by water, to buy and
sell free from all evil tolls, by the ancient and rightful customs, except in time of war, and if they are of a land at war
with us; and if such are found in our land at the beginning
of war, they shall be attached without injury to their bodies
or goods, until it shall be known from us or from our chief
justiciar in what way the merchants of our land are treated
who shall then be found in the country which is at war with
us; and if ours are safe there, the others shall be safe in
our land.

Foreign trade—both export and import—depended upon
royal permission in the Middle Ages, so that this chapter is a
natural concomitant of the series of economic and legal principles
being restated by Magna Carta. The original Article 31 of the
Barons simply stated that all merchants should have safe conduct
into and out of the kingdom, free of "evil" levies upon the goods
they bought and sold and subject only to long-established customs. The drafting of Chapter 41 in John's charter added a
detailed statement of international law, while the reissue added
the clause confirming the crown's paramount authority over foreign trade.

The net effect of this chapter was to guarantee several privileges to foreign merchants: security of person and property,
freedom to trade, and limitation of the excise levies to which they
were subject. To the extent that this curtailed the elaborate
restrictions upon mercantile competition which had been developed by the trading classes in London and other towns, this
chapter was a substantial limitation upon the promises contained
in Chapter 9, and by insuring freedom of movement, the present
chapter helped to perpetuate a monopoly in the carrying trade
between England and the Continent already enjoyed by Flemish,
Gascon, and Hanseatic groups.

Because entering or leaving the realm was a matter of which
the crown naturally would take cognizance—eloquently com-
mented upon in the following chapter in John's charter—the
feudal mind readily accepted the proposition that the king as
paramount lord of the land was entitled to levy a reasonable

amount upon any goods being brought into or out of the kingdom. This was a logical extension of the tolls and customs exacted by crown tenants and mesne lords with reference to commercial traffic touching their own lands;[141] and the safeguard sought in Chapter 30 (41 John) was "ancient and rightful customs." The established amounts of these levies was substantial enough—up to a tenth of the goods involved—and any amount greater than that was an "evil toll" (Lat. *mala tolta* or Fr. *maltolte*). John was not the first or last king to try to add to the excise revenues by one means or another; the final chapter in the *Confirmatio Cartarum* of 1297 embodied the promise of Edward I to rescind the surtax of forty shillings on every sack of wool export he had decreed shortly before.

The right of the crown to "tonnage and poundage" continued to the seventeenth century and became one of the explosive issues in the struggle with Charles I. Parliamentary lawyers uniformly cited Chapter 30 as fundamental evidence that the crown could not arbitrarily increase the customs duties, adding the authority of several fourteenth-century statutes which in their view went to establish that the requirement of Parliamentary consent dated at least from the time of Edward III.[142] The chapter has been continued among the statutes to the present, both as a policy statement on the right of the crown to tax exports and imports but also as an expression of the modern British principle of free trade.

[42]   *Writ ne Exeat*

[IT is allowed henceforth to any one to go out from our kingdom, and to return, safely and securely, by land and by water, saving their fidelity to us, except in time of war for some short time, for the common good of the kingdom; excepting persons imprisoned and outlawed according to the law of the land, and people of a land at war with us, and merchants, of whom it shall be done as is before said.]

In time of peace, and in cases of persons other than accused or convicted criminals, the right of the subject to depart from and return to the kingdom is seldom challenged in modern times, although the government retains the right to determine whether circumstances warrant the exercise of the power to order citizens not to leave (*ne exeat*). In feudal times, exile of persons out of favor with the crown was a common preliminary to plotting a hostile movement, and the writ *ne exeat* might be used as a means of forestalling such a project, or if the fugitive succeeded in making his way abroad, putting him on record as having violated the writ. The alternative medieval process was that of abjuration, whereby an accused person who had obtained sanctuary would confess his guilt to the coroner in return for a renouncing of allegiance and a safe-conduct to leave the realm.[143]

The chief objective of this chapter, promptly deleted from the reissue, appears to have been to permit ecclesiastics to come and go between Rome and the kingdom, without the king's permission, to lay their particular cases before the Holy See. In effect it rescinded a stipulation in the Constitutions of Clarendon which required clerics to obtain the king's license before leaving the land. The stipulation of 1166 more accurately reflected the feudal understanding of the right of the crown to control the movements of its subjects, however, and Henry's advisers accordingly removed this chapter from the reissue.

31 [43] *Escheated Baronies*

IF any one holds of an escheat, as of the honor of Wallingford, or Nottingham, or Boulogne, or Lancaster, or other escheats which are in our hands and are baronies, and he dies, his heir shall not give any other relief, nor do to us any other service than he would do to the baron, if *that* barony had been in the hands of the baron; and we will hold it in the same manner as the baron held it. *Nor shall we have, by occasion of such barony or escheat, any escheat or holding of any of our men, unless he who holds the barony or escheat otherwise held of us in chief.*

This characteristically feudal provision, abolished in 1660 and formally repealed in 1863, undertook to clarify the rights and liabilities of subtenants who held their estates of one of the great crown tenants. If the crown tenant died without heirs, his holding, an honor or a barony, escheated to the crown. Since the term "honor" in particular referred to the sum of services and obligations owed to the crown as conditions of the original grant, when the grant escheated to the crown it was held that the subtenancies ceased to exist, or that the holders under the escheat assumed all the obligations of the former crown tenant.

Not only did this work an unjust series of burdens upon the subtenants, but it contrasted with the condition of subtenants of a mesne lord, who were not held liable upon the escheat of the estate of their mesne lord for more than they formerly owed for their own holding. Thus if A, a tenant paravail, held of B, a mesne lord, by one knight's fee, the obligations involved in the knight's fee were the sum of A's obligations to B; if B then died and his estate escheated to C, subtenant A owed to C only what he had owed to B. However, if B held one of the vast baronies or honors —four of which are cited by name as examples—and his estate escheated to the crown, A was apt to be treated as a subtenant of the crown and subject to whatever arbitrary levies the crown might please to impose.[144]

This chapter sought to establish a more equitable practice which had developed under Henry II, and the reissue preserved and elaborated upon it. If A were a mesne lord and had made grants from his holdings, some of these might in due course have escheated to him; if B, the crown tenant and the grantor of A's estate, died and his holdings escheated to the king, the king was not to have any of A's holdings which had reverted to A by escheat. The only exception was in the case where A might hold some of his land directly from the crown; in such case, apparently (although authorities are divided), escheats to A by virtue of this tenancy could be reached by the king.

The chapter testifies to the complexities which arose in the course of feudalism when lands were successively granted, subinfeudated, placed in ward, forfeited or escheated, and regranted. The crown and the crown tenants, the principal grantors, were always disposed to define the chain of title to a particular estate to their advantage, or to forget (literally or as a matter of con-

venience) some of the intervening rights and obligations which
had developed in the course of changing tenancies. Later pur-
chasers of tracts of land found these escheat claims to cast grave
doubts on their own titles; Chapter 31 was relied upon as a means
of relieving them of some of these often unforeseeable liabilities.[145]

32   Alienation

*No freeman from henceforth shall give or sell any more
of his land, but that from the remainder of the land the lord
of the fee may have the service due him therefrom.*

The reissue added this chapter as a natural sequel to the
amendment to Chapter 31. The indefinite continuation of subinfeudation of land meant that it became substantially more difficult, as a practical matter, to hold someone liable for the original
obligations represented in the original grant. In the case of the
great baronies or "honors," feudal law recognized that every acre
of the estate retained a proportionate liability to the crown for
the obligations which were identified with that estate, and Chapter 31 primarily sought to reassure subtenants of those particular
estates that they would owe no more, upon escheat, than they
owed to the baron who had held the honor.

Chapter 32 recognized that in lands other than the great
"honors" the tenant in chief or the mesne lord might grant away
so much of his estate, and on such terms, that the remainder
of the land under his control would be insufficient to provide
the services due from the land to the lord of the fee. Thus A, the
original grantor and lord of the fee, might grant to B a certain
estate on the stipulation that it was to be held of A for twenty
knight's fees. B in the course of subinfeudation might be left with
land insufficient to meet this obligation, and B's grants to his own
subtenants might not provide enough services to make up the
difference.

In 1290 the Statute of Westminster III stipulated that "whereas buyers (*quia emptores*)" of land had theretofore held the title
under the terms set out by the immediate grantor, the buyers

were henceforth to hold of the lord of the fee. Although this legislation—known to modern times by the opening Latin words —sought to preserve a fundamental feudal property right for the benefit of the great lords, it actually prepared the way for the modern law of property, the right to substitute the new owner in his own place so far as the obligations to the lord of the fee were concerned. Thus B, in the example in the preceding paragraph, after the Statute *Quia Emptores* would not sell part of his land to C under services which C would owe to B, but rather would make C directly responsible to A for the services B had owed to A.

The limiting of subinfeudation thus substantially simplified the feudal structure at a point where it was in danger of collapsing under its growing complexities. At the same time, it further prepared the way for modern uses of land by making possible alternate means of granting interests in the land without permanently taking the title from B. Thus C might hold the estate for life or for a fixed term of years.

The tenurial concept of landholding long outlived the feudal system in which it was conceived, and was transferred to the American colonies through the charters to various proprietors. Thus, in the 1681 charter of Maryland from Charles II to Lord Baltimore, the Calverts were made lords of the colony "in free and common socage," and were to pay annually the token of two Indian arrows, with full rights of enfeoffment (granting of estates) to settlers. After the American Revolution, the continuing tenurial obligations traceable to the crown presumably were then transferred to the states; thus, in some states the theory of landholding is still tenurial, with all the complex considerations of common-law property rights which this involves. In most states, however, by constitutional declaration, landholding is allodial (outright ownership without external obligations). In England the Land Registry Act of 1862 led to the formal repeal of this chapter in 1887.[146]

[44] *Restraint of Forest Summons*

[MEN who dwell outside the forest shall not henceforth come before our justiciars of the forest, on general summons, unless they are impleaded or are sureties for any person or persons who are attached on account of the forest.]

The next five chapters of John's charter concern several interrelated matters; three of the five deal with the all-important subject of forest laws, another with the conduct of various royal officers in the forest and the rest of the countryside, while the fifth deals with the custody of vacant abbeys. Except for the last subject, which is totally out of context, the other chapters were transferred from the charter of 1215 to the separate Charter of the Forest in 1217. This charter, expanded to sixteen chapters, became the companion to the Great Charter and was regarded throughout the Middle Ages as equal in importance.

Chapter 44 thus becomes Chapter 2 of Carta de Foresta; it set a strict limit upon the jurisdiction of the forest courts and thus was a substantial grant of general liberty to the subject who dwelt "outside the forest" and sought the benefit of the common law rather than the forest law. The justiciars of the forest courts were not to reach such persons by a general summons, but could only compel their attendance if they were made parties to a specific action or were the sureties for someone who was.

Royal officers charged with administering forest laws were apt to be extortionists and petty tyrants; they performed their tasks out of the sight of superiors, under a system of law which took for granted the absolute rights of the crown within the forest and hence offered no safeguards for the accused, while the persons who dwelt within the forest and were subject to these officers were the humblest and most ignorant elements of the population for the most part. Many foresters held their positions as of fee— that is, by annual payments for the office—and like the sheriffs holding counties by similar rents, they were disposed to collect all they possibly could to recover their investment handsomely.

Forests—a term which included much open land within the "perambulation" or limits—covered a large part of England in medieval times, and from the time of the Conquest had been regarded as the king's exclusive property. All the beasts and verdure (vert) of the forest were his, the one to be reserved for his hunting pleasure, and the other to be the subject of periodic levies collected from the humble denizens who used them to feed livestock or gathered brush to sell in the villages. The Forest Charter set out the duties of the various officers: the *verdors* to watch for the cutting of vegetation, the *rangers*, who drove the wild beasts back into the depths of the greenwood and sought to apprehend poachers, and the *agistors*, who assessed the husbandmen for the number of their cattle pastured therein.

The Charter of the Forest recognized the complexities of administration: the types of game which humble men might hunt, the amount of cutting over of land which was permissible, the seasonal courts which were to be attended—and the abuses which were too often perpetrated. Having set out a safeguard for men "outside the forest" in this chapter, the Charter itself undertook to reform the administration by providing for itinerant justices who would presumably administer the forest laws more objectively. The separate courts and special jurisdictions were not abolished until 1817, and the Charter itself remains in the Statutes of the Realm as a general definition of the crown control, now administered in the general public interest.[147]

[45] *Appointment of Royal Officers*

[WE will not make justiciars, constables, sheriffs or bailiffs except of such as know the law of the realm and are well inclined to observe it.]

This somewhat plaintive statement of policy suffered the fate of all such pronouncements; it was ignored and dropped from the reissue. It reflected Article 42 of the Barons, a protest against some of John's appointees who were often incompetent or rapacious or both. It suggests an awareness that the law of the land had developed into a special body of knowledge which ought to be understood by those who were appointed to administer it, but this should not be taken too literally. Following as it did the first chapter on the forest laws, it may have been prompted by the general knowledge that these particular laws were administered harshly and often manifestly in ignorance of fundamental elements of justice. If so, the spirit of this chapter was incorporated into several of the provisions of the Forest Charter; the self-serving ambitions of the sheriffs were the object of a series of restricting laws during the rest of the thirteenth century, and restraints upon other royal officers were set out in other legislative proposals during the reign of several succeeding kings.

33 [46]   *Custody of Vacant Abbeys*

ALL [barons who have founded] *patrons of* abbeys for which they have charters of kings of England, or ancient tenure, *of advowson,* shall have their custody when they have come vacant, as they ought to have, *and as is aforesaid.*

Abbeys, as major ecclesiastical centers next in importance after cathedrals, were founded either by royal initiative or by action of wealthy tenants. When vacant, the wardship of the lay tenement which was part of the spiritual estate was normally claimed by the lord who had founded the abbey; but the king, as the nominal protector of the Church in the kingdom, appears frequently—before and after John's day—to have pre-empted the wardship. This chapter accordingly sought to insure that the custody of the vacant abbey would go to the founder.

The reissue of 1225 added a reference to the other privilege of a founder—advowson, the right to present the candidate for filling the vacancy. Because the abbot, as head of a powerful and wealthy monastery, was an important member of the ecclesiastical hierarchy, the right of presentment might outweigh the king's right of presentment in the case of some bishoprics. Yet the clear intent of the feudal law, as indicated in the writ of *darrein present-ment* with reference to lesser advowsons, was that this privilege should remain in the founder of the benefice.

Chapter 33 was rendered obsolete with Henry VIII's suppression of the religious houses in 1535 and was formally repealed in 1863.[148]

[47] *Disafforestation*

[ALL forests which have been afforested in our time shall be disafforested immediately; and so it shall be concerning river banks which in our time have been in "defense."]

The latter part of this chapter was incorporated into Chapter 16 of the reissue, while the first part was expanded in Chapter 3 of the Forest Charter to cover wrongful afforestations of Richard I as well as of John. The disafforestation provisions of Carta de Foresta went further, in fact; Chapter 1 extended the restitution process to the reign of Henry II. While an earnest effort was made to carry out the promises embodied in these two chapters, the practical difficulties involved and the reluctance of the crown to give up any more than it had to kept the issue alive for many years. It was finally settled in 1327, and neither Tudors nor Stuarts successfully modified the statutory limits set to the forests after that date.[149]

Under Henry III, "perambulations" were carried out, whereby veteran forest officials, royal justiciars, and "good and lawful men" of the neighborhood undertook to reconstruct the boundaries of particular forests at the time within their memory when Henry II or his sons had afforested particular areas. In the absence of documents or commonly recognized boundary features, it was obvious that the process would be slow, subject to disagreement, and ultimately less productive than the letter of the chapter had suggested.

[48] *Forests and Riverbanks*

[ALL the bad customs concerning forests and warrens and concerning foresters and warreners, sheriffs and their servants, river banks and their guardians shall be inquired into immediately in each county by twelve sworn knights of

the same county, who shall be elected by the honest men of
the same county, and within forty days after the inquisition
has been made, they shall be entirely destroyed by them,
never to be restored, provided that we be first informed of it,
or our justiciar, if we are not in England.]

John appears to have accommodated this demand at once;
writs implementing this chapter began issuing on June 19, the day
the final draft of Magna Carta was sealed. It was the excessive
zeal of the inquisitors—doubtless agents of the rebels—which
defeated the reform which was the object of this chapter. The
aim of the "twelve sworn knights" in each county was to cripple
or destroy the whole system of administration of the royal forests,
which was the primary subject of this chapter. Perceiving that
this chapter of the charter was thus being abused, the archbishops
of Canterbury and Dublin and six of the leading bishops of the
kingdom formally protested that "all those customs shall remain,
without which the forests cannot be preserved."[150]

The bad faith with which this chapter was carried out in all
probability was part of the evidence presented to Innocent III in
the recommendation to quash Magna Carta. The chapter was
omitted from the reissues; more specific reforms of forest procedures were written into the Forest Charter.

[49]   *Release of English Hostages*

[WE will give back immediately all hostages and
charters which have been liberated to us by Englishmen
as security for peace or for faithful service.]

Here begins the succession of chapters, all deleted from the
reissues, concerning specific concessions which the barons demanded of John. The taking of hostages and charters was a normal
enough medieval practice, as security for the good faith of the
parties to an agreement. Sons and daughters of vassals were
commonly placed in the lord's household, as a pledge for peace or

for faithful service. John's suspicion of everyone about him—
sometimes pathological, sometimes entirely justified—led him to
demand wholesale hostages as the tension of his reign increased.
Coupled with this was the grim knowledge of his ungovernable
rage when he was thwarted or betrayed, which had led to his
hanging of twenty-eight sons of Welsh nobles when he learned of
the rebellion of 1211.

The rebels would therefore wish to use this present advantage at Runnymede to obtain release of their relatives before John
could wreak his personal vengeance upon them. They also sought
the return of the charters by which the titles to their estates were
established.

[50] *Disability List*

[WE will remove absolutely from their bailiwicks the
relatives of Gerard de Athyes, so that for the future they
shall have no bailiwick in England; Engelard de Cygony,
Andrew, Peter and Gyon de Chancelles, Gyon de Cygony,
Geoffrey de Martin and his brothers, Philip Mark and his
brothers, and Geoffrey his nephew and their whole retinue.]

Another concern of the rebels was to strip the King of some of
the powerful professional soldiers who had remained in his service
after the loss of the major part of the Angevin empire. These men
were formidable warriors in their own right, and they commanded
Flemish mercenaries who gave John a considerable military
advantage when they could be thrown upon the rebels. But even
more irksome to the rebels were the administrative positions
which the exiles, mostly from the former province of Touraine,
held and rather effectively conducted in the latter years of John's
reign. Gerard de Athée had been one of Richard's most trusted
captains, and John had made him Sheriff of Herefordshire and
Gloucestershire in 1208; two years later he was replaced by his
cousin, Engelard de Cigogné.

Philip Mark was Sheriff of Nottingham and Derby, and
Geoffrey de Martin had been Constable of Northampton Castle.

The others mentioned in the list—a relatively short list, even when "their whole retinue" is included—held similar positions in John's kingdom, and there is little evidence that they were disliked by the people under them, or ruled with any heavier hand, than most other royal officers.[151] Most of them were retained by Henry III and gave loyal service to their master.

[51] *Dismissal of Mercenaries*

[AND immediately after the re-establishment of peace we will remove from the kingdom all foreign-born soldiers, crossbow men, servants, and mercenaries who have come with horses and arms for the injury of the realm.]

This provision aimed at further reducing the military strength on the side of the crown. While the number of mercenaries—including, presumably, the Poitevin troops which John had the right to use by color of his Angevin titles—is unknown, their battle-seasoned character made them a powerful threat to the rebels. The specific reference to soldiers trained to use the crossbow suggests the disadvantage which the barons sought to remove. All of this, in turn, adds up to the fact that the barons in June of 1215 held a very tenuous bargaining superiority; the king had well-distributed military resources, which he proceeded to use to reconquer much of the kingdom after the rebels revealed their own bad faith in refusing to abide by the Charter agreement.

The protestation that the use of foreign troops was "for the injury of the realm" did not deter the barons when they found the reconquest proceeding, and they applied to Prince Louis of France to send an invading host to help them recover the initiative.

[52] *Redress of Wrongful Disseisins*

[IF any one shall have been dispossessed or removed by us without legal judgment of his peers, from his lands, castles, franchises, or his right, we will restore them to him immediately; and if contention arises about this, then it shall be done according to the judgment of the twenty-five barons, of whom mention is made below concerning the security of the peace. Concerning all those things, however, from which any one has been removed or of which he has been deprived without legal judgment of his peers by King Henry our father, or by King Richard, our brother, which we have in our land, or which others hold, and which it is our duty to guarantee, we shall have respite till the usual term of crusaders; excepting those things about which the suit has been begun or the inquisition made by our writ before our assumption of the cross; when, however, we shall return from our journey or if by chance we desist from the journey, we will immediately show full justice in regard to them.]

In this chapter summarizing the restitutions which John is to be required to make, the Charter introduces the baronial plan for insuring the meeting of their demands. The authority of the twenty-five barons is set out in detail in Chapter 61; the group itself foreshadowed the conservators who assumed control of affairs from Henry III in 1258-59, and the Lords Ordainers who sought to dominate Edward II sixty years later. The original Article 25 of the Barons had dealt with this subject in the context of the several provisions on legal procedures and safeguards; as it appears in this spot in the Charter it reveals more clearly the strategy for reducing the King to a point where the rebels' will would prevail. First hostages were to be released, then the leading foreign professional soldiers and the mercenaries were to be sent away, then the King was to submit any disputes over the claims against him to a high commission made up of his bitterest enemies.

The rebels naturally had in mind, in the present chapter, the restitution of estates of various types which John had declared forfeit or had seized outright in the course of his disputes with his tenants. They took the opportunity, at the same time, to claim certain damages from actions by Richard and by Henry II. In each case, it should be noted, the test is whether the dispossession was "without legal judgment of his peers," which in this context obviously means the barons. The claims for restitution in the cases of wrongful acts by Richard or Henry were, in all probability, *pro forma;* in any event, the rebels were content to grant a stay in any action on them until "the usual term of crusaders," or three years. The disseisins attributed to John himself were to be remedied immediately.

[53]   *Crusader's Respite*

[WE shall, moreover, have the same respite and in the same manner about showing justice in regard to the forests which are to be disafforested or to remain forests, which Henry our father or Richard our brother made into forests; and concerning the custody of lands which are in the fief of another, custody of which we have until now had on account of a fief which any one has held from us by military service; and concerning the abbeys which have been founded in fiefs of others than ourselves, in which the lord of the fee has asserted for himself a right; and when we return or if we should desist from our journey we will immediately show full justice to those complaining in regard to them.]

This chapter introduces the proposition to disafforest certain areas which had been afforested by Henry II or Richard; this proposition was transferred from Magna Carta to the first and third chapters of the Forest Charter. The present chapter also implements the earlier Chapter 37 of John's charter on prerogative wardships, and Chapter 46 on wardship of vacant abbeys. In each instance the Crusader's respite is granted, but John is compelled to promise that "if we desist from our journey" the remedies will be provided without delay.

34 [54]   *Appeal of Women*

NO one shall be seized nor imprisoned on the appeal of a woman concerning the death of any one except her husband.

There is no logical explanation for the placing of this chapter at this particular point in the Charter; it belongs among the earlier chapters on procedural safeguards and general restatements of feudal law, and it has no counterpart among the Articles of the Barons. It is declaratory of the law, as witness Glanville's statement that "a woman is heard in this suit, accusing any one of her husband's death, if she speak as being an eye-witness to the fact, because husband and wife are one flesh."[152]

An appeal (criminal accusation) was still to be met, in the early thirteenth century, only by combat, and when the appeal was made by a woman, or an elderly or infirm person, a champion could be designated to meet the accused party. The present chapter, accordingly, limited the cases in which women could appeal or charge a felony since it was thought to give women an unfair advantage if they could compel a defendant to do combat with a champion on any matter. Even in these cases where an appeal was permitted, Glanville states that the accused party may "purge himself by the ordeal" (i.e., of fire or water).[153]

This chapter was rendered obsolete in 1819 with a general modernization of criminal procedures and was abolished in 1863.[154]

[55] *Remission of Unjust Fines*

[ALL fines which have been imposed unjustly and against the law of the land, and all penalties imposed unjustly and against the law of the land are altogether excused, or will be on the judgment of the twenty-five barons of whom mention is made below in connection with the security of the peace, or on the judgment of the majority of them, along with the aforesaid Stephen, archbishop of Canterbury, if he is able to be present, and others whom he may wish to call for this purpose along with him. And if he should not be able to be present, nevertheless the business shall go on without him, provided that if any one or more of the aforesaid twenty-five barons are in a similar suit they should be removed as far as this particular judgment goes, and others who shall be chosen and put upon oath, by the remainder of the twenty-five shall be sustituted for them for this purpose.]

This chapter resumes the enumeration of restitutions being demanded of John, and introduces three significant provisions: (1) All fines and other penalties imposed unjustly and "against the law of the land" are to be remitted; (2) a majority of the twenty-five barons, together with the Archbishop of Canterbury and others he may wish to have sit in on the case, are to decide the issues; and (3) any of the twenty-five who have an interest in the case under consideration will be disqualified for that case.

In the early feudal law, a fine was any final payment to settle a claim or to make an agreement binding. Under Richard I, John, and Henry III, however, the fine became a figure arbitrarily fixed at a heavy sum, and the king readily committed the victim to prison until he agreed to pay it. These unreasonable levies were now held to be "against the law of the land," or in disregard of ancient custom, and were to be submitted to a jury of at least thirteen persons, for review and determination. The presence of the Archbishop, and the requirement that no one should partici- pate in the judgment of his own case, was intended to give some degree of objectivity to the proceedings.

[56] *Restitution to Welshmen*

[IF we have dispossessed or removed any Welshmen from their lands, or franchises, or other things, without legal judgment of their peers, in England, or in Wales, they shall be immediately returned to them; and if a dispute shall have arisen over this, then it shall be settled in the borderland by judgment of their peers, concerning holdings of England according to the law of England, concerning holdings of Wales according to the law of Wales, and concerning hold- ings of the borderland according to the law of the borderland. The Welsh shall do the same to us and ours.]

The next three chapters undertake to encourage the Welsh to make common cause with the rebels, by promising remedies for wrongful seizures and return of hostages. The procedure, as set out in this chapter, is the judgment of peers and the law of the place of the complaint: English estates to be adjudicated by English law, Welsh estates by Welsh law, the estates of the borderland by the amalgam of English and Welsh custom which obtains in that area.

[57]   *Further Restitution*

[CONCERNING all those things, however, from which any one of the Welsh shall have been removed or dispossessed without legal judgment of his peers, by King Henry our father, or King Richard our brother, which we hold in our hands, or which others hold, and we are bound to warrant to them, we shall have respite till the usual period of crusaders, those being excepted about which suit was begun or inquisition made by our command before our assumption of the cross. When, however, we shall return or if by chance we shall desist from our journey, we will show full justice to them immediately, according to the laws of the Welsh and the aforesaid parts.]

This chapter extends the restitution to cover wrongful takings by Richard I or Henry II, and as in the case of the disafforestations by his predecessors, covered in Chapter 53, a Crusader's respite is granted.

[58]   *Further Restitution*

[WE will give back the son of Llewellyn immediately, and all the hostages from Wales and the charters which had been liberated to us as a security for peace.]

By compelling the return of Welsh hostages, including the son of the leading Welsh warrior, the barons were seeking to discharge an obligation to those Welshmen who had sporadically made common cause with them against the crown for a number of years. Llewellyn was Prince of North Wales, and the husband of John's illegitimate daughter Joan; the youngster stipulated in this chapter was therefore presumably the grandson of John. He was one of a number of hostages probably taken after the King had put down the most recent uprising in that kingdom, to replace the earlier hostages whom he had executed.

[59] *Restitution to Scots*

[WE will act toward Alexander, king of the Scots, concerning the return of his sisters and his hostages, and concerning his franchises and his right, according to the manner in which we shall act toward our other barons of England, unless it ought to be otherwise by the charters which we hold from William his father, formerly king of the Scots, and this shall be by the judgment of his peers in our court.]

The relationship between Scotland and England throughout the Middle Ages was a confused and chronically disputed one. After Glanville's troops had captured William the Lion in the course of his massive uprising against Henry II, the King of the Scots had done homage to the Plantagenet ruler and had compelled his lords to do the same. Richard I, in his reckless fundraising for his Crusade, had sold a rather vaguely defined independence back to William, and when John came to the throne he compelled the Scottish King to do homage again. William, however, reserved "his franchises and his right"—the one relating to certain baronies in England traditionally held by the King of the Scots, the other referring to the autonomy of Scottish rule north of the Tweed.

In 1209 during a new outbreak of border troubles John compelled the King's son Alexander to renew Scotland's homage, and required that the young Princesses Margaret and Isabel be delivered as hostages. The courteous treatment of the Princesses, and John's help to Alexander in securing his throne after William's death, held Scotland in the royal camp in 1215; Alan of Galway, a kind of deputy of the King for Scotland, was among the supporters of John mentioned in the preamble to Magna Carta. Thus the barons in this chapter were probing for an opportunity to weaken the Scots' ties with John while avoiding any concessions which would enhance their autonomy.

This accounts for the rather circumlocutory provisions in this chapter; Alexander is to be treated in the same way John is to treat "other barons of England," unless his feudal position has been qualified by some of the concessions John secured "from William his father." The unraveling of this tangled procedure was to be by judgment of his peers (i.e., the other barons of England) in the King's court.

This chapter came to nought; Scotland remained in the royal camp, and the Princesses eventually were married to vassals of Henry III—Margaret to Hubert de Burgh, the able Poitevin warrior and administrator, and Isabel to Roger Bigod, one of the rebels at Runnymede who later made his peace with the throne.

35 *County Court; Sheriff's Tourn, View of Frankpledge*

NO county court from henceforth shall be held but from month to month; and where greater time hath been used, there shall be greater; nor any sheriff nor his bailiff shall keep his term in the hundred but thrice in the year, and no where but in due place and accustomed; that is to say, once after Easter, and again after the Feast of St. Michael. And the view of frankpledge shall be likewise at the Feast of St. Michael, without hindrance; so that any man may have his liberties which he had or used to have in the time of King Henry our Grandfather, or which he hath purchased since.

The view of frankpledge shall be so done, that our peace may be kept; and that the tything be wholly kept, as it hath been accustomed; and that the sheriff shall not seek to trouble any, and that he be content with so much as the sheriff was wont to have for his view-making, in the time of King Henry our Grandfather.

This chapter—one of two added to the reissue at this point—contrasts strikingly with the passages in John's charter immediately preceding it. The latter are retributive and *ad hoc;* the present chapter reflects the character of the Great Charter as it emerged through the reissues, as a comprehensive statement of the common law of the time. This chapter is of further significance in extending the Charter's coverage to areas of local administration which were less the concern of the great landholders, the subject of so many of the other chapters, and more the concern of the yeomen and small tenants.

Three fundamental considerations of local government are the subject of Chapter 35 of the reissue: The reasonable schedule of terms of the county court, the sheriff's "tourn" or circuit of the hundred courts within the county, and the "view of frankpledge." All of these dealt with procedures dating back to Saxon times, which the Norman and Plantagenet kings and their successors were to leave largely undisturbed. They all were posited upon the universal participation of the adult male population in the business of the county as a whole, of the hundred, or of the neighborhood. Chronically there were complaints about the frequency with which it was necessary to do "suit of court," when all men of the county or hundred, as the case might be, were expected to be on hand to serve on juries of variable size dealing with administrative as much as with judicial matters.

The county court was the outgrowth of the ancient shire-moot, which in turn was a vestige of the courts attending the petty kingdoms from which the counties developed. They were thus roughly analogous to the advisors who were in attendance upon the king, with the sheriff in the place of the king at the county level. All of the men of standing in the county participated in the court, while the humble folk sought to avoid the burdens of attendance by sending a variable number of representatives.

The present chapter undertook to regularize the terms of the county courts at periods of once a month, unless local custom warranted a variation. It then sought to limit the sessions of the hundred courts—three a year are set as the maximum, but only two are specifically required, at spring and fall dates. These were sessions of the hundreds at which the sheriff or his representative was to be present; other sessions were also held monthly. The hundred court was roughly analogous to a "police court" of later centuries, being a gathering of men of the community to investigate local crimes and determine the appropriate action to be taken. When the sheriff made his "tourn," the hundred reeve and four of the "best men" of each vill in the hundred came before him to present information concerning all criminal matters in their jurisdiction. The graver charges resulted in arrests and detention in gaol until the coming of the royal justices; the lesser charges were the subject of amercements.

One of the most important functions of the sheriff at the fall "tourn" was the viewing of frankpledge. Frankpledge was an interlocking system of securities for debts, and perhaps for other forms of liability; each person was required to find another who would serve as his security to guarantee his discharge of a debt or his appearance in court if this became necessary. Various members of a family might provide this security for each other; a master would serve as security for his servants; a guild might find the security for its members. Or a group of ten men within a hundred might provide for a corporate security (tithing), and the tithing-man in charge of the group soon became the village constable. All of the records of these securities for the local keeping of the peace were to be inspected by the sheriff at the fall session of the hundred, with the fee due the sheriff on this occasion being limited to the amounts customary in the time of Henry II.

All men of the hundred, according to the chapter, were also to be reconfirmed in the liberties (freedom from certain feudal obligations) which they had enjoyed in the time of Henry II or had "purchased" (been granted unconditionally) since then.

Although some of the practices of the hundred courts fell into disuse—even in medieval times being supplanted by seignorial courts leet, which administered the business of the hundreds under a proprietary system—the general structure of county administration set out in Chapter 35 was not formally abolished until the Sheriff's Act of 1887.[155]

36 *Fraudulent Gifts in Mortmain*

IT shall not be lawful from henceforth to any to give his lands to any religious house, and to take the same land again, to hold of the same house; nor shall it be lawful to any house of religion so to take the lands of any to deliver the same land to him. If any from henceforth so give his lands to any religious house, and thereupon be convict, the gift shall be utterly void, and the land shall accrue to the lord of the fee.

This chapter, added to the charter in 1217, was intended to protect crown tenants and certain mesne lords from the loss of feudal obligations owing to them by a fraudulent gift of his estate by an undertenant. Thus a freeholder who owed his grantor certain annual rents and services might convey the title to his estate to a religious house; this terminated the temporal obligations attached to the estate. Thereafter the religious house would grant the same property to the freeholder, subject to the spiritual obligations which would thereafter be owing to the new grantor. The original lord's rights were thus cut off by the "dead hand" *(mortmain)* of the spiritual grantor.

Because this process, if permitted to accelerate, would break down the tenurial system itself, Edward I in 1285 undertook to implement Chapter 36 in the Statute of Mortmain (Chapter 32 of Westminster II), which in itself was an extension of his 1279 Statute *de Viris Religiosis* (on spiritual tenants). Gifts to ecclesiastical corporations were permitted where they did not cut off certain specified obligations to the original grantor, or later to the state. As the feudal age waned, and landholding became a matter of economics rather than military and political policy, mortmain continued to be a legal problem for different reasons. The extinguishing or diminishing of tax liabilities in cases where land was held by church corporations in trust for secular tenants led in modern times to the Mortmain Act of 1736, taking away the power to convey land by will to eleemosynary agencies. In 1888 the Mortmain and Charitable Uses Act repealed the 1736 law, but set up a code of controls over transfers of land ownership which tended to remove the land in perpetuity from the possibility of acquisition by other tenants.[156]

In the United States the common-law doctrine of mortmain was not generally recognized in the period of history when the supply of land seemed almost limitless. Later, a number of states found it desirable to enact legislation which came to have the generic title of "mortmain acts," and which aimed, as in England, at limiting grants of land to ecclesiastical and charitable owners except under well-defined limitations. By modern times, in both countries, the original force of Chapter 36 had long since been supplanted by other statutes, beginning with those of Edward I. Accordingly, this chapter of Magna Carta was repealed as obsolete in 1863.

37 [60]   Escuage; General Saving

ESCUAGE from henceforth shall be taken like as it was wont to be in the time of King Henry our Grandfather, reserving to all archbishops, bishops, abbots, priors, templars, hospitallers, earls, barons, and all persons as well spiritual as temporal, all their free liberties and free customs, which they had in time passed. [Moreover,] **AND all these customs and liberties aforesaid, which we have granted to be held in this our realm, as much as appertaineth to us *and our heirs*, we shall observe; and all men of this**

our realm, as well spiritual as temporal, as much as in them is, shall observe the same against all persons, in like wise.

The portion of this concluding chapter of 1225, relating to "shield money" *(escuage* or *scutage)* and transferred from Chapter 12 of 1215, was rendered obsolete with the abolition of feudal tenures in 1660 and was formally abolished in 1863. The remainder of the chapter, however, remains in force as a general policy statement and summary of the guarantees set out in the foregoing chapters of the charter.

While Coke exaggerated the significance of the last sentence of the chapter, taking it as evidence that Magna Carta in its reissue extended its benefits to all persons, the fact remains that by its retention to modern times this has indeed become the import of this chapter today. In 1225 it was important for admonishing that as the king was granting the various liberties and customs to his tenants, they in turn were to insure them "in like wise" to all their subtenants. As the tenurial system waned, the literal statement became properly susceptible of a broader application.

[61] *Forma Securitatis*

[SINCE, moreover, for the sake of God, and for the improvement of our kingdom, and for the better quieting of the hostility sprung up lately between us and our barons, we have made all these concessions; wishing them to enjoy these in a complete and firm stability forever, we make and concede to them the security described below; that is to say, that they shall elect twenty-five barons of the kingdom, whom they will, who ought with all their power to observe, hold, and cause to be observed, the peace and liberties which we have conceded to them, and by this our present charter confirmed to them; in this manner, that if we or our justiciar, or our bailiffs, or any of our servants shall have done wrong in any way toward any one, or shall have transgressed any of the articles of peace or security; and the wrong shall have been shown to four barons of the aforesaid twenty-five barons, let those four barons come to us or to our justiciar, if we are out of the kingdom, laying before us the transgression, and let them ask that we cause that transgression to be corrected without delay. And if we shall not have corrected the transgression or, if we shall be out of the kingdom, if our justiciar shall not have corrected it within a period of forty days, counting from the time in which it has been shown to us or to our justiciar, if we are out of the kingdom; the aforesaid four barons shall refer the matter to the remainder of the twenty-five barons, and let these twenty-five barons with the whole community of the country distress and injure us in every way they can; that is to say by the seizure of our castles, lands, possessions, and in such other ways as they can until it shall have been corrected according to their judgment, saving our person and that of our queen, and those of our children; and when the correction has been made, let them devote themselves to us as they did before. And let whoever in the country wishes to take an oath that in all the above-mentioned measures he will obey the orders of the aforesaid twenty-five barons, and that he will injure us as far as he is able with them, and we give permission to swear publicly and freely to each one who wishes to swear, and no one will we ever forbid to swear. All those, moreover, in the country who of themselves and their own will are unwilling to take an oath to the twenty-five barons as to distressing and injuring us along with them, we will compel to take the oath by our mandate, as before said. And if any one of the twenty-five barons shall have died or departed from the land or shall in any way be prevented from taking the above mentioned action, let the remainder of the aforesaid twenty-five barons choose another in his place, according to their judgment, who shall take an oath in the same way as the others. In all those things, moreover, which are committed to those five and twenty barons to carry out, if perhaps the twenty-five are present, and some disagreement arises among them about something, or if any of them when they have been summoned are not willing or are not able to be present, let that be considered valid and firm which the greater part of those who are present arrange or command, just as if the whole twenty-five had agreed in this; and let the aforesaid twenty-five swear that they will observe faithfully all the things which are said above, and with all their ability cause them to be observed. And we will obtain nothing from any one, either by ourselves or by another by which any of these concessions and liberties shall be revoked or diminished; and if any such thing shall have been obtained, let it be invalid and void, and we will never use it by ourselves or by another.]

By this remarkable chapter, the parties to the Charter sought —and failed—to find a practical procedure for insuring adherence to the concessions by the King. In part the plan was foredoomed by the character of the twenty-five barons who were to be John's overseers; they were not the type of magnates whom the rest of the kingdom would choose to trust with the welfare of the state. In part, too, the plan was foredoomed because it did not reach the basic constitutional problem; it merely replaced one tyrant with a directory and was unable to settle the matter of how to prevent any element in the structure of government from converting the structure into an instrument to serve its own ends.

The Charter does not include the names of the twenty-five barons; in all probability, they had not been finally settled upon by June 19. The most commonly accepted list is provided by the chronicler, Roger of Wendover, and includes the following: the earls of Aumâle, Gloucester, Hereford, Hertford, Norfolk, Oxford, and Winchester; Robert fitz Walter, the so-called marshal of the rebel army; William d'Albini and Geoffrey de Say, the only names in the lot who were reasonably sympathetic to John; William Marshal the younger, son of the Earl of Pembroke, who may have placed his family on both sides of the fence for "insurance" purposes; Eustace de Vesci, one of the oldest of the King's enemies; William Hardell, mayor of London; and Gilbert de Clare, son of Earl Richard of Hertford, who would in a few months succeed to the title and who would be one of the first to swear allegiance to Prince Louis of France.

Five were lesser barons of the northern part of the kingdom who were doubtless under the influence of some of the greater rebels from that area; they were John fitz Robert, John de Lacy, William de Mowbray, Richard de Percy, and Robert de Ros. Hugh Bigod was the son of Earl Roger of Norfolk; Roger de Montbegon was one of several who seem to have had family ties with some of the leaders. Four who had followed John on his ill-fated expedition to Poitou had been among the vassals who had refused to fight once they were there—William de Lanvelei, William Mallet, Richard de Montfichet, and William of Huntingfield.[157]

All of these men doubtless could point to entirely valid grievances at the hands of the King; but the personal histories of the more prominent among them make it clear that the wrongdoing was not one-sided. Moreover, their subsequent behavior dispelled whatever doubt there might have been about their ultimate bad faith. It is safe to assume that there were mixed motives on all sides, and that at this point in time most powerful men acted with self-serving ends in view. Indeed, considering the circumstances, Magna Carta as a whole has a remarkably high percentage of principles which would be beneficial to broadening segments of English society as the years passed. But Chapter 61 placed the entire document in jeopardy by attempting to make it self-executing through a perpetual right of rebellion.

The barons at Runnymede are not to be censured too severely for being limited to the psychology of their own age. They had no foreknowledge of parliamentary government or the separation of powers theory, or any guidance of experience in achieving a stable society. On the contrary, the only universal fact of the Middle Ages was the instability of human society, and the only effective political process known to them was the feudal system with its interlocking obligations and the rule of strength. Chapter 61 foredoomed the first issue of Magna Carta; it had indeed recapitulated most of the fundamental, understood principles of medieval law, but it could not give these the sanction of a higher loyalty. It offered only the alternative of a monarchy in being and a monarchy in suspense.

[62] *Letters Testimonial*

[AND all ill-will, grudges, and anger sprung up between us and our men, clergy and laymen, from the time of the dispute, we have full renounced and pardoned to all. Moreover, all transgressions committed on account of this dispute, from Easter in the sixteenth year of our reign till the restoration of peace, we have fully remitted to all, clergy and laymen, and as far as pertains to us, fully pardoned. And moreover we have caused to be made for them testimonial letters-patent of lord Stephen, archbishop of Canterbury, lord Henry, archbishop of Dublin, and of the aforesaid bishops and of master Pandulph, in respect to that security and the concessions named above.]

In a further attempt to restore peace, this chapter empowers the spiritual leaders, including those named in the preamble, to confirm to the realm that the concord between John and his barons had been agreed upon. The letters began going out promptly; copies of the charter and the letters under seals of the two archbishops and the papal legate were in all the cathedrals of the kingdom in a few weeks. When, with the passing of time, it became evident that the barons were not living up to the concord, the same group of spiritual lords proceeded to publish a protest which certified the ultimate collapse of the agreement.

[63] *Formal Clauses*

[WHEREFORE we will and firmly command that the Church of England shall be free, and that the men in our kingdom shall have and hold all the aforesaid liberties, rights and concessions, well and peacefully, freely and quietly, fully and completely, for themselves and their heirs, from us and our heirs, in all things and places, forever, as before said. It has been sworn, moreover, as well on our part as on the part of the barons, that all these things spoken of above shall be observed in good faith and without any evil intent. Witness the above named and many others. Given by our hand in the meadow which is called Runnymede, between Windsor and Staines, on the fifteenth day of June, in the seventeenth year of our reign.]

BIBLIOGRAPHIC ESSAY AND NOTES

Because Part I of this small work has been intended primarily to give the general reader a narrative description of the role played by Magna Carta in the history of English and American institutions, no attempt was made to document the text in detail. The notes for this portion of the book are, accordingly, an acknowledgment of the principal sources of the information incorporated into each chapter. On the other hand, it was felt that in Part II, where the text of the Great Charter itself was involved, and the annotation and interpretation was necessarily subject to more particular reference and authority, the more conventional method of citing specific sources should be employed.

BASIC GENERAL REFERENCES

The acknowledged scholarly authority on the Great Charter in modern times is W. S. McKechnie's *Magna Carta* (Glasgow, 2d ed., 1914; reprinted New York, 1958). The author wrote within a generation after the great outburst of critical research on early English legal and political institutions which was made possible by the nineteenth-century printing, under public and private auspices, of many ancient records. Beginning with the nine great volumes of the Statutes of the Realm from 1215 to 1714, published between 1810 and 1828 by the Records Commission, there had been a series of calendars and excerpted texts from a wide variety of medieval sources which continued to appear until well into the 1840's. Then, in 1858, began the systematic publishing of the Rolls Series, which was carried on for almost eighty years and which made available a priceless treasury of records for the thirteenth to the fifteenth centuries.

With the accessibility of these records, supplemented by fundamentally important editions of specific records by the Pipe Roll Society and the newly established Selden Society, a succession of studies began to appear, based upon the new perspectives of the Middle Ages provided by these primary sources. The writers of the time discovered that the great authorities upon whom they had customarily relied—

353

Sir Edward Coke, in particular—had erred substantially in their Elizabethan and early Stuart interpretations of the origins of English legal
institutions. The new historians, accordingly, wrote in the flush of a
reaction to the new discoveries, and as might be expected, followed
the pendulum swing to the opposite extreme. As a result, a work like
McKechnie's, while based upon a much larger and much more reliable
collection of primary source materials, tended to exaggerate or unduly
to depreciate the ultimate contribution of the various political forces
of the early thirteenth century to the subsequent development of legal
institutions.

The perspective needed to bring McKechnie's pioneer twentieth-
century work into focus was provided by two careful studies by Faith
Thompson of the University of Minnesota. *The First Century of Magna
Carta* (Minneapolis, 1929) drew upon materials which were still
coming to light when McKechnie published his second edition on the
eve of the seven hundredth anniversary of the Great Charter. This
work, addressed to the question of why Magna Carta persisted and
developed into a fundamental document in the critical years which saw
the establishment of Parliament and the beginning of systematic en-
rollment of statutes, was complemented two decades later by her
*Magna Carta: Its Role in the Making of the English Constitution,
1300-1629* (Minneapolis, 1948). Thus equipped with the two Thompson studies, and reading McKechnie with the qualifications that these
and later scholarly general histories suggest, the serious student of the
subject may proceed with confidence.

Although the plans were disrupted by the First World War, the
Royal Historical Society's observance of the seven hundredth anniversary eventually came to fruition in a volume of *Magna Carta Com-
memoration Essays* (London, 1917) under the general editorship of
H. E. Malden. Among the contributions of lasting significance in this
series were the discerning studies of Chapter 39 of John's charter by
Sir Paul Vinogradoff and of the phrases, "law of the land" and "judgment of peers," by F. M. Powicke, as well as Charles H. McIlwaine's
essay on the Charter and the common law, and H. D. Hazeltine's essay
on the influence of Magna Carta on American constitutional law. Thus,
although there is later and more detailed research on all of these subjects, these particular essays still provide much valuable and valid
insight into the content of Magna Carta and its heritage.

For the seven hundred fiftieth anniversary, the major work analogous to McKechnie promises to be the monograph by Professor J. C.
Holt of the University of Nottingham, *Magna Carta* (Cambridge,
1965), while the counterpart of Malden's volume is anticipated in a
series of *Magna Carta Essays* being prepared by the Virginia Magna
Carta Commission under the general editorship of Professor A. E. Dick
Howard of the University of Virginia. It is anticipated that these essays
will appear in individual paperbound editions throughout 1965, and

will then be gathered into a single clothbound volume. The first essay in this series is Howard's *Magna Carta: Text and Commentary* (Charlottesville, Va., 1965), which lists the other titles proposed for the series.

Professor Holt and Professor Sidney Painter of the Johns Hopkins University have, between them, produced the most important secondary studies of the people and events of the period. Holt's *King John* (London, 1963) and Painter's *The Reign of King John* (Baltimore, 1949)—complemented by W. L. Warren's *King John* (New York, 1961)—testify to the continuing interest in this period stimulated by the continuing discovery of additional data to confirm the prevalent scholarly view that John, with all his faults, has been the victim of folklore and overzealous apologists for the idea that the barons in arms of the early thirteenth century were selfless crusaders for general liberty.

Painter's research spanned more than two decades, from his early study of William Marshal in 1933 to his concise and excellent *History of the Middle Ages* (Baltimore, 1953). Holt's study of *The Northerners* (Oxford, 1961), concerning some of the baronial leaders, should be used to give prespective to some of Painter's conclusions, while Powicke's *Stephen Langton* (Oxford, 1928) makes a persuasive case for the role of the Archbishop of Canterbury in developing the Great Charter into a definitive restatement of fundamental law. *The History of English Law Before the Time of Edward I*, by Sir Frederick Pollock and F. M. Maitland (Cambridge, 2 vol., 1911, second ed., Washington, D. C., 1959), is also of fundamental importance in providing background for this period.

The second volume of the excellent series of English Historical Documents, covering the period 1042-1189, and edited by David Douglas and G. W. Greenaway, was published by Oxford University in 1953; unfortunately, the next volume on the thirteenth century has not yet been published, although later volumes, for the Puritan revolutionary period and the American colonial period, have fortunately appeared. Oxford University has also sponsored an excellent History of England, including volumes by A. L. Poole, *From Domesday Book to Magna Carta* (Oxford, 2d ed., 1955) and by Powicke, *The Thirteenth Century, 1216-1307* (Oxford, 1953). The second and third volumes of W. S. Holdsworth's *History of English Law* (Boston, 1922-23) cover the period from the Conquest to the end of the Middle Ages exhaustively.

Two recent works of fundamental importance are *The Governance of England from the Conquest to Magna Carta*, by H. G. Richardson and George O. Sayles (Edinburgh, 1963), and the Jayne Lectures of the American Philosophical Society given in 1963 by Lady Doris M. Stenton and published as *English Justice Between the Norman Conquest and the Great Charter* (Philadelphia, 1964).

Inasmuch as almost all of the general works cited here contain detailed and valuable bibliographies, it is not necessary to reiterate the numerous authorities covered therein. Professor Powicke has put most Americans in his debt by editing a *Handbook of British Chronology* in 1939; it has recently been reissued in revised form and happily orients the layman and the scholar in many details which persistently elude all but the most erudite. The excellent multivolume histories of medieval and modern Europe sponsored by Cambridge University are also welcome guides to Continental as well as English developments from feudalism to the nineteenth century.

GENERAL NOTES TO PART I

Chapter 1

To attempt to capture the feeling of the times, the opening chapters have relied heavily upon various medieval chronicles, available in a number of translations. Three versions of the Anglo-Saxon Chronicle (1042-1154) appear in the second volume of the English Historical Records cited above; a variant under the title of the Peterborough Chronicle, translated by H. A. Rositzke (New York, 1951), provided a particularly flavorful series of episodes and anecdotes.

The Douglas and Greenaway volume in the English Historical Records provides a most convenient compendium of the major chronicles and features a careful analysis of the Bayeux Tapestry. Among narratives collected in this volume are those, extending from the Conquest through the time of Henry II, of William of Poitiers, William of Malmesbury, Henry of Huntingdon, William of Newburgh, and Gerald of Wales. Many of the early writs, charters, and decrees of Norman and Plantagenet kings are also collected here, and there is an exceptionally illuminating documentary history of the famous quarrel between Henry II and Thomas à Becket. There are also a number of excerpts from the Domesday Book and other local records.

On feudalism itself, among many works available may be cited the legal histories by Pollock and Maitland and by Holdsworth, and for briefer but particularly enlightening discussion there is Theodore F. T. Plucknett's *Concise History of the Common Law* (Boston, 5th ed., 1956). Vinogradoff's chapter on feudalism in the third volume of the Cambridge Medieval History is a classic of concise information; and Sir Frank M. Stenton's *First Century of Feudalism* (Oxford, 2d ed., 1961) is a more detailed study of equal authority. Poole's volume in the Oxford History of England is also available, and the bibliographic sources in its appendix suggest a number of detailed studies of particular aspects of the subject.

Several old and modern works which cover personalities and events of the period are Edward A. Freeman's *History of the Norman*

Conquest (Oxford, 6 vol., 1867-79) and *The Reign of William Rufus and the Accession of Henry I* (Oxford, 2 vol., 1882); works such as H. W. C. Davis's *England Under the Normans and Angevins* (London, 8th ed., 1924) are useful complements. Lord Lyttleton's *History of the Life of King Henry II* (London, 4 vol., 1767) is rich in color and sometimes more persuasive than Thomas B. Costain's readable history of the Plantagenets (New York, 4 vol., 1962). C. H. Haskins's *Norman Institutions* (Cambridge, Mass., 1918) is a standard reference.

Biographical studies include Stenton's *William the Conqueror* (New York and London, 1915), J. H. Round, *Geoffrey de Mandeville* (London, 1892), and sketches in the Dictionary of National Biography.

Chapter 2

The most fruitful chronicle for this period is Roger of Wendover's *Flowers of History,* translated by J. A. Giles (London, 2 vol., 1849), supplemented and continued by the writings of Matthew Paris, also translated and edited by Giles (London, 3 vol., 1852). Bishop William Stubbs's extended research in early constitutional history is still of fundamental importance for this period; students need to rely continually upon his *Constitutional History of England* (Oxford, 3d ed., 2 vol., 1887) as importantly rounded out by Charles Petit-Dutaillis' *Studies and Notes Supplementary to Stubbs . . .* , translated by W. T. Waugh (Manchester, 2 vol., 1914). Stubbs' *Select Charters Illustrative of English Constitutional History,* as revised by H. W. C. Davis (Oxford, 9th ed., 1913), is still a basic reference, together with Charles Bémont's *Chartres des Libertés Anglaises* (Paris, 1892), one of a number of valuable French works on English legal development.

The Camden Society has published several volumes of political songs and poems which have been rich sources of contemporary comment: Thomas Wright's *Political Songs of England* (London, 1839) covers the thirteenth-century era. But the works of the Selden Society, each volume featuring a definitive introductory essay, are indispensable for the study of legal history of the Middle Ages. The most valuable for this period is Volume 77, *Royal Writs in England from the Conquest to Glanville,* edited by R. C. Van Caenengem (London, 1959), but mention should also be made of the first volume, edited by Maitland himself as *Select Pleas of the Crown* (London, 1887), covering the period 1200 to 1225, and the third volume, *Select Civil Pleas* (London, 1889), edited by A. P. Baildon and covering the period 1200-1203. Another important study for the period of Richard I and John is Volume 15, *Select Pleas, Starrs and Other Records from the Rolls of the Exchequer of the Jews* (London, 1901), edited by J. M. Rigg, even though much of its material covers the later thirteenth century.

Volumes 18 and 21 represent a subseries on *Borough Customs,* edited by Mary Bateson (London, 1904, 1906) which, like the preceding title, cover later documents but have valuable historical introductions which throw welcome light on many practices with which Magna Carta was concerned, but which are cryptic to the modern reader. In this same category is G. J. Turner's edited collection of *Select Pleas of the Forest* (London, 1899), the best commentary on the problems anticipated in the Great Charter and expanded in the Charter of the Forest. Sir Cyril Flower's *Introduction to the Curia Regis Rolls* (London, 1943) opens important scholarly vistas into a number of constitutional subjects for the period 1199-1230. Lady Stenton's *Pleas Before the King or his Justices* (London, 1948) provides important documentary evidence of the growth of judicial administration during John's reign.

The life and career of John, and the study of his contemporary age, has been the subject of a number of modern studies, led by the three biographies of John already mentioned.

Chapter 3

McKechnie, of course, is the fundamental source for information in this chapter. The legal histories by Pollock and Maitland and by Holdsworth are of primary importance, as is the volume by Powicke in the Oxford English History. Warren's volume on King John is especially valuable for its bibliography, and from the titles therein may especially be cited the contributions to scholarly journals by C. R. Cheney, Professor Holt, H. G. Richardson, and J. H. Round. Lady Stenton's study of English justice, published as the Jayne Lectures of the American Philosophical Society, as well as her documentary volume for the Selden Society mentioned above, establish the case for John's administrative contributions to government. Lady Stenton, and others, are also editors of *The Great Rolls of the Pipe, 1-14 John,* a series of monographs for the Pipe Roll Society (London, 1933-55) which corroborate the documentary evidence of the preceding works.

The primary documentation of the specific passages in Magna Carta is set out in the annotations in Part II.

Chapter 4

The first of Professor Thompson's two important monographs is basic to the period following the death of John. Kate Norgate's *The Minority of Henry the Third* (London, 1912) is better than her work on John himself, written, like McKechnie's volume, in a period of maximum depreciation of the King and the aggrandizement of the barons. G. W. Prothero's old *Life of Simon of Montfort* (London, 1877) provides most of the available information on that figure, while for Henry's later career the leading work is Powicke's *Henry III and the Lord Edward* (Oxford, 2 vol., 1947). Plucknett is the author of the definitive study of *The Legislation of Edward I* (Oxford, 1949), while Maitland's *Collected Papers,* edited by H. A. L. Fisher (Cambridge, 3 vol., 1911), contains a great deal of important information. So do the legal histories by Pollock and Maitland and by Holdsworth.

R. F. Treharne's *Baronial Plan of Reform, 1258-1263* (Manchester, 1932) provides valuable information on the developments pointing toward the first Parliament of 1265, while McIlwaine's *The High Court of Parliament* (New Haven, 1920) covers the judicial and legislative theories which developed around this branch of government in the later Middle Ages. Powicke's volume in the Oxford English History continues to be useful for this period.

Among the Selden Society volumes which provide background for the century following Runnymede are the opening numbers in the subseries on the Year Books of Edward II, although these are directed toward the fourteenth century for the most part. Maitland's introductory essay to the first of this series (London, 1903) has valuable information on the general development of legal procedure and "law French." There is also Sayles' *Select Cases in the Court of King's Bench Under Edward I* (London, 1936), with a definitive introductory essay on officers and attorneys of the court and a brief history of the court's development during the thirteenth century. Sayles continues this historical review in two other volumes in this subseries (London, 1938, 1939) with valuable material on pleading and procedure.

The student of legal history for this period will also find much information in Maitland's *Select Pleas in Manorial Courts* (London, 1888); the definitive edition of an early treatise, *The Mirror of Justices,* by Maitland and W. J. Whittaker (London, 1893); Maitland's *Selected Passages from the Works of Bracton and Azo* (London, 1894), documenting the influence of Roman law upon the developing common law; and Charles Gross's *Select Cases from the Coroners' Rolls* (London, 1896), extending from the thirteenth to the fifteenth centuries.

Equally important among the Selden Society volumes are Lady Stenton's *Rolls of the Justices in Eyre for Lincolnshire and Worcestershire* (London, 1934), covering the great judicial processes of the latter part of the minority of Henry III; and her companion volume editing *Rolls of the Justices in Eyre in Yorkshire* (London, 1937). Legal developments just prior to the final reissue of the Great Charter in her *Rolls of the Justices in Eyre for Gloucestershire, Warwickshire and Shropshire* (London, 1940) provide a useful basis of comparison with procedures in the later part of Henry's reign as edited by Richardson and Sayles in *Select Cases of Procedure Without Writ Under Henry III* (London, 1941). Turner and Plucknett collaborated on the editing of an important "form book" of this period, *Brevia Placitata*

(London, 1947), and this has a valuable companion study by W. H. Dunham, Jr., in *Casus Placitorum and Reports of Cases in the King's Courts* (London, 1950).

Chapter 5

For the general history of the late Middle Ages and the Tudor times, the corresponding volumes in the Oxford English History are of primary value: May McKisack's *The Fourteenth Century* (Oxford, 1959), and J. B. Black's *The Reign of Elizabeth* (Oxford, 1959). J. E. A. Jolliffe's *Constitutional History of Medieval England* (New York, 2d ed., 1958) is excellent for providing perspective on the constitutional issues of the period. The fundamental reference, of course, is Professor Thompson's second monograph on Magna Carta. The Holdsworth and Plucknett legal histories continue to be basic to the understanding of the legal developments.

Among the Selden Society publications, the twenty-four volumes in the Year Book subseries, published at various dates between 1903 and 1951, are invaluable for an understanding of the steady development of formal judicial institutions under the early Edwards. Chancery procedure is traced in Baildon's *Select Cases in the Court of Chancery* (London, 1896), covering much of the fourteenth and fifteenth centuries. A number of special courts established between the end of the fourteenth century and the middle of the sixteenth are the subject of half a dozen other volumes in the Society's series.

McIlwaine's *The Growth of Political Thought in the West* (New York, 1932) is an exceptionally helpful guide to changing concepts of law, and is a natural companion to S. B. Chrimes, *English Constitutional Ideas in the Fifteenth Century* (London, 1936). T. F. Tout's *The Place of Edward II* (Manchester, 1914) and A. Steele's *Richard II* (Cambridge, 1941) are studies of two periods of legal development which are still not adequately covered. Plucknett contributed a significant paper on the Lancastrian constitution to *Tudor Studies* (London, 1924), while Maitland's famous paper on English law and the Renaissance, reprinted in *Select Essays in Anglo-American Legal History* (Boston, 3 vol., 1907), is still an important introduction to this period. A. F. Pollard's *Evolution of Parliament* (London, New York, 1934) is useful for this general period, while K. Pickthorn's *Early Tudor Government* (Cambridge, 2 vol., 1934) examines respectively the administrative developments under Henry VII and Henry VIII. The same theme is found in G. R. Elton's *Tudor Revolution in Government* (Cambridge, 1953) and in J. R. Tanner's *Tudor Constitutional Documents* (Cambridge, 1930).

The later Tudor period is covered, from a political and legal standpoint, in J. E. Neale's *Elizabethan House of Commons* (New Haven, 1950) and *Elizabeth I and her Parliaments* (New York, 2 vol., 1953, 1958).

Chapter 6

Thompson's second monograph on Magna Carta carries the story to the eve of the English Revolution. The sixth volume of Holdsworth's history of law has a particularly thorough treatment of the legal issues of the period. Tanner is the author of two fundamental works: *Constitutional Documents of the Reign of James I* (Cambridge, 1930) and *English Constitutional Conflicts of the Seventeenth Century* (Cambridge, 1928). John W. Allen's *English Political Thought, 1603-1660* (London, 1938) and W. M. Mitchell's *Rise of the Revolutionary Party in the English House of Commons* (New York, 1957) are valuable recent studies. J. W. Gough's *Fundamental Law in English History* (Oxford, 1955) explores some of the constitutional theory of the time.

Godfrey Davis's *The Early Stuarts* (Oxford, 1959) and G. N. Clark's *The Later Stuarts* (Oxford, 1956) are companion volumes in the Oxford History of England, while Volume VIII of the English Historical Documents covers the Restoration and final constitutional settlement. Maurice Ashley's *England in the Seventeenth Century* (London, rev. ed., 1961) is an excellent general analysis. F. M. G. Higham has written the best study of *Charles I* (Manchester, 1932). David Ogg is the author of two studies of the Restoration and the "Glorious Revolution" and its aftermath: *England in the Reign of Charles II* (Oxford, 1955) and *England in the Reigns of James II and William III* (Oxford, 1955).

Most of the primary source materials are cited by title in the text of the chapter. Of many editions of Coke's second *Institute*, the present author has used the 1797 edition. Arguments in some of the early law cases are contained in the series of reports in *State Trials* (London, 10 vol., 1719-1766), while Parliamentary debates are reported in William Cobbett's early volumes of *Parliamentary History* (London, 1806-1820), in Wallace Notenstein's edition, with associates, of *Commons Debates, 1621* (New Haven, 7 vol., 1935), and *Commons Debates for 1629* (Minneapolis, 1921). Helen Relf edited the House of Lords debates for 1621, 1625, and 1628 for the Royal Historical Society in 1929, and is the author of the definitive monograph on *The Petition of Right* (Minneapolis, 1917). S. R. Gardiner, for the Camden Society, has edited several volumes on the debates in the House of Lords for this period.

Gardiner's *History of England* (London, 10 vol., 1883-84) is an exhaustive study of the decades from the accession of James I to the beginning of the English Civil War.

Chapter 7

As in the preceding chapter, most of the primary source materials are cited by title in the text of the chapter itself. Many of them are conveniently collected in the special volume in the Oxford History of England devoted to American colonial documents, edited by Merrill

Jensen. American legal history remains largely unwritten, with the conspicuous exception of some brilliant specialized studies and with the conspicuous absence of anything comparable to Holdsworth or Plucknett.

The three volumes of *Select Essays in Anglo-American Legal History* are of particular importance for this chapter. L. W. Labaree edited *Royal Instructions to British Colonial Governors, 1670-1776* (New York, 1935), which is indispensable in the study of colonial legal issues. An older work of value is Elmer B. Russell's *Review of American Colonial Legislation by the King in Council* (New York, 1915), while Lawrence A. Harper's *English Navigation Laws* (New York, 1939) studies the imperial controls which ultimately provoked colonial constitutional protest. With this should be read Carl Ubbeholde's *Vice-Admiralty Courts and the American Revolution* (Chapel Hill, 1960). Good background material is to be found in Richard B. Morris's *Studies in the History of American Law* (Philadelphia, 2d ed., 1959), while the evolution of a native jurisprudence is described in George L. Haskins's *Law and Authority in Early Massachusetts* (New York, 1960).

New York's colonial legal development has been better covered than most, from A. J. F. Van Laer's editing of the *Minutes of the Court of Albany* (Albany, 3 vol., 1926-32) to the study by Julius Goebel and T. R. McNaughton, *Law Enforcement in Colonial New York* (New York, 1944) and the project of Paul M. Hamlin and Charles E. Baker on *The Supreme Court of Judicature of the Province of New York* (New York, 3 vol., 1959). Joseph H. Smith has edited the Pynchon court records under the title of *Colonial Justice in Western Massachusetts* (Cambridge, Mass., 1961), and a number of administrative and judicial records have been edited and published in the Legal Records Series of the American Historical Association. The fact remains, however, that no extended work on colonial constitutional theory has yet been undertaken.

The constitutional dispute leading to the American Revolution has been extensively developed, on the other hand. J. F. Burns's *Controversies Between Royal Governors and Assemblies in the Northern Colonies* (Boston, 1923) was an early study which is still useful. Carl L. Becker's *Declaration of Independence* (New York, 1922, 1942) is a classic on the subject. Charles F. Mullett, *Fundamental Law and the American Revolution*, Benjamin F. Wright, *American Interpretations of Natural Law* (Cambridge, Mass., 1931) and McIlwain's *American Revolution: A Constitutional Interpretation* (New York, 1923) are standard background references. A. C. McLaughlin's *Foundations of American Constitutionalism* (New York, London, 1932) and his *Confederation and Constitution* (New York, London, 1905) are also basic reading. Allen Nevins's *The American States During and After the Revolution* (New York, 1927) contains the best description of the first state constitutional developments. For the Confederation, Merrill Jensen's *Articles of Confederation* (Madison, Wis., 1948) is outstanding.

On the American Constitutional Convention itself, the indispensable source is Max Farrand's *Records of the Federal Convention* (New Haven, rev. ed., 4 vol., 1937). Jonathon Elliott's *Debates . . . on the Adoption of the Federal Constitution* (Philadelphia, 2d ed., 5 vol., 1861), highly inadequate, is soon to be supplanted by a Documentary History of Ratification now being prepared under the auspices of the National Historical Publications Commission. A few equally inadequate state studies are represented by J. B. Walker's *New Hampshire Convention of 1788* (Boston, 1888), S. B. Harding, *Contest over Ratification in Massachusetts* (New York, London, 1896), C. E. Miner, *Ratification of the Federal Constitution in New York* (New York, 1921) and L. I. Trenholm, *Ratification of the Federal Constitution in North Carolina* (New York, 1932).

A recent book on colonial origins of the Bill of Rights is Helen Hill Miller's *The Case for Liberty* (Chapel Hill, 1965), while Robert A. Rutland's *Birth of the Bill of Rights* (Chapel Hill, 1955) remains the basic reference.

Two other references of importance to the student in this area are Edward S. Corwin's *Doctrine of Judicial Review* (New Haven, 1914) and Charles G. Haines's *American Doctrine of Judicial Supremacy* (Los Angeles, 1932, reprinted New York, 1959).

Chapter 8

As in the two preceding chapters, most of the primary sources for the text herein have been cited in the chapter itself or can be found in standard collections of the writings of the respective men quoted. It remains to recognize the substantial value of Rodney L. Mott's *Due Process of Law* (Indianapolis, 1927), and Elizabeth K. Bauer's *Commentaries on the Constitution, 1790-1860* (New York, 1952). Gough's *Fundamental Law in English History* is particularly enlightening for the contrast of American and British constitutional theory, particularly when read with Haines's work cited above. Most of the observations of Supreme Court justices are quotations from leading constitutional opinions.

NOTES TO PART II

The general bibliographical data on the original manuscript copies of Magna Carta, particularly the issue of 1215, are set out in McKechnie's treatise at Part V. The text for the 1215 issue used for the present book is modeled after that reprinted in Howard's *Magna Carta, Text and Commentary* and the text for the 1225 reissue has been translated from the Statutes of the Realm, vol. I and correlated, in the case of the ten extant chapters, with Halsbury's Statutes of England (London, 2d ed. by Sir Roland Burrows, 1948), vol. 4.

Thompson's second monograph has a useful interpolation, in

Latin, of the 1215 and 1225 texts, in Appendix A of the volume, while Stubbs's *Select Charters*, at pp. 336-39 and 341-44, sets out, also in Latin, the changes in the Charter in 1216 and 1217.

[1] The present writer has compiled the principal thirteenth-century documents into an annotated series to be published by the Virginia Magna Carta Commission as *Magna Carta Documents* (Charlottesville, Va., 1965).

[2] Contrast Edward Jenks's "The Myth of Magna Carta," *Indep. Rev.* 4:260 (1904) with Faith Thompson's two monographs.

[3] Cf. A. J. Robertson, *Anglo-Saxon Charters* (Cambridge, 2d ed. 1956), nos. ix, xi, xxiii, xlviii, lxxxii, xcv, cxiv.

[4] Cf. Douglas and Greenaway, *English Historical Documents, 1042-1189*, nos. 235-267.

[5] Cf. Painter, *Reign of King John*, p. 285 f.

[6] J. H. Round, "An Unknown Charter of Liberties," *Eng. Hist. Rev.*, v. viii, p. 288 (1893).

[7] Stat. of the Realm, I, p. 7.

[8] Data on the individuals named in the preamble have been derived from Painter, *op. cit.*, and from the Dictionary of National Biography, under the respective names in the indices.

[9] Cf. article on Pandulph (Pandulfus Masca, Bishop of Norwich) in the D. N. B. at vol. xliii, p. 174.

[10] Cf. note 8 on sources of individual data.

[11] Cf. Thompson, *Magna Carta* (1948 monog.), p. 10 n., citing forty-four confirmations from Edward III to Henry V; these are in addition to the considerable number from Henry III to Edward II.

[12] Cf. *Articuli Cleri*, 9 Ed. II, st. 1 (1315); 25 Ed. III, st. 6 (1351); 13 Ric. II, st. 1, c. 1 (1389); 23 Hen. VIII, c. 9, 20 (1531); etc.

[13] 7 & 8 Geo. IV, c. 28 (1827); cf. Plucknett, *Concise History of the Common Law*, p. 439.

[14] Maitland, *Domesday Book and Beyond* (Cambridge, 1921), p. 150 f.

[15] 12 Car. II, c. 24, s. 1-7 (1660).

[16] Halsbury's *Laws of England* (London, 3d ed. by Simonds, 1954), v. 7, p. 197 f.

[17] Cf. Edward S. Corwin, "The 'Higher Law' Background of American Constitutional Law," *Harv. L. Rev.* 42:149, 409 (1928-29).

[18] 26 & 27 Vict., c. 125 (1863).

[19] Thompson, *op. cit.*, p. 200 n.

[20] Plucknett, *op. cit.*, Bk. II, Pt. III, c. 1-6; Holdsworth, *History of English Law*, v. II, Bk. II, Pt. 2, s. 3; and cf. generally Bruce D. Lyon, *From Fief to Indenture* (Cambridge, Mass., 1957).

[21] Thompson, *op. cit.*, p. 21 n.

[22] Idem, p. 42 n.

[23] Pollock and Maitland, *History of English Law*, v. I, p. 326.

[24] 13 Edw. I, c. 16 (1285).

[25] Am. L. Inst., *Restatement of the Law of Property* (St. Paul, 1936), ss. 187-99.

[26] Year Book 3 Edw. II, p. 89 f (Selden Soc. v. 20, 1905), cited in Thompson, *op. cit.*, p. 52.

[27] Year Book 5 Edw. II, p. 185 (Selden Soc. v. 33, 1916).

[28] Edward Coke, *Institutes* (London, 1797), v. II, p. 14 f.

[29] Pollock and Maitland, *op. cit.*, v. I, p. 497 f; Holdsworth, *op. cit.*, v. III, p. 469 f.

[30] Thompson, *op. cit.*, p. 53.

[31] Cf. the several provisions on dower, estovers, and commons in Statute of Merton, 20 Henry III, c. 1, 2, 4 (1235).

[32] 6 Edw. I, c. 2-4, 11-14 (1278); 13 Edw. I, c. 46 (1285).

[33] 27 Hen. VIII, c. 10 (1536).

[34] 3 & 4 Will. IV, c. 105 (1833).

[35] Adm. of Estates Act, 1925, 15 Geo. V, c. 23, s. 56.

[36] Thompson, *op. cit.*, pp. 42, 173.

[37] Cf. Plucknett, *op. cit.*, p. 390 f.

[38] Pollock and Maitland, *op. cit.*, v. I, p. 471.

[39] Chapter 42 of the reissue of 1216 acknowledged that the chapters "in the prior charter" on "debtors of Jews and others" would be among those considered for reinstitution at a future date. Cf. Stubbs, *Select Charters*, p. 339; and cf. the mandates under Henry III set out as App. II-IV in Rigg, *Select Pleas, Starrs, etc.* (Selden Soc. v. 15, 1902).

[40] Pollock and Maitland, *op. cit.*, v. I, p. 473.

[41] Cf. William Blackstone, *Commentaries on the Laws of England* (Boston, ed. by Edward Christian, 1818), Bk. II, c. 4.

[42] Cf. George Norton, *The City of London, Its History, Constitution and Franchises* (London, 3d ed., 1869), *passim*.

[43] Cf. Painter, *op. cit.*, pp. 125-28.

[44] Cf. n. 15 *supra*.

[45] Thompson, *op. cit.*, ch. 4.

[46] *Ibid.*

[47] *Loc. cit.*, n. 4.

[48] Sir William R. Anson, *Law and Custom of the Constitution* (Oxford, 5th ed., 1922), p. 50.

[49] John Beames, trans., *Glanville's Treatise on the Laws and Customs of the Kingdom of England* (London, 1812), p. 234 n.

[50] Pollock and Maitland, *op. cit.*, v. I, p. 331.

[51] 18 Edw. I (1290).

[52] 11 & 12 Geo. VI, c. 62 (1948).

[53] Law of Property Act 1922, 12 & 13 Geo. V, c. 16, s. 128; Law of Property Act 1925, 15 & 16 Geo. V, c. 20, s. 56.

[54] Cf. Plucknett, *op. cit.*, p. 367 f.

[55] *Idem*, p. 383.

[56] Cf. Va. Code 1950, s. 8-586 f.

[57] Cf. esp. annotations to two following chapters of the Charter.

[58] Cf. Plucknett, *op. cit.*, Bk. II, Part II.

[59] Cf. the statement of Sir Frederick Pollock: "We may also say that Magna Carta gave England a capital." *Jurisprudence and Ethics* (London, 1882), p. 209.

[60] Glanville, *op. cit.* n. 49, Book I, c. III.

[61] Plucknett, *op. cit.*, p. 166.

[62] Cf. chs. 3 and 5 of *Articuli super Cartas*, 28 Ed. I (1300).

[63] Plucknett, *op. cit.*, p. 111 f, 118 f.

[64] Cf. Pollock and Maitland, *op. cit.*, v. I, p. 147 f.

[65] Civil Procedure Acts Repeal Act, 42 & 43 Vict., c. 59.

[66] Plucknett, *op. cit.*, p. 165 f.

[67] *Idem*, p. 360.

[68] Pollock and Maitland, *op. cit.*, v. I, p. 497 f.

[69] Year Book 5 Edw. II, p. 170 (Selden Soc. v. 31, 1915).

[70] Holdsworth, *op. cit.*, v. III, p. 138 f.

[71] Cf., generally, Morris, *Studies in the History of American Law.*

[72] Cf. Haskins, *Law and Authority in Early Massachusetts*, p. 69.

[73] Cf. Plucknett, *op. cit.*, p. 366 f.

[74] 3 & 4 Will. IV, c. 27, 42 (1833).

[75] Cf. Chapter 7 of Part I of the present volume.

[76] *Op. cit.*, n. 4, p. 400 ff.

[77] Pollock and Maitland, *op. cit.*, v. II, p. 513.

[78] *Op. cit.*, n. 49, 240 f.

[79] Cf. Maitland, N. W. Harcourt and W. C. Bolland, *The Great Eyre of Kent*, p. 1 (Selden Soc. v. 27, 1912).

[80] Cf. Thompson, *op. cit.*, p. 46.

[81] *Ibid.*

[82] Cf. N. J. Stat. Ann., 2A:15-21 *et seq.*; Gen. Stat. N. C., 114-11, 155-2, etc.; Page's Ohio Rev. Code, 2707.01 *et seq.*

[83] Cf. McKechnie, *Magna Carta*, p. 300 f.

[84] Coke, *op. cit.*, p. 30.

[85] 9 & 10 Vict., c. 24, 95 (1846).

[86] Cf. Plucknett, *op. cit.*, Bk. I, Part II, c. 11.

[87] 50 & 51 Vict., c. 55 (1887); 55 & 56 Vict., c. 19 (1892).

[88] Cf. McKechnie, *op. cit.*, p. 368 f.

[89] Cf. Plucknett, *op cit.*, p. 714 f.

[90] *Idem*, Bk. II, Part VI, c. 3.

[91] Thompson, *op. cit.*, p. 46.

[92] 7 Will. IV and 1 Vict., c. 26 (1837).

[93] 20 & 21 Vict., c. 77 (1857).

[94] 10 & 11 Geo. VI, c. 44, s. 39 (1947).

[95] Cf. Thompson, *op. cit.*, p. 21.

[96] Cf. generally, Plucknett, *op. cit.*, Bk. I, Part I, c. 7; Pt. II, c. 9, 10.

[97] Cf. n. 18 *supra.*

[98] Thompson, *op. cit.,* p. 247.

[99] Plucknett, *op. cit.,* p. 431.

[100] Holdsworth, *op. cit.,* v. III, p. 121 ff.

[101] 33 & 34 Vict., c. 23, s. 1; Admin. of Justice (Misc. Prov.) Act, 1 & 2 Geo. VI, c. 63, s. 12 (1938).

[102] Cf. Plucknett, *op. cit.,* p. 318 n. 3.

[103] Thompson, *op. cit.,* pp. 23-27.

[104] Glanville, *op. cit.,* n. 49, p. 6.

[105] Plucknett, *op. cit.,* p. 355 f, 375 f.

[106] Cf. McKechnie, *op. cit.,* p. 346 ff.

[107] 52 Hen. III, c. 29 (1267).

[108] Cf. n. 18 *supra.*

[109] Cf. Thompson, *op. cit.,* p. 27 ff, 116 ff.

[110] *Idem,* p. 116.

[111] 5 Geo. IV, c. 74 (1824); 41 & 42 Vict., c. 49, s. 3 (1878).

[112] Plucknett, *op. cit.,* p. 369.

[113] 9 Geo. IV, c. 31, s. 1 (1828).

[114] Plucknett, *op. cit.,* p. 126.

[115] *Idem,* Bk. II, Part II, c. 1.

[116] Cf. Plucknett, *op. cit.,* p. 433 f.

[117] *Idem,* p. 188 f.

[118] Cf. Chapter 6 of Part I of the present volume.

[119] Plucknett, *op. cit.,* p. 115 f, 363 f.

[120] Stubbs, *op. cit.,* p. 167 f.

[121] Mott, *Due Process of Law,* Parts I-IV.

[122] Cf. Coke, *op. cit.,* esp. p. 50.

[123] 25 Edw. III, st. 5, c. 4 (1352).

[124] Mott, *op. cit.,* p. 1.

[125] *Idem,* Parts I, II.

[126] Cf. McKechnie, *op. cit.,* p. 383 f.

[127] 5 Edw. III, c. 9 (1331).

[128] 28 Edw. III, c. 3 (1354).

[129] Cf. Thompson, *op. cit.,* c. 3.

[130] Cf. art. by Powicke in Malden, *Magna Carta Essays.*

[131] Pollock and Maitland, *op. cit.,* v. I, Bk. II, c. 2.

[132] Holdsworth, *op. cit.,* v. II, p. 215.

[133] Thompson, *op. cit.,* p. 71.

[134] Holdsworth, *op. cit.,* v. II, c. 3.

[135] 5 Edw. III, c. 9 (1331).

[136] 25 Edw. III, st. 5, c. 4 (1352).

[137] 28 Edw. III, c. 3 (1355).

[138] 36 Edw. III, c. 1, 9 (1362); 38 Edw. III, st. 1, c. 9 (1363).

[139] 42 Edw. III, c. 3 (1368).

[140] Thompson, *op. cit.,* p. 94.

[141] McKechnie, *op. cit.,* p. 402 f.

[142] Cf. Chapter 6 of Part I of the present volume.
[143] Pollock and Maitland, *op. cit.*, v. II, p. 590.
[144] Cf. Holdsworth, *op. cit.*, v. II, 67 f.
[145] Cf. Plucknett, *op. cit.*, p. 566 f.
[146] 25 & 26 Vict., c. 53 (1862); 50 & 51 Vict., c. 59 (1887).
[147] Cf. 57 Geo. III, c. 61 (1817).
[148] Cf. n. 18 *supra*.
[149] Cf. 1 Edw. III, st. 2, c. 2 (1327).
[150] Cf. McKechnie, *op. cit.*, p. 496 f.
[151] Painter, *op. cit.*, *sub nom.* March, etc.
[152] Glanville, *op. cit.*, pp. 355, 357.
[153] *Ibid.*
[154] Cf. 59 Geo. III, c. 27, 46, etc. (1817).
[155] 50 & 51 Vict., c. 55 (1887).
[156] Cf. 9 Geo. II, c. 36 (1736); 51 & 52 Vict., c. 42 (1888).
[157] Painter, *op. cit.*, *sub nom.* Lanvelei, *et al.*

Index